ROCKET MEN

ALSO BY JOHN EISENBERG

The League: How Five Rivals
Created the NFL and Launched a Sports Empire

The Streak: Lou Gehrig, Cal Ripken Jr.,
and Baseball's Most Historic Record

Ten-Gallon War: The NFL's Cowboys, the AFL's Texans,
and the Feud for Dallas's Pro Football Future

That First Season: How Vince Lombardi Took the Worst Team
in the NFL and Set It on the Path to Glory

My Guy Barbaro: A Jockey's Journey
Through Love, Triumph, and Heartbreak
(written with Edgar Prado)

The Great Match Race: When North Met South in
America's First Sports Spectacle

Native Dancer: The Grey Ghost, Hero of a Golden Age

From 33rd Street to Camden Yards:
An Oral History of the Baltimore Orioles

Cotton Bowl Days: Growing Up with Dallas
and the Cowboys in the 1960s

The Longest Shot: Lil E. Tee and the Kentucky Derby

ROCKET MEN

THE BLACK QUARTERBACKS WHO REVOLUTIONIZED PRO FOOTBALL

JOHN EISENBERG

BASIC BOOKS

NEW YORK

Basic Books
Hachette Book Group
1290 Avenue of the Americas, New York, NY 10104
www.basicbooks.com

Printed in the United States of America

First Edition: September 2023

Published by Basic Books, an imprint of Hachette Book Group, Inc.
The Basic Books name and logo is a trademark
of the Hachette Book Group.

The Hachette Speakers Bureau provides a wide range of authors for speaking
events. To find out more, go to hachettespeakersbureau.com or email
HachetteSpeakers@hbgusa.com.

Basic Books copies may be purchased in bulk for business, educational, or
promotional use. For information, please contact your local bookseller
or Hachette Book Group Special Markets Department at
special.markets@hbgusa.com.

The publisher is not responsible for websites (or their content) that are not
owned by the publisher.

Print book interior design by Jeff Williams.

Library of Congress Cataloging-in-Publication Data
Names: Eisenberg, John, 1956– author.
Title: Rocket men : the Black quarterbacks who revolutionized
pro football / John Eisenberg.
Description: First edition. | New York, N.Y. : Basic Books, 2023. | Includes
bibliographical references and index.
Identifiers: LCCN 2022059139 | ISBN 9781541600409 (hardcover) | ISBN
9781541600423 (ebook)
Subjects: LCSH: Quarterbacks (Football)—United States—History. | African
American football players—History. | Discrimination in sports—
United States—History.
Classification: LCC GV954 .E57 2023 | DDC 796.332092/2—dc23/eng/20221216

LC record available at https://lccn.loc.gov/2022059139

ISBNs: 9781541600409 (hardcover), 9781541600423 (ebook)

LSC-C

Printing 1, 2023

INTRODUCTION

When he was not selected until the eighth round of the 1969 NFL draft, James Harris considered quitting football altogether. He loved playing the sport and knew he was good at it, capable of out-playing many of the white quarterbacks who had been drafted ahead of him. But if it was going to be this hard for him to earn respect and make it as a Black quarterback in the pros, Harris wondered whether he was just wasting his time.

He stood six feet four and weighed 210 pounds—the ideal size for a pro quarterback—and possessed a powerful right arm capable of whipping tight spirals across the field. Mature and poised at age twenty-one, he had already operated a complex offense and won championships at Grambling, a historically Black college in Louisiana known for its powerhouse football team.

White quarterbacks with his size and college statistics usually were drafted in the first few rounds. But 191 other players had been selected before Harris went to the Buffalo Bills in the eighth round. It was a slap in the face.

Disgusted, Harris went to the football field at Grambling and sat by himself in the empty bleachers. Grambling's coach, Eddie Robinson, came and sat with him.

"Why bother?" Harris asked.[1]

Robinson, who had spent years grooming Harris to become the first Black quarterback to make it in the pros, answered carefully. "The decision is yours. But you're good enough to make it," Robinson said.[2]

Harris stared into the distance, listening.

"Don't expect it to be fair," Robinson said. "You're going to have to be better than the other quarterbacks. You're going to have to work harder, prepare more, throw more passes. Be the first one on the practice field and the last one to leave. You can't miss a day."

He paused for effect.

"But like I said," he continued, "you're good enough."[3]

Harris bit his tongue. The previous fall, another Black quarterback, Marlin Briscoe, had demonstrated in five starts for the American Football League's Denver Broncos that he *was* good enough to play in the pros; his scrambles and pinpoint passing electrified fans. But he was on the field only because the team's other quarterbacks were injured, and the Broncos had no intention of ever giving him another chance to play the position.

Briscoe's treatment in Denver discouraged Harris. There were still no Black quarterbacks in pro football. Nonetheless, after listening to Robinson, Harris decided to put aside his doubts, go to Buffalo, and try to make it with the Bills. His mother told him, "Just do your best," as she had before every game he played.[4] But she, too, prepared herself for disappointment.

Once in Buffalo, Harris experienced indignities that would have left almost anyone discouraged. During an introductory camp for rookies, the Bills put him up at a YMCA, in a room costing six dollars a night.[5] Some of his teammates had better accommodations.

When Harris told the Bills he needed spending money while Robinson negotiated his contract, they gave him a job cleaning his teammates' cleats.[6] When Robinson asked for more money than the Bills initially offered, they threatened to move Harris to wide receiver. Black quarterbacks coming out of college and trying to make it in the pros typically were turned into wide receivers or defensive backs. What went unstated was the assumption that they simply were not smart enough to play quarterback, the most complicated position in the game.

Harris was one of eight quarterbacks in Buffalo's training camp. The others included Jack Kemp, a veteran mainstay who had led the Bills to two championships, and Tom Flores, another veteran. Heeding

Robinson's advice, Harris studied and practiced hard, avoiding giving the coaches easy reasons to cut him. He prayed for windy days. The other quarterbacks' passes fluttered in drills, but Harris's arm was so strong that his balls zipped through the air on a line, undisturbed. He looked good in the wind and he knew it. It affirmed what Robinson had told him: *You're good enough.*

The Bills saw enough in Harris to give him a roster spot and start him in their season opener against the New York Jets, pro football's reigning champions. Few understood the extent of the miracle. The Associated Press buried it, reporting near the end of a story that Harris would break "a small barrier in sports by becoming the first Negro to open a season at quarterback in pro football history."[7]

The indignities continued. Several of Harris's white teammates complained to the coaches that they could not understand him when he called signals. When the coaches pulled him from the season-opening game before halftime, they explained that his diction was an issue.

After being pulled, Harris barely played again that season or ever again for the Bills. *Pro football obviously is still not ready for a Black quarterback,* Harris thought, just as he had told Robinson that day at Grambling. He took an office job in Washington, DC, and started getting on with the rest of his life. Then the Los Angeles Rams offered him a chance to try out for their practice squad. The job was on the fringes of the sport, but Harris sighed and gave it a shot, remembering once again what Robinson had told him: *You're good enough.*

His determination paid off. He made the practice squad, worked his way onto the roster, and wound up starting thirty regular-season and playoff games for the Rams over four seasons. There were triumphs, both measurable and intangible. The Rams won all but eight of his starts. Harris made play after play, earned an invitation to the Pro Bowl, and led the Rams to two conference championship games, the doorstep of the Super Bowl. Best of all, he earned his teammates' trust and respect. Yes, he *was* good enough to play quarterback in the NFL. All he had needed was a chance.

But his triumphs did not exempt him from being slighted and degraded. A white pro quarterback so successful was assured of a long leash of opportunity, but Harris was benched and traded, summarily rejected; in spite of his success, he failed to receive the support of team ownership. Harris retired at the relatively young age of thirty-two, frustrated by the NFL's outright racism and enduring disrespect for Black quarterbacks. He knew he would have played more, and probably won more, if he were white.

Pro football teams simply did not like giving Black quarterbacks a chance. This was an odious but indisputable reality at the heart of America's favorite sport. Starting in the 1930s, racist attitudes about Black inferiority were accepted among many team owners, coaches, scouts, and fans until professional football was purged of Black quarterbacks. Over time, the absence of Black players at the position became a conveniently circular excuse to continue blocking talented prospects, precluding Black pioneers and exemplars from arising to knock back the stereotypes, mentor the next generation, or inspire future prospects. And when Black quarterbacks finally did break down the walls, the progress was halting and painful. Baseball had one Jackie Robinson; pro football required many.

James Harris's opportunity, however limited and grudging, was one such starting point. Combined with Briscoe's performance during his brief stint in 1968, it demonstrated to other teams that they could play a Black quarterback and live to tell about it, even thrive. A trickle of others made it onto the field as a result, in the late 1970s and 1980s. Doug Williams, a first-round draft pick, took one team to the playoffs and won a Super Bowl for another. Randall Cunningham so stunned teammates, opponents, and fans with his ability to run as well as pass that *Sports Illustrated* labeled him "the ultimate weapon."[8] Warren Moon, cool and efficient as the league's highest-paid player, began a long career that would culminate with his induction into the Pro Football Hall of Fame.

Their success helped normalize the idea of Black men playing quarterback in the NFL and thoroughly disproved the racist myths about them that had prevailed for decades—namely, that they could not think, lead, focus, work hard, perform under pressure, or throw well enough. But while some Black quarterbacks were evaluated more fairly starting in the 1990s and opportunities increased, any declaration of victory over institutional racism was woefully inappropriate. Many teams still preferred white quarterbacks who stood tall in the pocket and gave comfort, not concern, to the owner as a face of the franchise. During the 1990 season, only four of the fifty-one quarterbacks who started games across the league were Black.[9] Heading into the 2000 season, more than a third of the teams, including some in existence for decades, still had never started a Black quarterback in a game.

In the early 2000s, Michael Vick broke stylistic ground, illustrating the advantages of having a quarterback who could frustrate opponents as a runner as well as a passer. But when Vick plummeted from being the league's highest-paid player to a cell in federal prison, the result of his having overseen a dogfighting ring, it reinforced the qualms about Black quarterbacks that quietly endured in the sport's all-white ownership ranks. Between 1999 and 2009, there was no increase in the number of Black starting quarterbacks across the league.

Not until the second decade of the 2000s did genuinely substantive change transpire. Doug Williams's Super Bowl victory, by now decades old, had represented progress, as had Vick's selection as the first overall draft pick. But this new example of change was more wide-ranging and irreversible. Colin Kaepernick, Russell Wilson, and Cam Newton continued to help redefine the position, taking their teams to Super Bowls with dazzling running, sharp passing, and breathtaking poise. Patrick Mahomes followed, earning immediate praise as one of the best pure passers ever. Lamar Jackson, brought to a fury by the opinion of some scouts that he was likelier to succeed as a wide receiver in the NFL, earned the league's Most Valuable Player award in just his second season. In 2022, Black starting quarterbacks squared off in the Super Bowl for the first time when Mahomes, with the Kansas City Chiefs, faced Jalen Hurts, with the Philadelphia Eagles.

The preeminence of these and other Black quarterbacks, including Dak Prescott and Kyler Murray, makes it clear that, as Mahomes said, "We should've been playing the whole time."[10] But still, any declaration of triumph is premature, as indicated by the doubts Jackson faced as his career began. In the NFL's generally towering history, by now a century old, the treatment of Black quarterbacks is a deplorable and enduring chapter. More than a half-century after his groundbreaking career began, James Harris considered the current circumstances in 2022 and said, "For so long, the question has been asked, 'Can a Black play quarterback?' It continues on; continues to be an issue."[11]

PART I

CHAPTER 1

On October 7, 1923, in a public park in Hammond, Indiana, near Chicago, the Hammond Pros and Dayton Triangles met in an NFL game seemingly destined to disappear into the mists of history. Neither team was a title contender; both would go out of business within a few years. A thousand or so fans watched on splintery bleachers, including some who just happened onto the scene while out for a Sunday stroll. But it just so happened to be the first NFL game in which a Black player started at quarterback.

Pro football was just getting started. Disorganized and obscure, with few fans and no traditions to speak of, it lived in the shadows of more popular sports such as baseball, horse racing, and boxing. Americans enjoyed watching high school and college football, but the pros had a dubious future. Franchises and leagues came and went. Players jumped from team to team. The men who ran the NFL, then four years old, had a single, modest goal: avoid extinction.

The Pros and Triangles sported dusky team sweaters, leather helmets, and thin pads over their shoulders and legs. It was hard to distinguish a Triangle from a Pro. Typical of the NFL's early years, the game was an indecipherable muddle, with most plays consisting of a back carrying the plump ball into a tangle of bodies at the line of scrimmage. There was a punt every few minutes, few passes, fewer points. The only score in the Pros' 7–0 victory came on a fumble return.

At the time, the events that took place in Hammond that afternoon were entirely forgettable. No one gave a thought to the fact that twenty-nine-year-old Frederick Douglass "Fritz" Pollard manned the quarterback position for the Pros. The presence of a Black player on the field was not newsworthy. Major league baseball was still for white players only, and NFL team owners would quietly enforce a color line between 1934 and 1945, but before that whitewashing of rosters, the league permitted Black players on its fields. A sprinkling had NFL careers in the early 1920s, including Duke Slater, a tackle, and ends Inky Williams, Bobby Marshall, and Paul Robeson—yes, the one destined for fame as an actor and activist. Pollard was the brightest backfield star, but the fact that he played quarterback for the Pros that day was not newsworthy at the time, either. With offensive strategy still in what amounted to a prehistoric age, the position was several decades away from becoming football's most pivotal and glamorous, deemed so complex and intellectually challenging that many in the NFL believed only white men could handle it.

Like most teams at every level of football in the 1920s, the Pros lined up in the single-wing formation on offense. Four players were positioned on one side of the backfield, creating a "wing" of potential ball carriers and blockers that included a tailback, a fullback, a halfback, and a quarterback. The tailback was the central figure; the offense ran through him as it would through the quarterback later. He lined up the farthest behind the line, received snaps in what would become known as the shotgun formation, and either ran with the ball, handed the ball to another back, or, occasionally, heaved a pass. The fullback and halfback touched the ball the most besides the tailback. The quarterback, so called because he lined up just a quarter of the way back to the tailback, was a blocker on many plays.

Playing quarterback that day in Hammond was, if anything, a comedown for Pollard. In an era when achieving good field position was regarded as more important than completing passes, the punter ranked ahead of the quarterback in the pecking order of positions that determined games. Three years earlier, as a darting single-wing tailback, Pollard had helped another team, the Akron Pros, win the league title; an award honoring the most valuable player in the league did not exist in 1920, but if it had, Pollard would have won it. Playing for Hammond in 1923, though, he occupied a lesser role.

Only later, beginning in the 1960s, would his start at quarterback for the long-forgotten Pros earn historical significance. Pro football had become infinitely more popular. Teams played games before stadiums packed with roaring fans and tens of millions of television viewers. Quarterbacks were at the forefront of the show, operating complex offenses that blended passing and running. Most talent evaluators in the NFL only wanted white players manning the position, fearing Blacks lacked the necessary mental acuity. Black quarterback prospects faced grim options. If they wanted to play in the NFL, they had to move to defensive back, wide receiver, or running back—positions deemed more suitable for them because less thinking supposedly was required. If they wanted to continue playing quarterback, they had to flee the country entirely for Canada, where pro football teams were more open-minded about what Black players could handle and achieve. When a challenge to the NFL's all-white quarterback bastion began to arise, Pollard's start for the Pros in 1923 was identified as a historical footnote. Though it was not an example of a Black player leading an offense, it literally illustrated that, yes, they could play quarterback.

None of the few newspaper reporters on hand in Hammond that day referenced Pollard's position in their articles. Only in an agate-type box score, which accompanied the game story in some papers, were lineups printed that indicated his position.[1]

He did not perform well, missing two field goal attempts and contributing no long runs as a ball carrier. "It is rumored there will be changes in the backfield" before the Pros' next game, reported the *Lake County Times* of Hammond, Indiana.[2] Inky Williams, Pollard's teammate, scooped up a fumble and raced to the end zone in the fourth quarter for the game's only score.

The *Lake County Times* praised the play of the Pros' linemen and suggested Hammond would have "a world beating club" with a better backfield.[3] Thus began the story of a century of Black quarterbacks in the NFL: fittingly, it was christened with an insult.

═══

Some social pioneers fall into it; others are born to it. Named for a famous abolitionist and born into a family that challenged perceived notions, Pollard was a natural.

His parents were the first Black homeowners in Rogers Park, Illinois, a prosperous suburban enclave near Chicago. John and Amanda Pollard arrived in 1886, knowing they were in for trouble but determined to see that their children received a quality education. According to family legend, Amanda never answered a knock at the door without a pistol tucked in her apron.

Born in 1895, Fritz would recall being taunted at a local beach and denied service at a drugstore counter. He and his eight siblings walked the fine line between seeking acceptance in the "white world" because of the advantages it afforded while supporting other Blacks who faced relentless oppression. Their parents taught them to interact respectfully with whites but also to stand up for themselves when necessary. Standout students and star athletes, they busted many racial barriers. Among the girls, Artemisia was Illinois's first Black registered nurse and Naomi was Northwestern University's first Black female graduate. The oldest of the boys, Luther, was a star high school athlete who worked in insurance and advertising before becoming a pioneering Black film producer; he launched the Ebony Film Corporation, a Chicago-based producer of movie shorts with all-Black casts. Among the other boys, Leslie played football at Dartmouth and became a New York sportswriter, and Hughes led a jazz combo that toured the world before he died at thirty-five from injuries resulting from a mustard gas attack during World War I.[4]

Fritz was the second youngest of the nine and became the best known because of football. Aside from being the NFL's first Black quarterback, he was the first Black player to participate in the game that became known as the Rose Bowl, the first Black back selected to a prestigious college All-America team, and the first Black head coach in the NFL. Decades later, he was among the first Black inductees in the College Football Hall of Fame.

None of that seemed possible when he was a high school sophomore standing four feet eleven and weighing eighty-nine pounds.

He made the varsity football team only because an older brother demanded it, but he kept growing, picked up speed, and became a playmaking ball carrier who could dodge tacklers and speed downfield for gains.

In 1915, as a college freshman at Brown, in Rhode Island, he was one of two Black students on campus. A football teammate from the Deep South cursed him with racial slurs until he started breaking long runs, which prompted the teammate to reverse course and encourage the coaches to give Pollard the ball. Brown won five games, lost three, and tied one that season with Pollard enduring constant derision from opposing fans. Yale's crowd chanted, "Bye-bye, Blackbird" when he carried the ball, a sound that would haunt him.[5]

The team's winning season prompted an invitation from the Tournament of Roses, an organization in Pasadena, California, that staged a New Year's Day celebration that included a parade and a college football game. Pollard and his teammates traveled across the country by train and lost to Washington State on a rainy afternoon as Pollard took a pounding from WSU's larger defenders.

His renown was sealed a year later when he was selected to the backfield of Walter Camp's All-America team. Camp had coached at Yale and Stanford in the late 1800s and was widely regarded as the father of the sport. On his All-America team, he had previously recognized Black players who blocked and tackled, but not any that carried the ball.

A stint in the army ended Pollard's college playing career before he could earn his degree. In 1918, he took a job as the head coach at Lincoln University, a historically Black institution near Philadelphia. The job did not pay much, and he took dentistry classes at Penn in his spare time. He was trying to figure out how to make a living. While at Brown, he had run a dry-cleaning business out of his dorm room and done tailoring work for summer tourists at Narragansett Pier. Pollard initially did not think pro football's ragtag franchises could pay him enough to make playing the game after college worth his while. But in 1919, Frank Nied, owner of the Akron Indians, a team in the Ohio League, offered him a salary too big to turn down.

Pollard arrived to find a city simmering with racial hostility. "Akron was a lot like Mississippi in those days," he said later.[6] At first, some of his teammates would not speak to him and he dressed for games in Nied's cigar store rather than in the locker room because Nied feared fans or players on other teams would try to injure him.

But Pollard's parents and siblings had taught him how to persevere. He made it through the season unscathed beyond the usual bruises and returned to Akron a year later, in the fall of 1920. Nied had given the team a new nickname (Pros) and joined a new league, the American Professional Football League, which would change its name to the NFL in 1922.

As a single-wing tailback, Pollard dominated with his running, passing, and kicking. The Pros won eight games and tied two heading into a December showdown with the Decatur Staleys, run by player-coach George Halas, one of the new league's primary organizers. The Staleys had a winning record and Halas saw the Pros as a competitor for the league title. (The title was determined not by playoff games, but by a vote of team owners at a league meeting after the season.)

Emotions ran high. Pollard and Halas had competed against each other as high school stars in Chicago. The game was played in the Windy City, at the home of baseball's Cubs, and drew twelve thousand fans. (The Staleys would relocate to Chicago after the season and become the Bears.) Flaunting league rules, Halas brought in a star player from another team for the one game; he did not want Pollard getting the best of him.

The Staleys' defense kept Pollard corralled and the game ended in a scoreless tie, but months later, the Pros were awarded the championship, embittering Halas, who would always believe his team had been denied a title it deserved.

Pollard returned to Akron in 1921 with added duties, sharing the job of coaching the team. He was at his peak as a player. White fans in Akron and other cities gladly paid to watch the speedy Black star they had read about in the paper. Pollard seldom disappointed. He carried the ball, caught and threw passes, and returned punts.

Defenders bearing down on him lunged to tackle him but grasped only air as Pollard swiveled his hips and sped by.

But opponents were out to get him. They twisted his ankles in piles, kicked him, scratched him. His injuries mounted and he played sparingly late in the season as the Pros faded from title contention. His time in Akron was up.

He settled in Chicago and looked beyond football to make a living. Having given up on dentistry, he opened one of the nation's first Black-owned investment firms. The Roaring Twenties were in full bloom, the stock market booming, and more Blacks needed to make the most of that, Pollard thought.

In 1922, he returned to the NFL, signing a contract to coach and play for a new team in Milwaukee. The owner also signed Robeson and Slater, hoping fans would pay to see the curious spectacle of so many Black players on one team. The Milwaukee Badgers started the season well, but problems arose when the owner and some players did not like taking orders from a Black man. Pollard left the team before the season ended with a new reputation as a troublemaker, a common label hung on the era's Black athletes.

As the 1923 season approached, Pollard's NFL playing career was now a lesser priority. He had an investment firm to run. He took a job coaching a high school team in Chicago. He signed to play for the Gilberton Catamounts, a minor-league team in northeastern Pennsylvania's hardscrabble coal-mining region. Pollard's paydays with the Catamounts were substantial enough to convince him to take weekend train trips between Illinois and Pennsylvania and play before many fans who had never seen a Black man, much less cheered for one. At one game, he was greeted with a hail of rocks and sticks.

It seemed Pollard had no time to coach or play in the NFL in the fall of 1923. But then he received an offer from Alva "Doc" Young, owner of the Hammond Pros, based near Chicago, where Pollard lived. The NFL was still so unorganized that teams set their own schedules, and Hammond only played a few games, so the time commitment was reasonable.

Pollard appreciated the chance to play for Young, a respected physician with a progressive attitude about race. Young had played semipro baseball as a teenager, and now, at age forty-two, he owned racehorses and promoted boxing and wrestling matches. He had provided medical services for Hammond's football team before buying the club in 1920 just as the league now known as the NFL launched. He was on hand for the league's birth at an organizational meeting in an auto showroom in Canton, Ohio, on September 17, 1920. Years later, Pollard told an interviewer that the idea of excluding Black players from the league was discussed at the meeting, but when Young and Akron's Frank Nied argued against it, the idea was tabled.

The Pros were not a franchise with serious designs on success. The only suitable field in Hammond was a reconfigured baseball park. Young settled for scheduling most of the team's games on the road, where league rules guaranteed him 25 percent of the proceeds from ticket sales. But even with that cash, he could not afford much bona fide talent. His players had other careers and busy workweeks, limiting their ability to practice. The Pros were overmatched against stronger squads such as the Canton Bulldogs.

With so few of their games in Hammond, the Pros could not develop a lasting following. A local semipro team drew bigger crowds. The fact that the Pros had Black players did not help. The Indiana countryside outside of Chicago was a notorious hotbed of intolerance; the state would have a quarter-million Ku Klux Klan members at one point in the 1920s. Doc Young was in the minority with his open-mindedness.

But that did not change how he ran his team. Of the more than three dozen franchises that competed in the NFL between 1920 and 1926, none suited up more Black players than Hammond. Pollard, Inky Williams, a back named Sol Butler, and a fullback named John Shelburne all played for the Pros during those years.

Pollard had good intentions when he joined the team in 1923. The Pros' head coach was Wally Hess, a versatile back who was from Hammond and had played at Indiana University. In the season opener,

Hess played quarterback and Pollard played halfback in a 17–0 loss to Canton. They swapped positions a week later in the October 7 win over Dayton. It is not known what prompted the move.

Regardless, as the press predicted, there were changes in the backfield in the next game. Hess was back at quarterback. Pollard did not suit up at all. In fact, Pollard did not play again for Hammond in 1923. He made more money with the Gilberton Catamounts. Some of his finest performances as a pro came as Gilberton's single-wing tailback in 1923 and 1924.

When a Pennsylvania coal strike threatened Gilberton's season in 1925, Doc Young asked Pollard to rejoin the Pros as their head coach and also a player. Pollard mostly coached, playing little, as Hammond began the season with a 14–0 loss to the Green Bay Packers.

After that game, Pollard received a call from Nied. He wanted Pollard to return to Akron, play for the team, and also help coach. Doc Young agreed to send him and several other players to Akron. Pollard's return to the team he had led to the league title in 1920 rekindled his fortunes in the NFL. Playing halfback and quarterback that fall, he helped Akron to a record of four wins, two losses, and two ties, good for fourth place in the twenty-team league.

He returned to Akron in 1926, and on October 10 of that season, there was an NFL game in which both teams started a Black quarterback, according to a box score in the *Akron Beacon Journal*.[7] Pollard manned the position for Akron. The Canton Bulldogs' quarterback was twenty-seven-year-old Sol Butler, who, like Pollard, had previously played for Hammond under Doc Young. One of America's finest all-around athletes, Butler had competed in the long jump at the Summer Olympics in 1920, pitched for three seasons in baseball's Negro leagues, and started at quarterback for four years at the University of Dubuque, in Iowa. He had manned a role in Hammond's backfield from 1923 through the start of the 1926 season.

Playing for Canton later in 1926, Butler shared a backfield with Jim Thorpe, the legendary Native American who was even more accomplished as an athlete. Though he was thirty-nine at the time, long past his prime, Thorpe had won Olympic gold medals, played major league baseball, and suited up for more than a half dozen NFL teams since the league's inception.

Seeing Thorpe and Butler together in Canton's backfield in 1926, a columnist for the *Pittsburgh Courier*, a Black newspaper, wrote that "we can't fail to marvel" at the idea of two people of color "usurping the spotlight" in "a white man's game." He was referring to pro football.[8]

Pollard and Butler were friends. In fact, it was Pollard who had talked Butler into trying the NFL in 1923. Both were fast and elusive, capable of dominating a game, but when they competed as rival quarterbacks on that October afternoon in 1926, they did not move sportswriters to wax poetic. Butler fumbled three punts in a row. Pollard was benched. The game ended in a scoreless tie.

Both Black quarterbacks were nearing the end of their time in the NFL. Within weeks, Nied cut Pollard for having "failed to play up to the form expected of him."[9] It was the final indignity Pollard had to endure in pro football, and around the same time Butler also experienced an event that helped him realize he was in the wrong place at the wrong time as a Black quarterback in the NFL.

It happened when the Bulldogs traveled to New York in November to play the Giants, then in their second season. Still on unsure footing in a city that cared far more about its baseball teams, the Giants were delighted when Thorpe's presence on Canton's roster helped draw thirty thousand fans to the Polo Grounds.

Butler was all set to play quarterback for the visitors, but the Giants had several players from the Deep South on their roster, which precipitated a revolt. It is not clear whether the Southerners refused to participate in a game with a Black player or Giants management feared the big crowd might witness a racial incident if the Southerners did play, but regardless, the Giants asked the Bulldogs to pull Butler from the game. Shortly before kickoff, Butler told his teammates to play without him rather than make a fuss and upset the fans.

The *New York Times* published a story about the game, which ended in a 7–7 tie, without mentioning Butler's absence. But later accounts in the Black press revealed the events that led to it, identifying the Southern players as the problem.[10]

Butler was back for the Bulldogs' next game and played out the season with the team, but he wanted no part of the NFL after that. He settled in Chicago, worked as a probation officer, wrote about sports for a Black newspaper, and added another sport to his repertoire when he joined Gilkerson's Colored Giants, an all-Black basketball team that toured through the Midwest.

With Pollard and Butler out of the league, NFL backfields were on the way to becoming all-white enclaves, destined to remain so for years. In fact, the league's entire playing population was white for a dozen years beginning in 1934, and by the time the tiniest trickle of Black players resurfaced after World War II, quarterback had evolved into football's most glamorous and complex position, deemed so important and challenging that owners and coaches would not dare trust a Black man with it.

Pollard continued to closely follow the NFL after his playing career ended. He succeeded in an array of business ventures, publishing a Black newspaper and becoming a prosperous tax consultant, but he seethed as he watched NFL talent evaluators dismiss Black players as potential quarterbacks after the war. If anything, Pollard, as a younger man, had demonstrated that Black players could think just as well as whites, and that it was racist, pure and simple, to put limits on them. But his darting runs and clever playmaking were just distant memories by then. Pollard had done as much as he could to open minds and doors, but it was not nearly enough.

CHAPTER 2

When the league that became the NFL launched in 1920, it did so with Jim Thorpe as its chief executive, holding the title of league president. The team owners gave him the job with the hope that his name would generate publicity, which they sorely needed. They disregarded the fact that he had zero management experience.

Thorpe was not cut out for the job. He kept playing for Canton while theoretically running the league, devoting little time, if any, to rules, paperwork, and the settling of disputes, duties that were central to keeping the nascent league intact. After a year, the owners replaced him with one of their own: Joe Carr, a former sportswriter from Columbus, Ohio. Not only had Carr run one of baseball's minor leagues, he owned and operated a football team of his own, the Columbus Panhandles—so nicknamed because many of the team's players worked for a division of the Pennsylvania Railroad known as the Panhandle.

Methodical and meticulous, Carr was partial to dark suits with high collars, wide-brim hats, and wire-rim spectacles, giving him a doctrinal air. The owners put their faith in his experience to organize and unify their haphazard start-up.

Football was a young sport and the NFL an even younger league, so Carr first set out to spread the word of pro football's existence. During those initial years, Carr was open to taking on any prospective team owner willing to join the NFL. By 1926, he had assembled a roster of twenty-two teams representing cities as large as New York, Chicago, and Detroit, and as small as Duluth, Minnesota; Racine, Wisconsin; and Pottsville, Pennsylvania.

It was a sprawling, messy brotherhood. When Carr stepped back and took stock in 1926, he recognized problems and confusion on multiple fronts. Teams handled their own scheduling with no guidelines from the league, so they could play however much, or little, they wanted. The Frankford (Pennsylvania) Yellow Jackets played seventeen games in 1926 while the Louisville Colonels played four. Screwy as that was, even stranger was the fact that the league title was not even decided on the field, but by a vote of the owners after the season.

Most troubling was the fact that the league was awash in red ink—even more so when a rival league arose in 1926, creating bidding wars for players and driving up salaries. If payrolls continued to rise, the only teams that could remain solvent would be those capable of selling more tickets and bringing in more money. Franchises in smaller cities would struggle to generate sufficient income playing in tiny stadiums before sparse crowds.

Given those circumstances, Carr reasoned that the NFL needed to become more of a big-city venture to have any chance of surviving and blossoming. It should establish roots in metropolitan areas with larger stadiums, more powerful media outlets, and more fans, while cutting ties with the smaller operations.

Moving boldly, Carr reshaped the league by kicking out a dozen franchises at an owners' meeting following the 1926 season. The Hammond Pros, Akron Indians, and Canton Bulldogs were among those shown the exit. But while doing so, Carr and the remaining owners appeared to give little, if any, thought to what this contraction meant for Black players.

The league did not have either a formal or a de facto policy of exclusion, as evidenced by the presence of Pollard, Butler, and several other Black players on the field. But none of the owners of the larger teams were interested in them. Between 1920 and 1926, every Black player but one suited up for Hammond, Akron, Canton, or the Rock Island (Illinois) Independents. Now those teams were gone, leaving Black players with nearly no one on their side.

In 1927, the newly streamlined NFL had twelve teams and a single Black player—Duke Slater, a lineman for the Chicago Cardinals.

He had been Pollard's teammate in Milwaukee in 1922 before joining Rock Island, where he earned a reputation as a fierce blocker. With Rock Island no longer an option, Slater had joined the Cardinals, who needed help as they competed with George Halas's more popular Bears for the favor of fans in Chicago.

Slater was an impressive figure, and not just on the field. While still playing with the Cardinals, he attended law school and became a practicing attorney, later becoming an assistant district attorney in Chicago, and finally, one of the city's first Black judges. His off-field career fully exposed the absurdity of the cruel lie that a Black man could not think or lead. On the field, Slater played without a helmet and loved to hit; he was with the Cardinals through 1931 and was the NFL's only Black player for most of that time. Only three others made appearances—guard Hal Bradley played in two games for the Cardinals in 1928, end Phil Scott played in eight games for the Orange (New Jersey) Tornadoes in 1929, and guard Dave Myers played for the Staten Island Stapletons in 1930 and the Brooklyn Dodgers in 1931. (Hoping to take advantage of baseball's popularity in the 1920s and 1930s, the Dodgers and several other NFL teams shared a nickname and home field with the major league baseball team in their market.) Myers's brief pro career was emblematic of the challenges Black quarterbacks would face in the coming years.

A New York native, Myers had been a backfield star on a Stuyvesant High School team that won the Manhattan-Bronx championship. His talent was impossible to miss. At NYU, he set records tossing the javelin for the track team and was described by reporters watching football practice as the fastest man on the roster. NYU's head coach, Chick Meehan, put his speed to work on defense, stationing him in the backfield and letting him return punts. But white players had always manned the offensive backfield at NYU, and Meehan, it seemed, was in no hurry to break with that tradition, so on offense Myers lined up at guard and blocked for others.

Myers's switch to quarterback came in his senior season. Meehan "experimented" with putting him at halfback at a preseason training camp, where the *New York Times* reported that he showed "real aptitude."[1] But he remained a guard until he replaced the white quarterback at a midweek practice in October. Three days later, he led NYU over Penn State before thirty thousand fans at Yankee Stadium, giving the offense "the punch it has lacked all season," the *Times* wrote.[2] He was a "star negro quarterback," and not the single-wing version.[3] Myers took snaps, ran with the ball, and threw passes, previewing what the job of a quarterback would entail several decades later, after changes in rules and general offensive philosophy made the position far more central.

But controversy soon overshadowed Myers's talent. Meehan had scheduled a home game against Georgia and initially told reporters Myers would not play because he "understood the feeling of Southern colleges in regard to playing against Negroes."[4] There was immediate blowback from the media. The *Brooklyn Daily Eagle* published an editorial cartoon with Myers depicted standing behind a "new Mason-Dixon line," located in New York.[5]

Meehan responded that Myers could not play anyway because he had an injured shoulder that might knock him out for the rest of the season. A team doctor confirmed the injury and Myers did not play against Georgia. Whatever Myers thought of his coach's lack of support, it was not enough for him to quit the team. He was back for the next game and played the rest of the season at quarterback.

In 1930, Myers signed with the Stapletons as the harsh realities of the Great Depression set in. The NFL was down to eleven teams and would soon shrink to eight. With roster spots becoming rarer, team owners did not want to take jobs away from white players. But Myers was too talented to pass up.

Joining the Stapletons, he hoped to earn a job in the backfield but was not given a chance to try out and ended up back where he started at NYU, playing in the line and blocking for others. There simply was no room for Myers in the backfield. Staten Island's tailback, Ken Strong, was a star, just beginning a long career that would include four All-Pro selections in the 1930s, and the team's player-coach, Doug Wycoff, took up another backfield spot as the fullback. Myers would play just one season with the Stapletons before moving on.

He suited up for the Dodgers in 1931, but even though their backfield was not as set, he still wound up at guard. Although he made second-team All-Pro, no easy feat for a player on a team that won just two games and lost twelve, it was becoming clear that an NFL career was a long-odds proposition for any Black player. The 1931 season was Myers's last.

Myers was a trailblazer, for better and for worse. Several decades later, it would become customary for Black college quarterbacks to have to switch positions in the pros. Myers was just the first of many.

═══

In the first half of a game between the Chicago Cardinals and Pittsburgh Pirates at Forbes Field in Pittsburgh on September 27, 1933, the Cardinals' single-wing tailback was easily the best player on the field. One of just two Black players in the NFL that season, Joe Lillard was big-shouldered and agile, nicknamed "the Midnight Express" by white reporters because he was so dark and fast.[6] He could do almost anything the game demanded, it seemed. In the first half in Pittsburgh, Lillard took snaps in what would become known as the shotgun formation, threw a touchdown pass, and repeatedly slashed through the Pirates' defense for gains. He also kicked an extra point, punted, and made tackles for the Cardinals' defense from his position in the secondary.

At halftime, with the Cardinals ahead, 13–0, both teams headed to their locker rooms to rest and adjust their strategy. Forrest "Jap" Douds, an offensive tackle for the Pirates who was also the team's head coach, stood before his players with a blunt prescription for getting back in the game. "We've got to get that damn nigger the hell out of there!" he said.[7]

None of the Pirates spoke up—it was the NFL in 1933, after all. But one player, Ray Kemp, a rookie tackle for the Pirates, was taken aback. He was the NFL's only other Black player besides Lillard.

Several minutes later, Douds pulled Kemp aside as the Pirates prepared to return to the field. "Ray, you know I didn't mean you," Douds said.[8]

Kemp was not one to make a fuss. A taciturn western Pennsylvanian, he had been the only Black player on his teams at Duquesne. He loved football and had ruefully accepted that he had to tolerate racial epithets if he wanted to play.

Lillard was different, more confrontational by nature. "An angry young man," Kemp would call him, and indeed, he had a lot to be angry about—his life had been filled with obstacles.[9] An Oklahoma native, he had been orphaned by age ten and sent to live with relatives in Iowa. A standout high school football player, he accepted a scholarship from the University of Minnesota only to see the coach leave for the University of Oregon. Lillard followed the coach to Oregon, but his career ended prematurely, and in controversy, when he was accused of having played for a semipro baseball team. Lillard claimed he had been paid only to drive the bus.

When he first played for the Cardinals in 1932, he performed well, but his playing time dwindled when the coaches and some white teammates claimed he had repeatedly skipped practices and meetings. Reporters for Black newspapers dismissed the allegations, attributing his benching purely to racism.

He was talented, though, and the Cardinals knew it. His 1933 season was already off to a great start through the first half in Pittsburgh. But when the second half began at Forbes Field, the Pirates would not rest until they had him kicked out of the game. "The players on other teams knew what would set Joe off," Kemp said later.[10] The Pirates taunted him and twisted his ankles when they tackled him. Finally, their fullback, Tony Holm, a Southerner who had played at the University of Alabama, irritated Lillard enough that a fight broke out.

Both players were ejected, which was fine with the Pirates. They rallied to win, 14–13, as the Cardinals sagged without their best player. Douds's strategy had worked. Sportswriters noted that a missed extra point attempt by Lillard in the first half wound up being the difference in the score.

A week later, against the Portsmouth Spartans in Ohio, Lillard threw a touchdown pass but missed another extra point while fans taunted him mercilessly. In the next game, he kicked the winning field goal against the Cincinnati Reds but was again ejected for fighting.

When the Cardinals faced their more popular crosstown rivals, the Bears, on an October Sunday at Wrigley Field, Lillard gave them an early lead on a breathtaking play. He fielded a punt near midfield, juked around several tacklers, and sped to the end zone while hugging the sideline. The Cardinals took a 9–0 lead, but the Bears overtook them and won, 12–9.

The Cardinals finished the season with just one win in eleven games, but what little hope they engineered along the way came courtesy of Lillard. He was their season leader in rushing yardage and passing completions and yardage, and was involved in over half of their touchdowns.

But he also was a source of friction with his penchant for getting into fights. Some teammates became frustrated with Lillard's volatile nature and did not always block their hardest for him. The coach elected not to play him in the season finale. The Cardinals had seen enough. They did not bring him back in 1934.

Kemp experienced a similar fate when he was cut from the Pirates shortly after the September game against the Cardinals. Kemp believed it was because he played the same position as Douds. "He had a lot of cronies on the team and I think it was just a combination of things," Kemp said. He complained to the Pirates' owner, Art Rooney, a cigar-smoking horseplayer who was known for supporting Black players. This time, however, Rooney refused to step in.

"He told me, 'Ray, I feel you're as good a player as we have on the club, but I'm not going over the head of the coach,'" Kemp recalled.[11]

Thinking he was through with the NFL, Kemp took a job in a steel mill. Then, to his surprise, the Pirates asked him to play in their season finale against the Giants in December 1933. Kemp traveled with the team to New York and played the entire game before twelve thousand fans at the Polo Grounds. It would be the last time until after World War II that a Black player was seen on an NFL field.

———

When George Preston Marshall agreed to start a new NFL franchise in 1932, he wanted to put it in Washington, DC, the city where he lived in a luxury hotel, rode around in a limousine, and owned a successful laundry business. Descended from Confederate officers, he was a proud son of Dixie who relished his hometown's segregated environment.

Joe Carr talked him into putting the team in a more northern home base, Boston, believing it would make for a better football market. As it turned out, Carr was mistaken. Marshall would endure five years of indifference from fans in Boston before he moved his team, the Redskins, to Washington, where they immediately took off, winning championships in a sold-out stadium.

But in 1932, his first year in the league, Marshall still hoped his team would succeed in Boston. He was encouraged to see a sizable and enthusiastic crowd attend a game against the Cardinals on October 3. His optimism quickly faded, though. The Cardinals beat his team easily, with Joe Lillard dominating the field. "Negro Star of the Chicago Eleven Thrills 18,000 by Dazzling Runs as Cardinals Down Boston," read the headline in the *Boston Globe*.[12] It was Marshall's worst nightmare. But he would exact his version of revenge soon enough. In a form of twisted logic, Lillard's superb performance in Boston that night in 1932 helped delay by decades the ascendance of Black players into offensive centerpieces in the NFL.

Blue-eyed and bombastic, Marshall came from a theater background that gave him ideas about how to make pro football a livelier sport. And though he was new to the NFL, he was unafraid to voice his opinions at meetings. The other owners liked his enthusiasm and vision, and they adopted many of his ideas, which included a postseason championship game and relaxing certain rules to make passing a larger part of offensive play. But Marshall is also widely credited with leading the owners into the most reprehensible epoch in the league's history. There is no official record of him speaking up at a meeting and formally suggesting that teams adopt a strict policy of segregation. Yet his attitude toward the exclusion of Black players was well known. However it happened, within two years of his arrival, the NFL was entirely white.

The league had never been welcoming to Black players—just thirteen had played between 1920 and 1933. But it is hard not to see

Marshall's fingerprints on the decision to draw a hard line. Even after other teams broke the color line following World War II, the Redskins played on without Black players until 1961.

Marshall could not create an entirely white league alone, though. In 1934, the NFL's ownership ranks included Pittsburgh's Art Rooney, the Bears' George Halas, the Giants' Tim Mara, and the Philadelphia Eagles' Bert Bell. They would become towering presences in pro football history and fiercely denied that the whitewashing of rosters was intentional. Yet none of them—nor any other NFL owner—gave a Black player a uniform for more than a decade starting in 1934.

The excuses they made were unconvincing, to say the least. Halas claimed it was the result of a lack of quality Black prospects coming out of college football. In fact, teams in the Big Ten and on the West Coast, where integrated rosters were becoming common, featured outstanding Black stars in the 1930s. The best known among them were backs who, like Lillard, could have become dominant tailbacks in the single-wing offenses that prevailed in the NFL. That would have positioned them to join the first generation of star quarterbacks.

Iowa's Oze Simmons was "the best I've ever seen," said a coach for Northwestern who had seen Red Grange and Fritz Pollard.[13] Dubbed "The Wizard of Oze" and "The Ebony Eel" by sportswriters, he set records as a rusher and kick returner, but he also threw touchdown passes—he had played quarterback in high school in Texas—and there is little doubt he could have confounded NFL defenses with his passing as well as his running, as Lillard did before being denied a place in the league. But Simmons never received so much as a tryout offer from an NFL team. After college, he played two years for the Paterson (New Jersey) Panthers of the American Association, a minor league, before giving up on football.

Kenny Washington projected as an even bigger NFL star than Lillard or Simmons. As a single-wing tailback for UCLA, he led the nation in total offense as a senior in 1939 and was described as "the greatest long passer ever" by his college football and baseball teammate, Jackie Robinson—yes, the one destined to make history by breaking the color line in major league baseball when he debuted with the Brooklyn Dodgers in 1947.[14]

Washington attained as much glory as Robinson, if not more, while at UCLA. He was such a difference-maker in football that Halas seriously contemplated signing him in 1940. It is fascinating to consider what might have happened had Washington received an opportunity. But he was never signed, presumably because Halas's fellow NFL owners discouraged it. "Amid the exclusion of all Black players from the NFL, the cause of Black quarterbacks certainly was set back with the likes of Kenny Washington never getting a shot," said Jack Silverstein, a Chicago sports historian who has researched the history of Black quarterbacks in pro football and published comprehensive findings in 2020.[15]

After being denied by the NFL in 1940, Washington joined the Los Angeles Police Department and, like Simmons, turned to minor-league football, playing for the Pacific Coast League's Hollywood Bears during World War II. When the NFL reintegrated in 1946, after the war had ended, he was the first Black player to sign a contract—the Los Angeles Rams took him on. But by then, knee injuries had robbed him of the playmaking skills that could have made him a major star. He gave the Rams three decent seasons in a hybrid role as a rusher, passer, and receiver, then retired and resumed his police career.

In time, Washington would be recalled as a racial barrier-buster, and thus, an important historical figure. But in a different time and under different circumstances, he also could have been the NFL's first great Black quarterback.

CHAPTER 3

The rise of the star NFL quarterback can be traced to a league meeting in Pittsburgh in February 1933. Joe Carr brought the owners there mostly because he wanted them to meet potential local investors—he wanted to put a new franchise in Pittsburgh. (Art Rooney's Pirates would debut that fall.) That possibility made news in western Pennsylvania, but nationally, the biggest headlines from the meeting involved rule changes.

Until that point, the NFL had used the college rulebook, the whole thing, cover to cover, instead of devising its own regulations. But with Marshall and Halas leading the way, the owners broke from the college game in fundamental ways during the two-day session in Pittsburgh. Their league was down to eight teams. Something had to change or pro football's days might be numbered.

According to the rules of college football, a player could not attempt a pass unless he was at least five yards behind the line of scrimmage. That resulted in more punting than scoring in many games. Hoping to inject more action into the pro game, the owners agreed to throw out the five-yard rule, hoping it would encourage more passing. From now on, a player could attempt a pass from anywhere behind the line.

Quarterbacks had almost always been complementary players, overshadowed by others, in the single-wing offenses most NFL teams employed. But they began their move to the spotlight with the rule change enacted in Pittsburgh.

The owners broke from the college rulebook in other ways during the meeting. Plays would now start nearer the middle of the field, instead of near the sidelines, giving offenses more room to maneuver. Goal posts would be stationed at the back of the end zone, instead of on the goal line, hopefully resulting in fewer field goals and more touchdowns. All the changes were aimed at enlivening the pro game and saving the NFL from shrinking any further.

But it was the opening of the passing game that set in motion a revolution in offensive strategy. Once it was easier to pass, teams opted to throw the ball more and move downfield faster. Offenses began gobbling up whopping chunks of territory on individual plays instead of just a few yards at a time on single-wing runs.

Pro games immediately became faster, higher scoring, and more dramatic. In 1932, the last season before the NFL dropped the five-yard rule, teams combined to score an average of 16.4 points per game. A year later, with players passing from anywhere behind the line, the teams in the inaugural championship game combined for forty-nine points.

A new kind of game required players with new skills. Two years after the rule change, the Green Bay Packers signed Don Hutson, a speedy end from Alabama who had run wild in the Rose Bowl. When the Packers played the Bears for the first time with Hutson, he lined up on the first play and raced downfield. The Bears' defenders let him go, thinking he had outrun the throwing range of any of Green Bay's backs, who shared the passing duties. But Arnie Herber, the tailback, launched a towering spiral that hit Hutson in stride and he sped to the end zone to complete an eighty-three-yard scoring play. The Bears were stunned. Green Bay wound up winning.

Pro football had never witnessed a weapon like Hutson, who would lead the Packers to two league titles and a run of winning seasons in his first five years. His rise further emphasized the importance of having an accurate and prolific passer; Hutson was nothing without one. Passing was becoming a skill too important just to leave to the tailback or halfback with the best arm.

Two years after Hutson entered the league, Marshall's Redskins drafted Sammy Baugh, a rangy single-wing tailback from Texas Christian University. He was a purposeful ball carrier, but his defining feature was a powerful and accurate throwing arm.

The NFL had never seen a passer with such confidence. When a receiver went out for a pass at Baugh's first pro practice, Ray Flaherty, the Redskins' head coach, challenged the rookie. "Let's see you hit that receiver in the eye," Flaherty said.

"Which eye?" Baugh replied.[1]

The Redskins would win their first NFL title that season with Baugh leading the league in passing as a single-wing tailback. But creative football minds had already begun scheming to move beyond the single-wing, which suddenly seemed old and slow. Halas and a coaching ally, Clark Shaughnessy, devised an offense that ran out of the "T formation," with the quarterback lined up directly behind the center, two backs behind him, and an end split wide as the primary receiving target. There had been a version of the T decades earlier, so Halas called his the "modern T." It put the quarterback at the center of the attack, with much more responsibility. He ran the huddle, called the plays, took every snap, handed the ball to backs, faked handoffs on some plays, and most importantly, threw all the passes.

The days of single-wing tailbacks throwing more than quarterbacks were about over.

In the late 1930s, Halas went searching for the right player to run the "modern T" for the Bears. He found Sid Luckman playing quarterback on losing teams at Columbia University in New York. Luckman was big and smart, a deft ball handler with a strong arm. Halas traded up to get him with the second overall pick in the 1939 NFL draft.

Luckman played halfback as a rookie with the Bears in 1939 while an older player, Bernie Masterson, played quarterback and threw more passes. But after the Packers won another title with Hutson leading the way that season, Halas had seen enough. In 1940, he committed to using the modern T with Luckman at quarterback. The Bears won a division title and faced the Redskins, and Baugh, in the league championship game. The matchup offered a stark contrast in offensive philosophies. The Redskins still used the single-wing even though Baugh was the NFL's top passer.

The game was played in Washington before a sellout crowd on a sunny Sunday afternoon in December. The Redskins had beaten the Bears during the season and were favored to claim the title. But the Bears scored on the second play of the game and went on to demolish Washington, 73–0. Although Luckman only attempted four passes due to the contest becoming so lopsided, the rout illustrated what could happen with a gifted quarterback at the helm of the T.

The NFL's move to the T became inexorable, and with that, quarterbacks became the central figure in offenses. Four years after they lost the championship game by seventy-three points, the Redskins finally adopted the T and put Baugh at quarterback. One of the finest passers ever, destined for the Pro Football Hall of Fame, he had spent the first seven years of his career at halfback, sharing the passing load. That would never happen again. By the end of World War II, the first generation of passing quarterbacks was dominating the pro game. The Bears had Luckman. The Redskins had Baugh. The Rams had Bob Waterfield, who threw two touchdown passes in a victory over the Redskins in the 1945 championship game.

Pro football had changed forever, become more modern, thrilling, and, soon enough, far more popular. It had previously been a slow-paced game of backs in leather helmets plunging into the line. Now, it was a game of dynamic quarterbacks.

═══

When the Rams defeated the Redskins in the 1945 championship, the game concluded a twelfth straight season of entirely white NFL rosters. It seemed unlikely the league would reintegrate anytime soon. Major league baseball was segregated. America's military was segregated. The NFL could coast in the shadow of those better-known entities, especially with so many local, state, and federal statutes effectively mandating segregation across the country.

Only later, in hindsight, would the whitewashing of the league become an embarrassing stain on its history. When the Bears celebrated their centennial by wearing "throwback" uniforms from 1936 in a 2019 game, Jack Silverstein, the local sports historian, noted in print that the Black players on the 2019 Bears would be the first Black players to don the uniform—an irrefutable fact that highlighted the NFL's shameful epoch from decades earlier.[2] George McCaskey, the Bears' chairman and Halas's grandson, did not try to skirt the issue. "Integration of the NFL and the Bears was too long in coming," McCaskey said in a video produced by the team.[3]

In the middle of the NFL's all-white era, Fritz Pollard, always interested in the greater good, fielded an all-star team of well-known Black players, including Joe Lillard, Ray Kemp, and Dave Myers. Pollard's aim with his squad, which he called the Brown Bombers, was to play NFL teams in exhibition games and hopefully show NFL owners that Black players were just as talented as white players, and also that Black and white players could compete harmoniously, without fighting.

It was telling that Lillard and Myers, by now in their thirties, manned the marquee positions in the Bombers' backfield. In the years when offensive strategy changed and T quarterbacks supplanted single-wing tailbacks as the focal point, there were no Black players in the NFL. Lacking a Black version of Luckman or Baugh, Pollard had no choice but to tap a prior generation's stars for the Brown Bombers.

Predictably, NFL teams would not play the Brown Bombers, who settled for playing minor-league squads in front of sparse crowds, almost always winning, before folding after three years due to a lack of attendance and revenues.

Inevitably, as NFL team owners searched for their versions of Luckman or Baugh, the ideal they imagined was a white player. The idea of putting a Black player at quarterback probably never even occurred to them, even after the NFL reintegrated starting in 1946.

When the color line was broken that year, it was certainly not because those in charge experienced a change of heart. The return of Black players to the NFL was almost an accident, coming as a byproduct of another move that received far more attention: the move of the Rams from Cleveland to Los Angeles.

Los Angeles had loomed as an attractive market for an NFL franchise as its population exploded in the 1930s and 1940s. A handful of prospective ownership groups had eyed it, but the league had hesitated to put a team there, especially after the United States became involved in World War II. But with the war ending, the Rams' owner, Dan Reeves, did not wait for league approval. He just said he was going.

Cleveland had never really warmed to the Rams, who began playing in 1937; with attendance a constant struggle, the franchise had lost money even while winning the title in 1945. Now, a rival pro league, the All-America Football Conference, was preparing to kick off in 1946 with a strong franchise in Cleveland called the Browns. Reeves wanted no part of a tough and costly fight for the hearts and minds of Cleveland's fans. He feared he would lose.

The AAFC was also establishing a team in Los Angeles, so the Rams would have to fight for fans there, too, but Reeves felt better about his chances in that challenge. He envisioned a rosy future for the Rams in Southern California. A young and impetuous scion of a family that had made a fortune in the grocery business, he dared his fellow NFL owners to stop him. They did not, approving the move on January 12, 1946.

Three days later, the Rams' general manager, Chile Walsh, appeared before a commission that oversaw the Los Angeles Coliseum, the city's massive stadium, which the Rams intended to use for their home games. Walsh was seeking a lease arrangement.

The Coliseum was a public venue, built with taxpayer dollars as a centerpiece for the 1932 Olympics, which Los Angeles had hosted. A three-man commission, featuring one representative apiece from the city, county, and state governments, oversaw the stadium's use. The commission meetings were public, and on the day the Rams asked for a lease, three sportswriters from Black newspapers were in the audience—Halley Harding from the *Los Angeles Tribune*, Herman Hill from the *Pittsburgh Courier*, and Abie Robinson from the *California Eagle*.

After Walsh announced the Rams wanted a lease, Harding asked to speak. Taking the floor, he gave the commissioners a tutorial on the

NFL's lamentable record on race, detailing the careers of Pollard, Lillard, and Sol Butler, and explaining that no Blacks had played in the league since 1934.

Harding, a former Negro leagues shortstop, told the commissioners it would be inappropriate to give a lease to a team in a segregated league—the taxes of both Black and white residents had built the Coliseum, he said. The commissioners agreed, and Walsh, turning pale, immediately stated that Kenny Washington, the former UCLA star from the 1930s, could try out for the Rams. Although now past his prime and playing on sore knees, he had a devoted following in Los Angeles. The Rams soon signed him to a three-year contract and also signed Woody Strode, another former UCLA star who was Black.

The signings of Washington and Strode were not received warmly around the NFL. "All hell broke loose," said Bob Snyder, a backfield coach for the Rams.[4] The other owners had no interest in following the Rams' lead. Some still believed fans would not buy tickets to see Black players. Some still believed Black and white teammates could not co-exist. Some still doubted whether Black players could help them win. Washington and Strode were the NFL's only Black players in 1946. Washington was the only one in 1947.

But the owners were tacking against a rising tide of historic change. Jackie Robinson integrated baseball's major leagues when he took the field for the Brooklyn Dodgers in 1947. President Harry Truman signed an executive order integrating the United States military in 1948.

Teams in the AAFC were more open to integrating their rosters. The Cleveland Browns had signed two Black players, fullback Marion Motley and guard Bill Willis, as soon as they opened for business in 1946. Both were immediately major contributors, and the Browns added a third Black player, a punter and end named Horace Gillom, in 1947. The Los Angeles Dons had three Black players that year. The New York Yankees' addition of Buddy Young, a crowd-pleasing Black halfback from the University of Illinois, showed NFL teams they were missing out on players who could help them win games and attract fans. Young had gone unselected in the NFL draft.

Ever so cautiously, other NFL teams began to sign Black players. In 1948, the Detroit Lions added Bob Mann, a wide receiver from the University of Michigan, and Melvin Groomes, a halfback from Indiana University. The Giants signed Emlen Tunnell, a single-wing tailback who had displayed a range of skills at the University of Iowa.

Tunnell had led his team in pass completions, pass receptions, and rushing yardage at different times but, like Buddy Young, had gone unselected in the NFL draft. Looking for a chance, he simply showed up at the Giants' offices in midtown Manhattan on a hot afternoon in July 1948 and asked to speak to Steve Owen, the team's head coach. Owen had never heard of him. The Giants' general manager vaguely recalled hearing about him. Tunnell wound up speaking to Wellington Mara, the son of the team's owner.

"I want a job," Tunnell said.

"What kind of a job?" Mara asked.

"Playing football. I play football," Tunnell replied.[5]

Impressed with Tunnell's gumption, Mara signed him. What happened next was telling. Tunnell could throw the ball, but the Giants had acquired a quarterback, Charlie Conerly, who had led the nation in passing at Ole Miss and fit the developing prototype of an NFL quarterback. He was tall and had a good throwing arm and could command an offense. The Giants shifted Tunnell to defense—a switch that would become typical for Blacks who had played quarterback or at least thrown passes in college.

For Tunnell, it was a good fit. He made an immediate impact as a defensive back and punt returner and became an All-Pro performer. He was later voted into the Pro Football Hall of Fame. But the exodus of potential Black quarterbacks to other positions was underway.

In 1949, the Bears became the first NFL team to draft a Black player. They took George Taliaferro, a single-wing halfback from Indiana, in the thirteenth round. But he did not play for the Bears. Aware of the NFL's record of discrimination, Taliaferro had assumed he would not get drafted even though he was one of college football's top players, a three-time All-American. He had signed with the AAFC's Los Angeles Dons before the NFL draft.

By 1950 the AAFC was out of business. The NFL had annexed its best teams, the Browns and San Francisco 49ers, along with the Baltimore Colts. Those additions significantly increased the number of Black players in the league. The Browns still had Motley, Willis, and Gillom, and had added Len Ford, an end destined for the Pro Football Hall of Fame.

On a Sunday afternoon in Cleveland in November 1951, the Browns thumped the Bears, whose roster was still entirely white. Watching Motley, Willis, Gillom, and Ford batter his team, Halas had seen enough. He drafted a Black running back, Eddie Macon, with a second-round pick in 1952. That fall, Macon became the Bears' first Black player—thirty-two years after the franchise's birth.

The Pittsburgh Steelers and Philadelphia Eagles also put Black players on the field for the first time in 1952. Ollie Matson, a Black halfback from the University of San Francisco, was the Chicago Cardinals' first-round draft pick, the third overall selection, and the league's Rookie of the Year in 1952.

Slowly, the number of Black players in the league rose, reaching nearly two dozen by 1955. It was an improvement, but the Black players still faced rampant discrimination. No team ever had more than three or four Black players in uniform at a time; it seemed there was still an unwritten agreement among the teams about not diving too deeply into this pool of talent.

There were also limitations on which positions Black players could play. It became clear that most teams wanted them at halfback, end, or defensive back, where, according to talent evaluators, success depended more on natural athleticism than on outthinking one's opponents. Thus, there were no Black centers or middle linebackers—positions where the job entailed calling signals on the field. Quite simply, coaches did not want to give Black players that much responsibility.

The ultimate thinking position was quarterback. Luckman, Baugh, and Waterfield, the great passers of the 1940s, had given way to a glittering new generation at the position that featured the Lions' Bobby Layne, the Browns' Otto Graham, and the Colts' Johnny Unitas. They all commanded their offenses with an army general's confidence, running huddles, calling plays, completing passes all over the field, and showing no fear in close games, and they emerged just as television, in its first decade as a mainstream medium, began broadcasting NFL games into dens across America.

The nation fell in love with these daring quarterbacks who ruled the NFL. And every last one of them was white.

CHAPTER 4

Paul Brown was pro football's most forward-thinking coach in the years after World War II. While leading the Cleveland Browns to seven championships—four in the AAFC and three in the NFL—he introduced a slew of innovations that became hallmarks of the modern game. He developed complex game plans. He hired staffs of assistants that included offensive and defensive coordinators. He used game film to scout college prospects. He used radio signals to relay play calls to his quarterback. Brown's advances helped make the pro game more sophisticated, fascinating, and popular.

He was also much quicker than most of his peers to move beyond the harsh discrimination that had prevailed in pro football. He put Black players in uniform as soon as his team was up and running, and he kept bringing in more. If there was an unwritten agreement among teams about limiting Blacks on their rosters, Brown did not adhere to it. Five Black players suited up for the Browns in 1952; other teams had far fewer.

But the great innovator only went so far; he balked when it came to actually playing a Black quarterback.

It initially seemed he was ahead of the curve. In 1951, the Browns became the first team to draft a Black quarterback, selecting Syracuse's Bernie Custis with an eleventh-round pick. Custis had been the first Black starting quarterback for a major college program, and he seemingly had the skills the NFL was now looking for, having passed for more than a thousand yards in a season.

He signed with the Browns, assuming they wanted him for the potential he had shown as a quarterback. But when he arrived at training camp, he discovered otherwise.

"I want you to play safety, try out for that position," Brown said.

Custis tried to hold his ground. "I want to try out at quarterback," he said.

"You're way ahead of your time," Brown replied, according to Custis's recollection of the conversation years later.[1]

It may not have been racism motivating Brown to move Custis. The Browns already had Otto Graham, a stellar quarterback in the prime of his career. Custis was not beating out Graham. But Brown likely thought Custis, savvy and talented, still could help the team at a different position.

Custis said later that he did not necessarily believe Brown bought the prevailing notion of Black quarterbacks in the NFL in the early 1950s—namely, that they were not smart enough to handle the position. "I respected Paul," Custis said.[2] But while negative stereotyping "was not something I ever zeroed in on," he added, "I certainly felt it."[3]

Unfortunately, as with his other inventions, Brown was laying down a footprint that other NFL teams would follow in the coming years: if they drafted a good college quarterback who was Black, they found another position for him.

Brown thought enough of Custis to propose a unique solution to their "situation." Brown said he would allow Custis to take a shot at playing quarterback elsewhere, but only if Custis agreed not to sign with another NFL team.

"I'll release you. But only to a Canadian team," Brown said.[4]

Pro football in Canada was just beginning to emerge as a viable alternative. There was a scattering of teams in the western half of the country and a handful more in the east. Within a decade, the groups would merge and become the Canadian Football League, playing by rules that sounded outlandish to American fans. The field was 110 yards long, not 100. Teams only had three downs, not four, to move the ball ten yards and retain possession. And just as different was the prevailing attitude on race. Most teams in Canada did not mind putting Black players in important positions that required them to use their minds, analyze situations, and call signals. Canada, as a result, would become a haven in the coming years for Black quarterbacks who had excelled in American college football but were denied a chance to play in the pros.

According to Custis, Brown had no problem finding a job for Custis in 1951. "He had numerous calls for me from Canadian teams," Custis said.[5] The young quarterback signed with a team in Hamilton, Ontario, known as the Tiger-Cats. They initially wanted him to play running back, but after Custis performed well at quarterback in a preseason game, fans clamored for him to get a shot. "The Negro pivot player has passed and ran himself into the minds of the fans," the *Hamilton Spectator* reported.[6]

On August 29, 1951, Custis stepped behind the center and took the snap on the first play of the Tiger-Cats' season-opening game against Montreal. Hamilton won easily, 37–6, delighting a home crowd of fourteen thousand fans. It had been four years since Jackie Robinson integrated baseball's major leagues and twenty-five years since a Black quarterback started a pro football game in North America. The last one before Custis was Sol Butler with the NFL's long-gone Canton Bulldogs in 1926—before Custis was born.

He wound up starting for Hamilton all season, earned his teammates' support, and seldom heard racist language from opponents, he said.[7] He also experienced few problems off the field while living in Hamilton. "I didn't find any real prejudice against me," Custis said.[8] "I think there was more a look of curiosity from the people. I sensed it, that people were looking, even when I was walking down the street. The Black population was just about nil."

Although the caliber of Canadian pro football was nowhere close to that in the NFL, Custis demonstrated that he was capable of being a pro quarterback in 1951. He led the Tiger-Cats to a winning record and made an all-star team.

Custis had been forced to cross the border because American pro football simply was not ready for him, but eventually Canadian football proved to be not quite ready at that point, either. Despite his success in 1951, Custis was moved to running back in 1952 and a white quarterback replaced him. A year later, the Tiger-Cats won the Grey Cup, Canada's championship game, with Custis as a running back. That was where he played until his career ended in 1956.

Still, even if his opportunity lasted only a single year, Custis had broken the color line and demonstrated that Canadian football was a viable alternative for Black quarterbacks shut out of the NFL. Many would follow his lead in the coming decades.

"I don't think of myself as a pioneer," Custis said later, "but there was a paving of the way."[9]

———

As he stalked the Bears' sideline in the second half of a game against the San Francisco 49ers on a Sunday afternoon in Chicago in October 1953, George Halas was increasingly furious. His team had started fast, taking a 21–0 lead, but the 49ers scored one touchdown, then another, and finally took the lead early in the fourth quarter. When George Blanda, the Bears' quarterback, lost a fumble while trying to turn things around, Halas spun toward the bench and barked at Willie Thrower, the Bears' backup quarterback, telling him to warm up and go in when the Bears regained possession.

By the time that moment came, the 49ers had scored another touchdown. The Bears had allowed thirty-five straight points and trailed by fourteen. But when the fans saw Thrower lead Chicago's offense onto the field, they stopped booing and cheered.

A rookie from Michigan State, Thrower was making his NFL debut. When he stepped under center and took a snap, he was just another young pro hoping to make a mark. But he made a mark just by taking that snap. He became the first Black quarterback to play in the NFL in twenty-seven years.

Another Black player, George Taliaferro, also had taken snaps from center and thrown passes in recent years. (After playing in the now-defunct AAFC as a professional rookie in 1949, he joined the NFL and played for the New York Yankees, Dallas Texans, and Baltimore

Colts.) But Taliaferro was a halfback who only occasionally lined up at quarterback as a tactical surprise, in what later became known as the "wildcat" formation. Thrower was a pure quarterback, tasked with running the huddle and calling plays.

His journey to the moment when he took a snap for the Bears illustrated the obstacles Black quarterbacks with NFL aspirations faced in the 1950s. Earlier, as a single-wing high school tailback in New Kensington, Pennsylvania, near Pittsburgh, Thrower had dominated opponents, losing just one game in three years. Scholarship offers from top college programs rolled in, but most were quickly rescinded when the schools discovered Thrower was Black.

He might never have played major college football if not for the enlightened perspective of Clarence "Biggie" Munn, the head coach at Michigan State. Munn offered Thrower a scholarship and kept him at quarterback after seeing his powerful arm.

Yes, Thrower was a thrower.

A Black quarterback had never played in the Big Ten until Thrower in 1950. A pair of white quarterbacks, Al Dorow and Tom Yewcic, were Michigan State's primary players at the position, but Thrower's talent earned him opportunities. "He probably threw the ball as good as anyone," Yewcic would recall.[10]

When an injury knocked Yewcic out of a game against Notre Dame in 1952, Thrower led the Spartans to a victory that preserved their unbeaten record. They would claim a national championship at the end of the season.

Soon after, the NFL held its annual draft of college talent. The league's thirteen teams each made thirty selections, theoretically dividing up the entire pool of college seniors ready for the pros. Top quarterback prospects such as Maryland's Jack Scarbath, Detroit Mercy's Ted Marchibroda, Georgia's Zeke Bratkowski, and Oklahoma's Eddie Crowder went in the first two rounds. Later, teams took chances on unheralded quarterbacks from the University of Chattanooga, William & Mary, and the Virginia Military Institute.

Thrower went unselected. Even though he had won games for a national champion, played well against top competition, and possessed a strong throwing arm, NFL scouts were dubious about Black quarterbacks.

Fortunately, going undrafted meant he could sign with any team willing to give him a shot. That he landed with the Bears was a bit of a surprise. They had never used a Black player until the year before, and one of Halas's closest friends, Redskins owner George Preston Marshall, was the NFL's most infamous bigot.

But Halas was experiencing what can only be described as an awakening on race and football. He had indicated before, at times with his actions more than his words, that he might be open-minded about taking on Black players. He had considered signing Kenny Washington in 1940. The Bears had drafted Taliaferro in 1949. But this was different. After watching Emlen Tunnell and Ollie Matson star for other teams, he realized he was missing out on a new pipeline of talent. He had drafted Black running backs with high picks in 1952 and 1953. Signing Thrower was another step.

When Halas put him in against the 49ers in 1953, it was with the hope that he might rally the Bears with his passing. Although Thrower tossed an interception to end his first possession in charge of the offense, Halas gave him another chance and he led a drive toward San Francisco's end zone. He completed a pass, scrambled for a first down, and completed another pass.

Halas did not trust him, though. With the ball at the 49ers' 4 yard line, the coach pulled Thrower from the game and put Blanda back in. The fans booed, wanting to see Thrower finish what he had started. But the boos tailed off when the Bears scored a touchdown.

Blanda was the quarterback for the rest of the game, which the 49ers won. In his brief opportunity, Thrower had attempted eight passes and completed three, good for twenty-seven yards. He had started a rally, giving the offense a spark. But he never threw another pass for the Bears that year and they cut him before the next season.

Believing he had no future as a quarterback in the NFL, he signed with a Canadian team, the Winnipeg Blue Bombers. But they also cut him. Thrower wound up playing for a semipro team in Toronto before an injury ended his career.

Years later, Thrower had settled into a quiet existence in western Pennsylvania. He had a wife and kids and owned a tavern. Few of his friends and neighbors knew he had played in the NFL. Then ABC aired a feature on him in 2001 as part of its Black History Month programming. "I was like the Jackie Robinson of pro football," Thrower said.[11]

That was an exaggeration in one respect. Robinson did more than just break baseball's color line; he played the game so well that he was inducted into baseball's Hall of Fame. Thrower's NFL career consisted of just one appearance and three pass completions.

But while he did not merit comparisons to Robinson as a player, Thrower was, indisputably, the first Black quarterback to play in the modern NFL, making him an important historical figure. His opportunity effectively represented the start of a brutal, decades-long journey for Black quarterbacks in the pros, a journey marked mostly by denial, discouragement, broken dreams, and incremental progress over time. Other important historical figures would rise along the way. Marlin Briscoe was the first Black quarterback to prove he could think and throw at the same time. James Harris was the first to start for several years and lead a team to a championship game. Doug Williams was the first to win a Super Bowl. Michael Vick was the first to get drafted first overall. Warren Moon was the first to make the Pro Football Hall of Fame. Steve McNair was the first to share the league Most Valuable Player award. Cam Newton was the first to win the MVP award outright—ninety-five years after the launch of the NFL.

They all could rightfully claim being a football version of Jackie Robinson. The NFL's quarterback color line did not fall on one day, so easily and conveniently celebrated—unlike baseball's, with Robinson, after his debut in 1947—but rather, it fell gradually, almost imperceptibly at times, in baby steps taken by a succession of trailblazers. Thrower took the first of those baby steps. Another Jackie Robinson, indeed.

═══

A month after Thrower's appearance in Chicago, George Taliaferro was walking out to practice with the Baltimore Colts one day when

Keith Molesworth, the team's head coach, pulled him aside and asked, "Have you ever played quarterback?"[12]

It was a simple question with a complicated answer. Taliaferro had played halfback almost exclusively in college, at Indiana, and also in the pros. But he occasionally took snaps from center, as a quarterback would, when his coaches sought to surprise opposing defenses and take advantage of his varied skill set.

In other words, he had played quarterback, but he was not a quarterback.

That was good enough for Molesworth. In their first year in Baltimore, the Colts were near the end of a losing season and running low on quarterbacks. Their starter, Fred Enke, was injured, as were several backups. Molesworth needed a quarterback for that Sunday's game against the Rams. He did not mind that Taliaferro had no experience operating a T-formation offense, which the Colts ran. "There's nothing to it. Just take a couple of snaps and you'll get used to it," Molesworth said.[13]

No Black quarterback had *started* a game for an NFL team since 1926. But in the moment, Taliaferro cared less about that than what he perceived as Molesworth's flippant attitude. "Needless to say, Coach Molesworth had never taken snaps under center," Taliaferro wrote later in an essay.[14] "It's not easy, and it takes a lot more than a couple of practice snaps to turn around and do it in a game."

He was not eager for the opportunity. "As much as I enjoyed the shotgun formation, I hated the T-quarterback slot. No one rooted more than I for Fred Enke to get healthy," he wrote.[15]

But Enke was unable to play. A thick fog hugged Baltimore's Memorial Stadium that Sunday as twenty-seven thousand fans watched Taliaferro lead the Colts against the Rams, one of the league's top teams.

Norm Van Brocklin, the Rams' quarterback, was a polished, modern quarterback. He completed eleven of seventeen passes during the game. Taliaferro completed just six of twenty-one with two interceptions. But he consistently gained yardage as a runner, which kept the ball moving and kept the score close. Baltimore led at halftime, 13–7, after Taliaferro ran forty-three yards for a touchdown.

The fans cheered, sensing an upset brewing. But the Rams took the lead on a Van Brocklin touchdown pass early in the fourth quarter, and the outcome was settled minutes later when Taliaferro threw an interception that the Rams returned for a touchdown.

Taliaferro emerged from the game with two bruised fingers on his throwing hand, but Molesworth started him anyway at home against the 49ers the next week. Baltimore was not known for being tolerant of Black athletes—fans there had heaped abuse on Jackie Robinson when he played there as a minor leaguer in 1946—but Taliaferro's turn at quarterback did not impact attendance. Twenty-six thousand fans came to Memorial Stadium.

The game was a dismal affair for the home team. The 49ers contained Taliaferro on the ground and he struggled as a passer. The Colts trailed at halftime, 24–0. It was 38–0 before Taliaferro threw two touchdown passes to make the final score more respectable.

Molesworth had seen enough. Taliaferro was back at halfback for the Colts' final two games. Only later did the significance of his achievement sink in. There would not be another instance of a Black quarterback starting a game for an NFL team until the 1970s.

"The coaches didn't think I could do it," he said later. "I showed them that I could."[16]

He was long accustomed to prejudice, as were all Black players in his era. Growing up in Gary, Indiana, Taliaferro had attended segregated schools, and then he was unable to live in an on-campus dorm as a college freshman because the dorms were for white students. Later, playing for the Dallas Texans in 1952, Taliaferro looked up at home games and saw the team's Black fans sitting in a "colored" section of the Cotton Bowl. He knew some of his teammates wished he was not playing at all.

That year, he met Gino Marchetti, a rookie with the Texans, when the hulking lineman sat down at his table at a banquet. Taliaferro had been sitting alone.

"Thank you," Taliaferro said.

"For what?" Marchetti said.

"For sitting with me," Taliaferro said.[17]

A lifelong friendship had begun.

In seven years as a pro, Taliaferro rushed for nearly 2,300 yards, completed ninety-two passes, and caught ninety-five. He also played defense, punted, ran back kicks, and made those two starts as a quarterback. The first Black player ever drafted by an NFL team had proved he was a worthwhile pick.

━━━

Halas commanded such respect in the NFL that most other teams followed his lead and began drafting Black players after the Bears selected Taliaferro in 1949. It quickly became a nonstory, for the most part, when a team took a Black player.

Still, eyebrows went up around the league when the Packers drafted Charlie Brackins, a quarterback from Prairie View A&M, in 1955. The selection went against two principles that NFL talent evaluators considered immutable. Prairie View was a historically Black institution, and pro teams saw Black college football as an inferior brand that produced few, if any, viable prospects at *any* position. Also, Brackins was a quarterback, and the NFL's position on Black players at *that* position was as fixed as the jutting jaw Halas displayed on the Bears' sideline on Sundays.

The doubts about the quality of Black college football were beginning to wane, however slightly. Paul "Tank" Younger, a fullback and linebacker from Grambling, was playing well for the Rams. The New York Giants had found an anchor for their offensive line at Morgan State, a historically Black college in Baltimore, when they drafted Roosevelt Brown.

But the out-of-hand dismissal of all Black quarterbacks sailed on, unchanged. Jack Vainisi, the Packers' chief scout, was thinking outside the box when he vouched for Brackins's potential to others in the organization before the 1955 draft. Vainisi had an open mind and a keen eye. Before he died of a heart attack in 1960, he would draft many of the players who would help the Packers win a succession of titles under Vince Lombardi.

Scouting in the 1950s was nothing like the analytical science it would become. There was little money in team budgets for scouts to travel, so they depended on college coaches' opinions and "bird dog" evaluators who were paid small sums to attend practices and games and deliver "eyeball" reports. It was a word-of-mouth business, and Vainisi heard that Brackins was so impressive that he was worth taking a chance on, even coming from Prairie View.

Brackins stood six feet two and weighed more than two hundred pounds. He was fast, an elusive runner, and could hurl passes far into the distance. He also punted, kicked field goals, and played defensive back, but he had dominated games as a quarterback while leading Prairie View to the pinnacle of Black college football. Sportswriters called him "Choo Choo" because he resembled an unstoppable locomotive on the field.

The Packers already had a starting quarterback, Tobin Rote, a chiseled Texan who stood six feet three, weighed 210 pounds, and in a nod to football's past, was just as happy running with the ball as throwing it. At age twenty-seven, he was in his prime.

But the Packers were open to making a change. They were on a long run of consecutive losing seasons. After they drafted Brackins, the *Green Bay Press-Gazette* published an article about the success that Black players were experiencing in pro football. "It's interesting to note that the league's top four rushers were Negroes" in 1954, the paper wrote, as were the league leaders in interceptions and punt returns.[18] "But no member of the Negro race has been able to make it as a quarterback," the paper pointed out, labeling the development "unusual" in light of the success Blacks were having at other positions. Brackins wanted to become the "first Negro quarterback regular" in the NFL, the paper reported.

How that impacted his relationship with Rote was never revealed. Both were Texans, but the Texas Brackins knew was far different from Rote's. A San Antonio native, Rote had played on all-white teams in high school and at Rice. Brackins had grown up in segregated South Dallas and attended all-Black Lincoln High School. His in-state college choices were limited to Black colleges because the powerhouse Southwest Conference was entirely white.

Beyond standard accounts of his performances in practices and games, little is known about Brackins's experience with the Packers. But it had to be jarring. In business since 1919, the Packers had not integrated their roster until 1950. Green Bay's Black population was almost nil. The Packers' head coach, Lisle Blackbourn, complained about Brackins lacking confidence, but what did he expect? Brackins had never played with white teammates, and now, in huddles, he was telling white teammates what to do.

But at least Brackins was given a chance to play quarterback, unlike Custis in Cleveland four years earlier. Early in training camp, he scored the winning touchdown in a rookie intrasquad game. Then, he threw two touchdown passes in an all-team intrasquad game. "He has the right physical and mental assets to really come through," Blackbourn said.[19]

Still, the coach had no trouble identifying reasons to doubt Brackins. "He's got to learn; he was never taught [how to play the position] correctly from the start," Blackbourn said.[20] Rote took most of the snaps during the exhibition season while Brackins handled kickoffs and received several brief opportunities at quarterback. He started the exhibition finale but was replaced after throwing an early interception.

"When Rote has a bad day or hits a slump, he works all the harder and eventually comes back. Brackins won't. He just doesn't seem to have any confidence that he can ever do better," Blackbourn said.[21] "He does have the potential. We certainly haven't given up on him."

Indeed, Brackins made the roster and handled kickoffs through the first month of the regular season. When Rote struggled in a loss to the Browns, Blackbourn pulled him and put in Brackins. But he was only in long enough to throw a pair of incompletions.

The Packers abruptly cut Brackins two weeks later, after a game against the Bears in Chicago. Dick Deschaine, the team's punter in 1955, said later, "They found him about four o'clock in the morning drunk in Chicago, passed out. He kicked off [against the Bears] and then they got rid of him on the train [ride home]. He had all the qualifications, but he screwed up."[22]

Talent evaluators around the league saw Brackins's dismissal as confirmation of their suspicion that the Packers had wasted a draft pick. Brackins arranged several tryouts in the coming years, but other teams only wanted him at positions other than quarterback. He never played in another regular-season NFL game. His second chance as a quarterback never materialized. It simply did not matter that he was as big or bigger than most of the white players who manned the position in the league, certainly was faster, and possessed a powerful throwing arm. His potential, apparent to anyone with an unjaundiced eye, was offset by his skin color. And with that, his opportunity just flittered away.

It is interesting to consider what might have happened if the Packers had tolerated his on-field and off-field mistakes, which white quarterbacks also made plenty of, and thrown the full force of the organization behind seeing that he succeeded—in short, given him the kind of support talented Black quarterbacks would receive decades later. But in the 1950s, when Brackins did not blossom as Vainisi hoped, it reinforced the racist stereotype about Black quarterbacks that had predominated in the NFL, ensuring that it would continue to predominate for several more decades. As Brackins spiraled out of the sport, the gains that Briscoe, Harris, Moon, and others would later register were as impossible to envision as an errant pass from the incomparable Unitas tumbling end over end through the air.

CHAPTER 5

It all started innocently enough. In the late 1950s, a young Texan named Lamar Hunt wanted to bring an NFL team to Dallas, where he lived. His father, oilman H. L. Hunt, was among the wealthiest men in America and expected Lamar to join him in the oil business after college. But Hunt liked football more. He had been a reserve end at Southern Methodist, and now, at age twenty-six, he wanted to own a team.

The older men who ran the NFL put him off. They liked his money and his pleasant demeanor, but they had already tried placing a team in Dallas and it failed miserably. They also did not want to expand the size of their league. After breaking even at best for more than three decades, they finally were making a profit thanks to contracts to televise games. They did not want to cut up their growing pie any more than they already were.

Their decision to put Hunt off set in motion a chain of events that would profoundly alter pro football.

Hunt reached out to football-loving businessmen in other cities who had tried, without success, to buy into the NFL. They started their own league in 1960, calling it the American Football League.

From the outset, the AFL distinguished itself from the NFL by offering a more wide-open, pass-happy game. Offenses in the NFL had come a long way since the 1930s, but the AFL cranked the excitement to new heights. The NFL still believed it was superior, and at least initially, it was. But it began to seem stodgy by comparison. And its claims to superiority did not hold up for long.

Perhaps not coincidentally, the AFL also distinguished itself from the NFL by aggressively signing Black college talent.

The NFL's position was steadfast; more than a decade after Kenny Washington joined the Rams, most teams still suited up only a few Black players at a time. The Redskins' roster was entirely white.

Teams in the AFL dug deeper into the pool of Black players. This was not necessarily the result of a more open-minded view; a better way to put it was the AFL was less closed-minded. "We never pretended that we were making a conscious effort to open things up [racially]," Lamar Hunt said later. "We just made a conscious effort to find the best players anywhere we could."[1]

In 1963, Hunt's team, the Kansas City Chiefs (they had moved after playing their first three seasons in Dallas as a team called the Texans), selected a towering lineman from Grambling, Buck Buchanan, with the first overall pick in the AFL draft. Talent evaluators in the NFL were shocked to see a player from a historically Black college go that high.

But while the AFL challenged the NFL's thinking and practices on many fronts, beginning a process that eventually would produce a merger between the leagues, the AFL did not challenge the NFL's longstanding belief that only white players should man the quarterback position.

Much like NFL teams, AFL teams latched onto signature quarterbacks who became associated with their franchises. The Chiefs had Len Dawson. The Buffalo Bills had Jack Kemp. Former NFL quarterbacks Tobin Rote and George Blanda won AFL titles with the San Diego Chargers and Houston Oilers.

In the early years of the AFL, every starting quarterback was white except for the Oakland Raiders' Tom Flores, who was Hispanic. Every backup was white, too. The new league's forward-thinking attitude on Black players did not extend to the most important position on the field. The rival leagues had many battles, but they were in agreement on the need for all quarterbacks to be white.

The lack of Black quarterbacks in the pro game was attributable to a set of enduring and racist generalizations entrenched in the minds of owners, general managers, coaches, and scouts. They not only believed that Blacks lacked the intelligence to run pro offenses but also that white teammates would not look up to them, that they could not pass adeptly enough, and that they were not as tough-minded, disciplined, or dependable as white quarterbacks.

Plenty of Black players had manned the quarterback position for college teams over the years, mostly at historically Black institutions, with a few at integrated major college programs. But when only a couple received legitimate opportunities in the pros, the contemptuous generalizations were allowed to stand unchallenged. In fact, they seemed stronger than ever in the early 1960s now that there were two leagues hewing to them.

If any quarterback had the potential to challenge the status quo in those years, it was the University of Minnesota's Sandy Stephens. A decade after Syracuse's Bernie Custis broke barriers, Stephens made a similar journey from a Pennsylvania high school to national prominence. Only his journey went even further.

Raised in Uniontown, southeast of Pittsburgh, Stephens was born to play sports. His parents met on a tennis court. His father was an all-around athlete. As a youngster, Stephens played sandlot baseball with Ernie Davis, who would become the first Black Heisman Trophy winner. Davis played third base while Stephens pitched. "That's where I got my arm for football," Stephens said later.[2]

Davis moved to New York before high school, but the light-skinned, broad-shouldered Stephens was an athlete for all seasons at Uniontown High School. He received sixty college scholarship offers from major programs, mostly in football, but also in basketball. Baseball's Philadelphia Phillies and Pittsburgh Pirates contacted him.

Stephens was the best player on any field or court he stepped onto, a hard worker, calm in tense situations, and a natural leader, always quick to provide encouragement to those who needed it. With all that going for him along with his bright smile and upbeat manner, his teammates, both Black and white, could not help but look up to him. "He always made people feel good," a college football teammate said.[3]

Given his many options, it was a surprise that he elected to play football at Minnesota. The Gophers had won five national titles in the 1930s and 1940s but were now also-rans in the Big Ten. What won Stephens over was a coach willing to let him play quarterback.

The coach, Murray Warmath, was widening his recruiting scope beyond the Midwest in an attempt to turn the program around. He would eventually land Stephens, fullback/linebacker Judge Dickson, and halfback Bill Munsey—three Black players from Pennsylvania who would lead the Gophers' dramatic return to the top of the Big Ten.

In the summer before he headed to Minnesota, Stephens played quarterback in a high school all-star game in Hershey, Pennsylvania. The game itself was forgettable, but Stephens would always remember being denied access to a pool where his white teammates went to relax after practice. The slight reminded him of the disingenuous smiles of recruiters who had talked to him about playing positions other than quarterback without ever telling him *why* they wanted him to switch.

"I went to Minnesota because I felt I would get a chance to play quarterback in the Big Ten," Stephens said later. "I wanted to go where I thought it was the toughest and roughest league because they felt like I couldn't play quarterback and I wanted to go where the toughest league was to disprove them."[4]

He became Minnesota's starting quarterback during his sophomore season in 1959, when it was impossible to envision better days just ahead for the Gophers. They won two of nine games and finished last in the Big Ten. Fans threw garbage on Warmath's lawn, hung him in effigy, and campaigned for the school to buy out the last two years of his contract.

Warmath kept his job, insisting the seeds of success had been planted, especially with Stephens as his quarterback. Though not a stellar passer, Stephens was a tough runner and indefatigable leader. "White or Black, Sandy gave all of his teammates the same promise: 'We're going to the Rose Bowl.' And then he took us there," Judge Dickson would recall.[5]

The Gophers opened the 1960 season by defeating a ranked opponent, Nebraska, then won five more games in a row to set up college football's most anticipated matchup of the year—undefeated Minnesota, ranked third in the country, against undefeated Iowa, ranked first in the country.

The stakes were high, with the winner likely to win the Big Ten and receive a bid to play in the Rose Bowl, college football's premier postseason contest. And that was not the only reason the game was notable. Both teams had Black quarterbacks—Stephens for Minnesota and Wilburn Hollis for Iowa.

Years later, Hollis said he gave little thought to that aspect of the matchup. "It's all in hindsight," he said. "Back then we never thought anything about race. Because we played in the Big Ten, and in the Big Ten they never had anything to do with race. It was always just put the best players on the field."[6]

Nonetheless, it was significant to see Black quarterbacks starting such an important game. Major college football was still strictly segregated in the Deep South and Southwest. The sight of Stephens and Hollis running offenses in an important game sent a message to teams in those regions that Black players could help them, much as they wanted to deny it.

Both quarterbacks were more effective as runners than passers. Stephens gave the Gophers the lead with a touchdown run in the second quarter and they went on to win. Although they lost to Purdue the next week, they ended the regular season ranked first in the Associated Press poll. The national championship was awarded in December, before the bowl games were played, so it did not hurt the Gophers when Washington upset them in the Rose Bowl. They rightfully claimed the national title.

A year later, the Gophers finished second to Ohio State in the Big Ten as Stephens completed his college career with a series of stellar performances. Against Michigan, he passed for a touchdown, ran for a touchdown, and preserved a comeback victory with a late interception on the goal line. (He also played defense due to limits on substitutions still in effect in college football.) When Ohio State declined the invitation to play in the Rose Bowl, the Gophers accepted and thrashed UCLA as Stephens ran for two touchdowns.

He finished fourth in the balloting for the Heisman Trophy, which was won by Ernie Davis, his childhood baseball teammate. Still friends, they marveled at the barriers they were breaking. Stephens was the first Black quarterback to earn first-team All-America honors.

There was little history of pro teams drafting Black quarterbacks, but none had presented themselves with such an impressive record. Stephens had led Minnesota from the bottom of the Big Ten to the top, won a national title, and made two Rose Bowl starts. He had led a team that was mostly white, giving his best performances in the biggest games. As a senior, he had rushed for more than five hundred yards and thrown for nearly nine hundred; it was clear he was developing as a passer, his skill set falling more in line with what pro scouts desired. How could those scouts not like him as a prospect?

In the early 1960s, the NFL and AFL held their drafts in December, after the college regular season but before the bowl games. The NFL's Browns took Stephens in the second round, with the twenty-fifth overall pick. The New York Titans took Stephens with the fifth overall selection in the AFL draft.

The idea of playing for the Browns excited Stephens. He had grown up rooting for them in western Pennsylvania, not far from Cleveland. Conveniently, they were looking for a new quarterback even though Milt Plum had led the NFL in completion percentage for three straight years. The Browns had missed the playoffs in those seasons. Accustomed to better, Paul Brown hoped a new quarterback would provide what the team needed to get back to the postseason.

A decade after denying Bernie Custis the chance to prove he was an NFL quarterback, Brown sounded ready to become the first pro coach to give a Black quarterback an opportunity to start. After watching Stephens dominate UCLA in the Rose Bowl, Brown said, "We definitely are thinking of Sandy as a quarterback. He looked sharp. He seems like a fellow who knows what's going on out there. I like that improvising."[7]

The Browns first had to sign Stephens, though. They made a contract offer, but so did the Titans and the Canadian Football League's Montreal Alouettes, who held his rights north of the border.

Surprisingly, Stephens signed with the Alouettes less than a week after the Rose Bowl. At the time, it was reported that negotiations between the Browns and Stephens had soured when Stephens asked that his contract include a no-trade clause. But Stephens said later that Jim Brown, the Browns' All-Pro running back and the league's most celebrated Black player, had called him and said, "Sandy, if you think you're going to be the quarterback of the Cleveland Browns, you're crazy."[8] Teams in the NFL just were not going to play Black quarterbacks, Brown told Stephens.

Disappointed, Stephens turned down pro football in the United States and became the Alouettes' starter as a rookie in 1962. He struggled as a passer, throwing twice as many interceptions as touchdown passes, which prompted the Alouettes to trade him. He soon abandoned Canada entirely, signing with the NFL's Minnesota Vikings, who had joined the league as an expansion team in 1961.

Stephens was optimistic that he would at least get a shot to play quarterback in the state where he had performed so heroically in college. But as training camp began, he was in an auto accident that left him severely injured. At first, doctors feared he might not walk again. He beat that prognosis but sat out two seasons. Finally, the Chiefs signed him going into the 1967 season. Their head coach, Hank Stram, fondly recalled Stephens's glory days at Minnesota.

The Chiefs listed Stephens as a quarterback on their training camp roster. Len Dawson was entrenched as the starter, but the backup job was open. Stephens played well in scrimmages, but his weight was up to 225 pounds and Stram thought he was more effective as a running back. Stephens was fine with the switch; at this point, he just wanted to play in the pros. But the Chiefs cut him before the season began.

At age twenty-seven, Stephens was done with football. He never played quarterback in either the NFL or AFL, a disappointment that, according to his testimonial plaque at the Fayette County (Pennsylvania) Sports Hall of Fame, "haunted him until the day he died."[9]

———

As a Black youngster in Jackson, Michigan, the heart of Big Ten country, in the early 1960s, Tony Dungy paid close attention to Sandy Stephens. "You watched him on black-and-white television in the Rose Bowl. He led his team to the national championship," Dungy said later.[10]

By the early 1970s, Dungy was a high school star who wanted to play quarterback in college. After meeting Stephens on a recruiting visit to the University of Minnesota, he signed with the Gophers.

"I had a dream. I wanted to play quarterback and I saw that this African-American had been able to do that and do it successfully at the highest level at Minnesota. That inspired me to go there and do it and try it," Dungy said. "I was 17 and just overwhelmed because that's what I wanted to do, be a quarterback who led my team to a national championship. I thought, 'It's happened once, at Minnesota. That might be the best place to do it again.'"[11]

Four years later, as he closed out his college career, Dungy again found himself in a position to emulate Stephens. Although he had not led the Gophers to a national title, he had passed and run for nearly five thousand yards and established a set of school passing records. Scouts from NFL teams liked him, but not as a quarterback.

"I led the Big Ten in passing and was told I needed to switch to defensive back or go to Canada," Dungy said. "I had a chance to go to Canada [and play quarterback] and could follow Sandy Stephens again in doing that."[12]

Dungy made a different decision. "I decided I wanted to play in the NFL, so I switched and became a safety," he said.[13]

After going undrafted, he made the Pittsburgh Steelers' roster in 1977 and played in thirty games as a safety over the next two seasons. (He did play quarterback in one game when injuries sidelined the

Steelers' starter and backup. Dungy attempted eight passes, completing three to his teammates and two to opponents.) After the Steelers cut him, he played one more year with the 49ers before retiring and starting what became a far more successful career as an NFL coach.

In thirteen years as the head coach of the Tampa Bay Buccaneers and Indianapolis Colts, Dungy compiled a .668 winning percentage and became the first Black coach to win a Super Bowl. He was coaching the Bucs in 2000 when Sandy Stephens died from a heart attack at age fifty-nine. Many fans across America had never heard of Stephens, partly because he did not follow up his brilliant college career with a stint in the NFL or AFL—or, more accurately, did not have the chance. But football insiders and fans of a certain age mourned the loss of a major historical figure. A letter from the Reverend Jesse Jackson, the famous Baptist minister and civil rights activist, was read at Sanders' memorial service. Jackson was the same age as Sanders. Both had played quarterback in high school and started their college careers in the Big Ten. Jackson lasted one year at Illinois before transferring to North Carolina A&T, a historically Black institution, where he started at quarterback and watched Sanders rise to the pinnacle of college football.

"Sandy made us feel so proud, with his poise and dignity, as well as his athletic ability," Jackson wrote. "I am convinced his dreams of having an even playing field for his skills to be demonstrated were broken, but his non-negotiable dignity and private pride were never broken."[14]

Before he died, Stephens cast his disappointing postcollege football experience in biblical terms. In an unpublished memoir, he wrote, "As a pioneer in the field, first of the consensus Black All-American quarterbacks, my experiences leave me feeling like the Moses of Black quarterbacks, able to see the promised land but unable to enter it."[15]

The "promised land" he referenced was the chance to step on an NFL field and play as a Black quarterback—a prospect that would not open up for several more decades after Stephens gave up trying. In his day, he was a rarity in that he even dared to dream it was possible. Because, quite simply, it was not.

"Sandy was a pioneer" who played in "a different era, a different time," before Blacks had a chance to play quarterback, Dungy said in a 2016 interview. "Then, years later, it kind of changed and we started seeing quarterbacks with this skillset get more of an opportunity in the NFL. We saw Robert Griffin and Russell Wilson and Dak Prescott and these guys have success. But Sandy Stephens, I would have to say, is the forerunner of all of that."[16]

CHAPTER 6

he legend of Eldridge Dickey began early in his life. In the late 1950s, when he was a youngster playing outside with friends in a Black neighborhood that would become part of Houston's Fourth Ward, he could throw a football clear over the power lines above his street. And he could do it throwing left-handed as well as right-handed.

Adults who saw him throw elbowed one another in the ribs. *Did you see that?*

In the early 1960s, crowds filled stadiums to watch Dickey play quarterback for the Golden Eagles of all-Black Booker T. Washington High School. Tall, fast, and poised, he donned showy white cleats, zipped tight spirals through the air—right-handed—and broke long runs for touchdowns. Houston's Black high school football scene had produced plenty of stars, but none like this.

He seemed to have it all. A preacher's son, Dickey led his teammates in prayer before games. It was rumored he had a 130 IQ. Had he been white, major college programs would have sought to lure him. But with college football still strictly segregated in the Southwest and Deep South, Dickey had limited options and chose to play at a historically Black institution. In a mild surprise, he signed with the Tigers of Tennessee A&I, in Nashville.

The Tigers had a winning tradition dating back to the 1930s, but lately they had fallen behind Grambling, Florida A&M, and other historically Black schools that were sending players to the NFL and AFL. Seeking to catch up, the school had hired "Big John" Merritt, a rotund, cigar-chomping former lineman who had built a winning program as the coach at Jackson State a decade earlier. A showman, Merritt took recruiting trips in a Cadillac and favored an offense built around a high-flying passing attack. He believed Dickey could lead Tennessee A&I back to glory.

Dickey did just that. The Tigers won thirty-three of thirty-nine games over the next four seasons, at one point going more than two years without a defeat. Running Merritt's pro-style offense, Dickey threw nearly seventy touchdown passes and accrued more than six thousand passing yards—astronomical numbers in an era when running games ruled college football.

But statistics alone do not convey the excitement Dickey generated. Fans filled the Tigers' stadium, built into a ravine on campus and known as "the Hole," and screeched as Dickey approached the line of scrimmage in his white cleats, surveyed the defense, and received the snap. What would he do? He might drop back and fling the ball to a receiver running far downfield. He might roll out and hit a halfback on a shorter route. Or he might take off running with the ball. Whatever option he chose, the defense seldom stopped him.

"Our stadium would hold about 18,000, and at game time there would be about 30,000 people in here, breaking every fire code you want to think about, but that's the way they came. They came from all over the country to see that young man play," said Joe Gilliam Sr., one of Merritt's assistants.[1]

Even just a decade earlier, pro scouts would have shown no interest in Dickey. The concept of Black inferiority at quarterback was baked into the minds of the all-white class of pro owners, general managers, coaches, and scouts. And with its firm judgment that Blacks were not fit for leadership positions or any job requiring intelligence, the NFL really was no different from the rest of America. The example of Karen Hastie, a Black student at an integrated middle school in Philadelphia in the 1950s, was illustrative. The daughter of a Harvard-educated lawyer and activist, she envisioned becoming a lawyer herself. But when she expressed that ambition to her school's guidance counselor, the counselor said she would make a good store clerk.[2] "That was the first time that I really was struck by the fact that there was, among many in the white population, a low expectation of what Blacks have the intellectual capacity to achieve and had the drive to go after," said Hastie, who later became a lawyer, the first Black woman hired as a Supreme Court clerk, and a partner at a powerhouse firm in Washington, DC.[3]

But dramatic changes shook up pro football scouting starting in the early 1960s, resulting in changes in how Black players, including quarterbacks, were perceived. Prior to that point, most teams had invested little time and money in scouting, relying instead on the opinions of college coaches and even sportswriters as they chose which players to draft. The Browns and Rams were the only teams with full-time scouts. But in the early 1960s, scouting became more comprehensive, scientific, competitive, and open-minded. The NFL's Dallas Cowboys began running their analysis of prospects through an IBM computer and finding starters in unusual places, demonstrating the value of quantifiable data and expanded searches. Teams hired full-time scouts, with the hires skewing younger, and paid for the scouts to travel to college campuses and study prospects. In this changing environment, more Blacks, including those at historically Black institutions, were given chances by the pros, and enough delivered that teams could no longer afford to ignore that talent pool, which included quarterbacks such as Dickey.

Upton Bell, a young scout for the Baltimore Colts, took a long driving trip through the South in 1963. "I was 26, which made me about 40 years younger than everyone else out there," Bell said.[4]

Bell's father, Bert, had been an instrumental figure in the NFL's growth. Bert founded the Philadelphia Eagles in 1933 and later served as the league's commissioner from 1946 until 1959, when he died from a heart attack during a game in Philadelphia. Upton had grown up in and around pro football and was beginning what he hoped was a long career in the sport.

Typical of the newer generation of scouts, he did not buy the old notions about Black players' limitations. "It was all bullshit," Bell said.[5]

As a youngster in 1950, he had accompanied his father to a season-opening game between the Eagles and Browns. The NFL had just merged with its rival, the All-America Football Conference. The

Eagles, champions of the NFL, had an all-white roster. Paul Brown's Browns had dominated the AAFC partly because they had Black players.

Watching the teams warm up, Upton noted the difference. "Dad, the Browns are going to kill the Eagles," he said.[6]

"Shut your mouth," Bert replied.

The Browns won, 35–10.

Starting in 1963, Upton's drive through the South became an annual part of his duties with the Colts. He stopped to see players at major colleges but also went to historically Black colleges.

"There was unbelievable talent that simply had gone unnoticed until recently for obvious reasons," he recalled.[7] When he studied the quarterbacks, he "saw a lot of talented guys who today would be Lamar Jackson or Deshaun Watson," Bell recalled. "I'd see a running quarterback with a good arm, but not a pocket passer, and I'd know what was coming. People would say, 'Well, he played quarterback but he's a good athlete; he'd be a great wide receiver.' That was the refrain."[8]

Starting in the mid-1960s, several teams went so far as to hire Black scouts who knew about Black college football. Lloyd Wells, a photographer from Houston who had sought to integrate press boxes, went to work for the Chiefs. The Houston Oilers hired Tom Williams, a former assistant coach at Grambling. The NFL's Steelers hired Bill Nunn, who, as the sports editor of the *Pittsburgh Courier*—one of the nation's most important Black newspapers—had selected a Black college football All-America team.

With new eyeballs assessing talent, new opinions arose. The Chiefs drafted Willie Lanier, a Black defensive star from Morgan State. Lanier played middle linebacker, a quintessential "thinking" position. The Chiefs won with him effectively running the defense, calling signals, and telling white teammates what to do.

When the Chiefs put a Black player at middle linebacker, the window of opportunity for Black quarterbacks cracked open ever so slightly.

Bell was one of many scouts who came to Nashville during the 1967 season to see Tennessee A&I's practices and games. Seven players from the program had been drafted the year before, and Eldridge Dickey, as a senior, was part of a class that included Claude Humphrey—a monstrous defensive lineman—and several speedy receivers. "Dickey was very exciting. He just had a ton of talent," Bell said.[9]

Even his opponents marveled at him. On a Saturday night in October that fall, the Tigers hosted Grambling before a full house at the Hole. Grambling's quarterback, James Harris, was a year younger than Dickey and not as well known, partly because he did not post such impressive passing statistics in Grambling's more conservative, run-oriented offense. Still, he admired Dickey. "He was just such a star," Harris said. "There were no Black quarterbacks at all in the NFL at the time, but there was no doubt in my mind that Dickey could play in the pros."[10] During pregame warm-ups, the two stood nearly back-to-back at midfield, throwing passes to teammates. Harris loved sharing the spotlight with Dickey.

Grambling's coach, Eddie Robinson, opened up his offense so Harris could compete with Dickey that night in Nashville. Two inches taller and twenty pounds heavier than Dickey, Harris passed for 264 yards and three touchdowns, the last of which came late and gave Grambling a 26–24 victory. Dickey threw five interceptions that night, but that did not stop scouts from raving about him. "Such an athlete. He seemed like a guy you could bring in and really develop," said Ron Wolf, a young, white scout for the Oakland Raiders in 1967.[11] On Wolf's recommendation, Al Davis, the Raiders' fiery managing general partner, scouted Dickey at a game and later helicoptered in to watch him practice.

A Black quarterback had not taken a snap in an NFL game since Charlie Brackins in 1955, and it had never happened in an AFL game. Dickey, so gifted that John Merritt nicknamed him "The Lord's Prayer," believed it was his destiny to break the color line. "His purpose in life is to prove that a Negro can be a successful pro quarterback," Merritt said.[12]

The AFL and NFL had agreed to merge in 1966, setting in motion a lengthy process of melding the two leagues into a single entity known as the NFL. For four years in the late 1960s, their respective champions met in an ultimate title game, soon to be known as the Super Bowl. They also now held a single draft, so only one team had the rights to each player. Previously, a team in each league had owned the rights and the bidding wars sent salaries skyrocketing to the point of almost putting everyone out of business.

On January 30, 1968, the NFL draft took place at the Belmont Plaza Hotel in New York City. The sport's deeper faith in Black college talent was immediately evident. The Atlanta Falcons selected Humphrey, Dickey's college teammate, with the third pick in the first round. Players from Morgan State, Jackson State, Grambling, and Mississippi Valley State also went in the first two rounds.

The Raiders took Dickey with their first-round pick, stunning the other teams. Few Black quarterbacks had ever been drafted, let alone this high. After decades of odious notions denying Black players this recognition—the definition of institutional racism—the Raiders, with a single pick, had effectively called bullshit on pro football's reflexive dismissal of Black quarterbacks.

The Raiders never would have drafted Dickey if they did not believe he was smart and tough enough, and enough of a leader, to become their quarterback. "We certainly had heard all of the theories about Black quarterbacks," Ron Wolf recalled. "The fact that we took Dickey with a first-round pick tells you what we thought of those theories."[13]

No one cheered louder than James Harris, Dickey's college rival, who would be eligible for the NFL draft in a year and wanted to play the position in the pros. "I jumped for joy," Harris said. "It gave me such hope to see a Black quarterback's talent get recognized."[14]

The pick came at a time when Black Americans were angry about the status quo in virtually every aspect of their lives, frustrated by police brutality, persistent poverty, and the dismal conditions of segregated housing and schools. The passage of the Civil Rights Act in 1964 had not made enough of a difference. Months before Dickey's selection, in the summer of 1967, social unrest had convulsed well over one hundred urban communities, usually triggered by a dispute between

Black citizens and white police officers. A Black quarterback being accorded respect was not going to ease the anger or alter any desperate realities, but it challenged a set of beliefs that had denied Black individuals, which made it a triumph.

That it was the Raiders engineering the challenge was no surprise. As sports franchises went, they were socially progressive, bordering on radical. They actively courted non-white fans, routinely drafted Pro Bowl–caliber talent from historically Black colleges, and would later hire the first Black head coach in modern NFL history, as well as the first female front office executive. For them, Dickey's selection was just another breakthrough, a classic move by Davis, who loved to zig when others zagged.

Reaction poured in, and, inevitably, not all of it was positive. "There was a lot of blowback," recalled Mark Davis, Al Davis's son, who was a teenager at the time.[15]

But the Raiders could handle it. Their rebellious image paired naturally with that of other Bay Area–based groups such as the Hells Angels, an outlaw motorcycle club, and the Black Panthers, a political organization that challenged police brutality against Blacks. Many members of those groups rooted for the Raiders. When they heard Davis say of Dickey, "I don't care if he's polka-dot," they thrust their fists in the air.[16]

Yet Dickey's path through pro football would not be smooth. That became apparent within hours of his selection, as the Raiders promptly drafted *another* quarterback, Ken Stabler, in the second round of the 1968 draft. Stabler had rushed and passed for more than three thousand yards at Alabama and led the Crimson Tide to an 11–0 record as a junior.

The back-to-back drafting of quarterbacks with high picks mystified fans. The Raiders had just won the AFL championship with Daryle Lamonica, a twenty-six-year-old quarterback nicknamed "The Mad Bomber" because he was such an effective deep passer. Although they had lost to Vince Lombardi's Packers in the Super Bowl, they appeared set for a long run of success with a roster built around Lamonica, winner of the AFL's Most Valuable Player award in 1967. They also had a quality backup quarterback, forty-year-old George Blanda, a longtime starter in the NFL and previous winner of the AFL's MVP award.

Their drafting of Dickey hinted at the possibility of historic change, but the reality was the Raiders did not need a quarterback. When Davis and the team's head coach, John Rauch, met with Dickey, they told him they liked his potential at quarterback but he probably would begin his pro career as a wide receiver. Dickey was disappointed, but publicly, he said he would do what the Raiders wanted, especially after he signed a four-year contract worth $150,000. Merritt tried to explain the Raiders' thinking to Dickey's fans across the country. "The pros don't think a college quarterback is ready to take over in their ranks for four or five years. Eldridge is too good an athlete to sit on the bench while he's learning to become a good enough pro quarterback," Merritt said.[17]

Undaunted, Dickey acted like a star. He made a memorable first impression at the Raiders' training camp in Santa Rosa, California, that summer. He drove a Cadillac Eldorado that he had bought with his signing bonus. He wore white playing cleats—the same shoes he had flashed for years while destroying defenses.

But the Raiders had Lamonica, Blanda, and thirty-seven-year-old Cotton Davidson, a former starter signed as insurance, and they did not think of asking Stabler to switch positions. It was truly an abundance of quarterback riches, leaving no room for Dickey.

"You've got all these quarterbacks; where are you going to put Eldridge Dickey? If he can't beat out any of them, you're going to play him where he has a chance to make the team," Rauch said later about moving Dickey to receiver.[18]

Rauch still gave him playing time at quarterback in practices, scrimmages, and preseason games. He gave teammates and fans a glimpse of the potential that had tantalized Davis and Wolf. Dickey was "one of the most talented players I've ever seen," said Art Shell, an offensive tackle who, like Dickey, was a rookie with the Raiders in 1968. "The guy could throw with his left hand just as good as he did with his right. I've never seen nothing like that. He could have done anything he wanted."[19]

But Dickey was erratic. He was prone to taking low-percentage chances with his powerful arm, which led to interceptions. And it worked against him that his playing style differed from Lamonica's. When Dickey dropped back into the "pocket" of linemen that formed around him and did not see an open receiver, he took off and ran. Lamonica never left the pocket. That was what the coaches wanted.

"It started going bad because the coaches wanted Dickey in the pocket," Gene Upshaw, a young offensive guard on the Raiders in 1968, said later. "They wanted to make him into a prototype quarterback. Dickey would stay in there for a while but then he'd say, 'Shit, I'm gone.'"[20]

Still, Dickey's exciting performances drew raves from fans. His prospects were a topic of conversation around the country; Black fans were especially anxious to see him break the color barrier at quarterback. The *Santa Rosa Press Democrat* reported that "black militants in the Oakland area" were pressuring Davis and Rauch to play Dickey, and that Dickey had been "counseled" to refuse to switch positions. But Dickey was "cooperating" with the Raiders rather than resisting, the paper reported.[21]

He had no choice. This was pro football, an environment effectively immune from the civil rights movement, even in the summer of 1968. White men ruled the sport, no questions asked, and any player who protested would likely soon be out of a job.

"A pro football team is not a democracy; it's a dictatorship," Davis said. "The organization reserves the right to play a man where he will make the greatest contribution. We never lied to [Dickey]. He knew all along what we had in mind for this year. We have a complex offense, a complete offense, and it's going to take time for anyone to learn it. Dickey will get more exposure as a receiver this year than he would have at quarterback and learning the pass routes will help him."[22]

Davis insisted that playing receiver as a rookie would not alter Dickey's eventual career path. "Dickey will play quarterback. He has great potential as a quarterback. I'm even more convinced of that now than I was before our training camp began," Davis said as the 1968 season began. "But we're dedicated to winning the championship and that's more important right now. If Dickey doesn't play quarterback in two or three years, then it will be an issue."[23]

As best as anyone could figure, the Raiders saw Stabler and Dickey as eventual competitors for the job of backing up Lamonica when Blanda retired, with the winner likely to become the team's starter at some point. If so, Dickey inched ahead early even though he was not even playing quarterback as a rookie in 1968. Stabler's rookie season was a disaster. He struggled to adjust to the pro game and the Raiders eventually sent him to Spokane, Washington, to gain experience while playing for a minor-league team.

Dickey, meanwhile, was in uniform when the Raiders opened the 1968 season in Buffalo, against the Bills, on a sunny September Sunday. A national television audience saw evidence of the team's offensive explosiveness. The Raiders led by twenty-one points in the first quarter, by thirty-one at halftime. It was 34–6 in the fourth quarter when Rauch pulled Lamonica in favor of a backup.

But to the disappointment of anyone who had tuned in hoping to see a Black quarterback in a pro game, Blanda trotted in instead of Dickey. "I could picture Negroes all over America turning off their television sets," a *Miami News* columnist wrote.[24] Dickey entered the game with Blanda, lined up at flanker, and immediately caught a pass for a thirty-four-yard gain. It was his first "touch" of the ball in a pro game, but the fact that he had caught it, not thrown it, tempered his celebration.

The Raiders would obliterate most of their opponents during the 1968 season. While winning twelve of fourteen games, they led the AFL in scoring, averaging more than thirty-two points per contest, as Lamonica developed connections with two young receivers, Warren Wells and Fred Biletnikoff, each of whom surpassed one thousand receiving yards. Even though Joe Namath and the New York Jets upset them in the AFL championship game (and went on to win the Super Bowl over the NFL's Baltimore Colts in an even bigger shocker), the Raiders had pro football's most dangerous offense.

That limited Dickey's opportunity. Lamonica seldom came off the field, and the same was true for Wells and Biletnikoff. Davis and the Raiders had envisioned Dickey helping them as a receiver, but he barely played. That one catch against the Bills turned out to be his only reception of the season.

=====

Relegated to the sidelines, Dickey found every game day disappointing during his rookie season. There was one Sunday in November that outdid them all, however.

The Raiders faced the Broncos in Denver, with Lamonica sitting out the game due to back spasms. Blanda stepped in and threw four touchdown passes as the Raiders raced to a 33–7 lead in the third quarter. The margin gave Rauch a chance to play another quarterback, but it was Davidson, not Dickey, who took snaps in the final minutes. Even more disappointing, another Black quarterback, playing for Denver, received the opportunity Dickey so craved. After falling behind, the Broncos pulled their starter and put in Marlin Briscoe, a rookie from the University of Omaha, in Nebraska.

It was not his first appearance. Briscoe had already played in five games as a quarterback that season, starting one. The Broncos had intended to use him strictly as a defensive back even though he had thrown fifty-two touchdown passes and won three conference titles in college. But injuries to the team's other quarterbacks had left Denver's head coach, Lou Saban, with no choice but to play Briscoe at quarterback from time to time.

On the Saturday night before the Raiders and Broncos played, Dickey went to Briscoe's apartment in Denver for a visit. "I could tell things didn't sit right with him," Briscoe recalled.[25] It was hard to believe which of them was playing. Dickey was three inches taller, thirty pounds heavier, and had been drafted 332 picks earlier than Briscoe that year. "He really wanted to be the first Black quarterback, and should have been, to be honest with you," Briscoe said. "But for some reason, divine intervention, whatever, he wasn't. You could see it in his demeanor, that something was denied him. He wasn't bitter toward me, but I sensed something in his body language."[26]

When the 1968 season ended, Merritt advised Dickey to remain optimistic and remember that the Raiders had told him it would take time for him to become a top pro quarterback. But Dickey doubted them now. He did not believe the pro game was so complex. Namath had started for the Jets as a rookie and developed quickly enough to win a Super Bowl in his fourth season.

Before the 1969 season, the Associated Press published a story about Black quarterbacks seeking to prove they could play in the pros, focusing on Dickey, Briscoe, and James Harris, now with the Buffalo Bills. The article did not mention that all three played for AFL teams. With the merger set to go into effect a year later, it was clear, however quietly, that skepticism about Black quarterbacks persisted in the front offices of NFL teams.

Dickey told the AP he was "a pioneer, that's the word for it," and the AP called him "admittedly impatient" to get on with his pioneering.[27] His goal for 1969 was to beat out Stabler and Blanda, now forty-one, for the job of backing up Lamonica. During training camp and the preseason, the Raiders' new head coach, John Madden, made good on Davis's pledge to give Dickey a chance at quarterback. In a rookie scrimmage against the Cowboys, Dickey played the first half and Stabler played the second half while Roger Staubach played quarterback for the Cowboys. Stabler and Staubach were destined for the Pro Football Hall of Fame, but Dickey outperformed them that day.

"This is for me," Dickey told reporters after the scrimmage, referencing the chance to play quarterback, not wide receiver. "I'll leave the pass catching to those 9.5 sprinters."[28]

His prospects seemingly rose when Stabler abruptly quit the team on the eve of the preseason, saying he was tired of playing football. Some teammates quietly wondered if Stabler feared being beaten out by Dickey. Stabler would sit out the 1969 season, rejoin the Raiders in 1970, and begin a slow ascension, eventually becoming the starter and one of the sport's top quarterbacks.

But for much of the 1969 preseason, Dickey seemingly was the one with a bright future. He was "the most exciting player on the field" in a preseason game against the Kansas City Chiefs, the *Oakland Tribune* reported, "sending 50-yard passes down the field with a flick of the wrist" and "making it look ridiculously easy to score a touchdown."[29]

Although he also threw three interceptions, he moved the ball. When a passing play broke down, he just tucked the ball under his shoulder and ran. Fans shrieked. Blanda grumped that Dickey's style was akin to high school football, but Hank Stram, the Chiefs' head coach, called Dickey "the best scrambling quarterback I have ever seen."[30]

When the game against the Chiefs ended, two players hoisted Dickey on their shoulders in celebration. Buck Buchanan and Ernie Ladd had come from Grambling and now played for the Chiefs, and even though they suited up for the other team that night, they were proud of Dickey, their fellow Black college football alum.[31] "I knew then that a door had been opened," Dickey said later.[32]

He had another solid outing against the Baltimore Colts the next week, passing for seventy-four yards and rushing for twenty-six, prompting praise from Don Shula, the Colts' head coach. "He can run with anybody," Shula said.[33]

But the Raiders were not so impressed. "We prefer our quarterbacks to drop back and throw the ball," Madden said.[34] Eventually, Dickey's prospects soured. He missed a practice, irritating Madden, and played poorly against the Chargers. His reputation had become inescapable: he was "spectacular but erratic," according to the *Oakland Tribune*.[35] Madden went with Blanda, who was steadier, and the Raiders cut Dickey at the end of the preseason. It was strictly a procedural move; they intended to keep him on their developmental "taxi squad" if he went unclaimed on waivers. But the Chiefs put in a claim, forcing the Raiders to rescind the move of putting him on waivers. He was still on their taxi squad but sulked and missed several more practices after learning he had been cut. An Oakland teammate, cornerback Willie Brown, later described his attitude as "adolescent."[36] Then he suffered a serious knee injury in practice, ending a disappointing season.

"Looking back on it, I think he was spoiled coming out of college," Art Shell said. "He didn't feel he needed to put forth the effort to become a quarterback in the NFL. He had his white buck shoes and his black Eldorado but I don't think he was ready to study. I don't think he was taught how to study."[37]

75

In 1970, Lamonica was still the starter, but Stabler was back on the team and exhibiting promise. Although Davis had said in 1968 that it would be "an issue" if Dickey was not playing quarterback in two or three years, the Raiders gave up on the idea. Madden broke the news to him in training camp: from now on, he was a receiver.

His teammates were encouraged to see him catch four passes in the first three preseason games and stay after practices to work on his routes. "He's a different person; he's concentrating on football," cornerback Dave Grayson said.[38] Dickey did not deny that his attitude was partly to blame for his stalled career thus far. "I guess it's partly my maturity," he said of his new approach.[39]

Long gone was his goal of making history. "I wanted to be remembered as the first and best Black quarterback in pro football. Now it may be as a top pass receiver or punt returner. I don't care as long as I'm the best," he said.[40]

But he was back on the taxi squad when the season began and stayed there all year. "They tried to make him a wide receiver, but he was never really the same; he wasn't a receiver," Upshaw said.[41] In 1971, his last year under contract, he made the roster as a receiver and caught a touchdown pass early in the season, but he started skipping practices, frustrated about his fading fortunes. Tired of his act, the Raiders cut him near the end of the season.

———

Before Dickey's senior season at Tennessee A&I in 1967, John Merritt told a reporter, "I've heard it said by several pro scouts that if a quarterback who could run well and throw at the same time ever came along, it could revolutionize their game. Dickey might just be the man to do that."[42]

The comment was prescient. Quarterbacks who could run and pass eventually gained a firm foothold in the pro game, with the likes of Michael Vick, Cam Newton, Russell Wilson, and Lamar Jackson revolutionizing offenses and bringing to life the future Merritt envisioned.

From the vantage point of a half-century later, it becomes clear that timing was Dickey's problem more than anything else. While the Raiders deserved credit for drafting a Black quarterback with a first-round pick, they thrust him into a no-win situation. Dickey was never going to beat out Lamonica, who was not only the quarterback the Raiders wanted, but also, as a pocket passer, the *kind* of quarterback the Raiders wanted.

The way pro rosters were shaped in the late 1960s also worked against Dickey. Teams were still able to stockpile players at positions, as the Raiders did at quarterback with Dickey and Stabler. Both would sign contracts, yet only one could play, with the other stranded on the bench, being paid not to play. The practice became impossible after 1994 when the NFL instituted a salary cap, putting limits on payrolls. With a cap in play, no team would ever select quarterbacks in the first and second rounds of the same draft.

In today's NFL, a team makes a statement when it drafts a quarterback with a first-round pick. That quarterback is the team's future. Barring an injury, he is almost surely going to get a chance to start and prove he was a worthy selection.

But Dickey never received that chance.

"I've always wondered what might have happened if Dickey had been given an opportunity and the organization's support. Would he have been Lamar Jackson?" Upton Bell said.[43]

Ron Wolf does not think so. "He was under such tremendous pressure because of his skin color. He just wanted to play football, but everyone saw him as a symbol. And unfortunately, the bottom line is he succumbed to that pressure," Wolf said. "He just was never good enough to man the quarterback position. I don't know how to put that any differently."[44]

Dickey still broke through the color line in one way. Only once in the next two decades would another Black quarterback get selected in the first round of the draft. But after failed tryouts as a receiver with the Colts and Chiefs in 1972, he went into a personal tailspin and battled drug addiction. Deeply religious, he eventually became a minister in Houston before dying from a stroke at age fifty.

"What happened to Eldridge Dickey has to be one of the greatest sports crimes ever committed," Hank Stram said later. "The entire sports world and Dickey were robbed by the Oakland Raiders. Dickey was special. He was fast, had a powerful arm, and could throw with both hands. He was truly one of the most accurate passers I've ever seen. I wanted him badly, but the Raiders selected him first. By the time I did get him four years later, Dickey really wanted out of the NFL. Deep down, he never forgave the Oakland Raiders."[45]

He dreamed of making history but never played quarterback in a regular-season pro game. "He was," Marlin Briscoe said, "the best quarterback we never saw."[46]

CHAPTER 7

hree other Black quarterbacks were drafted in 1968 after Eldridge Dickey went to the Raiders in the first round. The 49ers took Fisk University's Henry Johnson in the twelfth round. The Broncos took Marlin Briscoe in the fourteenth round. The Rams took Michigan State's Jimmy Raye in the sixteenth round.

Although it was a sign of progress that they were at least drafted instead of entirely ignored, all three were immediately dismissed as candidates to play quarterback. Johnson was switched to defensive back and cut almost immediately, as training camp opened in mid-July. Raye also was switched to defensive back even though he had rushed and passed for more than 2,600 yards at Michigan State and helped the Spartans win a share of a national championship. He was with the Rams for a year and played for the Philadelphia Eagles in 1969 before retiring and going into coaching.

Denial of opportunity was the standard experience for a Black quarterback in the late 1960s. If he wanted to play the position as a pro, his only option was joining a team in Canada. If he was set on playing in the NFL, he had to switch positions. That the Raiders even contemplated playing Dickey at quarterback qualified as rare and special treatment.

Black high school and college quarterbacks recognized the dead end that lay ahead, and their reactions differed. Dickey and James Harris plowed on, doggedly believing they had the talent to change minds and play quarterback in the NFL or AFL. But many others, such as Gene Washington, a Black quarterback at Stanford, switched positions while still in college. "It was strictly a matter of economics. I knew a Black quarterback would have little chance in the pros unless he was absolutely superb," Washington said.[1]

Washington had been a standout high school quarterback in Long Beach, California, but Southern Cal, the region's top college program, did not recruit him as a quarterback. Stanford did; his speed and ability to throw on the run made him a nice fit for the offense favored by the head coach, John Ralston. Washington won the starting job as a sophomore in 1966. In his first college start, he threw for two touchdowns and ran for another. He was ranked among the conference leaders in total offense until he suffered a shoulder injury that limited his ability to throw. Another hit to the same shoulder forced him to miss the last part of the season.

Washington was still the starter heading into his junior year in 1967, but just before the season opener, Ralston asked him to switch to receiver. The team's top pass catcher was injured. "Gene, our team would be better with you as a receiver," Ralston said. "We have another thrower, but we need the team speed. We would be better as a team if you switched to receiver."[2]

Washington agreed that the team probably was better with him catching passes from Chuck Williams, a senior quarterback. But Washington also took his pro prospects into account. "I knew that if I was going to play in the pros, I was going to be a receiver anyway," he said. "Here's what I saw: I wasn't going to be a pro-quality quarterback because I wasn't a great passer. There weren't many rollout-type quarterbacks in the pros."[3]

He would make more money, he reasoned, if he made the switch now. He knew Black quarterbacks were routinely lowballed in contract negotiations with NFL teams. "The pro team tells you that there's no place for you at quarterback, but they can use you as a defensive back or flanker. And then they tell you they can't give you as much money because you'd be learning a new position. I decided to beat them to it," Washington said.[4]

His position switch worked out well for him both financially and on the field. After two record-setting seasons as a receiver at Stanford,

Washington was selected by the 49ers in the first round of the 1969 NFL draft. He would catch 385 passes and earn four Pro Bowl selections during a distinguished pro career.

But the fact that he changed positions was emblematic of the predicament all Black quarterbacks faced in the late 1960s. After the Raiders drafted Dickey in the first round but moved even *him* to receiver, it seemed more unlikely than ever that a Black quarterback would get a shot in the pros.

———

Initially, Marlin Briscoe did not envision himself as a breakthrough candidate. Even though he had always played quarterback since his days as a peewee star in Omaha, Nebraska, and had set passing records and won titles in college, he was drafted as a defensive back. He recognized his size—five feet eleven and 185 pounds—was perfect for the secondary but atypical for a quarterback. He also could not just sling the ball sixty yards with a flick of his wrist, as Dickey could.

But he was not without qualities that gave him a chance to make it as a pro quarterback. He was an elusive runner and deadly accurate as a passer. He understood the leadership demands of the position. And his background encouraged him to believe anything was possible.

Born in California in 1945, he had moved to Omaha with his mother and sister when he was five and his parents split up. They settled in public housing near the city's stockyards. The meatpacking industry attracted Black families from around the country; it was gruesome work, but the industry was integrated and paid relatively well.

But Briscoe did not want to spend his life slaughtering livestock. "I said, 'There's no way in the world. I'm getting my education,'" he said. "Playing pro football was a fantasy. I wanted to get a [football] scholarship so I could go to college and get a good job."[5]

His football talents matured during a golden era for sports in Omaha. The city's Black community produced Bob Boozer, a basketball star who won an Olympic gold medal and played in the National Basketball Association; Bob Gibson, an ace pitcher for baseball's St. Louis Cardinals; and Gale Sayers, a transcendent running back for the Chicago Bears. In college, Briscoe met Gale's older brother, Roger, who was one of America's top track sprinters and encouraged Briscoe to focus on his classwork as a means of escaping the stockyards.

After seeing so many Black athletes from Omaha succeed, Briscoe began to believe he could, too. He had set numerous passing records as the starter at Omaha and earned the nickname "Marlin the Magician." At the suggestion of Omaha's head coach, Al Caniglia, Briscoe asked the Broncos to give him a three-day tryout at quarterback during training camp. The Broncos agreed to it, thinking it would not matter—they were already set at quarterback, having just traded two first-round draft picks to acquire Steve Tensi, a former Florida State star.

At training camp, Briscoe lined up with Tensi and six other quarterbacks during his tryout. He was always the last in line during drills and received fewer chances to throw, but he exhibited a strong arm. "They couldn't believe a kid this small could throw the ball that far," he said.[6]

The Broncos moved him back to cornerback after his tryout, and he began the season as a reserve, playing little. But Tensi suffered a broken collarbone in a preseason game, sidelining him for a period that included the first few games of the regular season. John McCormick, a veteran reserve, started the season opener, but the Broncos lost to the Cincinnati Bengals, an expansion team, and McCormick was so ineffective that Lou Saban, the Broncos' head coach, benched him during the game for Jim LeClair, a younger reserve.

LeClair started the next week but threw three interceptions in a lopsided road loss to the Chiefs. A week later, the largest crowd ever to watch the Broncos came to their home opener; their home stadium had been expanded to include an upper deck, and fans wanted to see it. LeClair started against the Boston Patriots but failed to move the offense as the Broncos fell behind and the crowd began to boo.

When LeClair threw his second interception early in the fourth quarter, Saban found Briscoe on the bench and told him to get ready to go in at quarterback. After the Broncos regained possession, Briscoe led the offense onto the field. A ripple of anticipation ran through the crowd as he called a play in the huddle and led the offense to the line.

A Black quarterback had never taken a snap in an AFL game. It had been thirteen years since a Black quarterback played in the NFL. "I was the only one that wasn't nervous," Briscoe said. "I had played that position since I was 10 years old. I just went out there and starting throwing."[7]

The Patriots led by ten points with nine minutes to play. On his first snap, Briscoe zipped a pass for a twenty-two-yard gain, eliciting cheers from the fans. That possession fizzled, but when the Broncos regained the ball, Briscoe led an eighty-yard drive that culminated with him scrambling for a touchdown. The cheers shook the stadium's new upper deck.

The Patriots held on to win, but Briscoe rushed and passed for nearly one hundred yards in his brief appearance.

"The support I got from my teammates and the fans was amazing," he recalled. "I had five white linemen, and I could hear them saying to each other, 'Nobody touches Marlin.' After the game, fans were coming up to me, wishing me well. Back then the fear was always that a Black quarterback would divide the team—some white players would have problems with it, and attendance would hurt because some white fans would stop coming. None of that happened."[8]

Wire service accounts noted that Briscoe was the first Black quarterback to play in an AFL game. Several days later, Saban said he would start the Broncos' next game, a rematch with the Bengals. Except for George Taliaferro's two emergency starts for the Baltimore Colts in 1953, a Black quarterback had not started a pro game in the United States since 1926. "My heart jumped. I couldn't believe it. I mean, it was just unbelievable," Briscoe said later.[9]

Yet the harsh reality of being a young Black male in America interrupted his dream. On his way home from a practice that same week, Briscoe and a teammate stopped at a department store to buy records. Briscoe purchased three, but when a security guard asked him to show receipts as he left the store, he could only find two in his pockets. He was arrested for shoplifting, booked at the Jefferson County Jail, and released on a personal recognizance bond. The charges were quickly dropped when he located the third receipt in his pocket, but the fact that he was a Black man playing quarterback in pro football, or trying to, made it newsworthy. Sports pages across the country printed articles about his arrest. No one in the mainstream media, a white bastion, was going to suggest Briscoe had been unfairly targeted because he was Black—that did not happen in the 1960s. But at least editors and reporters were starting to follow the Black quarterback story, some whiffing the scent of discrimination.

Rattled by his arrest, Briscoe did not make the most of his opportunity that Sunday, completing just four of eleven passes in the first half. With the Broncos trailing, Saban pulled him for Tensi, whose shoulder injury was healed. Tensi led two scoring drives and the Broncos rallied for their first win of the season.

A week later, Tensi started and passed for more than two hundred yards in a win over the New York Jets. It seemed the door of opportunity had slammed shut for Briscoe. But then Tensi took a hard hit on his shoulder in the second quarter of a game in San Diego, and Briscoe was back on the field. Although the Broncos trailed the Chargers when he came in and wound up losing by thirty-one points, Briscoe put on a show, passing for 237 yards and three touchdowns and also rushing for sixty-eight yards.

If any doubts about his abilities as a pro quarterback lingered, he quashed them in the Broncos' next game. Tensi started against the Dolphins in Denver, but he was ineffective as the Broncos fell two touchdowns behind in the first half. The fans cheered when Saban put in Briscoe, who began to move the ball. One possession culminated with him rushing for a touchdown. Another drive produced another touchdown that tied the score.

In the final minutes, Briscoe led the offense on a drive to Miami's 10 yard line. Approaching the line on first down, he read the defense, took the snap, and ran right up the middle for a touchdown that won the game.

"I changed the play at the line. Surprised my linemen. They told me later they couldn't understand what I was doing," Briscoe said, smiling. "But a safety and the middle linebacker were lined up on the outside, to shut off the outside stuff. There was nobody in the middle. I knew the play would work if I could get past the line."[10]

For his performance, Briscoe was named the AFL's offensive player of the week. He enjoyed the acclaim, but he was more excited that his teammates praised him for using his head on the game-winning play. He knew that a stereotypical criticism of Black quarterbacks was they were not smart enough to play the position. Briscoe shattered that myth. "Marlin's brain was probably his greatest strength," recalled Eric Crabtree, a receiver who caught passes from Briscoe in 1968. "He was always thinking. Even when he was talking to you, it seemed like he was deep in thought."[11]

Even after his success against the Dolphins, though, he still was not the Broncos' number one quarterback. Tensi started the next game and gave a strong performance in a rout of the Patriots. But two weeks later, a linebacker for the Oilers leveled Tensi as he threw a pass, breaking Tensi's collarbone again and ending his season. The Broncos had a 4–6 record and four games left to play. Saban's only choice was to start Briscoe.

A week later, Briscoe threw two early touchdown passes against the Bills in Denver. The Broncos held a comfortable lead, then staggered late. A fumble by Denver's top running back, Floyd Little, appeared to complete a collapse, enabling the Bills to kick a field goal giving them a one-point lead with eighteen seconds left.

The chances of Briscoe saving the game seemed remote. But he was nicknamed "Marlin the Magician" for a reason. The Bills blitzed him, but just before he was swarmed under, he hurled a pass far downfield for Little, who made the catch for a fifty-nine-yard gain. The Broncos' kicker trotted in and booted a game-winning field goal through the uprights.

"I wasn't ready to give up," Briscoe said in the locker room. "When I was in college, we won a number of games in the final seconds. That's how I got my nickname. I knew I just had to stay calm."[12]

The Broncos' final games were against playoff contenders. Briscoe threw three touchdown passes in a lopsided loss to the Chargers, then threw for 251 yards as the Broncos gamely matched the explosive Raiders score for score in Oakland until they lost by six points. A season-ending loss to the Chiefs was forgettable, but overall, it was impossible not to judge Briscoe's performance as a rookie quarterback as anything other than a smashing success. He had appeared in eleven games at the position, starting five. He had passed for fourteen touchdowns and sixteen hundred yards, rushed for more than three hundred yards, moved the offense, and shown that he was not overmatched against top competition. "The greatest thing in the world was giving Marlin the chance to play quarterback. We all thought he'd be our quarterback the next season," Floyd Little said.[13]

Briscoe's breakthrough unfolded during a searing year for Black America. Martin Luther King Jr. was assassinated in April, prompting more outbreaks of unrest in urban communities. Robert Kennedy, an outspoken proponent of racial justice, was assassinated in June, just as his presidential campaign gained momentum. Appointed by President Lyndon Johnson to pinpoint the cause of Black America's fury, the Kerner Commission described the country as inherently and thoroughly racist, with Blacks forced to live with "bad policing practices, a flawed justice system, unscrupulous consumer credit practices, poor or inadequate housing, high unemployment, voter suppression, and other culturally embedded forms of racial discrimination."[14] In October, two Black American track athletes, Tommie Smith and John Carlos, drew worldwide attention to the situation by raising black-fisted gloves in protest during the playing of the national anthem at the Summer Olympics in Mexico City. The episode illustrated the power of using sports as a symbolic platform.

Though Briscoe's performance in 1968 did not receive as much attention, it was celebrated in Black America. "I followed him closely, knew what he was doing, and took great pride in it," said James Harris, a senior quarterback at Grambling in the fall of 1968.[15]

But there was a problem. The Broncos were loath to commit to building their team around a quarterback who was not tall, big-armed, and white. Soon after the 1968 season, they signed Pete Liske, a former Penn State star who had played well in Canada for the Calgary

Stampeders. Looking ahead to 1969, Saban envisioned Liske starting and Tensi as the backup.

In early 1969, Briscoe was back in Omaha taking the classes he needed to finish his degree. A cousin was in Denver, staying at the apartment they had shared during the season. The cousin called to tell Briscoe the Denver media was reporting that Saban was holding off-season quarterback meetings with Liske, Tensi, and others. Briscoe had not received an invitation.

Confused, he flew to Denver, drove to the team office, and waited outside the room where Saban and the quarterbacks were meeting. When they emerged, Saban would not look him in the eye. Briscoe knew his career as a quarterback in Denver was over. "Saban was a quirky guy," Briscoe said later. "I've always been asked, was there racism? Well, first of all, he didn't have to put me in. I never understood what his motives were not to let me play once I established myself."[16]

Caniglia told him that even though he had proved he could do the job, and do it well, American pro teams just were not ready for a Black quarterback. Briscoe's choice, Caniglia said, was either play quarterback in Canada or stay in the AFL or NFL at another position.

Briscoe asked the Broncos to release him, which they did early in training camp. He arranged a tryout with Canada's British Columbia Lions but left after one practice, deciding Canadian football was not for him. He started calling American teams, letting them know he was ready to switch positions.

The Buffalo Bills had a veteran starting quarterback, Jack Kemp, who had led them to two AFL titles, and they also had drafted James Harris. They did not need another quarterback, especially another Black quarterback, but they were looking for wide receivers and signed Briscoe.

At the Bills' training camp, Briscoe roomed with Harris, touching off a lifelong friendship. "We had a lot of discussions, not only about football but about America and about the plight of Blacks and how the quarterback position was affected. It was interesting," Harris said. "I felt bad for Marlin. I figured that could be me, that could be my story."[17]

Harris later described Briscoe as bitter about having been denied the chance to continue playing quarterback in Denver, but Briscoe said later, "I wasn't bitter. Bitter people quit. I was disappointed. If I was bitter, I wouldn't have rolled up my sleeves and learned another position. I grew up in the '50s and '60s when Black people had a tough road no matter what career they pursued. We expected to have to go through closed doors. We expected not to get a fair shake."[18]

Briscoe certainly did not get a fair shake, but he became a productive wide receiver—quick and smart, with a knack for getting open. He caught thirty-two passes for the Bills in his first year as a receiver. The next year, he made the Pro Bowl.

In 1972, the Bills hired Lou Saban as their head coach and traded Briscoe to the Dolphins to avoid dealing with any lingering enmity between the two. Briscoe caught forty-six passes over the next two seasons as Miami won back-to-back Super Bowls. After brief tenures with the Chargers, Patriots, and Lions, he retired in 1976, having caught 224 passes as a pro.

At first, he was remembered mostly for having played on the Dolphins' championship teams. Eventually, though, his brief opportunity at quarterback in 1968 became the most significant aspect of his career. At a time when Black quarterbacks continued to be denied opportunities, Briscoe stood out as one of the few who had not only received a chance, but had taken advantage of it, even though he ended up being denied, too. "He could have been a great quarterback for a long time. But we have to be real about the time Marlin played," said Doug Williams, another pioneering Black quarterback, who came along a decade later.[19]

Briscoe experienced struggles after football. A cocaine addiction led to two jail terms in the 1980s. When Williams became the first Black quarterback to win a Super Bowl in January 1988, Briscoe watched the game from jail.

But he kicked his habit and straightened out his life. Living in Southern California, he became involved with his church, taught math, coached high school football, and finally, worked for more than a decade with the Boys & Girls Clubs of America, retiring from a job as a club director in Long Beach. Acclaim came his way. In 2009, he was recognized on the floor of the US House of Representatives as modern pro football's first Black starting quarterback. In 2014, during a White House ceremony honoring the Dolphins' undefeated 1972 Super Bowl team, President Barack Obama recognized him. "I know you. You're a trailblazer. You set the tone for Black quarterbacks," Obama told Briscoe as they shook hands.[20]

As he grew older, Briscoe, who died in 2022, said he most appreciated what his success did for others. "The very next year after I played, there were four Black quarterbacks drafted out of college. They had never done that before me," he said. "When I played, I played well, and at least it brought to mind that a Black man could think and throw the football at the same time."[21]

Dr. Charles K. Ross, a professor of history and African American studies at the University of Mississippi, who has authored books about race and pro football, compared Briscoe to another Black quarterback who played a half-century later—the Baltimore Ravens' Lamar Jackson. A dynamic runner and playmaker, Jackson won the Heisman Trophy as a sophomore at the University of Louisville, yet because he had an unusual throwing motion, many pro scouts doubted he would thrive as a pro. The Ravens took him with the last pick in the first round of the 2018 draft.

Like Briscoe, Jackson came off the bench in his rookie season to dazzle opponents with a skill set completely out of place with the pro game's norms. But where Briscoe was denied the chance to continue playing quarterback, Jackson was supported by the Ravens. They installed a new offense, tailored to his talents, and he won the NFL's Most Valuable Player award as a second-year player in 2019.

"Is there any real difference between these two players?" Dr. Ross said of Briscoe and Jackson. "We're talking about the same stature. We're talking about [both with] a lot of determination coming out of schools where they are coming in under the radar in terms of college football as a legacy institution. The only difference between them is opportunity."[22]

CHAPTER 8

For decades, the college football played at historically Black institutions was all but invisible to white fans and the mainstream media. It had legendary coaches, star players, and intense rivalries, all of which Black fans savored. But the white football world had zero interest.

When the flow of players from Black college football to the pros dramatically increased in the 1960s, the white football world began learning about Black football. Eddie Robinson, the coach at Grambling, was still relatively young, just forty-four, when one of his players, Buck Buchanan, was the first player selected in the 1963 AFL draft. But Robinson was already a towering figure in the Black community, having built a powerhouse over two decades at Grambling.

Robinson's background illustrated the challenges Black Americans faced. The woes of racism were ever present, impossible to dodge. A sharecropper's son, Robinson wanted to become a coach after playing quarterback and majoring in English at Leland College, in Baker, Louisiana, in the late 1930s. But most major college programs did not hire Black coaches. Robinson either had to invent a path into the profession or find another line of work.

He invented a path. The Louisiana Negro Normal and Industrial Institute, located in Grambling, was looking for a football coach in 1941. Robinson was twenty-two when he took a job that lacked every trapping considered customary in white college football. He had no assistants. He had to line the field before games, make sandwiches for the players to eat on road trips, and cover the team for the local newspaper. Oh, and he had to coach the offense and defense.

Most white coaches never would have agreed to such conditions, but then, they did not have to live with indignity, as Black coaches did. And the ultimate indignity, in a way, was the high bar they had to clear. If a Black football coach did not show he was truly exceptional, he would not last long in the profession. The coaching fraternity would not reflexively provide another opportunity, the safety net many white coaches tapped.

But it was clear from the outset that Robinson was exceptional. His 1942 team finished unbeaten, untied, and unscored upon, quite a feat, and he went on to develop a winning program after World War II, when the school's name was changed to Grambling. Black college football had other coaching icons such as Florida A&M's Jake Gaither and Jackson State's John Merritt, but Robinson bowed to none of them. By the 1960s, he was in his prime, square-jawed, handsome, and dressed in a coat and tie on the sidelines as he churned out championship teams and pro prospects. Although he sought acceptance from whites, putting him increasingly at odds with young Black Americans protesting the status quo, his Tigers integrated stadiums, hotels, and restaurants, introduced Black college football to white television audiences, and produced pros who obliterated racist myths about Black talent.

But one significant achievement eluded Robinson. By the mid-1960s, he still had not shattered the enduring stereotype about Black quarterbacks being unfit for pro football.

The subject came up when Robinson was in New York for an interview with Howard Cosell, the famous sportscaster. Cosell loved Robinson and wanted white fans to appreciate him, but he was also a legendary needler and could not help chiding Robinson: "You've produced so many great NFL players. Why can't you produce a quarterback?" Cosell asked.[1]

Robinson could have given Cosell a long answer about stereotyping from NFL talent evaluators denying Black quarterbacks even a chance to play, but rather than get into it, he just smiled uneasily.

Cosell had struck a nerve. "That stuck with him," recalled James Harris, at the time a high school quarterback in Monroe, Louisiana.[2]

Harris was being recruited by Michigan State after leading Monroe's all-Black Carroll High School to thirty-nine straight wins. "I thought about going to school up North to be on TV, to represent my neighborhood. That was appealing," Harris said.[3] But playing in the Big Ten would mean changing positions; he was so tall, at six feet four, that recruiters envisioned him playing tight end.

Eddie Robinson wanted him to play quarterback at Grambling. After scouting Harris on dimly lit high school fields, watching him elude defenders and throw strikes to receivers far downfield, Robinson believed Harris could be *the one*—the first Black quarterback to make it in the pros.

Upon returning to Louisiana from his interview with Cosell in New York, Robinson "got off the plane in Monroe [and] came straight to my house," Harris recalled. "He told me that if I came to Grambling, in four years I'd be ready for the NFL. He told me that he knew I could play quarterback. He said, 'Howard Cosell challenged me and I'm here to let you know I think you can do it.'"[4]

———

In the city of Monroe, Louisiana, where Harris was raised in the late 1950s and early 1960s, white supremacy was as constant as the smell emanating from the Brown Paper Mill. Crosses burned on the lawns of Monroe's Black churches. Black youngsters avoided even looking at whites, fearing what might go wrong. It was a world of strict segregation. Harris never attended church or school with whites, never played Little League baseball with whites, and learned from ragged textbooks deemed unsuitable for whites.

His parents took what they saw as the only navigable route through such an environment—be proud of who you are, but do not speak up and cause trouble. Harris's father, a sharecropper's son, worked in a furniture store and served as a pastor at night and on the weekends. His mother was a nurse in a white doctor's office. They did not originally think football could become an important factor in their son's life, but Harris was tall and fast and led his teammates from the peewee level on—a natural quarterback. College recruiters began calling the house.

Pondering his future, Harris noticed the scarcity of Black quarterbacks in the college and pro games he watched on television. A talented quarterback from his high school who was slightly older, Mike Howell, had made it in the NFL, but as a defensive back. Harris assumed he would eventually have to change positions, too. But after hearing a radio broadcast of Martin Luther King's "I Have a Dream" speech at age sixteen in 1963, he became resolved to play the position he loved. Robinson's recruiting pitch appealed to *his* dream.

"We recruited James Harris to play quarterback in the National Football League," Robinson said later. "I told him, 'Work hard and you could be the first.'"[5]

From the day Harris arrived on campus, Robinson sought to prepare him. Grambling had battered opponents for years with a dominant running game, but Robinson threw more with Harris at quarterback. Tank Younger, a former Grambling linebacker and fullback who in 1949 became the first player from a historically Black college to play in the NFL, came to campus and showed Harris how to learn from watching film, as pro quarterbacks did. "This is what you're aiming for," said Younger, now a scout with the Los Angeles Rams.[6] Robinson preached the importance of doing well in class because "the reasoning at the time was Black quarterbacks didn't have what it took upstairs," Robinson said.[7]

Harris mastered the offense and became a quiet but forceful team leader who won twenty-four of thirty starts in three seasons. His ability to focus was tested when protests roiled Grambling's campus in 1967; some students felt the school's emphasis on football was damaging its academic reputation. Harris helped keep his teammates on task and Grambling won a Black national championship. There were more protests in 1968; students were upset that the school's administration cooperated with an all-white state education board, and also felt the curriculum did not sufficiently address the Black experience in the South during the civil rights era. Harris approved of the pushback against the racist world he had grown up in, but he did not want to spoil his opportunity in pro football, which, he hoped, was almost at hand. He steered the Tigers through the tumult to another winning season.

In the spring of 1969, it was time to find out if Robinson's vision for Harris would come to fruition. Harris was increasingly skeptical as the NFL draft approached. He had "jumped for joy" when the Raiders took Eldridge Dickey in the first round the year before, but Dickey had been switched to receiver. "That was discouraging," Harris said. "It just seemed like the NFL was not ready for a Black quarterback."[8]

The Buffalo Bills drafted him, but only in the eighth round. The low pick left him considering quitting football altogether. Robinson convinced him to go to Buffalo and at least try out for the team.

"I didn't have a lot of faith that the NFL was ready for a Black quarterback, but I took a lot of confidence with me to Buffalo," Harris said. "I had worked out, worked hard, thrown a lot of balls. I was competitive. I was confident. . . As I got on the plane to Buffalo, my thinking was, 'How can they cut me?' Because I was really prepared. I was throwing the ball well. I understood football. I decided on that flight that I was going to leave behind all the reasons I might not make it, Blacks not being smart enough for quarterback, we couldn't lead, all that stuff. I was leaving that behind. When I got off the plane, I was prepared to compete."[9]

Harris was forced to put up with slights that a half-century later no pro athlete would tolerate. The Bills were in the national spotlight because they had drafted Southern Cal running back O. J. Simpson, one of the most explosive players in college football history, and when the team's rookies came to Buffalo to practice prior to training camp, Simpson stayed at the Hilton while Harris stayed at the YMCA. When he said he needed spending money while his contract was negotiated, the Bills paid him to clean his teammates' cleats. It was beyond demeaning, but having grown up under Jim Crow, Harris had long experience hiding the impact of insults.

There were eight quarterbacks in training camp, including Jack Kemp, who had led the Bills to back-to-back AFL titles a few years earlier, and Tom Flores, a former starter in the AFL, mostly for the Raiders. But Kemp was thirty-four and had sat out the prior season with a knee injury, and Flores was thirty-two, also near the end of his career.

"Would I get an opportunity? That was the question," Harris said. "A lot of guys before me could have made it if only they'd gotten the opportunity."[10]

He suffered a setback when he pulled a stomach muscle, forcing him to miss several practices and the first two preseason games. Harris called Robinson every night, fearing his opportunity was slipping away. Robinson told him to remain patient and keep learning the playbook so no one could accuse him of being dumb. "You're only going to get one chance," Robinson said. "Make the most of it."[11]

The Bills had hired John Rauch as their head coach and tasked him with rebuilding the team around Simpson. Having bolted from the Raiders after tiring of Al Davis, Rauch favored a complex offense. Kemp and the other veteran quarterbacks picked it up, but Harris did not have their experience. "I had to work extra hard just to keep up," he said. "If some of the guys wanted to go get a sandwich in the evening, I couldn't go. I felt very strongly that I had to study and prepare. If I got cut, the reason could NOT be I wasn't smart enough."[12]

When Marlin Briscoe joined the team as a wide receiver, fresh from being cut by the Broncos even though he had played well as a quarterback the year before, he warned Harris not to trust the coaches or the front office. "There's no question Marlin could have played quarterback in the NFL. I knew my future could be the same: someone who didn't get a chance," Harris said.[13]

But before a mid-August preseason game against the Lions in Detroit, Rauch pulled him aside and said, "You've got the second half."[14]

That night, in the stadium tunnel connecting the field and locker room, a small man smoking a cigar sought out Harris and introduced himself. It was Buddy Young, who had been one of the first Black players to reintegrate the NFL in the 1950s. Young now worked for the league as the director of player relations. His job was to help players find work when their careers ended, but he also monitored the status of Black players for NFL commissioner Pete Rozelle.

Three years earlier, Young had written a memo to Rozelle suggesting teams should strive harder to hire Black coaches and administrators and heed the concerns of the league's growing Black player population. Young was concerned about the lack of Black quarterbacks. "A lot of people are pulling for you," he told Harris before the game in Detroit.[15]

The Bills trailed by eight points when Harris came on in the second half. He did not lead a winning comeback, but he completed several passes, including one to Simpson for a long gain. When the game ended, Young sought him out again. "The way you played tonight, you can open up some opportunities," Young said.[16]

Rauch continued to give Harris playing time during the preseason. "I was fortunate that the coach believed in my ability and gave me some chances that other guys may not have gotten," Harris said.[17]

However, the indignities continued. An assistant coach told him that offensive linemen were moving before the snap, drawing penalties, because they could not understand him when he spoke. Searing hate mail arrived from fans who did not like seeing a Black man telling white players what to do.

Having Briscoe as a roommate helped. "He had been through some of the same things," Harris said.[18]

In the preseason finale, Harris performed "like a seasoned veteran," one newspaper reported.[19] Rauch decided to start him in the regular-season opener against the New York Jets. "I won the job," Harris said. "In the end, the coach thought I was the best option."[20]

It was a remarkable achievement. Harris had gone from cleaning his teammates' cleats to starting in the new pro football season's most anticipated game. The Jets were just months removed from their Super Bowl upset of the Baltimore Colts, a result that had sent the celebrity stock of their cocky quarterback, Joe Namath, soaring into the stratosphere. Now the Jets were beginning their title defense against Simpson, the sport's most ballyhooed rookie in years.

Buffalo's War Memorial Stadium was packed for the nationally televised game. Lost in the spotlight's glare was the fact that Harris was the first Black quarterback to start a season-opening game for a team in the AFL or modern NFL.

After he directed an early drive that produced a field goal, his performance spiraled downward. The Jets' defense seemed a step ahead of him. Several possessions went nowhere. He aggravated a sore groin muscle. Rauch pulled him at halftime with the Bills trailing, 16–3. Harris had completed just three of twelve passes.

"I was probably trying too hard to make things happen," Harris recalled. "It was such a big game, national TV, Joe Namath's first game after the Super Bowl. It didn't work out well."[21]

Kemp took over and led a rally; by early in the fourth quarter, the score was tied and the crowd was roaring. The Jets prevailed on the strength of two fourth-quarter touchdowns, but the Bills were encouraged. In a locker room swarming with reporters, Harris told an interviewer he expected to improve. He had no inkling his window of opportunity had just closed.

A week later, Kemp started and never came out even though he threw three interceptions in a loss to the Houston Oilers in which the offense failed to generate a touchdown. But Kemp threw for 249 yards and three touchdowns a week later as the Bills beat the Broncos. Harris came on late in a mop-up role and also took a few snaps in a win over Boston several weeks later.

With a 2–3 record, the Bills flew across the country to play the Raiders, who were unbeaten. It was a stunningly lopsided contest. The Raiders led 42–0 in the second quarter, and Kemp was being chased and knocked down whenever he dropped back to pass. Rauch switched quarterbacks, hoping Harris's youth and speed might invigorate the offense. Before halftime, Harris threw a thirty-nine-yard touchdown pass to Haven Moses, the Bills' top receiver.

Although the outcome of the game was not in doubt, Harris continued to move the offense after halftime, connecting with Moses and Briscoe on completions. He would total 156 passing yards during the game. "I was better prepared" than he was for the season opener, he said later. "I was more familiar with the offense, more comfortable.

There was never a doubt in my mind that I could play quarterback in the NFL."[22]

But late in the third quarter, two defenders brought him down hard and he stayed on the ground. He had injured his right knee. The Bills' trainers helped him off the field and he went on the injured list the next week. His season was over.

———

Heading into his second season in 1970, Harris had one key advantage that few, if any, other Black quarterbacks had experienced to that point. His coach actually liked him as a quarterback. "Rauch likes Harris [because] he really fires that ball; he has some arm," Haven Moses said.[23]

The team's roster of quarterbacks was drastically altered. Kemp had retired to enter politics. Flores had been released the year before. Dennis Shaw, a rookie from San Diego State, was considered the future starter after being drafted in the second round; broad-shouldered and white, he had thrown seven touchdown passes in one college start.

Shaw, Harris, and Dan Darragh, a third-year player from William & Mary, competed for the starting job during the preseason. Harris made some plays, but late in the preseason he failed to produce a point in back-to-back appearances. "There can be no disputing Rauch gave Harris every chance," one newspaper wrote.[24] Darragh won the job but lasted just two games, both losses, as the starter. Shaw took over and started for the rest of the season, and although he threw twice as many interceptions as touchdowns and fumbled nearly once a game, he finished seventh in the league in completion percentage and won the AP's Offensive Rookie of the Year award.

Harris appeared in seven games as a backup. His best opportunity came in a game against Boston in November. Shaw was shaken up with the Bills trailing late, 14–3. Harris came in and quickly threw for a touchdown. The Bills' defense forced a punt and the offense began a possession at their 21 yard line with seventy-four seconds to play. Harris completed a long pass to Briscoe. Another completion moved the ball to the Boston 16 yard line with only seconds to go. The Bills were out of time-outs so Harris fired an incompletion to stop the clock, leaving time for one more play. Incredibly, Rauch yanked Harris and sent in Shaw. The rookie threw a pass for Briscoe on the goal line, which fell incomplete.

Pressed about making a quarterback change on the final play after Harris had led the rally, Rauch explained that he could not get his desired play call in to Harris because of the lack of time-outs, so he just sent Shaw in to run the play.

Harris shrugged. After two years in the NFL, he was accustomed to being passed over. "You dream about playing in the NFL," he said later, "but if you dream of playing quarterback, it becomes a nightmare."[25]

———

In 1971, the Bills imploded. Rauch resigned. The team won just one game and lost thirteen. Shaw was the quarterback for most of it, but Harris started against the Dolphins in November. It was a tough assignment, on the road against a team that would play in the Super Bowl that season, and while Harris performed decently, completing eighteen of thirty passes, the Bills lost, 34–0. He started again the next week and threw a touchdown pass to Briscoe in a loss to the Patriots. It was his final start for the Bills, who released him after the season.

He had made three starts and played in eighteen games over three seasons, and while that was more of an opportunity than Dickey received with the Raiders, Harris took no solace. The Bills had drafted him because of his size and strong arm, but they drafted a white quarterback with size and a strong arm the following year and gave *him* what Harris wanted—a chance to play, through good performances and bad; a chance to develop.

Could Harris have become a starter with such support? The rest of the NFL did not think so. After the Bills cut him, he was out of pro football for a year. Eddie Robinson had told him that he would only get one chance, and in 1972 it seemed that chance had come and gone—until history proved Robinson wrong.

CHAPTER 9

As more open-minded thought swept America's college campuses in the late 1960s and 1970s, opinions about Black quarterbacks in major college football began to change. Previously denied at all but a few schools, they broke color lines, earned starting jobs, and won games, putting to shame the notion that they could not handle the job. Southern Cal's Jimmy Jones made the cover of *Sports Illustrated* in 1969. Three years later, Tennessee's Condredge Holloway became the first Black starting quarterback in the Southeastern Conference, the last bastion of resistance.

The NFL stubbornly balked at following the college game's lead. Until the late 1970s, James Harris was the only Black quarterback in pro football who started more than a few games. But the increase in Black quarterbacks in major college football produced an increase in viable Black prospects for the pros to consider in the 1970s. And at the same time, quarterbacks from historically Black institutions, previously dismissed as pro material, were at least taken more seriously, thanks mostly to Harris and Eldridge Dickey.

In effect, an entire generation of Black quarterbacks found itself knocking on the NFL's door with the hope that the door would magically open. Unfortunately for them, their timing was terrible. In the 1970s, the NFL still did not see its position on Black quarterbacks as outdated or racist, and with scant exceptions, the entire generation's NFL dreams were dashed.

But an alternate universe arose for Black quarterbacks, populated by those who did not want to just give up on the pros. They went to the

Canadian Football League, where, in several cases, glory beckoned, or they knocked around the American minor leagues, hoping they might eventually convince the NFL to answer that door knock if they hung around long enough.

Their efforts did not produce the desired result—a chance to play and thrive in the NFL. But in a backhanded way, the generation of denied Black quarterbacks did contribute to the cause of helping to open up their position. Taken together, their college and pro careers illuminated the enduring absurdity of the NFL's racist ideology.

On December 3, 1972, a Black quarterback with obvious skills and poise reached the pinnacle of Canadian pro football. A packed house at Ivor Wynne Stadium in Hamilton, Ontario, watched the Hamilton Tiger-Cats and Saskatchewan Roughriders play in the Grey Cup, the CFL's Super Bowl. With the score tied late, Hamilton's quarterback, Chuck Ealey, coolly directed a drive into Saskatchewan territory. On the game's final play, Hamilton's kicker booted a field goal through the uprights to give the Tiger-Cats the title.

As the home crowd cheered, Ealey's teammates took turns hugging him and shaking his hand. He had rushed and passed for more than 350 yards and steered his offense like a veteran on the game-winning drive. It was quite a performance by a rookie, and he was voted the game's Most Valuable Player for his efforts.

But he was accustomed to winning. It was all he had ever done, almost literally.

Ealey had grown up in Portsmouth, Ohio, in the 1960s, amid increasing racial turbulence. Living in public housing, he had whiled away countless hours hurling rocks at passing trains, unwittingly developing a strong passing arm in the process. At Notre Dame High School, he did not lose as the starting quarterback in either his junior or senior season. Major college recruiters were interested, but they wanted him to switch positions, so he signed with a lesser program at the University of Toledo, which said he could stay at quarterback. There, he would achieve a level of dominance that was rare at any level of football.

It was no secret why the major colleges wanted him to switch positions. At six feet one and nearly two hundred pounds, Ealey was an elusive runner, accurate passer, and innate playmaker, not unlike Russell Wilson decades later. He was a quarterback with talent and brains; an excellent student, he would enjoy a successful career as a financial advisor after football. But in the late 1960s, most major colleges still clung to the stereotypes about Black players lacking intelligence and leadership skills. They simply did not want Black quarterbacks.

Ealey's career at Toledo was an argument for change. He never lost a game in three seasons as the starter, leading the Rockets to thirty-five straight victories, three Mid-American Conference titles, and three Tangerine Bowl victories while setting a slew of school passing records. As a senior in 1971, he finished eighth in the Heisman Trophy voting, a feat for a player from a smaller school.

But a stellar college career did not translate to pro prospects. When NFL scouts weighed in on him before the 1972 draft, Ealey heard the same refrain that major college recruiters had conveyed four years earlier. He needed to switch positions if he wanted to play. "The NFL was looking for 6-foot-3 pocket passers. I was mobile and athletic," Ealey said later. "That was something that somebody could use against me. They built a reason against Black quarterbacks to move them to another position."[1]

Rather than indulge what he correctly perceived as blatant racial profiling, Ealey refused to play along. After observing the denial of opportunity that James Harris, Eldridge Dickey, and Marlin Briscoe experienced in the pros, he knew what fate awaited him. He sent a letter to NFL teams telling them not to bother drafting him if they were not willing to let him play quarterback.

"If you're going to draft me, draft me at quarterback," Ealey said later, recalling the text of the letter. "I wasn't bitter. I wasn't worried about it. I wasn't focused on playing pro ball when I was in college. I was just more practical to the reality that was taking place. I knew the NFL wasn't going to do anything about" giving Black quarterbacks a chance.[2]

Not surprisingly, he went undrafted. Upon graduating with an economics degree, he thought it might be time to begin a white-collar career. But when his agent received a Canadian offer, he changed his plans. The Hamilton Tiger-Cats were looking for a quarterback. Their starter, Joe Zuger, was out with a shoulder injury. His backup, Wally Gabler, did not project as a long-term solution.

Ealey reported to practice and began adjusting to the CFL's larger playing field and other rules unique to the Canadian game. Gabler started early in the season, but when he struggled as the Tiger-Cats lost three of their first four games, Ealey's chance arrived.

A pro team starting a Black quarterback would have generated headlines in the United States, but Ealey's opportunity was met with a shrug by fans in Canada and Ealey's teammates, emphasizing the difference in how many Canadians approached race. "There was never an issue that it would become a Black-white issue because it was not a segregated mindset [in Canada]," Ealey said later. "There was no one who put you in the mindset of being a Black quarterback. It was like college, it was liberating. I was immediately accepted by the team. There was no controversy. Nobody brought [race] up. That's a reflection of the country."[3]

Any potential for controversy was further quashed by Ealey's performance. He was more effective than Bernie Custis, Sandy Stephens, or any of the Black quarterbacks who had preceded him in the CFL. The Tiger-Cats won their last ten regular-season games with him in 1972. It was no surprise to anyone who had followed his career. Ealey had won in high school, won in college, and now, he was winning in the pros, too. His Grey Cup dramatics completed a rookie season that turned him into a Canadian football legend. He would play five more seasons in the CFL, finishing with eighty-two career touchdown passes and more than thirteen thousand passing yards.

A decade later, another Black quarterback from the United States, Warren Moon, would turn a successful career in Canada into an opportunity in the NFL after initially being snubbed. In the early 1970s, though, pro football in the United States persisted in subjecting Black quarterbacks to denial by stereotype. "The country just wasn't at a point where it saw African Americans as being able to intellectually handle the job. White privilege, ideology, all of those things were mixed in," said Dr. Charles K. Ross, University of Mississippi professor of history and African American studies. "You could make it as a safety, a wide receiver. But the idea that an NFL team was going to let you play quarterback and lead them on Monday Night Football, that wasn't going to happen."[4]

Ealey said later that he believed he "could have" been an NFL quarterback. "I would have had to go someplace and have somebody who could coach me in the right system. I think if that happened [today], I'd be given a shot. But that's the way society was then," he said.[5] He did not mind. He was so happy living in Canada that he settled in Hamilton after his football career ended. He married, started a family, and began his business career, eventually earning Canadian citizenship and becoming a dual citizen.

After Ealey's triumphant rookie season in 1972, more Black quarterbacks began to see Canada as a viable option. Jimmy Jones, the Southern Cal quarterback, and Karl Douglas, from Texas A&I University, signed with CFL teams in 1973, and Condredge Holloway joined them in 1975.

Jones had started for three seasons at Southern Cal, a national power. It was after his first start that he made the cover of *Sports Illustrated*, becoming the first Black quarterback to achieve what was then regarded as a high honor in the sports world. Although the cover did not reference his race, the image was powerful.

A year later, he played a key role in one of the most important games in college football history as the leader of an all-Black offensive backfield that helped USC dominate an all-white Alabama team in Birmingham—a result that helped illustrate to college coaches throughout the Deep South and Southwest that the era of Jim Crow football was over.

As fans and some Alabama players cursed Jones and his teammates with racial epithets, USC won by three touchdowns. "You felt great. You felt vindicated. Like you'd done something for yourself, but more importantly, for the whole African-American race," Jones said later.[6]

But even though he established school records in almost every passing statistic at USC, Jones, like Ealey, was not drafted in 1972. He signed with the Broncos but was switched to defensive back and cut. Three years removed from the cover of *Sports Illustrated*, Jones was out of football. But after sitting out the 1972 season, he joined the Montreal Alouettes in 1973 and helped them win a Grey Cup a year later. He would generate 14,306 yards of offense in seven CFL seasons.

Douglas was from a far smaller college, but he was held in higher regard by NFL scouts. The Baltimore Colts took him with a third-round pick in 1971 when Upton Bell was the team's scouting director and in charge of the draft.

"He was six feet two, a pocket passer who could really run," Bell recalled. "I looked at his films and also those of Dan Pastorini, Jim Plunkett, and Archie Manning, the high first-round guys that year, and I asked, 'How much better are they than Douglas?' He was bigger than all of them except Pastorini. This, to me, was a guy with a legitimate chance to be really good."[7]

The Colts needed new blood at quarterback. They still had Johnny Unitas, but he was thirty-eight, and his backup, Earl Morrall, was just a year younger. "We got to the third round of the draft and the best available player on our board was Douglas, so I took him," Bell said. "I would say, and I want to be careful with this, that I didn't necessarily get a warm reception."[8]

Bell would later wonder if he did Douglas a disservice. After the draft, he became the New England Patriots' general manager, which meant he was not in Baltimore later that year when the Colts made decisions about their roster. "Being the personnel guy, you can be in the room and argue for your [drafted] guys when cuts are being made," Bell said. "But I was gone. The Colts still had Unitas and Morrall, and in those days, you didn't keep three quarterbacks."[9]

Cut by the Colts and also by the Buffalo Bills a year later, Douglas went to Canada and played for the British Columbia Lions and Calgary Stampeders. On September 11, 1973, Douglas started for the Lions against Montreal, which started Jimmy Jones. The *Montreal Gazette* noted that the matchup marked "the first time that blacks have been the opposing starting quarterbacks in recognized professional football ranks," but it did so in the nineteenth paragraph of an article consisting of twenty-four paragraphs—a clear indication that the races of the quarterbacks was not headline-making news in Canada.[10]

Holloway's decision to join the CFL's Ottawa Rough Riders in 1975 best illustrated the firmness of the NFL's opposition to Black quarterbacks in the 1970s. Though just five feet eleven, Holloway started for three years at Tennessee and consistently confounded Southeastern Conference defenses with a blend of quickness, passing accuracy, and instinctive playmaking. Decades later, Kyler Murray, a Black quarterback with similar stature and skills, would be drafted first overall by the Arizona Cardinals. "I'd love to see Condredge Holloway playing in modern football, with the spread offense and the shotgun. He'd be devastating," Jon Gruden, a Super Bowl–winning coach, said in 2011.[11] In 1975, though, Holloway went undrafted until the New England Patriots took him in the twelfth round. Sensing the forces aligned against him, he went to Canada.

Holloway was familiar with racist stereotyping and racial symbolism, having grown up in Huntsville, Alabama, and attended a high school named for Robert E. Lee, the Confederate general. A painting of Lee, mounted on a horse and holding the Confederate flag, hung on the wall of the gym where Holloway led the high school's basketball team to glory.

But he also was familiar with the idea of shattering stereotypes. His mother worked at the Marshall Space Flight Center in Huntsville, making her the first Black employee of NASA.

A stellar all-around athlete, Holloway almost gave up on football entirely coming out of high school. Baseball's Montreal Expos drafted him with the fourth pick in the first round in 1971 and offered him a lucrative contract, envisioning him as their shortstop in a few years. Holloway was seventeen years old and sorely tempted to take the money. But his mother wanted him to attend college, so he focused on his football recruitment. In-state powers Alabama and Auburn both wanted him, but not as a quarterback. Alabama's Bear Bryant was brutally honest, telling him the state simply was not ready for a Black quarterback. "I respect Bear Bryant for telling me the truth," Holloway said later.[12]

Tennessee's program had made more inroads. Lester McClain, a wide receiver, had become the program's first Black player, and a fan favorite, a few years earlier. Bill Battle, the Volunteers' coach, had grown up in Birmingham and played for Bryant at Alabama, but he was more accepting of change. "He wanted to play quarterback. That wasn't a problem for me," Battle said later.[13]

Tennessee won twenty-five games over three seasons and went to a bowl game every year with Holloway, who rushed and passed for more than four thousand yards. Although he went winless against Alabama, he earned Bryant's respect. "The last time we played them," Holloway recalled, "he shook my hand and said, 'You had a great career and I sure am glad we don't have to chase you around anymore.'"[14]

Two years younger, Ozzie Newsome, an end for Alabama, would recall Holloway's efforts against the Crimson Tide. "If one man could win a game, Tennessee would have beaten Alabama; Condredge had that much of an impact," said Newsome, who became an All-Pro tight end for the NFL's Cleveland Browns, and later the NFL's first Black general manager.[15]

That apparently did not impress the Patriots, who drafted him in 1975 with plans to make him a defensive back. But as he did when he was leaving high school, Holloway chose to play where his skin color did not prevent him from manning his favorite position. He would thrive as a quarterback in Canada for more than a decade, leading a team to a Grey Cup title, winning the CFL's Most Outstanding Player award, and eventually earning the ultimate honor—induction into the Canadian Football Hall of Fame.

＝＝

The winding pro career of John Walton illustrated the challenges Black quarterbacks faced in the late 1960s and 1970s. But in the end, it also hinted at the possibility that the NFL's steadfast opposition to them was at least starting to wane ever so slightly, a development set in motion by the college game's embrace of Black quarterbacks and the impressive pro careers of Ealey, Holloway, and others in their generation.

Walton was the longest of shots to have any pro career at all. He played in college at Elizabeth City State, a historically Black institution in North Carolina that was so small it was seldom visited by pro scouts searching for prospects. But after going undrafted in 1969, Walton was thrown a lifeline by sheer happenstance. His college coach knew Tank Younger, the former Grambling star who now scouted for the Rams. Relying strictly on Younger's recommendation, the Rams signed Walton to a contract paying him the grand sum of $200.

His prospects were next to nil, it seemed. A year earlier, the Rams had drafted a Black quarterback, Michigan State's Jimmy Raye, but moved him to defensive back, and Walton was far less heralded. But he was the right size at six feet two and blessed with an arm so powerful he was nicknamed "the Rifle." Once he started flinging passes in training camp, the Rams forgot about making him a defensive back. "I was impressed with his arm and he had a good feeling of where to go with the ball," said Roman Gabriel, the Rams' veteran starting quarterback.[16]

In a preseason game that year, the Rams hosted the Buffalo Bills. James Harris, then a rookie trying to stick with the Bills, met Walton on the field and watched him during warm-ups. "He had a good delivery, was accurate, poised in the pocket with a bigtime NFL arm. All the things you look for in a quarterback," Harris recalled.[17]

But the Rams were playoff contenders with Gabriel and had a veteran backup they trusted, sealing Walton's fate. "I was raw," he said later.[18] But the Rams liked him. Though they cut him, they retained his rights and dispatched him to the minor leagues for seasoning. He promptly led the Indianapolis Capitals to the Continental League championship, then spent two years on the Rams' taxi squad, learning from assistant coaches Ted Marchibroda and Dick Vermeil, both future NFL head coaches.

After the Rams cut Walton for good in 1972, he was out of pro football for a year, his career seemingly over. But when the World Football League launched in 1974, seeking a slice of America's now-gargantuan pro football pie, Walton's career resumed. He landed a tryout with the Chicago Fire, and after the coaches saw him throw, he earned a job as a backup. The next year, he was starting for the San Antonio Wings when the WFL folded.

By 1976, Vermeil was the Philadelphia Eagles' head coach. He remembered the raw ability Walton had exhibited while on the Rams' taxi squad earlier in the decade. A tryout offer was extended, and remarkably, seven years after he became a pro by signing a $200 contract, Walton made an NFL roster—the terrain Sandy Stephens would call "the promised land." As a twenty-nine-year-old rookie backup quarterback, Walton played in three games for the Eagles in 1976. His tenure with the team extended through 1979.

He made it to the NFL because he was a pure talent, and because, against the odds, that finally mattered more than the fact that he was Black. "John Walton was definitely good enough to play in the league and certainly as good as some of the [white] guys who had long careers as backups," James Harris said.[19]

It was true that he was never more than a fringe NFL player, just as it was true that Ealey and Holloway were relegated to Canada, unable to crack the NFL's hard shell of quarterback stereotyping. But their careers chipped away at that hard shell. College football had changed—by 1981, even Alabama was starting a Black quarterback. And this was not just change for its own sake. Walton made an NFL roster and Holloway and Ealey played and won in Canada because they were adept at their position's many tasks and responsibilities. They could *play*. If the NFL persisted in finding them and their successors wholly unsuitable, it would become hard not to speculate that the problem lay less with the quarterbacks themselves than with the values underlying the NFL's judgment of them.

CHAPTER 10

As the middle rounds of the 1972 draft unfolded, the Pittsburgh Steelers' coaches, scouts, and front office executives huddled in a meeting room at Three Rivers Stadium in Pittsburgh. One of the scouts, Bill Nunn, lobbied for the team to take Joe Gilliam, a Black quarterback. "He's the best player available," Nunn told Chuck Noll, the Steelers' head coach.[1] A slender, wiry-strong prospect with a rapid throwing delivery, Gilliam had broken Eldridge Dickey's passing records at Tennessee State, formerly known as Tennessee A&I. His coach, John Merritt, had given him the nickname "Jefferson Street Joe" after the main street that ran through Nashville's Black community. It was just a playful turn on Joe Namath's "Broadway Joe" nickname, but the comparison to Namath was a compliment and seemed appropriate.

As the Steelers drafted other players in the seventh, eighth, ninth, and tenth rounds, Nunn continued to support Gilliam. "He's a steal," the scout told Art Rooney Jr., the team's personnel director, who had the final say.[2]

Nunn had been sports editor of the *Pittsburgh Courier*, one of the nation's most influential Black newspapers. The Steelers hired him as a scout because he was knowledgeable about Black players in college football. By 1972, he had led them to Joe Greene, a defensive lineman from North Texas State; Mel Blount, a defensive back from Southern; Dwight White, a defensive lineman from East Texas State; and Frank Lewis, a receiver from Grambling—all destined to play important roles on Pittsburgh's Super Bowl–winning teams.

Rooney respected Nunn's opinion but kept drafting players at other positions because the Steelers did not need a quarterback. They already had Terry Bradshaw, selected with the first overall pick in the 1970 draft, and a young backup, Terry Hanratty, a former Notre Dame star. Teams seldom kept three quarterbacks.

But as the eleventh round of the draft began, Nunn suggested the Steelers not consider the math. "Yes, he's another quarterback, but he's the best player available," Nunn said.[3] Rooney listened. The Steelers took Gilliam.

Players drafted in the eleventh round seldom generated buzz. But when the Steelers opened training camp that summer, it quickly became apparent that Gilliam was not a typical late-round selection. Franco Harris, the Steelers' first-round pick that year, had played with and against NFL-caliber talent during his career as a Penn State running back. Gilliam's raw passing talent mesmerized him.

Bradshaw and Gilliam eyed each other warily. Both were Southerners from smaller colleges. The Steelers had shocked the NFL when they took Bradshaw, from Louisiana Tech, with the first overall pick. When Gilliam joined the team, "I think it was future shock for both of us," Gilliam said later. "I'd never seen a white guy, anybody, throw like Terry Bradshaw. And I'm sure he had never seen a Black guy who could throw like me."[4]

Besides his powerful arm and cocksure attitude, Gilliam had a command of strategy. His father, Joe Gilliam Sr., was Tennessee State's defensive coordinator, a highly respected coach. Gilliam had grown up around practices and locker rooms. The stereotype about Blacks lacking the intelligence and instincts to play quarterback was absurdly inappropriate in his case. "He was just really impressive, had a lot of poise in the pocket, read the coverages. I mean, he did it all," Bradshaw said later.[5]

The Steelers paid him a compliment by giving him a roster spot and then paid him a higher compliment by not asking him to switch positions—the insulting fate other Black quarterbacks experienced in the 1970s. But Gilliam was not a wide receiver or a defensive back. It remained to be seen whether the NFL was ready for him, but Jefferson Street Joe was the quintessential quarterback.

━━

As a rookie in 1972, Gilliam was the only Black quarterback to throw a pass in an NFL game, and he threw fewer than a dozen in two brief appearances. But the fact that he was even in the league and on the field, however briefly, was a triumph. No one understood that better than his father.

Joe Sr. had also excelled as a quarterback in college. Born and raised in Steubenville, Ohio, just north of the Mason-Dixon Line, he had started out at Indiana University before transferring to West Virginia State, a historically Black institution, where he earned All-America honors. The Green Bay Packers brought him in for a look, but it was the early 1950s and they asked him to switch positions—a bitter disappointment that propelled him into a career in college coaching. Working under Merritt at Jackson State and Tennessee State, he became a defensive mastermind who authored popular coaching manuals and helped develop dozens of players who reached the NFL.

At home, with his wife, Ruth, Joe Sr. stressed the importance of education; an avid reader and classical music devotee, he quoted Aristotle in his manuals and took his four children to concerts as well as sporting events. Tragically, his daughter Sonia, a dean's list student and drum majorette at Tennessee State, battled depression before committing suicide on campus in the fall of 1967.[6]

The denial of talented Black quarterbacks was an enduring source of frustration for Joe Sr.; he was crushed when Dickey, whom he had coached, failed to make it with the Raiders. Now, it was his son trying to crack a barrier as resolute as any in football. And unlike Dickey, Jefferson Street Joe actually got somewhere. Even though he played little as a rookie in 1972, the Steelers kept him again in 1973, entranced by his potential. Their conviction paid off. A sore shoulder sidelined Bradshaw for weeks. Hanratty doggedly played on with bruised ribs, winning enough to keep the Steelers in playoff contention, but he suffered a sprained wrist at the outset of a game against the Cleveland

Browns in November. Suddenly, Gilliam was on the field in an important game.

The Steelers' history up to that point was depressing. Founded in 1933, they had never once played in a championship game over the course of almost forty years. But under Noll, with an emerging generation of talented players, they were on the verge of rewriting their narrative. They had made the playoffs for just the second time the year before, and they were good enough in 1973 to have a shot at returning to the postseason. Gilliam needed to come through.

He fared well against the Browns in what was, essentially, his first extended chance to play in the NFL. The Steelers lost, 21–16, but they generated their highest offensive yardage total of the past nine games; the ball moved steadily with Gilliam passing for nearly two hundred yards. With the game on the line late, he led a long drive, forcing the Browns to make a final stand to preserve the win.

He did not fare nearly as well a week later when he made his first start. Facing the Dolphins, the reigning Super Bowl champions, he looked lost. Of his first seven passes, four were incomplete and three were intercepted. Bradshaw replaced him and nearly brought the Steelers from far behind to a victory. Gilliam barely played the rest of the season. The Steelers made the playoffs but lost to the Raiders.

As the 1974 season neared, Bradshaw's grip on the starting job seemed secure. Though erratic and injury-prone, he had still led the Steelers to the playoffs in the past two seasons, winning nineteen of twenty-three starts. In a normal year, Noll would not have questioned whether he was the starter. But a unique set of circumstances intervened when the NFL players' union went on strike as training camps opened.

Labor strife was becoming commonplace in pro sports as players grew weary of ceding so much power to team owners. The NFL's players were seeking the right to change teams when their contracts expired, and the owners did not want them having such freedom. The impasse lasted two months as players boycotted practices and preseason games. The Steelers' quarterbacks all belonged to the union, which meant that Bradshaw and Hanratty dutifully participated in the strike.

Gilliam, however, did not. He crossed the picket line and reported to training camp. Desperate to prove himself, and unconcerned with what his teammates or fans thought, he wanted to play.

Noll was impressed by Gilliam's performance during camp, and Gilliam opened the preseason as the starter. The Steelers won. The strike eventually ended, and in August, Bradshaw and Hanratty rejoined the team. That meant that as the regular season approached, Noll faced a decision: Who was his starting quarterback? Bradshaw was the safe choice, but Gilliam was on a roll. In the Steelers' preseason finale, a nationally televised game against the Dallas Cowboys, he unleashed a stunning barrage of spectacular throws that included three touchdown passes before halftime. The Steelers won to finish the preseason with a perfect record of six wins and no losses. "It looks like we're going to have to go with Joe," Noll told reporters after the game.[7]

In the history of the NFL, in business since 1920, a Black quarterback had never started a season opener with the idea that the team's number one job was his. James Harris had started the Buffalo Bills' opener in 1969, but the Bills were still in the American Football League at the time, and they did not regard Harris, then a rookie, as a definitive answer by any means. He was on the bench before the end of the first half. The Steelers saw Gilliam as a more legitimate candidate to become their starter, provided he played well enough.

It was no surprise to Gilliam's rival for the job. "Joe had a phenomenal preseason; he won the starting job and I lost it," Bradshaw said later. "He played well and I got the axe."[8]

Nor was it a surprise that Noll was the first NFL coach to give a Black quarterback a real chance. In the 1950s, he had played offensive guard for the Browns and their forward-thinking coach, Paul Brown, who had similarly been more open to utilizing Black players than his contemporaries. Otto Graham was the Browns' quarterback in the 1950s, and although he was white, "if Otto Graham had been African American, he would have played quarterback for Paul Brown; that's the only coach I believe that about," said Upton Bell, the son of Bert Bell, the NFL's commissioner from 1946 through 1959.[9]

Noll and the younger Bell worked together in the 1960s when Bell was the Baltimore Colts' assistant scouting director and Noll was the team's defensive coordinator. "Noll was really much more attuned than a lot of coaches into the idea that an African American could play anyplace," Bell recalled. "It wasn't just quarterbacks. There weren't many [Black] linebackers or centers in those years, either. There were all sorts of prejudices, like that quarterbacks weren't pocket passers or intelligent enough to grasp the offense, which was pure bullshit. It wasn't so much prejudice. There was just a groupthink that they couldn't play these positions. My mind was different because I was a lot younger. Noll was similar. He believed in Black players."[10]

Noll's view would help turn the Steelers into a Super Bowl–winning team with Black players manning key roles. But the Steelers were still just playoff hopefuls when Noll made Gilliam the starting quarterback for the season opener in 1974.

Believing his coach had made a fateful decision, Bradshaw asked to be traded.

━━━

Gilliam's rookie season with the Steelers in 1972 coincided with the release of *Super Fly*, a movie about a Black drug dealer in New York seeking one final score. It was a popular example of the "blaxploitation" genre, which featured Black leads and served a Black moviegoing audience, though it also faced criticism for leaning heavily on stereotypes of Black drug dealers, pimps, and criminals. Nonetheless, *Super Fly* projected indelible images of Black swagger into America's mainstream culture. The lead character, played by Ron O'Neal, sported a wide-brimmed hat as he walked the streets of New York to an infectious soundtrack from soul musician Curtis Mayfield.

When Gilliam became the Steelers' starter in 1974, some fans saw him as a football Super Fly. He was irrepressible, supremely confident, and capable of playing with a swagger that many young, white quarterbacks simply could not conjure. He chattered nonstop on the field, trash-talking opponents and showering teammates with exhortations.

It seemed as if he did not have a care in the world as he called a play in the huddle, casually ambled to the line, dropped back, and flung balls far downfield. When a receiver caught one of his passes for a touchdown, Gilliam skipped toward the bench with a broad smile on his face.

Unfortunately, Gilliam had another commonality with Super Fly—he was a drug user. Some of his Pittsburgh teammates knew about it. Others had heard rumors and thought there were times when he *seemed* high, though it did not hinder his unique playing style. If anything, it explained why he missed several meetings and was late to others—ordinarily a no-no in Noll's book, which the coach tolerated in his case.

Gilliam was excited about opening the 1974 season against the Colts at Three Rivers Stadium. He wanted to show he was an NFL-caliber quarterback, regardless of his race. But it was impossible for him not to grasp the social significance of his opportunity. Media coverage leading up to the game was widespread and focused on the fact that he was breaking a barrier. Anchor Dan Rather even mentioned it on the *CBS Evening News*.

"Because of the racism that had always existed at the position, the few Black quarterbacks before him all felt, 'I'm probably not going to get a real opportunity.' But Gilliam is an interesting case. Look at Noll. Look at the Steelers of the 1970s. They're Black. Let's just be honest. That's the fundamental component of why they're so successful. They're instrumental in moving the needle [racially] at all positions," Dr. Charles K. Ross said. "So they even dabbled at the quarterback position. They had Gilliam, truly talented. And they said, 'We're going to give him this opportunity.'"[11]

Though outwardly nonchalant, Gilliam was nervous. It is hard to fathom now, but quarterbacks ran NFL offenses in the 1970s. The era of offensive coordinators calling plays was years away. Gilliam spent the week before the opener in meetings and practices with Noll and the other coaches, who offered ideas about what plays to call Sunday, knowing Gilliam had the final say.

On Sunday, his first five passes were incompletions. He threw an interception near the end of the first quarter. As murmurs of disapproval rippled through the crowd in Pittsburgh, Bradshaw, who had not been traded, watched from the sideline, ready if called upon.

But Gilliam had Noll's support. He was not coming out of the game. And he was undeterred. "I knew sooner or later I'd stop missing passes and start hitting them," he said later.[12] In the second quarter, he finished off a ninety-nine-yard touchdown drive with a fifty-four-yard strike to Lynn Swann, a rookie receiver. A few minutes later, he completed three passes that moved the ball sixty-four yards to another touchdown. Before coming out of the game in the fourth quarter because the Steelers were so far ahead, Gilliam passed for 257 yards. It was a withering disavowal of the many prejudices that had been used for so long to deny opportunities to Black quarterbacks. Gilliam was an effective pocket passer who had no problem calling plays or operating a complex offense. His white teammates had no problem taking cues from him.

The editors at *Sports Illustrated* had assigned one of the magazine's top football writers, Roy Blount Jr., to cover the game. Blount turned in a story that focused less on the racial implications of Gilliam's start than the quarterback's exuberant playing style: "Maybe 'classic' isn't exactly the word. Gilliam often seems to be throwing off the wrong foot or with both of them in the air. He tends to hold the ball down low instead of up by his ear before he throws, but his delivery is so quick that he gets the ball off faster than most anybody anyway. It is also not classic for a quarterback to smile and bounce around with both hands in the air after a successful play . . . but . . . so what?"[13]

A few days later, when readers of America's premier sports magazine reached for their copies in mailboxes and at newsstands across the country, they found Gilliam on the cover with the headline, "Pittsburgh's Black Quarterback."

Now everyone was paying attention.

The Steelers' second game was against the Broncos in Denver. Fired up, the home team attempted an onside kick on the opening kickoff, hoping to catch the favored Steelers napping. It did not work, but the Broncos soon led, 21–7, delighting a large crowd. Needing to lead a rally, Gilliam started throwing and did not stop until he had set the Steelers' franchise records for pass attempts and completions in a game.

His barrage provided the foundation of long drives that brought the Steelers back. They tied the score in the third quarter and held a 35–28 lead in the fourth quarter. But instead of finishing off a drive that would have sealed the win, Gilliam threw an interception, his third of the game. The Broncos converted the break into a touchdown that tied the score.

With little time remaining, Gilliam calmly maneuvered the offense deep into Denver territory, setting up what seemed an easy game-winning field goal attempt. But their kicker flubbed the attempt from twenty-five yards, forcing overtime. When neither team scored during the extra period, the final result was a tie.

Leaning back in his locker after the game, Gilliam looked spent as he spoke to the media. His offense had run ninety plays, a staggering figure. The Steelers were known for having a strong ground game led by Franco Harris, but the passing attack shot off fireworks with Gilliam. That day, he had completed thirty-one of fifty attempts for 348 yards in what Denver's head coach, John Ralston, called "possibly the finest performance I've ever seen by a quarterback."[14] His statistics sound normal decades later, but they were shocking in 1974. Quarterbacks in the NFL simply did not throw that much.

A week later, the Steelers' fierce rivals, the Oakland Raiders, came to Three Rivers Stadium for a nationally televised matchup of playoff contenders. The Raiders devised a special plan for Gilliam. "He has been doing a super job. We knew we had to stop their passing," said John Madden, Oakland's head coach.[15]

The visitors utilized what Madden called a "situational substitution" scheme.[16] Depending on the down and distance, the Raiders lined up with either three, four, or five defensive linemen and four or five defensive backs. They populated the secondary with as many as eight backs on some plays. Gilliam was confused by the constantly changing defense, and after Harris was injured on the Steelers' first offensive play, the quarterback could not rely on his running game. When the offense failed to move the ball early, the home crowd started to boo and turned on Gilliam, chanting, "We want Bradshaw!" Meanwhile, Oakland built a 17–0 lead.

The week before, in Denver, Gilliam had brought the Steelers from behind with his passing, and he tried the same approach in the second half against the Raiders. But Oakland's defense was much tougher. Gilliam finished with just eight completions in thirty-one pass attempts, a startling show of futility. But Noll stuck with him. Two of the Steelers' top receivers missed the game with injuries, and Oakland's defensive front harassed him seemingly every time he dropped back. "Someone asked me if I thought about taking him out. I didn't, but I did think about taking out the offensive line and receivers and about everyone else," Noll said.[17]

After the Raiders' victory, Gilliam was asked about being booed by his home crowd. He gave a diplomatic reply. "I understand about the crowd," he said. "They're fickle and they didn't understand what was happening. But they want to win as badly as us."[18]

Some fans were upset about the wide-open nature of the offense with Gilliam in charge. They wanted the Steelers to get back to running the ball and playing more physical football instead of throwing. But another source of the dissatisfaction with Gilliam had nothing to do with football. Some fans simply could not abide a Black quarterback starting for the Steelers. Gilliam was receiving hate mail. "We're going to cut your dick off. We're going to kill you and your nigger family. That kind of thing," Gilliam recalled.[19]

He would look back at the loss to the Raiders as a turning point. "Those guys beat me up pretty bad; my shoulder, my ankle, my ribs, my knees. They beat me pretty bad. And that's when I really started my first experience with hard drugs," Gilliam would recall.[20]

As he explained in an interview on HBO's *Real Sports with Bryant Gumbel* in 2000, an "acquaintance" who was not on the Steelers offered him crack cocaine and said, "Smoke some of this. It's going to make you sick but you aren't going to feel any pain. I knew initially that it wasn't the thing to do."[21]

Why do it?

"That's a fool," Gilliam said. "A fool does something that he knows is wrong and does it anyway."[22]

On the field, Gilliam recovered nicely from the Oakland debacle, leading the Steelers to a win in Houston a week later. But the running game, not his passing, carried the offense. Gilliam then completed just fourteen of thirty-six passes as the Steelers won against the Chiefs in Kansas City. He did toss a long touchdown pass that effectively clinched the win, but it was Pittsburgh's defense, which forced nine turnovers, that made the difference.

The Steelers were favored by two touchdowns in their next game, at home against the Browns, and they did win, but only by four points. And Gilliam had a terrible time, completing just five of eighteen pass attempts. Once again, many in the home crowd booed the quarterback and chanted for Bradshaw to replace him.

Noll defended his decision to stick with Gilliam, pointing out that Pittsburgh receivers had dropped several on-target throws. Continuity was important at quarterback, the coach said. But many fans disagreed. Al Abrams, a *Pittsburgh Post-Gazette* columnist, wrote that he was receiving "unsigned, bigoted letters from racists" demanding that Bradshaw or Hanratty take over. "These are sick people who cannot be cured," Abrams wrote.[23]

Gilliam had steered the Steelers to the top of their division with a record of four wins, one loss, and a tie. But despite the team's success, Noll was, in fact, ready to make a switch at quarterback. He let the players in on his decision at the start of a midweek practice several days after the Cleveland game. It was his ritual to let the starting quarterback take the first snap. "Terry, take it," he said, nodding to Bradshaw.[24]

It was a pivotal moment, rife with historical significance. Bradshaw wound up leading the Steelers to a division title and much more. The season ended with them beating the Minnesota Vikings in the

Super Bowl. Then they won another Super Bowl the next year. By the end of the decade, they had won four with Bradshaw.

Gilliam, meanwhile, was benched, and he never made another start in the NFL.

Circumspect by nature, Noll revealed little about his decision. "It was based on the facts. I don't always disclose those facts," he said.[25] Gilliam's statistics in his six starts offered insight. He had completed just 45 percent of his attempts, with four touchdown passes and eight interceptions. Although passer ratings were not in vogue yet, his 55.4 figure was well below average.

Noll surely did not like that the Steelers were passing more with Gilliam. He had attempted 198 passes in six games; Steeler quarterbacks had barely surpassed three hundred attempts in sixteen games the year before.

Even so, Gilliam had his team in first place. Yes, he was inconsistent, but was that a surprise considering he was receiving extended playing time for the first time as a pro? It was rare for a quarterback to play with a veteran's steadiness in his first starts. Bradshaw certainly had not.

Inevitably, some saw the fingerprints of racism. With a white coach preferring his offense in the hands of a white quarterback, Noll's decision seemed rooted in the same bias that had always helped forge the NFL's blanket dismissal of Black quarterbacks. But the Steelers' players did not think this decision boiled down to race, at least according to John Stallworth, a Black wide receiver who had joined the team in 1972, the same year as Gilliam.

"I don't think any of us thought it was a racial thing," Stallworth told author Michael MacCambridge in *Chuck Noll: His Life's Work*, a biography of the coach. "And I think it was because we knew Joe's [drug] habits, and I think partly because we knew Chuck. I mean, I think it was a big move to even start Joe in the beginning, to put him in there."[26]

If racism was evident anywhere in Gilliam's situation, it was in the fact that no one ever gave him another chance. Bradshaw had received numerous chances while struggling early in his career. A white quarterback who went 4–1–1 in his first chance to play surely would have received another opportunity. Gilliam never did.

Discouraged, Gilliam became a heavier drug user. "I kind of used the fact that I was benched as an excuse," he said. "All day, all night, I was using drugs."[27]

His habit hung over him as he tried to regain his footing in football. He spent one more year with the Steelers as a backup before being let go. The New Orleans Saints gave him a shot but eventually cut him. He spent time with semipro teams and played in four games, starting two, for the Washington Federals of the United States Football League, a spring league that rose and fell in the 1980s. Along the way, he was arrested multiple times on drug charges. His addictions to heroin and cocaine eventually left him homeless. For a time, Jefferson Street Joe lived on Jefferson Street in Nashville, with no roof over his head.

No one knows what might have happened if Gilliam had kept his starting job. But the Steelers were on the verge of a dynasty in 1974, and Bradshaw, for one, believes Gilliam could have steered them through it. "It easily could have been him instead of me. He absolutely had what it takes to lead the Steelers to those Super Bowls," Bradshaw said.[28]

Shortly before he died of a cocaine overdose on Christmas Day in 2000, Gilliam said as much in an interview: "Yeah, he won four Super Bowls and he was the quarterback. But he wasn't any better than me. I know it. He knows it."[29]

CHAPTER 11

James Harris thought his football career was over. After the Buffalo Bills cut him before the 1972 season and no team picked him up, he took a federal government job in Washington, DC, figuring it was time to get on with his life. He was confident he had what it took to be a starting NFL quarterback—his arm was strong and accurate, and he could evade blitzers, command a huddle, and operate an offense. But it seemed he would leave the NFL without getting a real chance to display those talents. He had made just three starts in three seasons with the Bills. Now, no one wanted him.

Though disappointing, it was hardly surprising. "As I drove to Washington, I had no hope of ever playing again. I didn't think there was any way," Harris said later. "There were no Black quarterbacks playing in the league anywhere. So there was no reason for me to have hope."[1]

He was headed to Washington to work at the Department of Commerce, which ran a management program for former NFL players. The yearly salary was far less than what he had made in the NFL, but Harris was glad to have a job to distract him from the fact that he was not playing football in the fall for the first time since he was a child.

Harris followed the NFL season from afar, but only a few months into his white-collar tenure, his phone rang with a surprising offer. The Los Angeles Rams wanted him to come to the West Coast for a tryout.

They did not need a quarterback. Their longtime starter, Roman Gabriel, was a three-time Pro Bowl selection and former winner of the league Most Valuable Player award, still playing well and winning games at age thirty-two. The Rams also had a capable veteran backup.

But Eddie Robinson, who had coached Harris at Grambling, thought it was a sporting crime that Harris was out of pro football at age twenty-five. Robinson had groomed Harris with the idea that he could become the NFL's first Black starting quarterback, and he refused to give up. He called Tank Younger, the former Grambling star who now worked in the Rams' front office. When Robinson asked if a tryout for Harris could be arranged, Younger made it happen. Harris flew to California and performed well enough that the Rams signed him to their taxi squad. He was back in the NFL, though not on an active roster.

The Rams were in playoff contention when Harris signed, but when they stumbled late in the season, winning just one of their last six games, the media speculated that major changes were coming. Earlier that year, a Chicago businessman, Robert Irsay, had purchased the team, and then, in a bizarre transaction, swapped franchises with Carroll Rosenbloom, owner of the Baltimore Colts. Now, Rosenbloom owned the Rams.

Rosenbloom had owned the Colts throughout Johnny Unitas's career, a period of great success, and wanted to put his stamp on the Rams. After the 1972 season, he fired the head coach and traded Gabriel. The new head coach, Chuck Knox, was a taciturn steelworker's son who had coached offensive lines as a pro and college assistant. Gabriel's replacement, obtained in a trade with the San Diego Chargers, was John Hadl, a balding thirty-three-year-old who had been a longtime starter in the AFL and NFL.

The new regime was an immediate hit. Knox believed in having a strong running game—he quickly earned the nickname "Ground Chuck"—and the Rams had a talented, young running back, Lawrence McCutcheon. Hadl, a shrewd veteran, knew how to use the run to set up the passing game. He threw thirteen touchdown passes as the Rams opened the 1973 season with six straight wins. They wound up easily winning their division, the NFC West, with a record of twelve wins and two defeats. Hadl was voted Player of the Year in the conference. (When the NFL and AFL merged in 1970, the league was divided into the National Football Conference and American Football Conference, each composed of thirteen teams. Each conference had three divisions, the East, Central, and West. With just a few exceptions, teams from the pre-merger NFL were now in the NFC and teams from the AFL were now in the AFC. The winners of the conference playoffs met in the Super Bowl.)

Harris spent the 1973 season as Hadl's backup. He had feared for his job after the Rams drafted a quarterback, Ron Jaworski, with a second-round pick that spring, obviously intending to develop him into their starter, but Jaworski was from a small college in Pennsylvania, Youngstown State, so he had a lot to learn. Harris was further along, and regardless, Knox liked him. "It was obvious he had the ability and had never gotten the chance," Knox said later.[2]

Unlike many coaches and executives in the league, Knox had no issue with using Black players at "thinking" positions. Though he never forced it, he understood the importance of proving that Black players had no limitations. He had started a Black center when he coached the Detroit Lions' offensive line. "Coach Knox was like the good coaches you had and respected who coached you at the recreation center when you were growing up and were concerned about you as a person," Harris said later.[3]

Though he played little in 1973, Harris enjoyed being on the Rams. He bonded with Hadl and Jaworski. They carpooled to work and ate breakfast together. Hadl, genial and generous, mentored the younger quarterbacks on fundamentals. "He was one of the guys in the league who was a genuine person," Harris said later about Hadl. "I didn't trust many people in the league. But I did trust Hadl."[4]

The Rams' season ended abruptly, with a playoff loss to the Cowboys. A year later, Knox kept all three quarterbacks on the roster and most experts picked the Rams to win the NFC West again. They started slowly, winning just three of their first five games as Hadl experienced arm soreness. When Hadl continued to struggle during a game in Green Bay, Knox pulled him for Harris.

Harris had not played meaningful snaps since 1971, and he completed just three of twelve passes, with two interceptions. He figured he was headed back to the bench—a Black quarterback's window of opportunity was seldom open for long—but several coaches pulled him aside on the flight home and told him they had liked what they saw. "In spite of the numbers, I had a good game," Harris said later.[5] Stunning fans, Knox started Harris the next week, and he had a big game, completing twelve of fifteen passes for 276 yards and three touchdowns as the Rams routed the 49ers.

They traded Hadl to Green Bay two days later. The Packers offered a staggering package—first-round, second-round, and third-round draft picks in 1975 and first-round and second-round picks in 1976—leaving the Rams almost no choice but to accept. The rest of the NFL could hardly believe it. Hadl was thirty-four and had been benched. What were the Packers thinking?

Harris had mixed emotions. Personally, he was sorry to lose Hadl as a teammate. The older quarterback had helped and supported him. "I had some sad feelings," Harris said later.[6] But Hadl's departure meant Harris was the now the starter. "When Chuck gave me the news, I'm thinking, 'Does he know I'm Black?'" Harris said.[7] He was shocked, having believed Hadl represented the Rams' present and Jaworski represented the team's future, leaving Harris without a niche. Suddenly, though, he had a chance to play and prove himself.

It had been two years since his infamous drive from Buffalo to Washington, when he believed his career was over. But he had persevered. That Sunday, he made his second straight start, and his first as the Rams' unquestioned starter. He only completed six of fifteen passes for forty-nine yards on the road against the Jets, but he rushed for forty-five yards and a touchdown and the Rams won. Then they kept winning and took command of the division as Harris settled into being the starter. When he kept his job after a dismal loss to the last-place New Orleans Saints, he realized Knox believed in him. "At a time when there were no other Black quarterbacks, having a coach like Coach Knox helped me relax," Harris said later.[8]

In late November, the Rams hosted the defending NFC champions, the Minnesota Vikings, who were in first place in their division. Minnesota's defense, known as "the Purple People Eaters," gave Harris fits. Minnesota led at halftime, 17–6, and that was still the score as the fourth quarter began. But Harris completed four straight passes on a long drive, then plunged one yard for a touchdown. Now the Rams trailed by four points. Their defense forced a punt, and as the clock ticked down, Harris again moved the Rams' offense into Minnesota territory. With a minute to play, he hit Jack Snow on an eight-yard touchdown pass that won the game.

Many of the ninety thousand fans who had attended the game left the Coliseum talking about Harris. He had outdueled the Vikings' Fran Tarkenton, one of the NFL's top quarterbacks, by passing for 249 yards and finishing with ten straight completions. The Los Angeles media had been speculating about Harris's job security even though he had been starting and winning for more than a month, but his status was no longer in doubt now. "Rams Find Themselves—And a Quarterback, Too," read a *Los Angeles Times* headline.[9]

They clinched the division title and won their regular-season finale against the Bills—a result Harris relished, given his history in Buffalo. On December 22, 1974, Harris became the first Black quarterback to start an NFL playoff game. The Rams faced the Washington Redskins before eighty thousand fans in Los Angeles.

Harris had the crowd's support. The Rams had won seven games and lost two with him as the starter. He had completed 53 percent of his passes and thrown eleven touchdowns to just six interceptions. His coaches and teammates believed in him.

The Redskins tried to unnerve him with a heavy blitz, and Harris misfired on several throws as the Redskins took a 10–7 lead. But then Harris led a drive that gave the Rams the lead in the third quarter, and the Rams' defense took over, intercepting three passes in the fourth quarter to preserve the win. Although the *New York Times* characterized Harris's play as "not especially good," he had helped the Rams to their first postseason win in twenty-three years.[10]

A week later, the Rams played the Vikings in the NFC championship game. Surprisingly, the game-time temperature in wintry Minneapolis was thirty degrees, relatively balmy. As many expected in a game with top defenses, points were hard to come by. The Rams trailed, 7–3, when they started a possession at their 1 yard line in the third quarter. But Harris completed a pass for a first down and then hit his favorite receiver, Harold Jackson, on a slant pattern. Jackson broke into the clear and raced to the Minnesota 2 yard line before being tackled.

It appeared the Rams were poised to take the lead when a run moved the ball within six inches of the goal line. Harris brought his offense to the line, barked his signals, and paused. When the pause lasted a beat longer than usual, the Vikings' star defensive tackle, Alan Page, lunged across the line. The officials blew their whistles and, surprisingly, flagged the Rams' center, Tom Mack, for moving before the snap.

Mack protested vehemently, claiming he had not moved. It did not matter. Now the ball was on the 6 yard line, and two plays later a short pass from Harris was deflected and intercepted. The Vikings wound up winning, 14–10.

Harris had been inches away from possibly taking a team to the Super Bowl. "I still go to sleep thinking about that game. I'm trying to figure out a way to win it," Harris said years later.[11] Had the Rams made it, they would have played the Pittsburgh Steelers, the champions of the AFC, who had started a Black quarterback, Joe Gilliam, earlier that season before turning to Terry Bradshaw.

Decades later, it is delicious to think about Harris and Gilliam dueling in a Super Bowl face-off. Both had already done a lot that season to debunk the racist myths about Black quarterbacks being unable to play in the pros; their teams had won eleven of their fifteen combined starts. A matchup of Black starting quarterbacks in the Super Bowl would have further illustrated the foolishness of the attitudes that had kept Black quarterbacks out of the NFL. In the end, though, Harris's team did not reach the Super Bowl and Gilliam watched from the sidelines as the Steelers defeated the Vikings with Bradshaw playing the position Gilliam had manned earlier that season.

Harris and Gilliam knew well that the road for Black quarterbacks had not gotten any easier, despite their success. Harris had received hate mail throughout the fall, especially after becoming the starter. Many fans supported him, but some could not stand that he was running an NFL offense. It was disturbing, but sadly, not surprising, and Harris was able to maintain his focus, helped by his teammates' support. But the mail became more spiteful after the season as the postmortem of the playoff loss focused on the critical penalty on Mack.

"Instead of blaming the ref, or even Mack, the fans and some media had the audacity to blame [Harris] for that call," Knox said later. "Blamed it on what they thought was his sometimes offbeat signal cadence. Can you imagine that? Maybe by then fans had realized that James Harris really was our starting quarterback and was going to be our starting quarterback until he lost his job. Since they didn't like him, they had to find something against him."[12]

Despite the disappointing playoff defeat and the criticism and vitriol aimed at him, Harris felt good about his season. When Tarkenton backed out of the Pro Bowl, Harris was added to the NFC squad. He became the first Black quarterback to appear in the game and earned the Most Valuable Player award when he led a rally that gave the NFC a 17–10 victory.

Harris's job as the Rams' starter was secure heading into the 1975 season. That was never more evident than at the outset of the season. The Rams lost their opener to the Cowboys with Harris completing just one of ten passes with three interceptions before Knox pulled him. But Harris kept starting and the Rams began to win. Two weeks after the opener, he completed sixteen of twenty-two passes for 295 yards and two touchdowns against the Colts.

The Rams wound up winning the NFC West again with a record of twelve wins and two defeats, with Harris starting every game except the finale due to a shoulder injury. After decades of denial, pro football truly had a Black starting quarterback. Harris was not just a fill-in or playing because he was on a team going nowhere. The Rams were championship contenders. Harris's teammates regarded him as smart, resilient, and capable of leading them to the Super Bowl. "He was the NFL's first Black regular quarterback, which didn't mean a thing to me," Knox said later. "However, he was the first quarterback that I developed, which did [matter to me]. I really liked James Harris."[13]

The Black community in Southern California savored the sight of Harris running the Rams' offense. Although the city's top sportswriters and radio talk-show hosts—a mostly white crew—seldom focused on the fact that Harris was Black, Black fans did, among them one of the city's top high school quarterbacks, Warren Moon, who also was Black. "I was a huge Rams fan, and to suddenly have an African American quarterback I could look up to was a great thing," Moon said later. "We'd go to training camp to watch him, and we used to sneak into the Coliseum through a fence to see him in preseason. He had this tremendous arm strength, but what I really tried to emulate was the way he stood in the pocket, so tall and calm."[14]

Jaworski started the Rams' first-round playoff game against the St. Louis Cardinals because Harris's shoulder was still sore. Jaworski threw for more than two hundred yards in a one-sided victory, and some fans clamored for Knox to start the younger quarterback in the NFC championship game against the Cowboys. Knox went with Harris, who had been cleared to resume playing.

More than eighty thousand fans came to the Coliseum, hopeful of seeing their team advance to the Super Bowl for the first time, but a disaster unfolded. The Cowboys intercepted Harris's first pass and took the lead. When the Rams' offense continued to sputter, Knox pulled Harris. But Jaworski fared no better. The Cowboys rolled to a 37–7 victory with Roger Staubach, their star quarterback, tossing four touchdown passes.

Speaking to the media after the game, Rosenbloom, the Rams' owner who had previously owned the Colts, called it his "second biggest disappointment since I've been in football," trailing only the Colts' shocking loss to the Jets in Super Bowl 3.[15] Palpably frustrated by the Rams' inability to take the last step needed to reach the Super Bowl, the owner said changes were coming. "We're going to be doing quite a few things we feel have to be done," he said.[16] At the top of his list was making the Rams more dynamic at quarterback. Although Harris had played well and helped the Rams win a lot of games, other quarterbacks had better statistics and generated more buzz. Rosenbloom wanted Los Angeles, a city of stars, to have a star quarterback.

That spring, the Rams drafted Pat Haden, a quarterback who was a local hero; he had been an All-American in high school in Los Angeles and helped Southern Cal to two national titles. A stellar student, he had spent the past year studying in England on a Rhodes scholarship while playing in the World Football League. Fans in Los Angeles were delighted that he would continue his NFL career with the Rams. "We picked up Haden, local guy, USC, Rhodes scholar, dearly loved by all. For whatever reason, James Harris was in trouble," Knox said later. "C. R. [Rosenbloom] invited [Knox's wife] Shirley and me to one of his infamous dinner parties at his house in Bel Air. I think maybe Jonathan Winters and Ricardo Montalbán were there. We all gathered in C. R.'s living room. With this spark in his eye, he said, 'Let's play a game. Let's vote on who we want for president this year, and then, just for fun, we'll vote on who we want for Rams quarterback.' So he passed around these little pieces of paper and everybody voted. Shirley and I were the only ones who voted for James Harris."[17]

The Rams' quarterback position was a circus that fall. Jaworski started the opener. Haden started the second game. Harris started the third. In Week 4, Harris threw for 436 yards and two touchdowns in a win over the Dolphins. But then he failed to generate a point in a loss to the 49ers a week later, and Jaworski took over.

As the quarterbacks rotated in and out, seemingly every week, Harris outperformed the other two. He would finish the season in a tie for the highest passer rating in the NFC. Knox and many teammates wanted him on the field.

But Rosenbloom had other ideas. Harris was benched in November. Haden wound up starting as the Rams secured another division title and reached the NFC championship game for the third straight year, only to lose again, this time to the Vikings.

The quarterbacks did not let the controversy interfere with their personal relationships. Following Hadl's example as the starting quarterback several years earlier, Harris and Jaworski took Haden under their wing, carpooled to work, bought him breakfast, and shared their expertise, especially when the rookie wound up on the field in the playoffs.

But it was a combustible situation, and it exploded after the season. A young sportswriter for the *Los Angeles Times*, Skip Bayless, wrote a series of articles about dysfunction in the Rams' organization. One article focused on the quarterback circus. Several veterans told Bayless the locker room had been solidly in favor of Harris starting all season. "He was certainly our best quarterback and one of the best in the league when he's healthy. I told him so after the season. I love the man dearly," Tom Mack, the Rams' center, said.[18]

Mack and others believed Harris had lost his job only because Rosenbloom had influenced Knox. The owner denied telling the coach he wanted Haden on the field. Knox declined comment.

Bayless's articles helped unleash anger that had slowly built in Los Angeles' Black community over Harris's benching. A Black member of the Los Angeles City Council introduced a resolution that praised Harris for keeping his dignity as he "had to fight his opponents as well as the Rams' front office." The resolution compared him to baseball's Jackie Robinson and claimed he had "suffered the pains and heartaches of a mostly vicious and biased press."[19]

The full city council did not endorse the resolution, citing technicalities, but Harris did not disagree with the resolution's depiction of the press. "Everything said about me [in the press] was always negative—I didn't have any mobility, I couldn't read defenses. The things other guys couldn't do were never pointed out. There was a double standard," he told Bayless.[20]

Undaunted, Rosenbloom instructed his front office to continue searching for more star power at quarterback. The Rams traded for Joe Namath, now thirty-four, sore-kneed, and barely able to play. They also drafted Nebraska's Vince Ferragamo with a fourth-round pick.

Harris was bitter about losing his job and fearful of what his situation said about the possibility of Black quarterbacks ever getting a chance in the NFL. After the Rams traded him to the Chargers on June 15, 1977, he said, "I'm not sure people will ever accept or write the fact that a Black quarterback can make it in pro football."[21] He said later, "Most teams, when you were part of a championship game, played in the Pro Bowl, you were the starter, [but] I had to go back and compete for the job each time. I felt that although I had played well for the Rams and accomplished some things, people were still asking, 'Could Blacks play quarterback in the NFL?' It meant to me that the NFL was just not ready for a Black quarterback."[22]

Lawrence McCutcheon, the Rams' running back, said later, "I totally understood the way he felt. He had done everything humanly possible to win the job. He was worn down by the whims of the front office; he was fed up with the racism of the fans. Any one of us would have said the same thing had we gone through what [Harris] went through. What's the use?"[23]

Harris considered retiring but ultimately joined the Chargers and started nine games for them in 1977 before a shoulder injury ended his season. He then backed up Dan Fouts, a future Pro Football Hall of Famer, in 1978 and 1979 before retiring.

"The Rams made me, but they also ruined me. I was never the same," Harris said later. "My passion, my motivation was gone. After all I'd been through, I didn't want to go through any more."[24]

He was worn out from having battled stereotypes and institutional racism for a decade. That he had forged a successful NFL career in spite of it all was miraculous. No other Black quarterback had ever done it. And because he had persevered, the pro football world Harris was leaving was different from the pro football world he had entered a decade earlier. Never again would it have what amounted to a zero tolerance policy on Black quarterbacks.

Change was coming, not that Harris or anyone else could tell in the late 1970s. It would be grudging and incremental change, with many gains offset by the persistence of old attitudes and the damage they could engineer. Truly significant change would not unfold until later, so far into the future that Harris would need decades to understand just how much his successors had benefited from his troubles. But benefit, they certainly did.

CHAPTER 12

The NFL's implicit bias against Black quarterbacks did not suddenly die out. It just slowly began to wane, ever so gradually, and become dated, at least in a few minds, for reasons as sweeping as general societal change and as minuscule as individual moves by the NFL and its teams that helped the cause of Black quarterbacks, sometimes by sheer chance.

Certainly, no one expected them to benefit from the league's launch of an expansion franchise in Tampa, Florida, in 1976. Racial animus was running as hot as ever in America's Deep South, and as Doug Williams, the Black quarterback who would lead the Tampa Bay Buccaneers, would say so succinctly, "You can't get any farther south than Florida."[1]

Hugh Culverhouse, a tax attorney who had made a fortune in real estate, paid $16 million to launch the Bucs. A cigar smoker with a backwoods Southern drawl and fondness for garish sports jackets, he exuded the plantation mentality. Culverhouse "would have been the perfect slave owner," Williams wrote in *Quarterblack*, an autobiography published in 1990.[2]

But while a team in the Deep South, owned by Culverhouse, did not seem a likely source of progress on any racial front, the Bucs, from their first day forward, were more open to Black quarterbacks than the rest of the NFL.

Culverhouse had plenty of money and wanted to win. He lured one of college football's most successful coaches, John McKay, to Tampa Bay. McKay had churned out championship-caliber teams at

Southern Cal for fifteen years with Black players, including quarter-backs Jimmy Jones and Vince Evans, frequently leading the way.

In his haste to give the Bucs an immediate identity with a well-known coach, Culverhouse surely gave little thought, if any, to the fact that McKay's opinion of Black quarterbacks differed from the general opinion that had prevailed in the NFL for decades. But it did, and that difference would result in significant progress for all Black quarterbacks.

McKay's presence did not automatically guarantee a Black quarterback would be in charge of the Bucs' offense. A team of personnel administrators shaped the roster, with input from scouts. Steve Spurrier, a thirty-one-year-old white quarterback who had won the Heisman Trophy at the University of Florida, started for the Bucs in their inaugural season.

But the fact that McKay was so enthusiastic about Black quarterbacks was not lost on the members of the personnel department. It meant they did not need to take race into account in their evaluations of quarterback prospects. If they found a Black quarterback who, they believed, could help the Bucs, they could grab him without fearing they were wasting their time.

In the Bucs' inaugural draft, in the spring of 1976, they selected Parnell Dickinson in the seventh round. Dickinson was Black, a quarterback from Mississippi Valley State. Tall and long-legged, he made the team as Spurrier's backup and played in several games early in the 1976 season because the Bucs usually were so far behind. Then an injury sidelined Spurrier, and Dickinson started against the Miami Dolphins in Week 7.

The Bucs were swimming against a powerful current. The NFL had twenty-eight teams, but only five had started a Black quarterback in a game. George Taliaferro had started two for the Colts in 1953. James Harris had made starts for the Bills and Rams. Joe Gilliam had started six games for the Steelers in 1974. J. J. Jones, a rookie backup, had started a single game for the New York Jets in 1975.

Twenty-three NFL teams, including many in existence for decades, had never started a Black quarterback in a game. But the Bucs broke the color line in their inaugural season. And Dickinson made the most of his opportunity early in his start against the Dolphins, completing his first four passes, including one for a touchdown. But then a foot injury knocked him out of the game, forcing McKay to use another quarterback. Spurrier returned to the lineup the next week, and Dickinson suffered a serious knee injury in practice later that season, effectively ending his career. "We thought we had a good one with Dickinson," said Ron Wolf, a personnel executive with the Bucs that season. "We liked him because he was mobile and had the ability to scramble out of trouble. Unfortunately, he got hurt doing just that."[3]

The Bucs were outmanned at many positions. All fourteen of their games in 1976 and their first twelve games in 1977 ended in defeat. McKay was unaccustomed to such failure, but he did not lose his sense of humor. At one point, a reporter asked him what he thought of his team's execution. "I'm in favor of it," he deadpanned.[4]

They were outmanned at quarterback as much as at any position. After releasing Spurrier following the 1976 season, they used three quarterbacks who combined to throw thirty interceptions and just three touchdown passes in 1977. Seldom had an NFL team needed a quarterback more than the Bucs heading into the 1978 draft. And they were in position to do something about it as the holders of the first overall pick, courtesy of their lamentable record.

Pitt's Matt Cavanaugh, Brigham Young's Gifford Nielsen, and Stanford's Guy Benjamin headlined the crop of quarterbacks available that year. They were all white. Doug Williams, from Grambling, also was available. He stood six feet three, weighed 225 pounds, and had finished fourth in the Heisman Trophy vote, having led the NCAA in touchdown passes and passing yardage. "If I was coming out today, I'd be the first pick. But there was zero chance of that happening in 1978," Williams said years later, laughing. "I can laugh about it now, but I laugh to keep from crying."[5]

It was impossible for NFL scouts not to like his arm, but few put stock in his accomplishments at Grambling, believing he had attained them while facing lesser competition in Black college football.

The Bucs' talent evaluators disagreed. After their initial review of the quarterback crop, they narrowed their options down to Cavanaugh, Benjamin, and Williams. McKay asked his offensive coordinator, Joe Gibbs, to study them and decide which he liked most. Gibbs traveled to Grambling and spent a week with Williams. They discussed family and offensive strategy. They ate together at McDonald's. Gibbs watched Williams work out and throw to receivers. Williams gave him all the time he wanted. No other NFL team sent a scout or coach to Grambling before the draft.

Gibbs was impressed. He returned to Tampa and told McKay that, in his opinion, Williams could start in the NFL and effectively lead a team. Gibbs also spent time with Cavanaugh, who had helped Pitt win a national championship, and Benjamin, an All-American. But Gibbs told McKay that Williams was the best of the three.

When the personnel department told Culverhouse it was considering drafting Williams, Culverhouse was aghast. Selling tickets was already a challenge after two miserable seasons. Making a Black quarterback the face of the Bucs would further alienate some fans in the Deep South.

But McKay's support for the idea, backed by Gibbs, carried the day. McKay trusted Gibbs and resented the racist nonsense about Black quarterbacks that he had heard in the NFL.

Knowing other teams were not interested in Williams, the Bucs could afford to trade the first overall pick, move back in the draft, and still get him. They fielded offers and wound up sending the pick to the Houston Oilers for a tight end, Jimmie Giles, and several draft picks, including Houston's first-round pick that year—the seventeenth overall selection.

The first round of the draft was held on May 2 at the Roosevelt Hotel in New York City. When NFL commissioner Pete Rozelle announced the Bucs were taking Williams, the shock in the room was palpable. No NFL team had ever drafted a Black quarterback in the first round. "People don't realize that Joe Gibbs changed the face of the NFL by having the courage to say, in a Southern town at that time, that Doug Williams is the guy we should take," Tony Dungy said later. "When they drafted Doug, it shocked the whole country that they took this unknown from Grambling over those stars from Pitt and Stanford."[6]

Before the draft, a television interviewer had asked Grambling's Eddie Robinson what Williams "needed" to succeed in the NFL. "An opportunity to play," Robinson said.[7]

Those four words were all he needed to say.

=====

Growing up in Zachary, Louisiana, near Baton Rouge, in the 1960s and early 1970s, Williams knew to avoid certain intersections on Friday nights and knew where weekly cross burnings attracted crowds. He was warned not to leave the house when LSU hosted Ole Miss in football. It was just too dangerous for him with so much hatred loose on the streets.

Williams was the sixth of eight children. His father, who had been wounded at Pearl Harbor, did construction work and managed a nightclub. His mother was a school cook. Their house did not have plumbing until Williams was fourteen. His parents jumped at the chance to send their athletic son to Grambling when Robinson recruited him to play quarterback and offered a scholarship.

They did not consider Williams's pro prospects. "We didn't think about it," Williams said. "Coach Rob was Coach Rob. We didn't know the world was watching. He told my mama that I would be going to class, and church every Sunday, and get a degree, and that's all she wanted to hear."[8]

Robinson held up his end of the deal: Williams graduated before the NFL draft. When the Bucs offered what he thought was an inadequate contract after drafting him in the first round, he held out. In the segregated world he had grown up in, white people always believed he should happily settle for less. He was done with that.

The gambit worked. After sitting out a week, he signed when the Bucs bumped the terms of their offer from three years to five and from $70,000 to $100,000 per year.

When he reported, Williams knew he would be closely scrutinized, but he was not nervous. "James Harris came to Grambling all the time while I was there, and he would tell me, 'Man, if you can throw it here, you can throw it anywhere. It doesn't matter where you're playing or what color you are. It ain't no different. You can do it,'" Williams said. "I was aware of what he and Marlin Briscoe had been through. I just wanted to play."[9]

He was buoyed by the experience of having played in the Senior Bowl, a postseason all-star game for players headed to the NFL. "I'd played with the big boys. Ozzie Newsome was my tight end at the Senior Bowl. It didn't feel any different being in the huddle with them, going to meetings with them, eating with them," Williams said. "Maybe they thought I was a Black quarterback from a small college, but I was their quarterback. I think that helped."[10]

At his first practice with the Bucs, an assistant coach sharply criticized him for a mistake. Gibbs ran from the other end of the practice field to calm the coach down. "If I hadn't had the home training and southern mentality of being Black, I couldn't have handled it," Williams wrote.[11]

In his home preseason debut, he intentionally sailed his first pass far over the receiver's head, just to showcase his arm. The fans cheered. Later in the preseason, he made several nice throws against the Atlanta Falcons, who had drafted their starting quarterback, Steve Bartkowski, with the first overall pick in 1975. "June Jones was Steve's backup, and after the game, June came over to me and said, 'Man, you should have gone first overall like Steve,'" Williams said.[12]

He started the regular season opener but was out before halftime with an injured shoulder that forced him to miss the next game. Returning a week later, he completed just five of nineteen passes against the Vikings. But the Bucs, with a career record of two wins and twenty-eight defeats at that point, upset a team that had dominated the NFC during the 1970s. The Bucs then won again a week later, beating the Falcons before a delighted home crowd.

Williams settled in. He completed fourteen of twenty-three passes in a win over the Chiefs and eleven of nineteen with two touchdowns in a win over the Bears. By early November, the Bucs had four wins and four defeats and were in the race for the NFC Central title. "Tampa was really fired up over the team. We had come a long way," Williams wrote.[13]

His effect on the rest of the team was undeniable. After he broke his jaw in early November, putting him on the sidelines until the final week of the season, the Bucs fell apart. They ended the season with a record of five wins and eleven defeats. But with Williams at quarterback, they won four and lost four.

McKay believed in him. And no doubt, Williams needed the faith. As the 1979 season began, the NFL had just three other Black quarterbacks, all backups: John Walton with the Eagles, Vince Evans with the Bears, and James Harris with the Chargers. Williams was the only starter. But the Bucs were more committed to him than any NFL team had ever been to any Black quarterback.

Some fans were fine with that, but Williams also routinely received racist letters along with fan mail. He knew if the envelope did not include a return address, it probably was nasty. One day he opened a box to find a rotten watermelon and a note that read, "Try throwing this to your niggers. Maybe they can catch this."[14]

McKay also was a target due to his support for Williams and the Bucs' other Black players. According to Williams's autobiography, as the Bucs left the field after one game, a fan shouted that McKay should "go back to Southern Cal and take your niggers with you."[15] McKay wanted to go into the stands and confront the fan, Williams wrote, but kept walking. The racism of the team's redneck fans "was one problem [McKay] couldn't solve," Williams wrote.[16]

The Bucs started fast in 1979. Their defense dominated. Their star running back, Ricky Bell, bulled through opposing defenses for gains. Williams made plays with his arm. The Bucs won their first four games before heading to Chicago to face the Bears in what became a historic occasion when Evans started at quarterback for the Bears. It was the first NFL game featuring two Black starting quarterbacks.

Evans had taken an improbable journey to the moment. As a twelve-year-old in Greensboro, North Carolina, in 1967, he had watched Southern Cal play on television and fallen in love. When he told his father he wanted to go to USC, located on the opposite coast, his father said, "Boy, you done lost your mind."[17] But six years later, he rejected a football scholarship to North Carolina Central and enrolled at Los Angeles City College, and a year after that, he realized his dream and signed with the Trojans. He started as a junior, operating McKay's run-oriented offense.

McKay left for the Bucs before Evans's senior season, and the new coach, John Robinson, brought in more of a pass-minded offensive coordinator, Paul Hackett, who taught Evans to drop back, read pass coverages, and run a pro-style offense. As a senior in 1976, he led the Trojans to the Pac-8 title and a Rose Bowl victory.

After the Bears drafted him in 1977, he was so sure he could play quarterback in the NFL that he had a clause inserted in his contract forcing the Bears to play him there. Then he mostly sat on the bench for two years before receiving his opportunity in 1979. The Bears had lost twice with him as their starter heading into the game against Williams and the Bucs.

Before the game, there was a smattering of media commentary about both quarterbacks being Black. "There will be no speeches or blare of trumpets, but mankind will take another step forward Sunday," a *St. Petersburg Times* columnist wrote.[18] Generally, though, there was little fuss. "Nobody is picketing. Nobody is boycotting. Nobody is writing angry letters to the editor. Nobody seems to care," the *Chicago Sun-Times* reported.[19]

That was not entirely true. Williams and Evans cared. "We were well aware of what it meant. We had a lot of respect for each other," Williams said.[20] James Harris told the *Sun-Times*, "Maybe there's some progress. Maybe some other guy coming along will get the opportunity, too."[21]

With fifty-five thousand fans watching on a Sunday afternoon in Chicago, neither quarterback performed especially well. The Bucs led at halftime, 10–3, but the Bears took the lead in the fourth quarter when their running back, Walter Payton, ran sixty-five yards for a touchdown with a screen pass. The Bucs were on the ropes.

Down by three, Williams and the Tampa Bay offense began a possession near midfield. On a third-and-2 play, Bell ran for a first down. Williams converted another third down with a completion. The ball moved deep into Chicago territory and Williams threw a touchdown pass. The Bucs won, 17–13. After the game, they learned they had the NFL's best record.

"Our confidence level was sky high. We were the only undefeated team in the NFL and we didn't think we could be beat," Williams wrote.[22]

Their invincible feeling did not last long. They lost to the Giants. The lowly Saints beat them by twenty-eight points in Tampa. But Williams helped end the slump, throwing two touchdown passes in a win over the Packers, and in early December, the Bucs had nine wins and three defeats and seemingly were zeroing in on the NFC Central title.

But after a missed extra point and a blocked field goal cost them in a one-point loss to the Vikings, they fell into a funk. Williams threw four interceptions in a loss to the Bears. Then he threw five interceptions in a loss to the 49ers. "Brent Musburger on CBS made the statement that 'Doug Williams is killing the Bucs.' That one stuck with me," Williams said. "I think a lot of fans wanted a new quarterback."[23]

McKay stuck with him. The Bucs needed to beat the Chiefs in their season finale to take the division title and make the playoffs for the first time. If they lost, their season was over.

A driving rainstorm turned their home field into a mud pit. Neither offense could move the ball. The game was scoreless deep into the fourth quarter. With the season on the line, Williams completed several passes to move the ball into Kansas City territory. The Bucs' Neil O'Donoghue lined up for a nineteen-yard field goal and booted the ball up and into the storm. It spun through the uprights, giving the Bucs the win and a division title.

A week later, in perfect weather and in front of a roaring crowd in Tampa, the Bucs won a first-round playoff game over the Eagles. It was a heady moment. In just their fourth season, they were in the NFC championship game, one win from the Super Bowl.

The title game was in Tampa, against the Rams, whom the Bucs had beaten by fifteen points earlier in the season. "We had them where we wanted them; we were on the verge of going from the worst team in pro sports to the Super Bowl in a matter of two years," Williams wrote.[24]

The Bucs were confident—too confident. The Rams had improved, and they were a team of veterans accustomed to playoff pressure. Their defense shut down Bell and overwhelmed Williams, who completed just two of thirteen passes before being knocked out of the game with a torn bicep muscle. The Bucs' defense kept the score close, but the Rams moved the ball enough to kick three field goals. Final score: Rams 9, Bucs 0.

It was a bitter disappointment, but the loss did not lessen the sense of accomplishment the Bucs felt for having come so far so quickly. The rest of the NFL now saw them as a rising power, their roster brimming with talented, young players.

But Williams still generated a mixed reaction among fans and the media. Some of the doubt stemmed from his unconventional playing style. He preferred taking risky, downfield shots to settling for short, safe completions. The reward was higher, but in 1979 he completed just 41 percent of his passes, a low figure. He also threw more interceptions than touchdown passes. His statistics gave ammunition to fans who wanted him gone.

But Williams also delivered in pressure situations and was sacked just seven times during the season, a league low among starters, despite having dropped back to pass more than four hundred times. His style was unique, but it was effective.

Only twenty-four, Williams was proud of his team and his performance and excited about what lay ahead. His starting job was secure. McKay and his teammates believed in him. But he wanted to be regarded as an NFL quarterback, period, not just a Black NFL quarterback, and that was not going to happen. The politics of race continually hung over him. "It was there every day," Williams said.[25]

That was never more evident than early in the 1980 season. Picked to go far, the Bucs stumbled, going five weeks without a win at one point. Behind-the-scenes problems arose. Some players had sought new contracts in the wake of the team's success and were furious when Culverhouse rebuffed them. Several players had drug habits. Williams was not the issue. He had no interest in drugs and was not seeking a raise despite being unhappy with his contract. He was playing well, yet he was under the most scrutiny.

In Week 3, he threw for 258 yards in a loss to the Cowboys, but his receivers dropped several important passes, helping seal the Bucs' fate. McKay ripped into the media after the game. During the week, a Texas newspaper had published an interview with Williams and sought to replicate his Southern dialect. McKay was furious to see Williams treated like Mark Twain's Jim character in the novel *The Adventures of Huckleberry Finn*. The paper wanted to make Williams look stupid, McKay believed. "He doesn't go anywhere where he's treated like a football player," McKay said. "Doug Williams is a young quarterback. He's not a Black quarterback. No more than David Lewis is a Black linebacker or O. J. Simpson was a Black running back. It's time people grow up. Every time I read something [about Williams] he's a Black quarterback."[26]

A week later, Williams was brilliant against the Browns, completing thirty of fifty-six passes for 343 yards and three touchdowns. After the Browns built an eighteen-point lead in the third quarter, Williams fell just short of bringing the Bucs all the way back with his scrambling and passing. When the final gun sounded, a dozen Browns, including Ozzie Newsome, took turns shaking his hand, showing appreciation for his gallant effort. But every one of the Browns who shook his hand was Black, according to the *Washington Post*'s John Feinstein, who viewed the scene.[27] None of Cleveland's white players made the gesture.

Feinstein published a feature on Williams in the *Post* several days later, focusing on the challenges he faced because he was Black. "Sportswriters in Tampa say they are sometimes subjected to phone calls and letters from people asking, 'When is McKay going to get the Black guy out of there?'" Feinstein wrote.[28]

Williams's affable, level-headed personality gave him the tools to endure. "If I play for 20 years, I'm still going to be a Black quarterback. I know that," he told Feinstein. "Every morning when I wake up and look in the mirror, I know I'm a Black quarterback."[29]

After a losing season in 1980, the Bucs bounced back. With Williams starting every game, they won a division title in 1981 and made the NFC playoffs as a wild card qualifier in 1982. Although the Cowboys eliminated them from the playoffs both times, they were closer to the top of the NFC than the bottom.

Williams's contract expired after the 1982 season, but he was confident he would sign a new deal. The Bucs were a laughingstock when they drafted him, but in five years with him as their quarterback, they had won two division titles, made three trips to the playoffs, and reached the NFC championship game. Although he had completed less than 50 percent of his passes, he had thrown one hundred touchdown passes and accumulated more than twelve thousand passing yards. "I thought I was on a team headed to the top," he wrote. "I wanted to win in the NFL and I wanted to do it in Tampa."[30]

He also wanted to be paid better. Although he had seldom complained, he was still upset about Culverhouse getting him to sign a below-market deal when he was a rookie. That contract had hung over him like a dark cloud. Even though he was one of twenty-eight starting quarterbacks in the NFL in 1982, fifty-three other quarterbacks in the league made more money. "I wasn't going to be their slave anymore," he wrote, referring to the Bucs.[31]

Pro football salaries were rising due to a new source of competition for talent—the United States Football League, a start-up scheduled to launch in 1983, playing games in the spring and summer. After earning $120,000 in 1982, Williams asked for a new contract paying him $600,000 a year. Culverhouse, scoffing, offered an annual salary of $400,000. Williams refused to consider it. Culverhouse tried to intimidate him with tough talk in the media and then, in a bizarre twist, tried to convince Williams to invest in one of the owner's real estate ventures in lieu of pay. Williams said no.

"It was very, very insulting, what happened to him," Dr. Charles K. Ross said. "He just wanted a contract that put him in a respectable place within the economic framework of the position. But it was like the Bucs said, 'We don't want you to be here. We know we've been horrible, one of the worst franchises in NFL history, and you've come in and changed our whole history . . . but you're Black, so it's hard for us to put our arms around you. We can't love you and squeeze you and love you. It's hard for us to do that.'"[32]

The stalemate continued even after Williams suffered a personal tragedy when his wife died of an aneurism shortly after undergoing surgery to remove a brain tumor. "Racism was definitely involved," Williams said.[33] "Culverhouse thought I was a good ole black boy who'd never had nothing and would go along with whatever he wanted. He was not going to pay a Black quarterback what white quarterbacks were making."[34]

The Bucs moved on, and Williams, grieving, went home to Zachary. His disgust with Culverhouse, the Bucs, and the whole business of football was so acute that he took a job as a substitute middle school teacher and did not play football in 1983. Even though he had proven he was a winning NFL quarterback, he wondered if the league would ever accept a Black quarterback. "I didn't care at that point," he wrote. "My wife had died and I had a little girl to take care of and I just didn't care about playing in the National Football League."[35]

Sensing an opportunity, the USFL's Oklahoma Outlaws called his agent. They were willing to pay him what he wanted. Williams did not mull the offer long. He signed. With a stroke of a pen, the only Black quarterback who had ever held an NFL starting job for long bid the league farewell and good riddance.

His departure put Black quarterbacks in the NFL back where they had started in the modern era, possessing minimal opportunity and impact. Evans was the only one to start a game in 1983, and he started just three for the Bears, winning one. Despite the efforts of Williams, Evans, and those who had played before them, Black quarterbacks were effectively shut out of the NFL.

CHAPTER 13

Warren Moon was stereotyped as a football player for the first time in the early 1970s, at the outset of his career at Hamilton High School in Los Angeles. He already had a bit of a pedigree at that point, having played quarterback for a youth football powerhouse, but that did not sway Hamilton's junior varsity coach. "The guy just didn't want to play me at quarterback," Moon said.[1]

It was a typical experience—at all levels of football, not just in the pros—for Black players who wanted to play quarterback in the early 1970s. "Times were different, people were different, the thought process was different," Moon would say later.[2] One of the sport's accepted and enduring precepts was that white players would do a better job of commanding a huddle, calling signals, and shouldering the responsibility of winning games.

Moon was fleet enough to play defensive back or running back, as his coach wanted, but when he refused to switch to one of those positions, he sat on the bench as a sophomore. "All I wanted was an opportunity to show what I could do at the position I loved," he said.[3]

His father had died of liver and heart disease when he was seven, influencing the person and athlete he would become. "You're the man of the house now," his mother, a nurse, told him.[4] Moon took her words to heart. He worried about his six sisters. He made sure the trash was on the curb on the right day. "I had to take on more responsibility," he said.[5] His friends called him "Pops" or "Daddy" because "I was always reminding everybody what to do right and what not to do wrong," he said.

Moon's youth football coaches spotted his maturity, strong throwing arm, and knack for leadership and put him at quarterback. "A lot of guys didn't want to deal with the responsibility, but because I was being raised with that responsibility around the house, I didn't have any problems with wanting to do the things a quarterback was going to be asked to do, which was lead a football team, make the big decisions at the right time, motivate guys, get them to play within one goal; all those different things that come with playing quarterback," Moon said. "And then I was blessed with a very good arm and that helped."[6]

He saw few Black quarterbacks in the pro and college games he watched on television, leading him to wonder if he had a future at the position. His high school junior varsity experience redoubled his doubts. But Jack Epstein, Hamilton's varsity coach, recognized that he was naturally suited to playing quarterback and made him the starter. Moon thrived for two seasons, earning All-City honors as a senior and attracting interest from major college programs.

But then he was stereotyped again. Although college football became a landscape of opportunity for Black quarterbacks starting in the 1970s, they were still mostly identified as effective runners, but not passers—labels that Moon could not dispel, no matter how hard he tried. He could drop straight back and throw passes all over the field, but the colleges recruiting him as a quarterback favored run-oriented offenses such as the wishbone or the veer while the colleges that favored "pro-style" passing offenses wanted him to switch positions.

The dismissal of his throwing arm particularly frustrated Moon, who would later pass for nearly seventy thousand yards in his pro career. "I was a good athlete for a quarterback, but I was not a fast and elusive Lamar Jackson by any means," he said. "But the colleges had me pegged as an option quarterback."[7]

He signed with Arizona State, which had recruited him as a quarterback until two other players at the position, both more highly regarded and white, also signed. "They said they'd honor my scholarship, but only if I changed positions," Moon said.[8]

Moon decided to spend the year at West Los Angeles College, a junior college where Epstein now coached. After a season in which he set passing records, he sought again to attract interest from passing-oriented programs such as Stanford or Cal-Berkeley, but they still wanted him to play positions other than quarterback. Then he heard from the University of Washington, which had a new head coach, Don James, whose offensive coordinator had seen film of Moon flinging passes for West Los Angeles. James offered Moon the chance to compete for the starting quarterback job.

Moon signed and won the starting job as a sophomore in 1975. But after he struggled in the season opener, a loss at Arizona State, he was booed a week later in the home opener, a loss to Texas. Moon eventually split time with another quarterback as the Huskies went 6–5. A year later, they went 5–6 with Moon as the full-time starter. Fans continued to boo him, and Moon's friends, sitting in the stands, heard racial slurs hurled at him.

"Those were some bittersweet days for me," Moon wrote later. "I learned a lot about people, and I also learned about how tough I could be. I never expressed my bitterness or lashed out. I never complained about it, never used it as an excuse."[9]

But while he appeared unflappable, he was upset about being a target of racial taunts. "I should have won an Oscar," he wrote.[10] The support of his friends helped him endure.

By the start of Moon's senior season, the Huskies had a solid defense and a strong running game. Moon's job was to manage the offense and make some plays while throwing on the run. The Huskies lost three of their first four games but then blasted Stanford, beat Cal and Southern Cal, and won the Pac-8 title with a season-ending win over Washington State. The boos and taunts quieted, replaced by cheers.

Washington fans flocked to Pasadena, California, for the Rose Bowl. The Huskies were not expected to beat Michigan, ranked fourth in the country, but Moon, playing near where he grew up, ran for one touchdown in the first quarter and another in the second quarter. When he tossed a twenty-eight-yard touchdown pass in the third quarter, the Huskies had a 24–0 lead. They held off a late rally and won.

Moon had passed for nearly 1,600 yards and rushed for six touchdowns as a senior, and though those were not spectacular numbers,

Moon thought he would at least receive consideration from NFL teams, especially after his fine showing in the Rose Bowl. He hired an agent, Leigh Steinberg, who had also attended Hamilton High School.

Several months before the 1978 draft, Steinberg contacted teams to gauge their interest in Moon. "A number asked if he was willing to play running back or receiver," Steinberg said. "When I met with him, I said, 'Warren, we're getting a lot of responses about you switching positions. I want you to think seriously about this.' He said, 'I don't have to think about it.' In terms of switching positions, he said, 'Never. I was born to play quarterback.'"[11]

Teams were not entirely uninterested in him as a quarterback. "They were telling me he might go in the fourth round, maybe the sixth, maybe later," Steinberg said. "But it didn't look like anyone was willing to have him compete for a starting role."[12]

Moon was being stereotyped again. "They would say things like I didn't come out of a pro-style offense, or my arm wasn't strong enough, or I was too small or too short," Moon said. "All just excuses that you knew were excuses. My arm strength was probably my best attribute. They weren't going to blatantly come out and say it was because of the color of my skin, or 'We don't think you can lead,' or 'We don't think he can think,' or all the other things they thought about African American quarterbacks . . . they were not going to come out and say those things. That's too blatantly racist."[13]

If he decided not to play pro football, he had a backup plan. "If I didn't get a chance to play quarterback somewhere, I was going to go to law school," he said.[14] But Steinberg heard from the Canadian Football League's Edmonton Eskimos. Their head coach, Hugh Campbell, came to Seattle, worked Moon out, and interviewed him. Campbell liked his arm, mobility, and maturity. The Eskimos were a winning team, but their quarterbacks were aging and Campbell envisioned Moon as a replacement.

On Campbell's recommendation, the Eskimos offered Moon a three-year contract worth an average of $55,000 per season—a deal a second-round pick in the NFL might command.

So much for law school.

"Edmonton was telling me, 'We think you can be a star in both the CFL and the NFL. We don't understand why they're not giving you a more serious shot down there, but we want you,'" Moon said. "When they paid me the money of a second-round pick in the NFL, that was enough for me. I'm going to go play football."[15]

Moon signed with the Eskimos on April 12, 1978, three weeks before the NFL draft. "Feeling that a black quarterback's chances of survival in the National Football League resemble a snowball's chance in Alabama, Warren Moon has become an Eskimo," the *Edmonton Journal* wrote.[16]

Signing with the Eskimos put Moon in the awkward position of hoping he would not get selected in the NFL draft. If he was drafted, the team that took him would control his rights if he wanted to return to the NFL. But if he went undrafted, he could sign with any team if he decided to come back. "Most guys had their fingers crossed in hope of being drafted [but] mine were crossed in hope of not being drafted," Moon wrote.[17]

His luck held. Sixteen quarterbacks were drafted, including Doug Williams in the first round, Pitt's Matt Cavanaugh and Stanford's Guy Benjamin in the second round, and later, prospects from smaller schools such as Lehigh and Santa Clara. But not Moon.

Instead, he joined the Eskimos in 1978. As a rookie, he backed up Tom Wilkinson, a veteran, even though it was clear Moon was more mobile and had a stronger arm. Campbell, a rising star in coaching, found a way to use them both. Wilkinson was the No. 1, but Moon passed for more than a thousand yards. The Eskimos won the Grey Cup, then won it again in 1979 with Moon and Wilkinson sharing their position.

It was "the first time in my career when race wasn't an issue," Moon would write. "It was funny that I had to go to another country, to an overwhelmingly white city, to feel I was a player being judged simply on the merits of my performance."[18]

With its wider and longer field, fewer downs in a series, and fewer limits on pre-snap motion, CFL football was more wide-open than American football, and Moon, with his mobility and powerful arm, was ideal for it. He began shouldering the full snap load at quarterback in 1980, and the Eskimos blew away the league, averaging thirty-one points per game. Moon terrorized opponents with long passes to receivers Brian Kelly and Tom Scott and kept defenses honest by rushing for more than 350 yards. The Eskimos finished the season by routing the Hamilton Tiger-Cats in the Grey Cup, with Moon honored as the game's MVP.

The Eskimos were even more dominant in 1981, losing just once during the regular season while averaging thirty-six points per game. Moon's passer rating for the season set a league record. In the Grey Cup that year, the Eskimos faced the Ottawa Rough Riders, who also had a young Black quarterback from America, J. C. Watts, who had been spurned by the NFL after starring at Oklahoma. Heavily favored, Moon and the Eskimos fell behind by nineteen points before rallying to win on a last-second field goal.

In 1982, Campbell announced it was his last season in Edmonton and the Eskimos won just three of their first eight games. But Moon put them on his back and carried them, becoming the first pro quarterback to produce five thousand passing yards in a season. An eight-game winning streak put the Eskimos in the playoffs, and after surviving an upset scare in the first round, they won their fifth straight Grey Cup with ease over Toronto.

Now twenty-six, Moon had married and started a family. He lived year-round in Edmonton, where the National Hockey League's Edmonton Oilers, led by Wayne Gretzky, were on the verge of dominating their sport. "There was a lot of winning going on. It was a great sports city. We were treated like royalty," Moon said.[19]

After winning five Grey Cups and setting numerous CFL passing records, Moon, through Steinberg, began hearing from NFL teams. They had shunned him before, but now they were interested. Moon enjoyed their about-face and considered just ignoring it. He had signed a ten-year contract with the Eskimos in 1980. Chuck Ealey, another Black quarterback from America, had stayed in Canada to work and raise his family after retiring from the CFL.

"There was a good life for you there if you could get adjusted," Moon said. "I never experienced any of the racial discrimination I had dealt with in America. That was so refreshing. I had dealt with so much of it in college, which I never really talked about until later. To then go to Canada and get booed only because some fan wanted the other team to win, that was nice. At one point, I thought I might spend my whole career there. That's how much I enjoyed it."[20]

But the Canadian winters were cold, and when the CFL season ended in November and Moon settled on his couch, it was NFL games that he kept watching. He realized he needed to come back to America and play. "I really didn't know how good I was, even though I was dominating that league. I wondered, 'How good of a quarterback am I?' Until you play against the best, you don't know," he said. "The only reason I came back was my curiosity. [Edmonton] was offering me a long-term, lifetime deal with a big insurance package and all this stuff to stay. So it wasn't money. It was just the fact that I was curious if I could play with the best players in the world or not."[21]

He had renegotiated his contract with the Eskimos after the 1981 season, signing a one-year deal for 1982 that included an option to play for the team in 1983. He decided to exercise that option, play one more year in Canada, and take stock. It was hard to leave with the Eskimos being compared to the NFL's Green Bay Packers, pro basketball's Boston Celtics, college basketball's UCLA Bruins, and other teams that had fashioned sports dynasties. But with Campbell gone, they were not the same in 1983. Moon had his finest individual season, passing for nearly six thousand yards, but the Eskimos finished with a .500 record and lost in the Western Conference playoffs.

Moon was now in the unique position of being able to choose where he wanted to play. Owners of teams in the USFL, the new league challenging the NFL, were luring big-name players with sizable contracts. The Eskimos still wanted him. And Moon could sign with any NFL team since no team held his rights after he went undrafted in 1978. "We had a three-league thing going," Steinberg said.

The USFL's Los Angeles Express and the NFL's New York Giants, Seattle Seahawks, Houston Oilers, Tampa Bay Buccaneers, New Orleans Saints, and Los Angeles Raiders all pursued him. Moon and Steinberg took a high-profile cross-country tour to visit them and gauge interest in the early weeks of 1984.

In Houston, the Oilers sent a stretch limousine to pick them up at the airport. At a dinner with team executives, a fan sitting across the restaurant sent over a bottle of Dom Pérignon. "We want you in Houston," read a note attached to the bottle.[22] Bud Adams, the oilman who owned the Oilers, took Moon on a drive to see his oil wells. "You see those? If you sign here, you can have one," Adams said.[23]

In New Orleans, the Saints' owner, John Mecom, took Moon for a sailboat ride. "They looked back at the city skyline and Mecom said, 'All that can be yours,'" Steinberg said.[24]

The Bucs' owner, Hugh Culverhouse, was desperate; his team had collapsed in 1983 after Culverhouse refused to meet Doug Williams's contract demands a year earlier. Culverhouse offered Moon a piece of a real estate project.

In New York, Moon and Steinberg spent an evening at Studio 54 and took a phone call from the owner of the USFL's New Jersey Generals, Donald Trump, who encouraged Moon to sign with the Express. If he did, Moon said later, Trump promised him "the free use of an apartment in Trump Tower anytime I wanted."[25]

The New York tabloids splashed Moon's visit across their back pages, reserved for the day's biggest sports news. "*Sports Illustrated* and all the newspapers covered what we were doing," Steinberg said. "No one had ever seen such a competitive situation to sign a player."[26]

The significance was not lost on Moon. The quarterback being pursued was Black and had gone undrafted just a few years earlier. "It's not my personality to say, 'I told you so,'" Moon said, "but I was determined to get the most out of the situation. I was an African American quarterback. I didn't know how long I'd be playing."[27]

He narrowed his choice down to the Oilers and Seahawks. Moon now lived in Seattle in the off-season. The Seahawks' head coach, Chuck Knox, had supported James Harris with the Rams when so many other NFL teams did not even have a Black quarterback. That was appealing.

But the Oilers went all out and hired Hugh Campbell as their head coach; he had coached in the USFL for a year after leaving Edmonton. "That was massive," Steinberg said. "Seattle was offering him $5.5 million for five years, which at that point was the biggest NFL contract ever, but their deal was like $1.2 million in signing bonus, with big yearly salaries. Houston was offering him the same amount, but with $4.5 million in [signing] bonus, so from the standpoint of security and safety, that was a better deal."[28]

In a phone conversation with Ladd Herzeg, the Oilers' general manager, Moon said, "I think you've got yourself a quarterback."[29]

━━━

The status of Black quarterbacks in the NFL was forever altered by Moon signing with the Oilers in 1984, beginning a second act of his career that would continue into the next century.

"I could make an argument that he's one of the best pure passers ever," Dr. Charles K. Ross said. "He could make all the throws, particularly the deep ball. People can take issue with me on this, but there isn't a big difference, in terms of pocket passing, between Warren Moon and Patrick Mahomes. Yet he had to spend five years in freaking Canada and win all those Grey Cups before Houston finally decides, 'OK, we'll give him this shot.' How did the league not see him for what he was coming out of college? Why didn't he get the opportunity then?"[30]

But once Moon settled in Houston in 1984 and began to demonstrate his talents, the NFL was never entirely without Black starting quarterbacks again. Minds began to change and, ever so slowly, other opportunities opened at last.

Only once before had an NFL team anointed a Black quarterback as its starter and public face, and the Tampa Bay Buccaneers had pulled the plug on the idea five years after they drafted Doug Williams, even though Williams had helped turn the franchise from a laughingstock into a contender. Initially, Moon doubted he would last even that long in Houston. The Oilers were a losing team, certain to continue to lose for several more years. Any quarterback in that situation would face criticism—it was all but customary on losing NFL teams—but a Black quarterback in Texas would be subjected to extraordinary disparagement. "People don't have the patience with a Black quarterback. I know in Houston I won't be given the same amount of time" to start winning as a white quarterback, Moon said when he signed.[31]

He cited the example of Joe Theismann, the veteran quarterback who started eighty-one regular-season games for the Washington Redskins over six seasons before he finally took them to the play-offs and led them to a Super Bowl victory at age thirty-two. "Theismann was thirty-two when he got a team into the Super Bowl. I'm twenty-seven now. By twenty-nine, I better have [the Oilers] in the Super Bowl," Moon said.[32]

But his fears about a limited opportunity were unfounded, it turned out. With Moon as their starter, the Oilers won just three games in 1984, four in 1985, and five in 1986, a year in which Moon threw a league-leading twenty-six interceptions and was sacked forty-one times. But he kept his starting job. Unlike Culverhouse with Doug Williams, the Oilers' owner, Bud Adams, did not run out of patience. There was too much to like about Moon. He threw a beautiful deep ball, zipped completions between defenders over the middle, commanded the huddle. The Oilers could see that their Black quarterback was not the reason they were losing. They just needed a better team around him.

Not surprisingly, a slice of the fan base still blamed Moon, largely because of the color of his skin. Two decades earlier, the Oilers had been one of the last pro teams to fully integrate their stadium; Black fans had sat in separate sections in the team's first years. Vestiges of that attitude persisted.

"In the south, you're not going to make everybody happy. There's a lot of bigotry and a lot of racism," Moon said. "I had gone through it in college. But now I had three kids and they were dealing with it. One time, my son came up to me in my locker room after a game. We had lost and he's crying, and I'm like, 'It's okay, man, we'll win the next one.'

But he's like, 'No, I want to know why these people are calling you all those names.' "[33]

The Oilers' fortunes changed in 1987. They won five of their first seven games, endured a midseason slump, and finished with back-to-back wins that clinched a playoff berth. Then they won their first-round playoff game before being eliminated. It was the start of something, the first of seven straight playoff appearances for the Oilers, all with Moon at quarterback. That he had started his NFL career so late did not keep him from piling up accomplishments. Three times, he led the league in completions. Twice he ranked first in passing yardage. He became one of the game's top quarterbacks and put his stature to work, launching an education-based charitable organization and mentoring a new generation of younger Black quarterbacks eyeing the pros. Steinberg nicknamed him Yoda, after the all-knowing Jedi master in *Star Wars*.

"He was handsome and articulate, a role model, and the publicity surrounding him and his success spawned a younger generation of Black quarterbacks who believed for the first time that they could play the position in the NFL," Steinberg said. "When I would go into their homes, trying to recruit them [as clients], I'd see two pictures on the wall. One was Martin Luther King. The other was Warren Moon."[34]

CHAPTER 14

The NFL that Warren Moon entered in 1984 was as determinedly white as ever at the quarterback position. The drafts that preceded Moon's arrival illustrated the challenge Black quarterbacks still faced in trying to gain even the slightest foothold.

After the Tampa Bay Buccaneers selected Doug Williams in the first round in 1978, thirteen more quarterbacks were drafted that year. They all were white. A year later, none of the fifteen quarterbacks selected were Black. In 1980, seventeen were selected—all white.

Three of the seventeen quarterbacks selected in 1981 were Black: Oklahoma's J. C. Watts went to the New York Jets in the eighth round, Tulane's Nickie Hall went to the Green Bay Packers in the tenth round, and Tennessee State's Joe Adams went to the San Francisco 49ers in the seventeenth round. None ever played in a regular-season NFL game.

In 1982, none of the fifteen quarterbacks selected were Black. A year later, a legendary class of quarterbacks dominated the first round, with John Elway, Jim Kelly, and Dan Marino, all future Pro Football Hall of Fame inductees, among six quarterbacks selected. The six first-round picks and nine of the ten other quarterbacks taken that year shared one trait. They were white. (The lone Black quarterback drafted in 1983, Reggie Collier of Southern Mississippi, went to the Dallas Cowboys in the sixth round but signed with the USFL's Birmingham Stallions.)

After fifteen quarterbacks, all white, were drafted in 1984, this was the latest math: of the 108 quarterbacks drafted since Williams in 1978, only four were Black. And none of those four had ever played in the NFL as of 1984.

The racial makeup of rosters around the league had changed dramatically since the 1950s, when teams had only a few Black players (and the Washington Redskins had none). By 1984, more than half of the league was Black. But the quarterback position was stuck in the old days. Moon was the league's only Black starter in 1984. Seventeen of the other twenty-seven teams had never started a Black quarterback in a game, including the New York Giants, Green Bay Packers, and St. Louis Cardinals, in business since the 1920s.

When pressed to explain the absence of Black quarterbacks, some NFL personnel executives dismissed it as a purely stylistic issue— Black quarterbacks who were fast and elusive runners were a poor match for NFL offenses designed for classic pocket passers, they said.

But Moon did not buy that rationale, not for a second. "I don't think mobility had anything to do with it; it was all about what was between your ears, and then, what your skin color looked like," he said. "We were always told that we didn't have the intelligence or the ability to play under pressure. And then you were going to be asked to be the face of a franchise and most franchises that were owned by white owners didn't want an African American being the face, representative of the franchise."[1]

Mobile *white* quarterbacks had flourished for years in the NFL. Fran Tarkenton, of the Minnesota Vikings and Giants, confounded defenses with his scrambling. The Dallas Cowboys' Roger Staubach won Super Bowls partly because he so effectively eluded blitzes. The Chicago Bears' Bobby Douglass and Detroit Lions' Greg Landry combined to rush for 1,492 yards in 1972.

Mobile white quarterbacks had a place in the NFL, but mobile Black quarterbacks still did not in the late 1970s and early 1980s.

Thomas Lott led Oklahoma to thirty wins and three straight Big Eight titles from 1976 through 1978. Confident and dynamic, he wore a bandanna under his helmet to keep his Afro from getting rumpled, which some white fans perceived as cockiness. Black fans loved his display of individualism. The furor did not interest NFL scouts, who dismissed Lott as a quarterback prospect because he seldom threw passes in Oklahoma's option offense. The Cardinals drafted him in the sixth round in 1979 and turned him into a running back and kick returner. He lasted one year in the NFL.

Watts, who followed Lott at Oklahoma, passed for nearly two thousand yards in three seasons as a starter. But he signed with the CFL's Ottawa Rough Riders after the Jets spoke to him about switching positions at a rookie camp. He would accrue more than twelve thousand passing yards in five seasons as a CFL quarterback, leaving little doubt that he deserved at least a chance to prove what he could do in the NFL. But that chance never came. Watts retired, went into politics, and became a US congressman.

Turner Gill never lost a conference game as Nebraska's starting quarterback. As a senior in 1983, he rushed and passed for more than two thousand yards and finished fourth in the Heisman Trophy vote. But after seeing what happened to other Black quarterbacks, he signed with the CFL's Montreal Concordes before the NFL draft. He was emerging as an effective quarterback in the CFL, able to run and pass, when he had to retire at age twenty-three because he had suffered several serious concussions.

The situation was bleak, and heading into the 1985 draft it seemed unlikely to change. The best-known quarterbacks in that year's class were all white. Doug Flutie had won the Heisman Trophy after a dramatic senior season at Boston College that included a Hail Mary pass that took down top-ranked Miami. Maryland's Frank Reich and UCLA's Steve Bono were among the other top prospects.

There also was a Black quarterback under consideration in 1985. Tall, long-limbed, and agile, Randall Cunningham had set records at Nevada–Las Vegas, becoming just the third major college quarterback (Flutie and Elway being the others) to surpass 2,500 passing yards in three consecutive seasons. He also had led the nation in punting.

Predictably, NFL scouts were unsure. One scout for BLESTO, a service shared by a dozen teams, ranked Cunningham as the twelfth-best prospect in the entire draft, but most teams thought he was no better than the fourth-best or fifth-best quarterback in a mediocre crop. They thought his delivery was too slow because of his long arms. They questioned his statistics because he had not faced top competition. The consensus was he probably would not get selected until somewhere in the middle rounds.

Still, the Philadelphia Eagles were intrigued by Cunningham. Their longtime starter, Ron Jaworski, had led them to four playoff appearances and a trip to the Super Bowl at his peak, but now, after three straight losing seasons, the team was quietly looking for a replacement. Jaworski was thirty-four.

Lynn Stiles, the Eagles' personnel director, scrutinized Cunningham's game films and "spent more time in Las Vegas than Amarillo Slim," the famous professional poker player, the *Philadelphia Daily News* reported later.[2] Stiles asked his scouts to weigh in. Some liked Cunningham. Others feared his delivery was too slow and preferred Bono, a classic pocket passer.

The Eagles' offensive coordinator, Ted Marchibroda, borrowed an office projector and painstakingly studied film of Cunningham, Jaworski, and Marino. Marchibroda determined that Marino, who played for the Dolphins, had the fastest delivery, but Jaworski was close behind and Cunningham was just as fast as Jaworski. That sealed it for Stiles. He was ready to draft Cunningham.

In business since 1933, the Eagles were among the many teams that had never started a Black quarterback in a game, although John Walton did make fifteen appearances for them from 1976 to 1979. But the team was being sold to Norman Braman, a Philadelphia native who owned a chain of car dealerships in South Florida. New to football, he did not subscribe to the disparaging stereotype of Black quarterbacks that had prevailed for decades in the NFL.

In the first round of the 1985 draft, held at the Omni Park Central Hotel in New York on April 30, seven of the first eight selections were offensive or defensive linemen—a clear reflection of where teams thought games were decided in the 1980s. With the ninth overall pick, the Eagles continued the trend, taking Kevin Allen, an offensive tackle from Indiana. The selection would go down as one of the worst in the history of the draft. Allen played just one year with the Eagles and went to jail on a rape charge.

In the second round, the Eagles surprised the football world by taking Cunningham with the number thirty-seven overall selection. It was just the second time in the history of the draft, which began in 1936, that a Black quarterback had gone before any white quarterbacks.

Cunningham was not at home in Las Vegas when Stiles called him to say the Eagles drafted him. He had grown frustrated while watching twenty-eight other players become first-round picks on ESPN's broadcast. When the round ended, Cunningham headed to a mall. Stiles left a message on his answering machine asking Cunningham to call him back.

Cunningham had hoped to go to the Oakland Raiders or another team on the West Coast; he had grown up in Santa Barbara, California. But he was well aware that college football's best Black quarterbacks had been drafted late or not at all in recent years. He was thrilled when he returned from the mall and a roommate congratulated him on going to the Eagles in the second round. A day later, he was on a flight to Philadelphia.

Initially, his contract status made headlines. Concerned that he might not get selected in the NFL draft until a late round, he had jumped the gun and signed with the USFL's Tampa Bay Bandits. But the contract included an escape clause. Cunningham would play for the Eagles.

When asked how it felt to be "a Black quarterback in Philadelphia" in his first session with the local media, he skirted the issue. "Being in South Philadelphia, I thought I was Italian," he said.[3] He joked about it because he was not prepared to talk about it; as he flew east from Las Vegas, he had not even considered that the subject might come up. Growing up in Santa Barbara, he had not lived with as much searing racism as James Harris or Doug Williams, who were from the Deep South. Cunningham knew that few Black quarterbacks had played in the NFL, but breaking barriers was not on his mind.

When Cunningham joined the Eagles for a minicamp shortly after he was drafted and took the field in scrimmages, the team's veterans could not believe thirty-six players had been drafted before him. He evaded tacklers with a skip and whipped on-target passes with a flick of his wrist. Scouts clearly had misjudged this kid, the Eagles' veterans told one another.

Cunningham had been overlooked before. Growing up, he was not even the best football player in his family. His oldest brother went straight from plowing over tacklers for Santa Barbara High School in the late 1960s to plowing over them for Southern Cal in the early 1970s. The New England Patriots drafted Sam "Bam" Cunningham in the first round in 1973, and he would rush for more than five thousand yards in a decade in the NFL.

Randall also had two other older brothers, Anthony and Bruce, who played college football—Anthony at Boise State and Bruce at Nevada–Las Vegas. Randall was the classic little brother, following his older siblings around and sneaking into their pickup contests. No one paid him much attention until he sprouted lean and limber, with the ability to hurl a football. The brothers realized the baby of the family might be the most gifted. "We knew his potential," Anthony said later, "so we worked him and worked him and worked him."[4]

From his first days in organized football, Randall Cunningham played quarterback. At every level, his coaches wanted the ball in his hands; no one else made so many plays. The fact that he was Black seldom came up. "I could not have picked a better place to grow up," Sam Cunningham said later about Santa Barbara.[5]

As a high school senior, Randall led his team to thirteen straight wins before a defeat in a regional championship game. College recruiters were on to him, but Southern Cal, his first choice, did not want him as a quarterback. The Trojans had started Black quarterbacks before, so that was not the issue. They just thought Sam's little brother could help them more at another position. "I don't know if it was the black quarterback issue, but they wanted him as a defensive back," Sam Cunningham said. "My feeling was, 'All you've ever played was quarterback. Go where they'll let you do that.'"[6]

Randall followed Bruce to UNLV, where the offense was wide open and there was a history of using Black quarterbacks. During his first year, both of his parents died, his mother from cancer, his father from a heart attack. Cunningham was depressed and distracted and did not perform well on the junior varsity. His brothers helped him steady his emotions.

He was a fourth-stringer on the varsity at the start of his sophomore season, but his opportunity to play soon arrived when those ahead of him struggled. He took full advantage, making plays and winning games. In the season finale, he passed for more than four hundred yards.

He continued to pile up big statistics in his junior and senior seasons while leading UNLV to eighteen wins. When NFL scouts called Harvey Hyde, UNLV's head coach, to discuss Cunningham, Hyde told them all the same thing: "Draft him or he'll beat you."[7]

After the Eagles took him and then saw his vast upside on the practice field in the spring of 1985, they were relieved they had not succumbed to doubts about his delivery or concerns that he had not played in a top conference, which had scared off many teams. The Eagles set out to help him maximize his talent. Their head coach, Marion Campbell, brought in seventy-four-year-old Sid Gillman, a legendary passing-game guru who had gone into the Pro Football Hall of Fame two years earlier. Gillman's job was to tutor Cunningham on the fine points of being an NFL quarterback.

Gillman lectured the rookie on offensive and defensive concepts, various strategies, and the art of decision-making. Seemingly a willing pupil, Cunningham took notes, asked questions, and conversed animatedly. But it all went out the window once he was on the field in training camp scrimmages and preseason games. If he did not recognize a defense or see a play unfold as drawn on the blackboard, he just took off running. And good things happened. "He took a very sophisticated position and narrowed it down," said John Spagnola, a veteran tight end on the team. "If the receiver is covered, he just takes off and runs 50 yards. Maybe we shouldn't worry so much about strong and weak zones and everything else."[8]

Jaworski started the season opener, but after he was sacked eight times in a loss to the Giants, Campbell started Cunningham in Week 2, hoping his mobility would help him elude the defenders overwhelming the Eagles' weak offensive line. It wound up being a significant opportunity: Cunningham started four straight games. But the Eagles lost three. Cunningham was not ready to take on top pro defenses. Jaworski reclaimed the starting job in Week 6 and kept it for the rest of the season. The Eagles had a shot at a playoff berth until a losing streak late in the season ended their hopes.

Braman fired Campbell and his staff after the season and hired Buddy Ryan, architect of a Super Bowl–winning defense for the Chicago Bears. An Oklahoma native who lived in Kentucky, Ryan had a background similar to coaches who had denied opportunities to Black quarterbacks for years. But Ryan was their opposite, an inveterate rebel who loved thumbing his nose at establishment dictates. Jaworski was still around, but Ryan wanted Cunningham to play and devised a unique scheme. Jaworski ran the offense on first and second down. Cunningham took over on third down.

The Eagles won just five games.

In the season finale, Ryan abandoned the project and let Cunningham play the whole game. Looking poised, he passed for 153 yards and rushed for thirty-three yards and a touchdown. The Eagles lost, but Cunningham's time had arrived. Ryan turned him loose starting in 1987. The coach's long-term vision for the team was simple: build a kick-ass defense and depend on Cunningham to generate enough offense. Ryan told him to do what came naturally. If he wanted to pass, pass. If he wanted to run, run. The result was quarterback play the likes of which the NFL had never seen.

That fall, Cunningham threw twenty-three touchdown passes and twelve interceptions, a superb ratio, and averaged 232 passing yards per game. But he was just as dangerous as a runner, averaging more than seven yards per carry and totaling 505 yards on the ground. That was more than any of the team's running backs.

His potential as a runner had not been evident in college because UNLV ran a short-route passing game, which meant the ball was in the air quickly, limiting his opportunities to tuck the ball under his arm and run. But Ryan encouraged it, knowing how hard it would be for defenses to contain. "Buddy allowed me to be the player I believed I could be," Cunningham said later. "He saw something in me and allowed me to flourish as an athlete, not just a quarterback, [and] to really take it to a whole, other level."[9]

The Eagles did not make the playoffs in 1987, mostly because they stumbled during an early-season labor stoppage; for three weeks, the league forced teams to use players willing to cross a picket line, and the Eagles went winless. But once the regulars were back on the field, they looked like a playoff team with a unique and dangerous quarterback.

A new era had begun. In the late 1960s, Marlin Briscoe had lost the chance to play quarterback in Denver, at least theoretically, because he was fast and elusive; the Broncos, like other teams in those years, preferred quarterbacks who dropped straight back into the pocket. But times were changing. The Eagles did not run from Cunningham's mobility. They embraced it.

CHAPTER 15

On April 6, 1987, ABC's popular late-night television news program, *Nightline*, devoted an episode to the fortieth anniversary of Jackie Robinson's first game in baseball's major leagues—a seminal moment in American sports history. The producers planned a testimonial with a slate of guests that included Al Campanis, a seventy-year-old executive with the Los Angeles Dodgers, who had mentored Robinson during his playing days in the 1940s. The commemoration unexpectedly ended up producing its own seminal moment in sports history.

Campanis's interview veered off course and into troubling terrain when the host, Ted Koppel, asked why baseball still had no Black club owners and so few Black managers and general managers forty years after Robinson integrated the sport on the field. "Is there still that much prejudice in baseball today?" Koppel asked.[1]

"I don't believe it's prejudice," Campanis replied. "I believe they may not have some of the necessities to be, let's say, a field manager. How many quarterbacks do you have that are Black? How many pitchers do you have that are Black?"

Shocked, Koppel called his explanation "garbage." But Campanis doubled down on his racial profiling, suggesting there were not many good Black swimmers "because they lack buoyancy." Later in the interview, he said Black athletes in general are "gifted with great musculature and various other things. They're fleet of foot and this is why there are a lot of Black major league ballplayers."

Campanis was soon out of a job, as media figures and fans decried his use of "necessities," a word many saw as code for nonphysical qualities such as intelligence and discipline—qualities many white decision-makers in sports had long doubted were present in Black athletes. In the sports world Campanis depicted, Black athletes succeeded only because of their bodies, not their minds.

Two months later, baseball sought to address the controversy by hiring Harry Edwards, a Black sociologist and civil rights activist, to lead an initiative to increase diversity among the sport's leadership.

Though baseball faced a racial reckoning, discrimination in football was also part of the story, thanks to Campanis's reference to the lack of Black quarterbacks. Indeed, there had been only one starter in the NFL as recently as 1984. The situation was only incrementally better in 1986 with Moon and Cunningham starting and Doug Williams back in the league as a backup with the Redskins.

After failing to land a new deal with the Tampa Bay Bucs following the 1982 season, Williams had sat out a year and then played in the USFL for two seasons. As the quarterback of the Outlaws, who played in Oklahoma in 1984 and Arizona in 1985, he threw thirty-eight interceptions and thirty-six touchdowns. "I got beat up a lot," he said.[2] When the USFL folded, Williams sought to return to the NFL at age thirty. But only one team called. Joe Gibbs, so instrumental in the Bucs' decision to draft him eight years earlier, was now the Redskins' head coach. They had won a Super Bowl and made three playoff appearances in five years with him in charge. Gibbs explained to Williams that he was committed to Jay Schroeder, a twenty-five-year-old former third-round pick from UCLA, as his starting quarterback, but he needed a backup.

"Coach asked me if I could be a backup. I said, 'Coach, I can be anything you want me to be because I don't have a job otherwise,'" Williams said. "I didn't have a choice. We're talking about a time when Black quarterbacks didn't have much of a choice about anything. They couldn't tell anyone what they wanted to do. I couldn't say I wanted to be the starter."[3]

The Redskins secured Williams's rights and signed him. Williams was elated to be back in the NFL with a winning team. "I was glad he called," Williams said of Gibbs, "because no one else did. If he hadn't,

I would have just sat at home, and quite possibly, a lot of good things wouldn't have happened."[4]

Gibbs told Williams not to expect to play much. Sure enough, Schroeder started every game and barely came off the field as the Redskins went 12–4 in 1986 and advanced to the NFC championship game. Williams threw one pass all season.

But Schroeder struggled in the championship game. The New York Giants' defense battered him on the way to a 17–0 victory. After a tackler drove him to the turf especially hard in the fourth quarter, Schroeder's head hit the ground. He knelt on one knee and paused before trying to stand. Gibbs sent Williams onto the field, thinking Schroeder was too shaken up to play. But Schroeder waved Williams off the field.

Williams was furious. "It was one of the most embarrassing moments of my life," he said.[5] It would motivate him.

The two quarterbacks were not close. They barely spoke outside of the position meetings they shared during the season. It was easy to assume race was the issue, but Williams later wrote in his memoir that he believed Schroeder was cool to him because Williams was such an obvious threat to his job; Williams was more experienced and had shown he could lead a team.

Despite the rough ending to his season, Schroeder made the Pro Bowl and signed a new contract, seemingly confirming that he was the Redskins' quarterback. The Redskins nearly traded Williams to the Raiders before the 1987 season, but Gibbs called off the deal at the last minute. Williams later surmised that the coach quietly feared Schroeder might not work out as well as many expected; the younger quarterback had thrown as many interceptions as touchdowns during his Pro Bowl season.

In the 1987 season opener, Schroeder suffered a shoulder injury and Williams came in, having not played significant minutes in an NFL game in five years. He threw two touchdown passes and the Redskins whipped the Eagles. "Coach knew that I was a veteran who had won in the league, and at any given time, I was a guy he could call on to do the job," Williams said.[6]

When Schroeder's injury lingered, Williams started the next game and threw three touchdown passes, but the Redskins lost to the Falcons. Then he and Schroeder were both out when a labor stoppage interrupted the season for three games and teams of "replacement" players took the field.

Schroeder, healthy again, reclaimed the starting job when the regular players returned. But he was ineffective early against the Lions in Week 10, and Williams stepped in and threw two touchdown passes in a comeback victory. Gibbs started him against the Rams the next week. Heavily favored at home, the Redskins fell far behind. Williams threw for two touchdowns and ran for another as the Redskins rallied late, but they fell just short.

Williams was considered the starter heading into the next game, at home against the Giants, but he tweaked his back in practice and Schroeder stepped in and passed for 331 yards and three touchdowns as the Redskins won. Gibbs gave Schroeder the starting job back.

Several of Williams's Black teammates were upset, suggesting to Williams that he was a victim of the mistrust of Black quarterbacks that had long prevailed in the NFL. Williams did not agree. "I refused to believe it was a Black thing. I respected Coach Gibbs too much for that," he wrote. "But a lot of my teammates told me that's why I wasn't starting."[7]

By late in the season, the Redskins had secured the NFC East title with Schroeder starting. But in the season finale against the Vikings, he threw an interception on his first pass and continued to struggle. With the score tied in the third quarter, Gibbs subbed in Williams, who threw a touchdown pass to put the Redskins ahead. The Vikings rallied and led late, but Williams threw another touchdown pass to force overtime and then led a drive that produced a game-winning field goal.

After that game, it was clear even to Schroeder that Williams would start in the playoffs. Gibbs soon made it official, telling the media that Williams would quarterback the Redskins in the postseason.

They opened with a daunting challenge, a divisional-round game against the Bears on a day when the windchill in Chicago was below zero. The Bears started fast, taking a 14–0 lead. Two years removed from winning a Super Bowl, they still had one of the NFL's top defenses. But the Redskins were a team of veterans, accustomed to challenges. "It didn't bother us to fall behind," Williams wrote. "We just stuck with our game plan and things began to work."[8]

A long completion to Ricky Sanders set up one touchdown, and a few minutes later, Williams hit a tight end, Clint Didier, for a touchdown that tied the score. With the defenses dominating and points hard to come by, the game came down to avoiding mistakes. Williams threw passes away rather than take sacks and risk interceptions, and his cautiousness paid off when the Redskins' Darrell Green ran a punt back for a decisive touchdown.

A week later, Williams had his hands full in the NFC championship game against the Vikings. Minnesota's defensive backs had his receivers blanketed. But Williams stuck to his strategy of throwing the ball away rather than risking mistakes. He gave the Redskins the lead with a touchdown pass and threw another to break a late tie. "It was a terrible day from a statistical standpoint but a great day for results," Williams said.[9]

Final score: Washington 17, Minnesota 10.

In the locker room after the game, reporters peppered Williams with questions about being the first Black quarterback to start in the Super Bowl. Only nine months had passed since Al Campanis's interview on *Nightline* revealed enduring prejudices against Black athletes, none more persistent than the idea that they lacked the "necessities" to lead. If a Black quarterback could help a team win the ultimate football game, it would serve as a powerful rebuke.

But immediately after the Minnesota game, Williams did not want to focus on the racial aspect of his Super Bowl appearance. "I'm not a Black quarterback. I'm the Washington Redskins' quarterback," he told reporters.[10]

A day later, warming to the idea, he served as the grand marshal at a parade in Washington honoring Martin Luther King and told a cheering crowd, "I'm just glad that I'm going to be one part of Martin Luther King's dream."[11]

He said later, "It took about a day for it to sink in. I thought about all of the things I'd been through to get that far, all of the trouble I'd overcome, all of the opportunities I'd been denied because I was Black, how they'd treated me in Tampa. Then I began to realize everything I'd worked for had come true. I was in the Super Bowl."[12]

The Redskins would face the Denver Broncos, champions of the AFC, at Jack Murphy Stadium in San Diego. The Broncos were in their second straight Super Bowl, having lost to the Giants the year before. They were favored. Their quarterback, John Elway, was a former first overall draft pick, widely acknowledged as one of the NFL's top quarterbacks. He directed his offense like a military general and zipped laser-like passes. No one wondered whether he had the necessities. He was white, after all.

The game followed two weeks of mounting suspense. The Redskins practiced in chilly Washington for a week and then flew to San Diego. The players looked forward to spending a week in California sunshine. As soon as they arrived, reporters questioned Williams about the historical significance of being the first Black quarterback to start in the Super Bowl. Butch John, a sportswriter for Jackson, Mississippi's *Clarion-Ledger*, saw Williams growing tired of the subject. He tried a different approach. "Doug, it's obvious you've been a Black quarterback for some time. When did it start to matter?" John asked.[13]

Williams did not hear the question correctly. "What? How long have I been a Black quarterback?" he asked.

The next day, the *San Diego Union-Tribune* reported that Williams had been asked how long he had been a Black quarterback. An urban legend was born, and though the reality was that the question was never asked exactly as the legend depicted, it continues to be remembered as the dumbest question ever asked at a Super Bowl press conference.

As the week progressed, reporters continued to ask Williams more about being a Black quarterback in the Super Bowl than about the Redskins' chances of winning. Williams spent much of the week in his hotel room, studying his playbook and watching television. "I knew what color I was. I didn't need anybody telling me what color I was," he said. "My whole thing was trying to find a way to win the game."[14]

On the Washington Football Team's *Women of Washington* podcast in 2021, Williams said, "All of the emphasis was put on myself being Black and the history part of it and everything, and I understood the significance of being the first to play in the Super Bowl, but I couldn't go into the game looking at it from that standpoint. I had to go and prepare from a standpoint of finding a way to win the game. I always said that when the game was over and we won, you can paint me any color you want to, but I still was the starting quarterback of the Washington Redskins."[15]

At a barbecue on Saturday, the day before the Super Bowl, one of his teeth began to ache. Williams went to the team dentist, who prescribed a root canal procedure lasting four hours. The dentist predicted Williams would be in too much pain to play, but he felt fine Sunday morning.

The first quarter of the game was tantamount to another root canal procedure for Williams. The Redskins opened the game with a three-and-out possession. Looking larger than life, Elway trotted onto the field and hurled a fifty-six-yard touchdown pass on the Broncos' first play.

The score was 10–0 later in the quarter when Williams slipped on a loose piece of sod while dropping back to pass. He fell to the ground, in pain, and needed help from trainers to walk off the field; it would turn out he had strained a knee ligament. Gibbs sent in Schroeder. The backup was sacked on his first play and then threw an incompletion, ending the possession.

Williams jogged on the sideline, seeing if he could tolerate the pain in his knee. He was determined to get back on the field. If he could handle a root canal, he told himself, he could handle this.

He also was motivated not to cede the spotlight to Schroeder. Williams had not forgotten the embarrassment he felt when Schroeder waved him off the field in the NFC championship game the year before. "Payback is a mother," Williams said. "He wasn't going to play no more—not if I could help it."[16]

He told Gibbs he could play. When the Redskins' defense forced a punt, Williams returned to the field as the second quarter began. On first down at his 20 yard line, he faked a handoff, dropped back, and arched a pass to his right, far downfield, toward Ricky Sanders, who was behind a cornerback along the sideline. Sanders grabbed the pass, which hit him in stride, and sprinted to the end zone to complete an eighty-yard touchdown play.

The score gave the Redskins momentum, which they would ride for the rest of the quarter. After their defense forced a punt, Williams led another scoring drive that he completed with a twenty-seven-yard touchdown pass to Gary Clark. Suddenly, the Redskins were ahead.

The change in momentum unsettled the Broncos. Their normally reliable kicker, Rich Karlis, missed a field goal on the next possession, and the Redskins needed just two plays to score again. Timmy Smith, a rookie back, ran fifty-eight yards for a touchdown.

Now down by eleven points, the Broncos needed Elway to make things happen. But their offense went three and out, their punter sliced a short kick, and Williams was right back in, scanning the Broncos' reeling defense for openings. He tossed a short completion to Sanders and then found Sanders running free deep and threw him a strike. The fifty-yard touchdown put the Redskins ahead 28–10. They had scored four touchdowns in the quarter and added a fifth just before halftime on a pass from Williams to Didier.

The football world was stunned as the teams headed to their locker rooms. Washington had a 35–10 lead. After nearly being knocked out of the game with a knee injury, Williams had knocked out the Broncos, completing nine of eleven passes for 228 yards and four touchdowns in the second quarter. "As a player, you don't think about being in the zone. That's for announcers and the media," Williams said. "As a player you're just trying to carry out the game plan. It was almost like, 'Let's go get the ball and score again.' After the game, you think about it and say, 'Damn, how in the world did we do that?'"[17]

In the locker room at halftime, Gibbs offered Williams the option of coming out of the game because of his knee, but ever the competitor, he took a cortisone shot to dull the pain and kept playing. The

Redskins mostly sat on their lead in the second half, and in the final minutes of their 42–10 win, it was announced Williams had been selected the game's Most Valuable Player.

Williams was exhilarated for himself and his team, and for what his triumph signified. Black quarterbacks still faced searing discrimination. Millions of fans and some NFL executives still had doubts about their ability to think and lead. Williams's performance would open some of those closed minds.

"There was a lot of pressure on Doug Williams. He did a good job of trying to downplay that. But I know he laid in bed and thought about it a lot leading up to the game; thinking, 'I can't throw four or five interceptions and we get blown out, I just can't do that,'" Dr. Charles K. Ross said. "But he did a phenomenal job, and I think it was a relief for white America. He was so successful that there was an unwritten, unspoken understanding that America is kind of ready now. It's okay for us to begin to open this door up" for more Black quarterbacks in the NFL.[18]

As Williams jogged off the field in San Diego, he spotted a familiar face waiting for him in the tunnel—Eddie Robinson, his coach at Grambling, who had put Williams's journey to this moment in motion by recruiting him to play quarterback, not another position. "I didn't even know he was at the game," Williams said.[19] As they hugged, both men started to cry. Robinson said, "Doug, you don't realize the impact you made today. You're Jackie Robinson. You're the Jackie Robinson of football."[20]

CHAPTER 16

By the late 1980s, the performances of Doug Williams, Warren Moon, and Randall Cunningham had effectively lectured any NFL team skeptical about Black quarterbacks that they were living in the past. The success of several Black quarterbacks had made it easier to believe that others might soon get drafted higher and receive opportunities to play.

But while it was encouraging to see Williams, Moon, and Cunningham each start their team's season opener in 1988, they were still vastly outnumbered by the twenty-five *white* quarterbacks who also started that weekend. The spout of opportunity was open, but barely. Thirteen teams, almost half of the league, still had never started a Black quarterback in a game. And there was little evidence of a new generation gearing up to try to further move the needle.

The upshot was Williams, Moon, and Cunningham needed to continue to play well. No one ever considered the performance of a white quarterback as a statement about the abilities of all white quarterbacks, but fairly or not, Black quarterbacks playing in the NFL were regarded as representative of all Black quarterbacks, especially in the minds of the skeptical. For the sake of the next generation, whenever it arrived, Williams, Moon, and Cunningham could not afford to let down. And they did not, Cunningham and Moon especially.

Williams had received a new contract from the Redskins as a reward for his Super Bowl triumph—basically, the contract Hugh Culverhouse refused to give him—and his status as their starter was assured when they traded Jay Schroeder. In the season opener in 1988,

Williams passed for 288 yards against the New York Giants, but Washington lost—the first of many disappointments the season would bring.

Moon, meanwhile, was typically sharp in the first half of the Houston Oilers' 1988 opener, hitting eleven of fifteen passes against the Indianapolis Colts. Coming off a season in which he had helped Houston make the playoffs for the first time in seven years, he was considered one of the NFL's most effective quarterbacks at age thirty-two. The Oilers won, but in the second half, Moon took a hard hit that broke a bone in his throwing shoulder. He was expected to be out for a month.

At age twenty-five, Cunningham was the youngest of the three Black starters, beginning just his second full season as the Philadelphia Eagles' number-one quarterback. His innate explosiveness was emerging into view. He threw two touchdown passes in the first quarter of the Eagles' opener as they routed the Tampa Bay Bucs. A week later, he passed for 261 yards and rushed for eighty-five against the Cincinnati Bengals. His throws were on target, and whenever his pocket collapsed, he took off downfield, daring the defense to corral him and astonishing fans and insiders with his speed, balance, and elusiveness.

But the Eagles lost that day, then also lost their next two games, one an ugly, mistake-filled contest against Williams and the Redskins. The fact that the game pitted two Black starting quarterbacks against each other was given scant attention.

With a 1–3 record, the Eagles faced the Oilers in Philadelphia, needing to win; with another defeat, they would become long shots to make the playoffs. Moon was still out with a shoulder injury, but his backup, Cody Carlson, started fast. Houston had a 16–0 lead early in the second quarter. The Eagles' fans booed.

Cunningham put the team on his shoulders. He completed passes, ran for gains, moved his offense. He threw one touchdown pass, then another, and the Eagles took the lead. In the third quarter, he led a drive to Houston's 33 yard line, took a snap, and rolled to his left, looking downfield for a receiver. Seeing no one open, he reversed field and sprinted back to his right while waving his left hand to direct his blockers. Picking up speed, he angled downfield, cut between two tacklers, and sprinted to the end zone. Veterans Stadium vibrated with the cheers from fans who had been booing an hour earlier.

The Eagles won, giving them a 2–3 record heading into a home game against the Giants on Monday Night Football. They had lost six straight games to their rivals in the NFC East. They also had not played on a Monday night in seven years. Fans in Philadelphia viewed the scheduling of the marquee prime-time game as symbolic of their team's return to relevance.

The game effectively served as Cunningham's introduction to the wider pro football world. Since he had become a starter the year before, most of the Eagles' games had only been televised regionally. Fans across the country had read about his playmaking, but most had only seen him in highlights on ESPN. This was their chance to see him live.

After a slow start, Cunningham led a long drive in the second quarter. On a third down at the Giants' 4 yard line, he took a snap and rolled to his right, looking for a receiver in the end zone. Carl Banks, a linebacker for the Giants, read the quarterback's eyes and ran toward him rather than drop into coverage. Without a blocker to beat, Banks was quickly on Cunningham and hit him hard below the waist, practically knocking him parallel to the ground. The hit would have upended most other quarterbacks and probably caused a fumble, but Cunningham did not go down and did not fumble. He put his left hand on the turf to keep his balance, stood upright, and continued to roll to his right.

Almost immediately, Banks's teammate, Harry Carson, a perennial Pro Bowl selection, was in the quarterback's face, set to deliver a blow. But just before he absorbed the hit, Cunningham unleashed a pass aimed at his tight end, Jimmie Giles, who was open along the sideline in the end zone.

Touchdown.

Amazing touchdown.

As the home crowd roared, the Monday Night Football broadcast crew tried to put the play in perspective. One of the analysts, Dan Dierdorf, a former All-Pro tackle, said, "Ladies and gentlemen,

Randall Cunningham IS a ready-for-prime-time player. The guy has not been seen by many national audiences before, but I think you're starting to get the drift of what kind of football player they have playing here in Philadelphia. That is a big-time play."[1]

Cunningham threw another touchdown pass before halftime, and later, his third of the night sealed an important win for the Eagles. Against one of the NFL's top defenses, he completed thirty-one of forty-one passes for 369 yards and three touchdowns.

But all anyone wanted to talk about after the game was how he had somehow kept his balance and thrown a touchdown pass after Banks sent him sprawling. "The most unbelievable play I've ever seen a quarterback make," Giles said.[2]

Even Cunningham could scarcely believe it. "Things like that aren't supposed to happen," he said. "When a 248-pound linebacker hits you, you're supposed to go down. My knee was half a foot from the ground. But I just knew I had to try to make the play."[3]

Banks just shook his head when asked about his inability to bring Cunningham down. "I played my technique perfectly. I go in to make a routine tackle and he turns into Stretch Armstrong," Banks said later, referencing a comic book character with elastic limbs. "It was one hell of a football play. No other quarterback could make that play. It was like Michael Jordan. You get a hand in his face and he still hits the shot."[4]

The four-yard touchdown pass did not look special in a box score, but decades later, when the NFL selected the top one hundred plays of its first one hundred years, Cunningham's pass to Giles made the list. "It's one of the greatest plays I've ever been involved in," Banks said later. "I can honestly say that even though it went against us."[5]

Doug Williams's Super Bowl triumph had changed the narrative about Black quarterbacks, but Cunningham's play was almost as impactful. Millions watched it on Monday Night Football. And many of those millions had never seen an NFL quarterback make such a play. With but a few exceptions, the quarterbacks had long conformed to a white stereotype, dropping straight into the pocket and passing. Doug Williams was out of that mold, a classic pocket passer who seldom actually ran with the ball. Cunningham was different—fast, unpredictable, instinctive. An entirely new breed, able to dodge and improvise and, yes, do the impossible. "He had everyone in the neighborhood dropping back saying 'Randall Cunningham, Randall Cunningham!'" said Michael Vick, a future star quarterback who was an eight-year-old in Newport News, Virginia, on the night of Cunningham's play against the Giants.[6]

Cunningham was the first Black quarterback to achieve widespread success by departing from the classic mold, and by being *allowed* to depart from the classic mold. The Eagles never tried to shoehorn him into being something he was not; they embraced who he was. The rest of his 1988 season illustrated his potential. Week after week, he electrified crowds and made big plays. He threw three touchdown passes against the Rams, brought the Eagles from behind four times during a win in Pittsburgh. The Eagles won the NFC East for the first time in eight years as Cunningham set franchise records for pass attempts, completions, and passing yardage in a season while also leading the team in rushing for the second straight season. Not since the Packers' Tobin Rote in the early 1950s had a quarterback led his team in rushing in back-to-back seasons.

The Associated Press named him the league's Offensive Player of the Year. He started for the NFC in the Pro Bowl and earned the game's Most Valuable Player award. The next fall, he was on the cover of *Sports Illustrated*'s pro football preview, photographed jumping high, with his helmet off, his throwing arm cocked, his legs spread-eagled. The headline read, "The Ultimate Weapon: Philadelphia's Randall Cunningham, the Quarterback for the 90s."

The magazine had used hyperbole before to conflate a quarterback. In 1971, when Greg Landry became the first NFL quarterback to throw for more than two thousand yards and rush for more than five hundred yards in a season, *Sports Illustrated* said the Lions were running "the offense of the future." That was true, but it was the distant future; at the time, no other teams copied Detroit's blueprint. Drop-back passers, mostly all white, continued to rule.

In Cunningham's case, the hyperbole was justified. In 1989, he passed for 3,400 yards and rushed for 621. In 1990, he passed for 3,466 yards, rushed for 942, and led the league with a whopping per-carry average of 8.0 yards. In both seasons, the Eagles posted double-digit wins and made the playoffs.

Some of the shine dulled when the Eagles lost in the first round of the playoffs in both years, which, inevitably, led to Cunningham being criticized for generating more flash than substance. He was among the sport's highest-paid players by then, and some of his teammates quietly believed he had become self-absorbed.

But his impact was undeniable. Before he turned thirty, Cunningham had forever broadened the concept of how NFL quarterbacks looked and played. "You knew there was something special about Randall," said Eric Allen, a defensive back who joined the Eagles in 1988. He was "extremely athletic, played with a great sense of self, understood that he was good, understood that he could do a lot of things other quarterbacks in the game could not do, and he had a great deal of confidence."[7]

An injury that sidelined him for the 1991 season robbed him of some of his speed and elusiveness, but he came back and played in the NFL for another decade—sixteen years in all, a period of sweeping change. When Cunningham's career began, the NFL was shocked to see a team draft a Black quarterback in the second round. By the time he retired in 2001, Black quarterbacks routinely went even higher in the draft and received chances to play. No one helped that evolution along more than Cunningham.

═══

On October 30, 1988, Moon's Oilers faced Williams's Redskins on ESPN's *Sunday Night Football*. That the matchup of playoff contenders featured two Black starting quarterbacks mattered less now, Moon told reporters, because he, Williams, and Cunningham were normalizing the idea of Black quarterbacks in the NFL. "You don't hear that term, Black quarterback, being used as much," Moon said before the game. "Now, when they mention our names, we're just quarterbacks, which is good."[8]

Williams's post–Super Bowl MVP season had not gone as planned. After three games, he underwent an appendectomy that sidelined him for a month, and while he was out, his rookie backup, Mark Rypien, performed so well that Joe Gibbs considered keeping Rypien as the starter when Williams returned. But then a shoulder injury sidelined Rypien and Williams shredded the Packers, completing twenty-five of forty-two passes for 225 yards and two touchdowns. He was still the starter.

The Oilers were coming off a brutal loss in which they fell behind the Cincinnati Bengals, 28–0, in Moon's second game back from the shoulder injury he had suffered in the season opener. He expected to play better against the Redskins. A rowdy crowd filled Houston's Astrodome to see if the Oilers could take down the reigning Super Bowl champions, creating a daunting environment for any visitor. Early in the game, Williams fumbled in his territory, the Oilers recovered, and Moon immediately tossed a touchdown pass. Moon then ran for a touchdown and threw for another while Williams lost a second fumble. Houston had a 24–3 lead at halftime.

Trying to start a rally, Williams led a touchdown drive in the third quarter. But Moon had no problem finding open receivers gallivanting through Washington's leaky secondary. By the fourth quarter, the score was 41–10 and Gibbs took out Williams, who had thrown an interception, lost two fumbles, and been sacked three times. Final score: 41–17.

It was a thorough shellacking, but the Redskins had gone to the playoffs five times and won the Super Bowl twice in the past six years, so there was reason to believe they would recover and go on a late-season surge. Sure enough, they won their next game, beating the Saints, with Williams running for a touchdown, throwing for two, and completing twenty of twenty-eight passes for 299 yards.

This time, though, there was no late-season surge. The Bears put the Redskins in their place, taking a 20–0 lead on the way to a 34–14 victory in Washington. Williams was ineffective, completing just six of nineteen passes before Gibbs pulled him. A week later, the Redskins lost badly to the 49ers. A year removed from winning the Super Bowl, they missed the playoffs. "To finish 7–9 that season was probably the most disappointing thing that ever happened to me in football," Williams wrote later. "We were the champions, and everyone was coming after us."[9]

Gibbs said he expected Williams and Rypien to compete for the starting job the next year, but Williams experienced back pain before training camp and underwent surgery to repair a disc, sidelining him for the first half of the season. The Redskins hovered around .500, with Rypien inconsistent as the starter. In his first game back, Williams attempted fifty-two passes and the Redskins scored just three points in a loss to the Cowboys. A week later, they beat the Eagles, but Philadelphia's defense battered Williams and his hip hurt after the game, knocking him out of practice. Gibbs went back to Rypien as the starter for the rest of the season, and the younger quarterback played far better as the Redskins won their last five games to finish 10–6.

Williams had lost his starting job. Forever. The Redskins cut him in May 1990. They went with Rypien as the starter and signed a white backup, thirty-three-year-old Jeff Rutledge, who had made just nine starts in a decade with the Rams and Giants. "Coach Gibbs was honest with me. He said, 'I'm going to bring in Jeff Rutledge.' I said, 'Coach, a banged-up Doug Williams could outplay Jeff Rutledge any day,'" Williams said. "Coach said, 'Well, with your popularity in this town, anytime Rypien doesn't play well, I don't want to hear the fans chanting, "We want Doug!" from the stands.' He told me that!"[10]

He was just twenty-eight months removed from earning MVP honors in a Super Bowl victory, but pro football was done with him. Williams never signed with another team, never received a chance to extend his career as a backup. He was thirty-four.

It was unlikely a white quarterback who had been at the pinnacle so recently would experience such disdain. But the abrupt end of Williams's career revealed a different barrier Black quarterbacks would now face. Those with obvious talent such as Williams, Moon, and Cunningham would continue to receive more opportunities in the coming years, but the market for Black backups would not open as freely. "If you weren't good enough to start, there usually wasn't a place for you on the roster," Williams said.[11]

In the 1990s, a Black quarterback had almost no chance of forging the kind of career Rutledge had molded, lasting a decade in the league without being a starter. The job demanded that he master his playbook and possess the professionalism to prepare to play in every game even though the chances of him getting on the field were slim. It was not unusual for a head coach to rely on his backup quarterback as an extra set of discerning eyes, almost another coach, free to proffer opinions in practices and in sideline huddles during games. That few Black players had such a role indicated a lack of trust, one of the hallmarks of the doubts that had denied Black quarterbacks for so long. "It was the same old thing, really, just demonstrated in a different way," Williams said.[12]

The lack of Black backup quarterbacks would receive little attention as Black star quarterbacks gradually filtered into the sport, reflecting progress. But the dearth of Black backups would persist well into the twenty-first century. "Honestly," Williams said in 2022, "it's still kind of going on."[13]

There were similarities in the paths Moon and Williams took to the Sunday night game in October 1988 when they opposed each other as starting quarterbacks in Houston. Both were in their thirties. Both had performed well in the NFL but also had spent years in other pro leagues—Moon in the CFL, Williams in the USFL—because of the disdain for Black quarterbacks that prevailed in the NFL.

Moon and Williams liked and respected each other, but before the game, Moon acknowledged feeling a pang of jealousy. "It was a goal of mine to be the first Black quarterback to win the Super Bowl," he said.[14] Williams had beaten him to it.

But Moon recognized that the impact of Williams's triumph outweighed his personal concerns. "It did a lot for other Black quarterbacks, letting people see a Black quarterback can perform in the biggest game of the year," Moon said. "That was always a rap against us, that we don't play well in big games. He proved it was a fallacy."[15]

The Oilers' rout of the Redskins that night in Houston symbolized where the quarterbacks' careers were headed. While Williams was nearer the end than anyone imagined, Moon, in a way, was just getting started. He led the Oilers to a second straight playoff appearance that season, and their streak would extend to seven straight appearances in the coming years. In 1991, they went 11–5 and won their first division title in twenty-four years. In 1993, they went 12–4 and won another division title.

Williams had beaten Moon to the mantel of being the first Black quarterback to win a Super Bowl, but when Williams threw his last NFL pass in 1989, Moon still had his best years ahead of him. His production skyrocketed after Jack Pardee became the Oilers' head coach in 1990. Pardee, a fifty-four-year-old former NFL linebacker, was known for running conservative offenses in his prior stops as a head coach with the Bears and Redskins. But he now believed in a wide-open, high-risk offense known as the "run and shoot."

In Moon's first season in that system, he led the NFL in pass attempts, completions, passing yardage, and touchdown passes. The next year, he repeated as the league leader in every category except touchdown passes. The Oilers were almost impossible to defend on some days, yet success in the playoffs eluded them. They never made a deep run, and their owner, Bud Adams, eventually grew weary of being disappointed and broke up the team. Moon was cut loose after the 1993 season, after a decade in Houston.

Even then, he was not finished. Canada had been his first act as a pro and Houston had been his second act, but a third act awaited. In 1994, at age thirty-eight, Moon became the first Black quarterback to start a game for the Minnesota Vikings, led them to the playoffs, and made the Pro Bowl. A year later, still in Minnesota, he led the NFL in completions and made the Pro Bowl again. In 1997, at age forty-one, he became the first Black quarterback to start a game for the Seattle Seahawks and made the Pro Bowl for the ninth and final time. He finally retired after the 2000 season, at age forty-four, after a season in which he became the first Black quarterback to start a game for the Kansas City Chiefs—the fourth NFL franchise for which he had broken that barrier. "That's amazing when you think back on it. Just shows where the league was for so long, the mindset, the mentality," Moon said. "I feel good about having been the guy to break the barriers, the guy that teams felt confident enough about to sign to a contract when they never had [a Black quarterback] before. It's something to feel good about."[16]

The past, present, and future of Black quarterbacks in the NFL intersected at the Pro Bowl after the 1988 season.

Cunningham started for the NFC. Moon started for the AFC. To that point in the history of the annual all-star game, first played in 1951, only one Black quarterback had taken a snap—James Harris in 1975. Now, Black quarterbacks were starting for both teams in the game that celebrated the NFL's best.

The news value of the race angle would soon cease. For Cunningham, this was the first of three straight Pro Bowl appearances. For Moon, it was the first of nine straight. Cunningham had to be goaded into commenting. He always downplayed the racial implications of his position. "I'm sure for Blacks there is a sense of accomplishment," he said. "The way I look at it, I'm proud to be here, number one, and I've tried to downplay the black-white thing by saying I'm an Italian from South Philly, but it does give us a sense of pride. We don't think in terms of, 'Hey, we're Black.' It doesn't work that way. I think what we're saying is things are changing and they're allowing you the opportunity to go out and play, regardless of the color you are. I think that's great."[17]

The opening up of the quarterback position in the NFL was just one piece of a larger wave of racial barrier breaking in the late 1980s. In 1987, Dr. Clifton R. Wharton Jr. became the first Black chairman and CEO of a major US corporation when he took command of the Teachers Insurance and Annuity Association of America (TIAA). In 1989, Colin

Powell became the first Black chairman of the Joint Chiefs of Staff, the US Department of Defense's highest military position. That same year, Art Shell became the first Black head coach in the modern NFL, with the Raiders. A year later, Virginia's Douglas Wilder became America's first elected Black governor.

These milestones reflected progress, but it was coming more than two hundred years after America's birth—a clear reflection of the fierce and unyielding discrimination Black Americans had always faced as they sought to attain any leadership position. Like the other milestones, the presence of two Black starting quarterbacks in the Pro Bowl exemplified that, as Cunningham put it, "things are changing." But the different reactions of Cunningham and Moon indicated how recent the change was. Cunningham, seven years younger, could joke about getting a chance as a Black quarterback at least partly because he had not experienced the denial by stereotype that had forced Moon to Canada as a first-year pro in 1978. A decade later, Moon still could not joke about it.

During a practice the week before the Pro Bowl, Moon arranged for a photographer to take his picture with Cunningham. "We were saying, 'Yeah, this is history, and we're proud of it,' something that has never happened, two Black quarterbacks in the Pro Bowl," Moon said. "I want the kid who sees this to realize that if this is something he wants to do, be a quarterback, if he's Black, looking at us shows him that he's got a chance to do it."

Moon recalled never seeing such a photograph when he was younger. "When I was a kid, I couldn't say, 'Hey there's a guy playing who was named to the Pro Bowl,'" he said. "But [today's kid] has role models and I think that would keep him fighting. And that's what it is, a fight. There are a lot of hurdles to overcome. But when you see it has been done before, you say you've got a chance. And that's all we want, a chance."[18]

Cunningham's NFC teammate, Mike Singletary, a Black linebacker for the Bears, was moved to comment. "It just goes to show how, when you give the opportunity, when people stop making excuses, a lot of good things can happen," he said. "That's the difference. Acceptance plays a big part of it. When you're successful, when good things happen, when you live your life in a class way, after a while people see he isn't just an 'acceptable Black quarterback,' he is a quality quarterback. And that's what it takes sometimes to break down the old barriers, the clichés, whatever you want to call them."[19]

Cunningham and Moon—and Williams—had been "given the opportunity and utilized it," Singletary said. "That opens whole new doors. So we'll go from here."

With that short remark at an innocuous Pro Bowl practice, Singletary, a future NFL head coach, summed up the conflicting themes that ruled the Black quarterback story heading into the 1990s. Williams, Moon, and Cunningham deserved to be celebrated for having blazed a trail, for effectively having created something where nothing had existed before. But their success did not mean Black quarterbacks could declare victory over the institutional racism that had denied them a place in the NFL for so long. The road that lay ahead of them was still lined with potential trouble that could slow their progress, even halt it, and continue to limit them in the same manner they had always known. Some talent evaluators still doubted them and bypassed them more readily than white prospects, failing to grasp the effectiveness of their strengths. It was unclear how many owners, all of whom were white, actually would commit to them being the face of their franchise. And woe unto any young, Black quarterback who did not immediately soar in the NFL. When Singletary said they would "go from here," he meant they would continue to fight for respect and a level playing field—a fight in which their success was hardly assured.

PART II

CHAPTER 17

For anyone seeking evidence that white and Black quarterbacks still were judged differently by NFL talent evaluators as the 1990s approached, the outcomes that two prospects experienced in the 1989 draft offered compelling evidence.

UCLA's Troy Aikman fit the profile of a winning quarterback that had prevailed for decades. Tall, broad-chested, and white, he was a classic pocket passer who had thrown strikes to receivers all over the field while winning twenty-two games, including two bowls, in two years as a starter. As a senior, he won the Davey O'Brien Award, given to the nation's top quarterback.

Across town from UCLA, Southern Cal's Rodney Peete had a comparable resume. He had won the Johnny Unitas Golden Arm Award, given to the nation's top senior quarterback, and had led the Trojans to two Rose Bowl appearances while setting school records for pass attempts, completions, and passing yardage. But offsetting his many similarities to Aikman was one difference that still mattered in 1989: Peete was Black.

When their teams met in 1987 and 1988 to determine bragging rights in Los Angeles, Peete's Trojans defeated Aikman's Bruins twice. Peete was more mobile, able to escape the pocket, and throw accurately on the run. He received more Heisman Trophy votes than Aikman in 1988, finishing second to Barry Sanders, a running back from Oklahoma State. But when it came to the 1989 draft, Aikman went to the Dallas Cowboys with the first overall pick and Peete had to wait, and wait, to hear his name called while a succession of less-accomplished quarterbacks, all white, went before him. Wake Forest's Mike Elkins and Texas Tech's Billy Joe Tolliver were selected in the second round. Oregon State's Erik Wilhelm and Duke's Anthony Dilweg went in the third round. Long Beach State's Jeff Graham and Weber State's Jeff Carlson went in the fourth round. Peete went unselected until the Detroit Lions finally took him in the sixth round.

Peete understood why Aikman went before him, but not the others. "I felt I should have been taken second among all quarterbacks. I don't take a back seat to any quarterback in the draft. I wish someone would explain it," Peete said.[1] Asked if he believed he had slid because he was Black, he said, "I hope that's not the case because I can't do anything about the color of my skin."[2]

Several NFL general managers and scouts dismissed the idea, offering football-based rationales. They noted that Peete was relatively short for the NFL at just over six feet tall and that he had not performed well at the scouting combine or in several important games. Elkins had a higher ceiling, they said, because he was six feet three with a strong arm. Tolliver also was more promising, they said; he had thrown for nearly seven thousand yards in college. But none of that explained why a quarterback just as accomplished as Aikman had gone 140 picks later, a stunning disparity.

It would turn out Aikman was a deserving top pick; he led the Cowboys to three Super Bowl victories and made the Pro Football Hall of Fame. Otherwise, though, the NFL's appraisal apparatus was dead wrong about Peete and the other quarterbacks in the 1989 draft. Elkins played in one NFL game. Tolliver lasted a decade but won just fifteen games as a starter. Dilweg, Carlson, and Wilhelm made just eleven starts between them in their careers. Graham never threw a pass in the regular season. Peete, drafted after all of them, played in the NFL for fifteen years, his reputation as a savvy contributor enabling him to sign contract after contract. In 1994, he led the Eagles to a playoff berth and a playoff victory. In 2002, thirteen years after he was drafted, he was the Carolina Panthers' starting quarterback.

In the late 1980s and early 1990s, most Black quarterbacks faced a version of the same, quiet disparagement coming out of college. Even with trailblazers Doug Williams, Warren Moon, and Randall Cunningham having demonstrated that Black quarterbacks could thrive in the NFL, talent evaluators still tended to find reasons not to like them while always finding reasons to draft white quarterbacks. The playing field was nowhere close to level.

Based on his stellar career at West Virginia, Major Harris should have been a high pick in 1990. A unique and dynamic Black quarterback, he rushed and passed for twenty touchdowns as a sophomore while leading the Mountaineers to an undefeated season and a place in the national championship game. On one run, he juked past seven Penn State defenders on his way to the end zone. But scouts questioned his throwing mechanics and believed his relatively slow forty-yard-dash time meant he would not dodge defenders as easily in the pros. He also gave up his final year of college eligibility to turn pro, an uncommon move at the time, unpopular with some evaluators.

Harris found the criticism laughably absurd. Asked to identify his strengths as a player, he deadpanned, "Getting the ball into the end zone."[3]

But he knew before the draft that he would not have an opportunity to play quarterback in the NFL. "I could tell I wasn't going to get taken," he said.[4] He was so sure that he did not watch ESPN's coverage and did not know the Raiders had taken him in the final round until a *Pittsburgh Post-Gazette* sportswriter called for a reaction. "Major, did you hear? The Raiders drafted you," the sportswriter said.[5]

"What round, fifteenth?" Harris joked.

"Twelfth," the reporter said. That was the last round.

"Oh, well, I look at it this way. They saved the best for last," Harris said, laughing.

Eighteen quarterbacks had been taken before him, including Pacific Lutheran's Craig Kupp, Stephen F. Austin's Todd Hammel, and Western Illinois's Gene Benhart—white quarterbacks whose college resumes could not begin to compare with his. "It has to do with my race, you can't deny that," Harris told the *Post-Gazette*. "I think I'm a different type of quarterback. If they let me in the league, it would change the whole league. The NFL doesn't change. [A Black quarterback] is just something they're not ready for."[6]

It was hard to argue with his notion that the NFL did not change and was "not ready for" a Black quarterback. Williams, Moon, and Cunningham had not changed enough minds, it seemed. Rather than try to make it with the Raiders, Harris signed with Canada's British Columbia Lions and was their backup quarterback for one season. He then spent years with an assortment of indoor and minor-league teams before giving up on football.

Two years before Harris, Don McPherson was the most accomplished quarterback in the 1988 draft class. He had thrown for nearly six thousand yards at Syracuse and finished second in the Heisman voting as a senior. A fast forty-yard-dash time at the combine seemingly burnished his prospects. But scouts thought he was too small, an inaccurate passer, and not explosive as a runner. He went to the Eagles in the sixth round and never threw a pass in the NFL.

Tulane's Terrence Jones went one round after McPherson that year. He stood six feet three, weighed 210 pounds, was fast, and could throw. The Chargers took him as a cornerback. He went to the CFL and played quarterback for seven years.

Clemente Gordon was Grambling's best quarterback prospect since Doug Williams; he went in the eleventh round in 1990. Reggie Slack led Auburn to two Southeastern Conference titles; he went in the twelfth round in 1990. As a senior at Virginia, Shawn Moore received more Heisman votes than any player in the history of the Atlantic Coast Conference; he went in the eleventh round in 1991.

The only Black quarterback talent evaluators liked in these years was Andre Ware, from the University of Houston. As a senior in 1989, he posted statistics so astronomical—365 completions, 46 touchdowns, 4,699 yards—that he made history as the first Black quarterback to win the Heisman Trophy. The Lions took him with the seventh overall pick, believing he could lead them to their first NFL championship since the 1950s. It was the highest a Black quarterback had ever been drafted.

But Ware was a bust.

Initially, the Lions seemed like an ideal landing spot for him. He had run up his gaudy statistics operating Houston's wide-open "run-and-shoot" offense, and the Lions' offensive coordinator, Mouse Davis, also favored the run-and-shoot. Ware seemingly would face a gentle learning curve as a young pro.

But as a rookie, he was beaten out by Peete, then in his second pro season. Ware did not even win the backup job. The seventh pick in the draft was a third-stringer in Detroit. Soon, it was being whispered in league circles that his huge college numbers were due more to the gimmicky offense than his natural talent.

Ware hung around Detroit for four years, but Wayne Fontes, the Lions' head coach, continually vacillated between Peete, Ware, and Erik Kramer, a white quarterback who led the team to the 1991 NFC championship game. When Ware's contract expired, the Lions did not re-sign him. He had started six games in four years.

Ware never threw another pass in the NFL after leaving Detroit. The skepticism that prevailed in the league about putting Black quarterbacks in the backup role brought his career to an end. During a failed attempt to land a job with the Jacksonville Jaguars, an expansion team, in 1995, he told a reporter, "As a Black quarterback, you have to succeed right away or things are automatically different for you after the first year, and you become a bust."[7]

Jeff Blake's story was the same until it was not. He was a Black quarterback who soared in college but did not at first receive the opportunity in the NFL that he seemed to deserve. When his chance finally came, however, he did so much with it that one could only wonder what other Black quarterbacks might have done with the same chance.

In college, at East Carolina, Blake set passing records while leading the Pirates' long-shot rise to the top ten. He threw a beautiful deep ball, but in a familiar refrain, scouts were lukewarm about him, believing he was too small and had not faced top competition. The Jets drafted him with a sixth-round pick in 1992, buried him on the bench for two years, and cut him.

When the Cincinnati Bengals picked him up as the 1994 season began, they saw him strictly as insurance. They already had a quarterback they were building around—David Klingler, from the University of Houston, drafted two years earlier with a first-round pick.

But Klingler, who was white, had not blossomed, and on October 23, 1994, he was injured during a loss to the Cleveland Browns. His backup, Don Hollas, replaced him but also went out with an injury. The Bengals had no choice but to start Blake in their next game, at home against the Cowboys.

The pro football world assumed a disaster was coming. The Cowboys had won the past two Super Bowls and appeared capable of winning another; Aikman, their quarterback, had been a Super Bowl MVP. The Bengals, meanwhile, had an 0–7 record, and Blake was a third-year pro making his first career start; he had completed four passes in the NFL.

But Blake was not a typical novice. His father had played in the CFL and coached him in high school in Seminole, Florida; Blake was a savvy coach's kid. Also, while he was with the Jets in 1992 and 1993, their head coach, Bruce Coslet, had taken him on as a project, teaching him how to read defenses and make adjustments. Fired by the Jets after the 1993 season, Coslet was now the Bengals' offensive coordinator; the Bengals had signed Blake strictly on his recommendation.

When Blake trotted onto the field against the Cowboys on October 30, 1994, he became the first Black quarterback to start a game for the Bengals, who had been in existence for twenty-six years. Their white-only history at football's most important position was not unusual. At the time, ten of the NFL's twenty-seven franchises still had never started a Black quarterback in a game.

Blake's debut would drive home the point that maybe, just maybe, something had been missing from the league's quarterback population.

Midway through the first quarter, Blake dropped back to pass and saw Darnay Scott, one of his receivers, facing single coverage far downfield. Before his pocket collapsed, Blake unleashed a long pass that hit Scott in stride. Scott fought off the defender and sprinted to the end zone to complete a sixty-seven-yard scoring play. The Cowboys were stunned. And Blake was not done. Early in the second quarter, he spotted Scott open again, this time behind the whole defense. His pass was on target and Scott raced to the end zone, completing the fifty-five-yard touchdown.

Bengals 14, Cowboys 0.

The Cowboys were shocked. Fans at Cincinnati's Riverfront Stadium were shocked. Fans across the country were shocked when they saw the partial score from Cincinnati.

Not surprisingly, the Cowboys rallied. Aikman hurled completions. The defense confused Blake with new alignments. The Cowboys took the lead and withstood a late rally to win, 23–20. But it did not feel like a defeat to the Bengals or their fans. In the next day's *Cincinnati Enquirer*, Coslet and Blake were pictured leaving the field with broad smiles. "Hope Emerges," a headline read. Columnists wrote that Blake deserved to keep the starting job. "He did a hell of a job, didn't he?" said David Shula, the Bengals' head coach.[8]

Blake had been so worried about holding his own that he had not thought much about his situation from a racial perspective. Being Black certainly had impacted his career years earlier when he was selecting a college. Miami and Florida State had wanted him only as a cornerback or wide receiver; their lack of interest in him as a quarterback had prompted him to go to East Carolina. He also believed he had slipped in the NFL draft at least partly because he was Black.

He quickly discovered that a Black quarterback actually getting a chance to play in the NFL was a newsworthy development. He received a phone call from Spike Lee, the Black film director, and realized Black fans across the country were rooting for him.

Blake continued to start and continued to shine. He completed thirty-one of forty-three passes for 387 yards the next week as the Bengals won for the first time in 1994, beating the Seahawks in Seattle. He was even better a week later, completing twenty-three of thirty-three passes for 354 yards and four touchdowns in a win over the Oilers in Cincinnati.

Late in the game against the Oilers, with the Bengals trailing, Blake suffered a bruised ankle and went to the locker room for X-rays. The Bengals were just starting a last-gasp possession when he returned to the field in a golf cart, cleared to play. He hopped off the cart, ran onto the field, and tossed two long completions that set up a game-winning field goal.

The Bengals had lost too many games to make the playoffs, but that did not stop Cincinnati from going wild over Blake. One fan sold T-shirts extolling the "Shake and Blake" phenomenon. Another fan recorded a rap video. Blake just smiled and shook his head. "I love to prove people wrong," he told one interviewer. "People said I'd be another statistic, another guy who didn't get a chance to prove what he could do in the NFL."[9] He later told another interviewer, "The stigma of the Black quarterback, there's nothing I can do about it. The only thing I can do is keep playing good. If I do, I'll open up doors for others."[10]

He would spend the next decade demonstrating what can happen when an opportunity is extended.

The next year, he started every game and passed for 3,822 yards and twenty-eight touchdowns. The Bengals went 7–9, a considerable improvement. Blake was selected to the Pro Bowl. Klingler was his backup.

He continued to start and play well in 1996, but the Bengals still hovered around .500 and support for Blake waned inside the organization. That off-season, the Bengals traded for Boomer Esiason, a popular veteran who had led them to a Super Bowl appearance in 1988. The plan was for Esiason, now thirty-six, to back up Blake, and indeed, Blake started the first eleven games in 1997. But the Bengals went 3–8, and Coslet, now the head coach, benched Blake. Esiason led the team to a 4–1 record down the stretch.

When Esiason retired to become a broadcaster after that season, the Bengals traded for another veteran quarterback, thirty-two-year-old Neil O'Donnell, who had taken the Steelers to the Super Bowl a few years earlier.

Blake left Cincinnati after the 1999 season but remained in demand, playing for five teams over the next six years. He started eleven games for the New Orleans Saints in 2000, ten games for the Baltimore Ravens in 2002, and thirteen games for the Arizona Cardinals in 2003. Although he wound up with a losing career record as a starter, that was a reflection of the teams he played for more than his performance. He threw thirty-five more touchdowns than interceptions during his career, a superb ratio.

Blake belonged to a small generation of Black quarterbacks who began playing in the mid-1990s—a generation that also included Steve McNair and Kordell Stewart and served as a bridge between the first wave of trailblazers and a generation for which the door of opportunity opened wide starting in 1999.

Blake's era was one of measurable progress. Opportunities were still rare for Black quarterbacks when the Bengals gave him a chance in 1994. By the time he retired, enough were playing that the concept of a Black franchise quarterback, embraced by ownership, had been mainstreamed.

But as usual, the measurable gains did not signal the end of the forces that had held back Black quarterbacks for so long. The arc of Blake's career told that tale, too. A white starter so effective for a team likely would not have been undermined as quickly as Blake was by the Bengals, who fell back on veteran white starters after just a few years, leaving Blake with little choice but to become a vagabond, moving from team to team in his final years. "The whole time I was [in Cincinnati], I never got the feeling they were going to build a whole team around me," Blake said later. "Because I wasn't supposed to be there."[11]

The lesson? He had received an opportunity, but it did not come with trust.

CHAPTER 18

O ne month before Jeff Blake shocked the Cowboys in his first NFL start in 1994, another Black quarterback made the cover of *Sports Illustrated*. If any of the magazine's subscribers had not known before about Steve McNair, they did now. And when they read the magazine's profile of him, they knew McNair was unlike any marquee quarterback who had made the cover before.

Standing six feet two and weighing 220 pounds, with a broad chest, thick neck, and sturdy trunk, he could easily pass for a linebacker who had mistakenly wandered into the offensive huddle. He played like a linebacker, too, dishing out as much contact as he absorbed while rumbling around the field.

But McNair was unique as a cover subject mainly because he was the quarterback at Alcorn State, a historically Black college in Mississippi—far off the brightly lit paths of major college football.

Alcorn played in the Southwestern Athletic Conference, a league of historically Black schools in Division I-AA, a tier below college football's top level. SWAC football featured tradition, pageantry, and intense competition, and it had produced Doug Williams, Walter Payton, and many other NFL stars. But overall, the caliber of play did not compare with Division I-A.

No player from the SWAC or Division I-AA had ever come close to winning the Heisman Trophy, college football's highest individual award. But when *Sports Illustrated* put McNair on the cover in September 1994, it did so with the provocative headline, "Hand Him the Heisman," inferring that he was so good it did not matter where he played.

It was hard to disagree. In the first weeks of the 1994 season, McNair played a brand of football seemingly borrowed from a video game. In his first three years at Alcorn, he had posted impressive statistics while helping the Braves compete with Grambling, Southern, Jackson State, and other SWAC powers. But those years were merely a prelude to his spectacular senior season in 1994.

In the opener at Grambling, he passed for 534 yards and five touchdowns and rushed for ninety-nine yards, helping Alcorn score fifty-six points. The only problem was Grambling scored sixty-two. Eddie Robinson, Grambling's legendary coach, hugged McNair when the game ended. "Son, you're a great quarterback. You're the best. I love you," Robinson said.[1]

A week later, McNair was even better against the Moccasins of Tennessee-Chattanooga. He easily outran defenders, threw with a strong and accurate arm, and played with a calmness that suggested he *knew* he could prevail in pressure situations. As scouts from a half-dozen NFL teams watched, he passed for 491 yards and rushed for 156 as the Braves scored fifty-four points—this time, enough to win. The Moccasins' defensive coordinator, Rick Whitt, did not hold back in his praise, saying McNair was "better than anyone I've ever seen" at quarterback.[2]

Why was he playing at Alcorn and not the highest levels of college football? It was a fair question with a familiar answer. McNair was in Division I-AA because he was Black. Yes, that still mattered in 1994, just as it had in 1964.

With a population of less than one thousand, Mount Olive, Mississippi, was one of those small Southern towns where everyone knew everyone. Yet the residents had a hard time distinguishing Lucille McNair's five sons from one another. They were all good athletes with bright smiles. They were all polite and helped their mother make ends meet.

Their father long ago left the job of raising them to Lucille alone. She worked the overnight shift in a fluorescent light factory to keep the tin roof of their small house over their heads. Fred, the oldest son, assumed the father's role. "Fred has taught me absolutely everything that I know. I can't thank him enough," Steve said later.[3]

Fred was the family's first quarterback, such an effective passer at Mount Olive High School and Alcorn State that he was nicknamed "Air" McNair. Once Steve came along, though, it was clear he was the best athlete in the family. In high school, he led Mount Olive to a state title as a quarterback and also played defensive back, started at point guard in basketball, and earned all-state honors in baseball.

Not surprisingly, Steve had many options after high school. Baseball's Seattle Mariners drafted him. College basketball recruiters called. College football powers LSU, Miami, Ohio State, and Nebraska all offered scholarships. But they wanted him as a defensive back. If he wanted to play quarterback, he had to go to a smaller school—the same predicament so many Black quarterbacks before him had faced.

He was tempted to choose baseball and start drawing a paycheck, which would help Lucille. But he loved football most of all. "I like physical contact," Steve said later. "There are things you can do on the football field that you can't do on the baseball field in a physical way."[4]

When he sought Fred's advice, Fred suggested following *his* path to Alcorn. It might hurt Steve's chances of playing in the NFL, as it had hurt Fred's (Fred was playing in an indoor pro league), but that was hardly a serious consideration given how few Black quarterbacks received opportunities in the NFL, even by the 1990s. Steve chose Alcorn.

Cardell Jones, the school's head coach, was delighted to land another McNair. He planned to break him in slowly, but that plan was quickly scotched. McNair, as a freshman, completed nine straight passes in a preseason scrimmage, then came off the bench and threw three touchdown passes in a comeback win against Grambling in the season opener. "He was mature at a very young age," Jones said later.[5]

He started for the rest of that season and the next two, piling up records and awards and earning the nickname "Air II." It was clear the major college programs had underestimated his potential as a quarterback. Pro scouts began following him when he was a sophomore. That was unusual for a quarterback playing at a historically Black institution, but McNair's powerful throwing arm was tantalizing, as was the way he led a huddle, played through injuries, and consistently delivered in close games.

After his junior year, McNair seriously considered going pro. One of the best white quarterbacks in the South, Tennessee's Heath Shuler, was in the same situation and decided to forgo his final college season. It worked out for him. The Washington Redskins took Shuler with the third overall pick and signed him to a $19.25 million contract.

But McNair knew the history of Black quarterbacks being disappointed in the draft. He asked the NFL's Draft Advisory Board for a recommendation. The Board, a panel of scouts and personnel executives that helped prospects decide what to do, told McNair he probably would get selected late in the first round or somewhere in the second round. That was encouraging, but McNair would not be able to demand nearly as many millions as Shuler.

The Board's recommendation helped him decide to return to Alcorn for his final season in 1994. Lucille was happy to hear he would stay in school and earn his degree. McNair felt better about the decision as he watched the drama surrounding another Black quarterback, Charlie Ward, that spring.

In the fall of 1993, Ward had led Florida State to an unbeaten season and a national championship. Playing with uncanny poise, he became the second Black quarterback to win the Heisman, after Andre Ware four years earlier. Decades later, people who know the game believe Ward would have thrived in the NFL. "The thing about him, if you're a quarterback and you're cool, calm, and collected, you can make a lot of things happen in the NFL," said Jameis Winston, a Black quarterback who also went to Florida State, won the Heisman, and was drafted first overall in 2015.[6]

But in the buildup to the 1994 draft, scouts had doubts about Ward's arm strength and questioned his commitment to football, since he also played point guard on Florida State's basketball team. When he skipped the combine to play basketball, his draft stock plummeted. The reigning Heisman Trophy winner wound up not being selected at all. Fortunately, he did become a first-round selection in the NBA draft and went on to play a decade of pro basketball.

After seeing what happened to Ward, McNair felt good about returning to Alcorn for his senior season. If he played well, scouts would not be able to dismiss him as casually as they did Ward.

It so happened that offensive strategy in college football was beginning to change, with passing games becoming more popular. When Alcorn went with a shotgun-style attack in 1994, it unleashed McNair to dominate Division I-AA opponents. The week he was on the cover of *Sports Illustrated*, he passed for 395 yards against Sam Houston State. As the season progressed, he gave more spectacular performances. In one game, he faced second-and-40 in the final minute, with Alcorn down by three points, and still engineered a winning drive. In another game, he rallied the Braves to a win after they trailed by twenty-nine points in the third quarter. Against Troy, a ranked opponent, he led a winning rally from eleven points down.

"If people do what's right, Steve wins the Heisman," Doug Williams said. "But like I told him, there are an awful lot of things in America that aren't fair, and this might be one of them."[7]

With his name in the Heisman race, the SWAC went wild for him. Wherever Alcorn played, the stadium was sold out and fans cheered for McNair. Several games even were televised, a rarity in the SWAC. The national media awakened to McNair's talent. A sportswriter for the *New York Times* spent the fall with him and wrote a series of features. The *Baltimore Sun* wrote that it was "ludicrous" to give the Heisman to anyone else.[8]

McNair mostly shrugged off the fuss. "No matter what happens, I'm just Steve, the country boy from Mount Olive," he told the *New York Times*.[9]

But could he really win the Heisman? Not unlike the primary phase of a presidential election, the award had a campaign season in which institutions mounted expensive publicity campaigns in an effort to sway the eight hundred sportswriters, broadcasters, and college experts who cast votes. Alcorn could not afford to do that for McNair, but it did produce a video that included highlights, a smiling McNair asking for votes, and a rap song.

McNair ended up averaging 442 passing yards per game while setting the Division I-AA record for most total yards (passing and rushing) in a season. Alcorn earned a bid to the I-AA national playoffs. The Braves lost badly to powerful Youngstown State in their opener, but McNair put on a show. Playing with a sore hamstring, he completed fifty-two of eighty-two passes for 517 yards.

"Hopefully, this game didn't hurt my chances for the Heisman. I think I'm still in the hunt," McNair said.[10]

His optimism was admirable, but the fact that he played at a smaller school impacted voters. "When McNair made his decision to attend Alcorn State, he 99 percent eliminated himself from the Heisman," ESPN's Lee Corso said.[11] Although he received 111 first-place votes, a respectable total, he finished a distant third in the balloting behind the winner, Rashaan Salaam, a running back from Colorado, and Ki-Jana Carter, a running back from Penn State.

It was disappointing, but McNair did not despair for long. It turned out his stellar senior season did, in fact, bolster his NFL draft stock. Scouts loved his decision-making, his toughness, his calm demeanor in the face of a rush, and his arm. "In terms of pure throwing ability, I had never seen anyone like Steve McNair, and I still haven't except for Patrick Mahomes," Bill Polian, the Carolina Panthers' general manager in 1995, said years later. "When you think of natural, incredibly gifted throwers, I think of Brett Favre, Mahomes, and Steve McNair. Dan Marino is probably in there somewhere. Steve, in my mind, is still the best."[12] Jeff Fisher, who would coach McNair in the NFL, said, "There were so many qualities that Steve possessed, and they were there even when we were scouting him. We saw them. The ability to just take a game over early, or late in a game, the ability to pull that thing out of a hat."[13]

Talent evaluators in the NFL usually had no trouble finding reasons not to like Black quarterbacks, but McNair's poise, on top of his arm, made him a quarterback you seemingly were going to be able to trust as a starter—a positive projection that Black players at the position had seldom received and, in McNair's case, proved 100 percent accurate.

The only lingering question about McNair before the 1995 draft was whether he could thrive against the top competition he had not faced in college. His performance in the Senior Bowl, against major college players, took care of that. "There was more pressure on him at the Senior Bowl than on anyone I've ever seen, and he put on a show," Polian said.[14]

Heading into the draft, McNair and Penn State's Kerry Collins were the top quarterback prospects. Collins had the major college bona fides McNair lacked; as a senior, he had set passing records and led Penn State to an undefeated season and a Rose Bowl victory. Nonetheless, Mel Kiper Jr., ESPN's draft analyst, ranked McNair higher. For weeks, it appeared McNair, like Andre Ware in 1990, would avoid the vague, negative assessments that had sent so many Black quarterbacks plummeting in the draft.

In fact, as the Panthers, who held the first overall pick, discussed McNair and other prospects, it came up that McNair might help sell tickets because he was so popular, especially among Black fans, who relished the fact that he was a top quarterback prospect from a historically Black college.

Then, the day before the draft, Kiper reported that McNair's stock might be falling due to "questions about his low-key approach and quiet demeanor."[15] His supporters regarded that as code for the old-fashioned, discriminatory doubts about whether Black quarterbacks were intelligent enough to operate an NFL offense. "I don't know where this tag came from," said Glenn Cumbee, the Houston Oilers' director of college scouting, "but we put him through extensive classroom work and he's one of the most intelligent players I've seen."[16]

McNair and his mother traveled to New York for the draft. After deliberating for months, Polian still could not decide between McNair and Collins. Though he loved McNair, the Panthers wanted a young quarterback who could start at some point in his rookie season, and it seemed inevitable that McNair, being from Alcorn, would need a longer apprenticeship.

In the end, the Panthers traded the first pick to the Cincinnati Bengals, who took Ki-Jana Carter. The Jacksonville Jaguars, who held the second pick, already had a starting quarterback, Steve Beuerlein, picked up during an expansion draft (in which the Jaguars and Panthers selected players made available by other teams), so they drafted a tackle, Tony Boselli.

Next up were the Oilers, a franchise in transition in 1995. They had a new general manager, Floyd Reese; a new head coach, Fisher; and they would soon leave Houston, where they had played since 1960, for Tennessee. A new quarterback would complete the organizational overhaul. The year before, they had used three journeymen who completed just 47 percent of their passes, with more interceptions than touchdowns, during a two-win season.

One year removed from parting ways with Warren Moon, the Oilers could engineer a reset at quarterback with the third pick. They scrutinized McNair, Collins, and other prospects for months. Years later, ESPN's Chris Mortensen reported that their offensive coordinator, Jerry Rhome, favored drafting a wide receiver from Colorado, Michael Westbrook. If so, Reese overruled him. It did not matter to the GM that McNair was from a small school, or that he was Black. Reese called him "the Michael Jordan of the draft," the highest possible compliment for an athlete in the peak years of Jordan's career.[17]

At New York's Marriott Marquis, NFL Commissioner Paul Tagliabue stepped to the podium and announced the Oilers were drafting McNair. Dressed in a fashionable suit, McNair smiled broadly, accepted a kiss from his mother, dipped his head, and headed for the podium, where he donned an Oilers cap. Even though he had been optimistic about how high he might go, he was still stunned. A Black quarterback had never gone as high as third overall.

Reese was excited until he began fielding calls from other general managers congratulating him on making a pick so "gutsy."[18] He did not think it was gutsy in the least. But if this many other teams did, was it?

No, he soon learned. McNair held out before signing a $28.7 million contract that made him the team's highest-paid player. Once he joined the team, he held up well in practices and scrimmages and cultivated respect with his humble approach.

Reese and Fisher still wanted to bring him along slowly. The coach and GM wanted to build a winning team with tough, no-nonsense players. McNair was their ideal quarterback, but they thought he needed to learn more about playing the position in the pros.

Prior to the draft, the Oilers had signed Chris Chandler, a twenty-nine-year-old journeyman, expecting him to be their starting quarterback in 1995. The drafting of McNair "was something I didn't expect or want to happen," Chandler said later.[19] Although he got along with McNair, he viewed the rookie as a threat to his job and career. Chandler said later that he "possibly" could have been more generous in helping mentor McNair.[20]

That job fell to Rhome, a laconic Texan known as an effective mentor of young quarterbacks. As a player in the 1960s, he had been coached for six years by Tom Landry on the Dallas Cowboys, helping propel him into a second career as a coach. Joe Theismann and Troy Aikman were among his top successes. He began working with McNair on how to read defenses and make adjustments.

The idea that McNair would stand on the sideline and watch Chandler play in 1995 had the potential to cause problems. For starters, McNair was not thrilled. "It was a little rocky," Fisher said later.[21] Also, some owners might demand to see their highest-paid player on the field. But Reese and Fisher convinced Bud Adams that McNair would benefit from waiting until he was more ready.

In the Oilers' first thirteen games in 1995, McNair was on the field just once, for four plays, and did not attempt a pass. Then an opportunity arose when Chandler contracted mononucleosis in early December. He still started against the Detroit Lions, but when he struggled, Fisher put in McNair, who completed sixteen of twenty-seven passes for 203 yards and a touchdown in the last two quarters.

Encouraged, Fisher started McNair in the final two games of the season, and the Oilers won both, prompting speculation that he would become the starter in 1996. But Fisher stuck to his plan. McNair sat behind Chandler again in 1996. "We clearly had a plan and that was to bring him along slowly," Fisher said later.[22]

The 1996 season was a tumultuous time in Houston. Adams announced the team would leave for Nashville, where local officials had agreed to build the new stadium Adams wanted. (Adams and Houston officials had clashed over how to get a stadium built there.) Sparse crowds of bitter fans attended the team's final home games at the Astrodome.

The tumult continued after the franchise moved to Tennessee for the 1997 season. The new stadium was not ready, so the Oilers practiced in Nashville and played their home games at the Liberty Bowl in Memphis. A year later, they played at Vanderbilt's on-campus stadium in Nashville.

McNair's developmental timeline was not affected. Reese and Fisher believed he was ready to start after two years on the bench. They traded Chandler. Beginning in 1997, McNair was the starter for a team known as the Tennessee Oilers. The front office was excited. Black quarterbacks had long faced vague, unsubstantiated doubts about their ability to think, lead, or win close games. Fisher believed McNair would put that nonsense to bed forever. "If you were going to put together a list of all the things you can't coach—poise, ability to lead, competitiveness, responsibility—Steve has them all," Fisher said later.[23]

In the season opener in 1997, he rallied the Oilers to an overtime victory over the Los Angeles Raiders at the Liberty Bowl. A four-game losing streak followed, but then McNair began to settle in. He threw three touchdown passes in a win over the Bengals. He rushed for seventy yards and threw two touchdown passes in a win over the Cardinals. The Oilers finished the season with an 8–8 record.

They went 8–8 again in 1998 as Reese and Fisher continued to assemble the physical, hard-hitting team they had sought to build. They had a strong defense and a run-based offense built around Eddie George, an All-Pro back. The passing game went in and out as a priority. McNair completed just nine passes in one game and attempted forty-nine in another. When defenders swarmed him in the pocket, he met them head-on, gladly absorbing punishment if it meant moving the ball forward. His bruises added up, but he did not miss a start.

The new stadium in Nashville opened in 1999. The team now known as the Tennessee Titans was ready to launch. McNair passed for 341 yards and three touchdowns in the season opener against the Bengals, yet the fans booed him after he fumbled late to set up a field goal that gave the Bengals the lead. Booed again when he returned to the field for a last-chance possession, he coolly led the offense on a drive that produced a game-winning field goal.

Five days later, he ruptured a disc in his back in practice. The disc lodged against his spinal cord, producing pain so intense that he had no choice but to undergo surgery. His doctors said he would miss at least two months, possibly more, but he missed just five games. His backup, veteran Neil O'Donnell, helped the Titans win four.

McNair's return, coming earlier than expected, was dramatic. In his first game back, he threw two touchdown passes and ran for a touchdown in the first quarter. The Titans, who had a 5–1 record, were hosting the St. Louis Rams, who had a 6–0 record. McNair's early flurry stunned the Rams, who later rallied, but Tennessee held on to win, 24–21.

After the game, McNair's teammates and the Titans' coaches praised the quarterback's toughness. "I watched one of the great competitors of all time do whatever it took to stay on the field," Fisher said later.[24]

A week later, though, McNair fell flat in a prime-time game in Miami; he threw three interceptions in a loss. The up-and-down nature of his play indicated that he was still not that polished and efficient in his fifth NFL season.

But no quarterback was tougher. "Halfway through the season," Fisher said later, "someone asked me, 'Do you think Steve McNair is a top ten quarterback?' I said, 'I don't know, but I do know he's a top three football player.' That's what Steve brought early on, was the ability to play football. Years later, he polished up the ability to play quarterback."[25]

The loss in Miami was the first of six straight games in which he did not throw a touchdown pass and averaged fewer than two hundred passing yards per game. But he rushed for five touchdowns in those games and the Titans won enough to build one of the AFC's best records. Although the Jacksonville Jaguars nosed them out for the AFC Central title, they earned a wild card ticket to the playoffs.

Their opening round game, at home against the Buffalo Bills, was not McNair's finest hour. He threw for just seventy-six yards. He did rush for a touchdown, helping the Titans take a twelve-point lead at halftime, but the Bills rallied and appeared to win on a field goal that gave them a 16–15 lead with sixteen seconds left.

One of the most famous plays in NFL history saved the Titans. They had practiced a "gadget" kickoff return in which the ball carrier headed in one direction, stopped, and lateraled the ball across the field to another runner. The goal was to catch the coverage team overcommitting to the original runner, leaving the receiver of the lateral with an open field to run through.

The Titans called the play "Homerun Throwback." It worked perfectly against the Bills. Lorenzo Neal, a fullback for the Titans, caught the kickoff and handed the ball to Frank Wycheck, a tight end. Wycheck headed to his right, drawing the coverage, then stopped and tossed the ball across the field to Kevin Dyson, a receiver. The field was clear in front of him and he sprinted seventy-five yards to a touchdown that won the game.

After being saved by what became known as "The Music City Miracle," the Titans played like they knew fate was on their side. They beat the Colts in Indianapolis and routed the Jaguars in Jacksonville in the AFC championship game.

McNair passed for only 112 yards against the Colts but directed five scoring drives. Against the Jaguars, playing with a sore toe, he again passed for just 112 yards, but rushed for ninety-one and two touchdowns as the Titans blew out their rivals and advanced to a Super Bowl date with the Rams.

The quarterback matchup for Super Bowl 34 on January 30, 2000, was arguably the most improbable in the game's history. McNair was just the game's second Black starter, a dozen years after Doug Williams became the first. And though any Black quarterback in the NFL was an underdog, the Rams' white quarterback, Kurt Warner, had beaten even longer odds to reach this pinnacle.

A decade earlier, Warner, now twenty-eight, had received little interest from Division I programs when he was coming out of high school in Cedar Rapids, Iowa. He landed at Northern Iowa and posted big passing numbers, but no NFL team drafted him in 1994 and the Packers quickly cut him after a training camp tryout. Warner took a job stocking shelves at a supermarket. Still believing he could make it in the NFL, he played so well in an indoor league that the Rams signed him to a tryout deal. He became their backup in 1998 and starter in 1999 by showing off a potent arm and cool pocket presence.

Utilizing the Rams' other star playmakers, including running back Marshall Faulk and receivers Isaac Bruce and Torry Holt, Warner blew away the NFL during the 1999 regular season. He had the highest completion percentage in the league, the most touchdown passes, and the highest quarterback rating. McNair had entered the league with a higher profile as the third overall pick in his draft, but in 1999, McNair threw twelve touchdown passes and Warner threw forty-one.

Inevitably, the comparison prompted criticism that McNair was not living up to his high draft status, even though the Titans had made it to the Super Bowl. Never mind that Fisher wanted McNair handing off more than throwing. "We do have a very conservative offense," McNair said. "It's all about running the ball first, and we'll pass if we have to."[26]

McNair's teammates bristled at any harsh commentary directed at their quarterback. "He's heard a lot of criticism, that he can't do this or that," Eddie George said. "But we're going to a Super Bowl because of the things he does. Steve is a warrior."[27]

The Rams, favored by a touchdown, dominated early, taking a 9–0 lead at halftime. Then Warner completed passes of thirty-one and sixteen yards on a drive that produced a touchdown and a 16–0 lead for the Rams midway through the third quarter.

To that point, the game had only been a source of frustration for McNair. But his innate competitiveness emerged. He completed three passes and gained twenty-three yards on a scramble to highlight a touchdown drive. A two-point conversion attempt failed, but after Tennessee's defense forced a three-and-out, McNair led his offense on a methodical drive early in the fourth quarter. He completed a pass to convert a third down into a first. On fourth-and-2 at midfield, he ran for a first down. The Titans' offense boiled down to basics. Either George or McNair ran with the ball or McNair threw it. The Rams knew it but could not stop the drive. Twice, McNair hit receivers for twenty-one-yard gains, setting up a short touchdown run by George.

After the extra point, the Titans trailed by just three points, and when their defense quickly forced another punt, the crowd in Atlanta's Georgia Dome roared. McNair, with help from George, had taken over the game. He ran for eleven yards, completed a pass for six. The ball reached the Rams' 25 yard line, putting the Titans in position to take the lead. When the Rams' defense finally made a stop, the Titans' kicker tied the score at 16–16 with a field goal.

With the crowd imploring Tennessee's defense to make another stop, the Rams' offense took the field. On first down, Warner dropped back and saw Bruce open down the right sideline. His pass was on target and Bruce reeled in the ball, shook off a tackler, and sprinted to the end zone to complete a seventy-three-yard touchdown play.

It seemed the Rams had delivered a knockout blow. The clock showed less than two minutes to play. The Titans needed a touchdown to tie the score, and a holding penalty on the kickoff meant they would start the possession at their 12 yard line. McNair had to drive the offense eighty-eight yards. He completed a pass for nine yards, another for seven, then picked up twelve on a scramble, and when a defender grabbed his face mask, the ball moved fifteen more yards in the right direction. The noise in the dome was shattering. McNair had something going.

With twenty-two seconds remaining and the ball at the Rams' 26, he took the snap in the shotgun and looked downfield. He paused, finding no receivers open, and defenders closed on him for a sack that would all but settle the game. But he eluded their grasp, spun, sprinted to his right, and fired a pass for Dyson, who grabbed it at the 10. Fisher called a time-out. McNair's great escape gave them one final chance. There were five seconds left.

"Probably the final play of the game . . . in regulation," announcer Al Michaels said on the broadcast.[28]

It was no time for indecision. Lined up in the shotgun, McNair took the snap, briefly scanned the field, and saw Dyson break open over the middle on a slant pattern. Dyson grabbed the pass at the five and angled toward the end zone, holding the ball in his right hand in hopes of getting it to the goal line. He only had one defender to beat, but that defender, Mike Jones, brought him to the ground with a text-book tackle.

The ball, in Dyson's outstretched right hand, wound up one yard short of the goal line.

Needing eighty-eight yards, McNair had picked up eighty-seven.

The game was over.

Warner, the winning quarterback, was selected MVP, but McNair had earned the respect of the football world and demolished the tired criticism about Black quarterbacks lacking leadership and toughness and wilting in the clutch. Talent evaluators at all levels had underval-ued them for decades by using those and other disparagements, many times without basis. The best, perhaps only, way for Black quarter-backs to prove those evaluators wrong was by dazzling on the most public stages, in the most dramatic ways, and McNair had done that. Even in defeat, his gallant effort sent the message that he was a quar-terback you could trust. All Black quarterbacks would profit from the damage he had done to the notion of inevitable white superiority at football's most important position.

No one received the message about McNair more clearly than Warner. McNair's dramatic performance "just spoke to how he was as a player and how he was as a leader for that team," Warner said years later.[29]

Destined for the Pro Football Hall of Fame and a subsequent career as an NFL broadcaster and analyst, Warner would recall his Super Bowl opponent as a great quarterback, period, not as a Black quarterback who happened to be great.

"Steve was an incredible competitor, and he really was ahead of the game with how he played," Warner said. "He was a great in-pocket passer, with the unique ability to make plays with his feet and arm outside that pocket, kind of like Aaron Rodgers. I don't think we've seen a lot of guys that have been as talented both in the pocket and outside the pocket. And what he did in that game, and on that final drive, it's what Steve McNair was all about."[30]

CHAPTER 19

For sixty-two years, from when pro football teams first began drafting college talent in 1936 through 1998, only five Black quarterbacks were selected with first-round picks. No matter what happened on the field in the fall, the draft was an annual reminder that discriminatory thinking, whether conscious or unconscious, significantly influenced who played quarterback in the NFL.

That was what made the 1999 draft so stunning. Out of nowhere, Black quarterback prospects suddenly were sought after. On a Saturday afternoon in April at Madison Square Garden in New York, almost as many were taken in the first round as had been taken in the prior sixty-two drafts combined. The Philadelphia Eagles took Syracuse's Donovan McNabb with the second overall pick. The Cincinnati Bengals took Oregon's Akili Smith third overall. The Minnesota Vikings took Central Florida's Daunte Culpepper eleventh overall.

To that point, Black quarterbacks had settled for making just occasional, and mostly modest, gains after pro teams allowed a door of opportunity to creak open ever so slightly. But three of the first eleven picks in a single draft was a lot more than a modest gain. It indicated "the NFL was looking at things with more of an open mind," Doug Williams said, sending the clearest signal yet that the noxious opinion in the league about Blacks not being intelligent enough to play quarterback finally was being widely seen for precisely what it was—racist nonsense.[1] "What Doug Williams did in the Super Bowl was a breakthrough. The 1999 draft was on par with that," agent Leigh Steinberg said.[2]

For so long, the holes in the resumes of Black quarterbacks had set their draft stock; no matter what they accomplished in college, their prospects plummeted if they had not faced the toughest opponents, did not exhibit the strongest throwing arm, or were not that fast. "Basically, you had to be perfect," James Harris said.[3]

But McNabb, Smith, and Culpepper all went high despite questions talent evaluators had about them. McNabb had run an option-style offense in college; could he operate a pro-style offense? Smith had only made eleven starts in college; was he experienced enough? Culpepper had not played against top competition; was he ready for the NFL? Such questions would have ended the pro careers of many Black quarterbacks before them. But this time, McNabb's, Smith's, and Culpepper's positive attributes outweighed any doubts.

Also finally ebbing, it seemed, was the quiet hypothesis about white owners not wanting to make Black quarterbacks the face of their franchises. When a team drafted a quarterback as high as McNabb, Smith, and Culpepper went, it was clear the team expected that quarterback to become the team's most prominent player, hopefully sooner rather than later. McNabb, Smith, and Culpepper all attended the draft in New York, and when their names were called, they all smiled and walked to the podium, hugged the commissioner, and donned the caps of the team that had selected them. White fans paid no mind, but to Black fans, the symbolism was powerful—at last, Black quarterbacks were being swept into the NFL's resolutely white power structure.

———

The 1999 draft did not come completely out of nowhere. During the decade leading up to it, the NFL had slowly become a better place for Black quarterbacks.

Most significantly, the style of play at their position underwent a revolution of sorts, or at least, the start of one. It became more acceptable for NFL quarterbacks to leave the pocket and use their legs to frustrate defenses and move the ball—a skill many Black quarterbacks possessed.

Eldridge Dickey's prospects had suffered in the late 1960s and 1970s because he *could* escape the pocket and run for gains. The Oakland Raiders wanted him playing their way—dropping straight back and staying in the pocket until the ball was airborne. And the Raiders were not unique; every team wanted quarterbacks who played that way. "It was a game of pocket passers," Ron Wolf, then a scout for the Raiders, said later.[4]

Dickey's mobility actually was a detriment. "Those of us in those [personnel] positions at that time, we had to learn that there was value in someone at the quarterback position being able to move," Wolf said. "As it evolved, we had to educate ourselves on the advantages of having a mobile quarterback."[5]

Inevitably, since the quarterback position in the NFL was still overwhelmingly white in the 1980s and early 1990s, it took white quarterbacks illustrating the advantages of mobility for teams to wake up to the idea—and for Black quarterbacks to begin to benefit. The San Francisco 49ers' Steve Young and the Denver Broncos' John Elway led the way. "They play the position more like the stereotypical black quarterback, and they've been successful and won," Tony Dungy said in the late 1990s. "They've won with athletic ability. They've won with mobility. They've won with creativity. They've become what the NFL looks for in a quarterback. We've said it's all right to be in that mode now, where it's even looked at as a positive if you can move around and make someone miss and still throw the ball 70 yards up the field on the run."[6]

Young was a twenty-seven-year-old backup in San Francisco when he signaled the change was coming by producing one of the most dazzling plays by a quarterback in NFL history—with his legs, not his arm. No one knew at the time, but it was a forerunner of the future at his position.

The 49ers were playing at home and seeking revenge against the Minnesota Vikings, who had upset them in the playoffs the year before. Having recently won two Super Bowls with Joe Montana as their quarterback, they were a powerhouse that took their rare disappointments personally. But the Vikings were on the verge of frustrating them again on October 30, 1988, leading, 21–17, late in the fourth quarter.

With Montana sidelined by an injury, it was up to Young to save the game. The 49ers had the ball at the Minnesota 49 yard line. On a third down, needing two yards for a first, Young took the snap, dropped back, and scanned the field. His receivers were covered. Minnesota's pass rush closed in, seemingly leaving him no avenue of escape. But Young ducked his head, spun out of the pocket, and began to run.

Standing just over six feet tall, Young had been an effective runner since his days as a high school star in Greenwich, Connecticut. Recruited by college programs that favored option offenses, he ended up at BYU, which favored a prolific passing offense. The fact that he was Mormon influenced his choice, and also, eventually, his game. Young developed his arm strength and accuracy and became a dangerous passer. But he could still run.

Expected to go first overall in the 1984 NFL draft, he was lured to the USFL by a huge contract with the Los Angeles Express. He exhibited his dual-threat talents—in one game, he passed for more than three hundred yards and rushed for more than one hundred yards, a feat no NFL quarterback had ever achieved. When the USFL folded, he joined the Tampa Bay Bucs in a supplemental draft and immediately became their starter in 1985. But they were among the league's worst teams, and they traded Young to the 49ers after two losing seasons.

Young seemed fated to have a disappointing pro career; the 49ers wanted him to back up Montana, the NFL's preeminent quarterback, who was winning titles with the pass-centric "West Coast" offense favored by Bill Walsh, the 49ers' head coach. But Montana never could run like Young did when he broke out of the pocket near midfield against the Vikings that day in 1988.

As he began to make his way downfield, weaving back and forth across the grass, five Vikings had clear shots at him. Joey Browner and Jesse Solomon missed him at midfield. Carl Lee missed him at the 40. Browner missed him again. Near the 30, Young stiff-armed Solomon.

In the press box, the 49ers' radio broadcaster, Lon Simmons, growled a classic play-by-play call: "Young back to throw. In trouble. He's going to be sacked. No! He gets away. He runs. Gets away again! Goes to the 40. Gets away again. To the 35! Cuts back to the 30!"[7]

The crowd was standing and screaming. Shaking off a final would-be tackler, Young broke into the clear at the 15, stumbled, staggered, and fell across the goal line.

"To the 15! To the 10! Young is exhausted! He dives! Touchdown 49ers!" Simmons shouted.

His run won the game and began a push by the 49ers that ended with them winning their third Super Bowl with Montana. Young's epic play was an unforgettable turning point. Fans of the NFL had never seen a quarterback make a mad dash halfway across the field, shedding tackles and eluding defenders.

It was just one play, but to any scouts, coaches, or general managers clinging to the notion about quarterbacks needing to stay in the pocket, it was an eye-opener. A quarterback's ability to move had turned a broken play into a game-winner. Maybe, just maybe, that was a skill worth pursuing.

———

Young became the 49ers' full-time starter at age thirty, in 1991, when Montana sat out the entire season with an injury. Young earned a triple-figure quarterback rating, indicative of superior passing. Two years later, after Montana was traded to the Kansas City Chiefs, Young ranked among the league leaders in passing and finished second on the team in rushing.

He was not the only mobile quarterback in the league. Randall Cunningham had been using his legs for nearly a decade by 1994. Elway, by then a decade into his career with the Denver Broncos, was known for his arm and daring, but also for his quick feet and knack for knowing when to scramble.

Cunningham's postseason struggles—he only had one playoff win—could be wielded by critics doubting mobile quarterbacks. But Elway had taken the Broncos to three Super Bowls by 1994. And that year, at age thirty-three, Young forever quashed the doubts about quarterbacks who could run as well as throw. He completed 70 percent of his passes, threw for thirty-five touchdowns, and rushed for nearly five hundred yards. The 49ers rolled through the regular season and playoffs and routed the San Diego Chargers in the Super Bowl, where Young threw six touchdown passes and bedeviled the defense with his agility.

It was official: the mobile quarterback had been mainstreamed in the NFL. Not coincidentally, Black players at the position finally began to receive more opportunities. Jeff Blake emerged in Cincinnati in 1994. A year later, the Houston Oilers used the draft's third overall pick to take Steve McNair, who could run over defenders as well as dodge them, and the Pittsburgh Steelers drafted Colorado's Kordell Stewart in the second round.

Stewart was easily as dangerous running with the ball as throwing it. He had run the forty-yard dash in 4.4 seconds at the combine. But his arm also stood out. He was best known in college for having heaved a sixty-four-yard "Hail Mary" pass to beat Michigan.

Stewart's early career in Pittsburgh reflected improving conditions for Black quarterbacks. The Steelers had drafted him even though they already had Neil O'Donnell and Mike Tomczak, two veteran (and white) quarterbacks. "A lot of teams had talked to him before the draft about switching positions. It was a lot like what Warren [Moon] faced, and Kordell had the same response: 'I'm a quarterback,'" said Leigh Steinberg, who represented Stewart.[8] But unlike Moon, Stewart still was drafted high and achieved his dream of being an NFL starting quarterback relatively quickly.

He was on the bench at the outset of his rookie season in 1995, but midway through the season, the Steelers' head coach, Bill Cowher, could no longer stand having a player so talented on the sideline. Stewart grudgingly agreed to try different positions. "I'll play whatever position they want me to play," he said.[9] The coaches devised a package of plays in which he ran with the ball, caught passes, and threw passes. He immediately began causing problems for opposing defenses. By the end of the season, he had run for a touchdown, caught a touchdown pass, thrown a touchdown pass, and earned the nickname "Slash," as in quarterback, slash, receiver, slash, running back.

With O'Donnell at quarterback, Jerome Bettis at fullback, and Stewart in a unique role, the Steelers won their division and made it to the Super Bowl; Stewart caught a touchdown pass in the AFC championship game.

The football world was enthralled. "He's bubbly, he's enthusiastic, he's bright-eyed. I think anyone who spends any time with Kordell will walk away thinking, 'Isn't it refreshing to see a player like that in the NFL?'" Cowher said.[10]

But behind Stewart's smiling demeanor was an athlete who had not given up on his goal. "I'm convinced I can play quarterback in this league," he said, "but I also know it's not my time. It's a tough thing to come into this league and play quarterback right away."[11]

As excited as he was to be "Slash," he believed the role had roots in the discrimination Black quarterbacks faced in the NFL. "I just don't know why a quarterback has to be 6'8" and 230 pounds, with blond hair and blue eyes," he said late in his rookie season. "A team will invest in someone like that and say that he's going to be its quarterback six years down the road. But why can't a team do that with a guy who is 6'1" and Black? People still think a Black guy isn't going to be a smart quarterback, and that's BS."[12]

In the end, even though he was contributing on a winning team, Stewart was not satisfied. "People have said to me, 'Once they move you to wide receiver, they won't let you play quarterback again.' Well, I will do all I can to play quarterback again," he said.[13]

He would have to wait another year, but Cowher saw enough potential to make him the Steelers' starting quarterback in 1997. It was the right move at the right time. In his third season, Stewart was comfortable reading defenses and trusting his talent. One week, he passed for three touchdowns and ran for two as the Steelers overcame a twenty-one-point deficit to beat the Ravens. By the end of the season, he had passed for more than three thousand yards, rushed for nearly five hundred, and helped the Steelers win a division title. It was the start of a six-year run in which he proved himself as a conventional and successful NFL quarterback, winning forty-six of seventy-five starts.

One year after the Steelers drafted Stewart, the St. Louis Rams also drafted a Black quarterback, Michigan State's Tony Banks, with a second-round pick. Although Banks was more of a classic pocket passer at six feet four with a powerful right arm, he nimbly avoided blitzes. The start of his pro career also reflected the widening door of opportunity for Black quarterbacks in the 1990s. His predecessors would have relished the near-immediate chance to start and the relatively long leash the Rams gave him.

The Rams had moved from Los Angeles in 1995, the year before they drafted Banks, and they wanted to start fresh; they posted their sixth straight losing season when they went 7–9 in their first year in St. Louis. Heading into the 1996 draft, they zeroed in on Banks because of his size, arm, and intelligence. He was the first quarterback selected that year, and by the fourth game of his rookie season, he was starting.

He received an extended opportunity, starting the final thirteen games of his rookie season, all sixteen games as a second-year player, and the first fourteen games of his third season—forty-three straight games. Only a knee injury knocked him out of the lineup. He made a lot of mistakes, throwing forty-two interceptions and fumbling forty-six times in those forty-three starts. He also was sacked 142 times as the Rams won just six, five, and four games in those seasons. But they still believed in him. In 1997, the Rams had two chances to draft Jake Plummer, a star white quarterback from Arizona State. They passed twice.

Banks became so confident in the team's faith that he took advantage of it. Instead of focusing on honing his craft, he brought a rottweiler puppy to training camp in 1997. The puppy's name was Felony, part of Banks's full-on embrace of the "thug" prototype emanating from the hip-hop culture he had grown up with in California. His earrings, tattoos, and bandanna were, at least partly, a response to the segregated environment he had encountered in St. Louis, which shocked the young California native. "It might not have been the ideal city for a Black quarterback back then," Banks said later. "I had never really seen a city like that at the time, a city so separated."[14]

He took his response too far, he admitted later. He did not fly home with his teammates after one road loss and did not come to the team's practice facility the next day. "Not what a starting quarterback should be doing," he said later.[15]

Still, the Rams' faith endured.

"I think I had the best arm, by far, during my era of playing," Banks said later. "I feel that, deep down in my soul, that's the reason that I was given so many opportunities, because I had that 'wild' factor with my arm. I just don't know if I had the 'wild' factor with my preparation."[16]

During the 1998 season, Stewart, Banks, and McNair all were starters, as was Charlie Batch, a rookie Black quarterback for the Detroit Lions, and Warren Moon, now with the Seattle Seahawks. Randall Cunningham, now with the Vikings, gave one of his finest performances that season at age thirty-five. Nearly a decade after *Sports Illustrated* anointed him "the ultimate weapon," he threw thirty-four touchdown passes for a team that lost just one regular-season game.

The NFL's surging use of Black quarterbacks in 1998 was, in effect, a prelude to the 1999 draft. Even more were selected after McNabb, Smith, and Culpepper went so high in the first round. The Tampa Bay Bucs took Tulane's Shaun King in the second round. The Green Bay Packers took Virginia's Aaron Brooks in the fourth round. The New England Patriots took Kansas State's Michael Bishop in the seventh round.

The six Black quarterbacks drafted in 1999 would form the heart of a transformative generation. Five years before they were drafted, only four Black quarterbacks had started games during the 1994 season. But during the 2000 season, as the 1999 draft class became established and moved into prominent roles, fourteen Black quarterbacks started games across the league. It was a massive spike.

The six Black quarterbacks drafted in 1999 would combine for more than fifty miles of passing yardage in the coming years and win nearly two hundred regular-season games and more than a dozen playoff games. Between them, they would make seven starts in conference championship games and one start in the Super Bowl.

Not all of them thrived. The doubts about Smith's lack of experience were founded, it turned out. He started just four games for the Bengals over four seasons. Bishop appeared in just one game before joining the CFL's Toronto Argonauts.

But the range of outcomes was, in itself, an indication that the latest generation of Black quarterbacks was entering a pro football world more open-minded than the one their predecessors inhabited. For so long, there were so few Black quarterbacks that the career of each one that received a chance was regarded as a referendum on *all* Black quarterbacks; they had to succeed or teams would become skeptical about taking a chance on another. Besides not being fair, this was blatantly discriminatory; the white quarterback population had long provided a wide range of career outcomes without the failures discouraging teams from drafting more white quarterbacks.

In the wake of the 1999 draft, Black quarterbacks were no longer tasked with proving the bona fides of every Black player at the position. They were accepted as more typical members of the NFL's overall playing population, and thus, subjected to the same career probabilities as players at all positions. Some were going to soar. Some were going to crash. It was unfair to expect anything else.

CHAPTER 20

Surrounded by family and friends, Shaun King sat in the living room of his parents' house in St. Petersburg, Florida, watching ESPN's coverage of the 1999 draft. Although he was not expected to go high in the first round—he would have been in New York if so—his draft stock had gone up after he led Tulane to an undefeated season as a senior, in the process setting an NCAA record for passing efficiency.

King was thrilled to see Donovan McNabb, Akili Smith, and Daunte Culpepper all get selected among the first eleven picks; clearly, whatever prejudice had denied Black quarterbacks in the draft before, it was not in effect this year.

Shortly after Culpepper was picked eleventh overall, the phone rang in King's house. He picked up the receiver and his mouth fell open. The caller identified himself as Tony Dungy, head coach of the Tampa Bay Bucs, who held the fifteenth overall pick. Was it possible King's hometown team was taking him *in the first round*?

King stammered a greeting, paused, and then broke up laughing. He had been pranked. A younger brother was on the line, pretending to be Dungy.

But a few hours later, it happened again. The phone rang. King answered. The caller identified himself as Dungy, and this time, it was not a prank. The real Dungy was calling to say the Bucs were taking King in the second round.

After he hung up, grinning, King's family smothered him with hugs. They cheered so loudly they could be heard down the street. King was staying home to play in the NFL.

He knew the draft had seldom produced good outcomes for Black quarterbacks, and he was grateful to be among the unusually large group of players selected that milestone year. King's career was a study in the ways in which the underlying conditions for Black quarterbacks were shifting for the better.

On his journey to this moment, unlike so many Black quarterbacks before him, King had never been asked to switch positions due to a coach tacitly questioning whether he was intelligent enough to play quarterback. To the contrary, he played other positions at the youth level; his high school and college coaches were the ones who believed he belonged at quarterback. And it was not because he was physically dominant. He was just six feet tall and a little heavy at 225 pounds, which was why he had ended up at Tulane rather than Florida State or Florida after a stellar high school career in St. Petersburg.

King's best qualities as a quarterback were not physical. He was smart, clutch, confident, a leader—qualities that many NFL coaches and scouts had long doubted Black quarterbacks possessed. Tulane had gone 19–4 with King at quarterback in his last two seasons. When he was a senior, the team went 12–0 with King leading the way.

It was true he had not faced the highest caliber of opposition, but unlike many Black quarterbacks who preceded him, that had not dragged down his draft stock. The Bucs had believed in him enough to take him with the fiftieth overall pick.

It surely helped that Dungy, one of the NFL's few Black head coaches, saw a bit of himself in King. Dungy, too, had been a productive college quarterback but had gone undrafted after setting passing records at Minnesota in the 1970s; it still bothered him that NFL teams had only wanted him as a defensive back. Now, as a head coach, his job depended on him putting the best players on the field, regardless of skin color. But if he could promote the cause of Black quarterbacks *while* doing that, he surely would.

Dungy told King not to expect to play at first. The Bucs' starting quarterback, Trent Dilfer, was a former high first-round pick who had not missed a start in four years. Although he had not always met the expectations that came with being taken sixth overall, he was entrenched. The Bucs also had acquired a veteran backup, Eric Zeier.

King began his career as a third-stringer and did not take a snap in the first ten weeks of the 1999 season as the Bucs hovered around .500 amid increasing uncertainty and drama at quarterback. Several uninspiring performances by Dilfer convinced Dungy to bench him after seventy straight starts and go with Zeier. But Zeier immediately suffered a rib injury, and Dilfer became the starter again, to the fans' dismay. But the Bucs started to win.

In late November, Dilfer suffered a broken collarbone during a game in Seattle. Zeier was not healed, so Dungy put in King. It was his first time on an NFL field, and he struggled, but one of his few completions went for a touchdown that secured the win.

A week later, against the Vikings on Monday Night Football, Dungy started King instead of Zeier. Unfazed by the prospect of making his first pro start before a national audience in prime time, in the Bucs' home stadium, where he had attended games as a fan, King threw two touchdown passes, securing a Tampa Bay victory once again.

Impressed with his calm demeanor, his veteran teammates gave him a new nickname—Smoothie King. He more than lived up to it in his second start. Facing the Detroit Lions in Tampa, with first place in the NFC Central at stake, King was harassed for three quarters by one of the NFL's toughest defenses. But he did not succumb. "I thought we would get to him a bit more," the Lions' head coach, Bobby Ross, said later.

Trailing 16–9 early in the fourth quarter, King faced third-and-17 at his 28 yard line. He zipped a completion between four defenders for a thirty-yard gain and the Bucs went on to score a touchdown. After a turnover gave the Bucs the ball again, King hurled a touchdown pass that won the game and gave the Bucs control of the division race.

They had most recently won a division title with Doug Williams as their quarterback in 1981, and since had recorded just two winning seasons. Some fans attributed the long dry spell to the team's nasty divorce from Williams, who later became the first Black quarterback to win a Super Bowl. It qualified as poetic justice when King, another

Black quarterback, helped them secure a division title in 1999 with strong performances in the team's final two games.

"Shaun would never qualify for any quarterback beauty pageants," Rich McKay, the Bucs' general manager, said. "He's short, he's somewhat pudgy, he's not the fastest guy. He's a good athlete, but not a great one. But he's a winner. Whatever the 'it' is that makes a quarterback special, Shaun has it."[1]

On January 15, 2000, King started for the Bucs in a playoff game against the Redskins in Tampa. The three Black quarterbacks drafted so high in the first round the previous spring were reduced to watching him on television; two were on teams not in the playoffs and the other was a backup. King was the one in the spotlight. But he was in a challenging situation. A rookie starter had not won an NFL playoff game in twenty-three years.

The Redskins took advantage of his inexperience early. He completed just four of his first sixteen passes as the Bucs fell behind, 13–0, in the third quarter. Eight of their first nine offensive possessions ended with a punt; an interception ended the other. "I was just a little off," King said later. "They did a good job of giving me different looks. It took me a while to adjust."[2]

Dungy resisted making a change and eventually was rewarded. Late in the third quarter, King completed three passes on a seventy-three-yard touchdown drive. Then, after a turnover gave the Bucs the ball in Washington territory, he overcame two sacks and produced a game-winning touchdown.

The Redskins tipped their caps. "I saw an NFL quarterback out there. I didn't see a rookie," cornerback Darrell Green said.[3]

A week later, nine months removed from having been pranked by his brother during the draft, King started in the NFC championship game.

Facing the Rams in St. Louis, the Bucs were solid underdogs; the Rams had terrorized opponents during the season with an offense so potent it was nicknamed "the Greatest Show on Turf." But the Bucs were a dangerous opponent for them with their stout defense, led by tackle Warren Sapp and linebacker Derrick Brooks, and a straight-ahead running game led by fullback Mike Alstott. Their seemingly nerveless rookie quarterback completed the picture.

The Bucs immediately made it clear they would not go quietly when they intercepted the first pass thrown by Rams quarterback Kurt Warner. King moved the Bucs' offense inside the St. Louis 10 yard line before settling for a field goal.

The Rams kicked a field goal to tie the score and took the lead on a freakish play early in the second quarter. An errant snap sailed past King when he was lined up in the shotgun in his own territory. All he could do was retreat and dejectedly bat the ball out of the end zone, giving the Rams a safety and a 5–3 lead.

Early in the third quarter, King completed a thirty-yard pass to set up a short field goal. The Bucs now led, 6–5, and with their defense dominant, it seemed the baseball-like score might hold up until Warner finally delivered a big play, a thirty-yard touchdown pass with less than five minutes to play.

After the Rams' two-point conversion try failed, King and his offense began a possession at their 23, trailing by the strangest of scores, 11–6. To that point, the Rams' defense had intercepted King twice, sacked him three times, and kept him out of the end zone. But as Tampa fans knew, King was dangerous when a game was on the line.

Alstott rushed for gains of nine and eight yards. King passed for eight, four, and nine. After losing five yards on a sack, he completed a pass for twenty-two yards. The ball was on the Rams' 22 yard line with less than ninety seconds to play. King was positioned to strike. He was sacked on first down, losing thirteen yards, but seemed to make back most of the lost yardage on the next play when he hit one of his receivers, Bert Emanuel, for a twelve-yard gain on a crossing pattern.

The ball was at the 23. Dungy called a time-out. King fully believed he would finish the job. Since the start of his senior season at Tulane, he had won seventeen of eighteen games as a starting quarterback. (Twelve straight at Tulane and five of six with the Bucs.) His Tampa teammates had faith in him.

"Are you ready to go to the Super Bowl?" Dungy said to Emanuel during the time-out.

"I'm ready," Emanuel replied.[4]

But Dungy was stunned when the head referee informed him during the time-out that Emanuel's catch was being reviewed.

"What are you reviewing?" Dungy cried.[5]

Although Emanuel had clearly controlled the ball as he hit the ground, a tip of the ball hit the ground as he fell. The side judge had called it a catch. John Madden agreed on Fox's broadcast. "You can't take that one away," Madden said after watching a replay.[6] The Rams were not challenging the call. But under the rules of instant replay, a league official could initiate a challenge in the final two minutes.

It was determined the ground had helped Emanuel control the ball. The catch was overturned, the pass ruled incomplete, the ball moved back to the 35. King was in a tough spot now, facing third-and-23. After two incompletions, the Rams began to celebrate.

Saying he was "flabbergasted" by the pivotal replay decision, Dungy complained to the league the next day. "This has been a catch for one hundred years and it will always be a catch," he said.[7] The league agreed. That off-season, the rules of what constituted a catch were altered. If a tip of the ball hit the ground but the receiver had full control, it was a catch. This clause became known as the "Bert Emanuel Rule."

Bizarre events had stopped King's rookie season just short of the Super Bowl, preventing a historic matchup. On the day the Rams beat the Bucs, the Tennessee Titans, with Steve McNair at quarterback, scored an easy win over the Jacksonville Jaguars in the AFC championship game. If not for just a few plays that went against King and the Bucs, the Super Bowl could have matched two Black quarterbacks.

———

When Daunte Culpepper joined the Vikings in 1999, their head coach, offensive coordinator, quarterbacks coach, and starting quarterback all were Black—a rare example of legitimate inclusion in a league where most decisions were made by white coaches, white personnel executives, and white owners. It did not guarantee Culpepper success, but never had a Black quarterback started his pro career so clearly understanding that he would not be subjected to racial stereotyping. "I'm lucky enough never to have faced that kind of an issue. But I'm aware of what went on in history," he said as a rookie.[8]

The Vikings also were an opportune landing spot because of their powerful offense. Their head coach, Denny Green, had taken them to the playoffs six times in his seven years on the job, and his offensive system was a key to their success. It was based on having a fast running back, fast receivers, and a quarterback with the arm to make it all work. Green's Vikings had gone to the playoffs with Warren Moon and also with Randall Cunningham. The year before Culpepper was drafted, they had overwhelmed opponents with Cunningham throwing to Cris Carter and Randy Moss, a dangerous pair of wide receivers.

Drafted to replace Cunningham eventually, Culpepper served the briefest of apprenticeships; he had the starting job a year later when Cunningham tailed off at age thirty-six. As a second-year pro and first-year starter in 2000, Culpepper started flinging passes to Carter and Moss. He was an immediate sensation, winning his first seven starts, leading the league in touchdown passes, making the Pro Bowl, and helping the Vikings win a division title.

Aside from having great receivers to throw to and coaches who believed in him, he did not feel the burden of having to represent all Black quarterbacks as they sought to gain widespread acceptance. "The age has changed," Culpepper said. "People are looking at the position as just a quarterback. You're not called a Black quarterback anymore. You're just a quarterback."[9]

He was already familiar with good fortune; it had altered the course of his life. His biological mother, a troubled teenager named Barbara Henderson, had delivered him in a jail cell in Ocala, Florida; she was incarcerated for armed robbery. It was no way to start a life, but an employee at the jail, Emma Culpepper, adopted the infant, diverting Daunte from a path strewn with uncertainty. "It was the best thing that happened to me in my whole life," Culpepper said. "If not for her, I don't know where I'd be."[10]

Aunt Dolly, as he called her, qualified as an angel on earth. She raised fifteen children, none of whom were hers biologically. Four were adopted. Eleven came from family members. Daunte was the youngest, adopted the year Emma's husband died. "I never really had a man in my life. She was my mother and my father," Culpepper said.[11]

While Aunt Dolly gave him a loving home, his biological mother gave him the bones and blood for sports, especially football; her brother, Thomas Henderson, had been a star linebacker for the Dallas Cowboys.

At Ocala's Vanguard High School, Culpepper had started out as a wide receiver, but the coaches' view of him changed after a long pass intended for him in practice fell to the ground. Culpepper picked up the ball and fired a sixty-yard spiral back to the coaches. Pretty soon, he was playing quarterback. Tall and broad-chested, he had a powerful arm, nimble feet, and a knack for making big plays. Facing fourth-and-20 late in a tightly contested state championship game, he ran for a first down to set up a potential game-winning field goal attempt, only to watch the kicker miss it.

Florida's powerhouse college programs recruited him until his spotty academic record cooled their interest. He landed at Central Florida, at the time barely more than a decade removed from membership in the NCAA's non-scholarship Division III. Culpepper showed off a powerful arm and put up huge statistics as pro scouts locked onto him as a prospect; even though he was not facing premier opposition, he was built like a linebacker, threw like Dan Marino, and ran like Steve McNair.

By the start of the 2000 playoffs, it appeared Minnesota would receive a grand reward for having overlooked the caliber of Culpepper's college opposition in favor of his surpassing talent; the Vikings had serious Super Bowl aspirations, and their young quarterback was one of the primary reasons.

The field for the 2000 NFC playoffs provided another clear indication that the landscape for Black quarterbacks was changing in the NFL. Minnesota had won a division title with Culpepper. The Bucs also had won a division title, their second straight with King. The

Eagles had earned a wild card berth with McNabb starting every game. Aaron Brooks had led the Saints to a division title after becoming their starter in November; originally drafted by the Packers, he had joined the Saints in a trade before the season.

The Vikings received a first-round bye and hosted New Orleans in a second-round game. Before the 2000 season, the Saints had never won a playoff game—quite a record of futility considering their history dated to 1967—and also had never started a Black quarterback in a game. By the time they faced the Vikings in the playoffs, they had checked off those boxes.

The Saints had signed Jeff Blake in free agency during the off-season, thinking he would become their starter. Blake had made history as the first Black quarterback to start a game for the Bengals in 1994, and now, six years later, at age thirty, he became the first Black quarterback to start for the Saints when he took the field against the Lions on September 3, 2000. The Saints lost that day and soon had a 1–3 record as their fans grumpily settled in for another long season. But this was not a typical year. Supported by a star running back, Ricky Williams, a Pro Bowl–caliber receiver named Joe Horn, and a solid defense, Blake started winning games. By mid-November, the Saints had one of the NFL's best records.

The good vibe was interrupted by a November loss to the Raiders in which Blake suffered a fractured ankle, ending his season. Suddenly, it was up to his backup, Brooks, to keep the Saints in the playoff hunt. "I was like, 'Wow this is my moment,'" Brooks said.[12]

Brooks had grown up in public housing in Newport News, Virginia, avoiding trouble as drugs overtook his neighborhood. With a level-headed nature and superior athletic talent, he became the starting quarterback at the University of Virginia, and in 1999, an NFL draft pick.

Later, he would express pride about having helped integrate the quarterback position for the Saints. At the time, though, he did not even know Blake was the first Black quarterback to start for the team. "I was just trying to take advantage of the situation," Brooks said.[13]

Though he had long legs that helped him scramble for gains, Brooks was a pocket passer at heart; he preferred to drop straight back and use his arm to move the ball. When asked why, he replied, "Because I can throw the ball. You ain't seen my arm?"[14]

He was an instant sensation once he became a starter, averaging nearly three hundred passing yards per game as the Saints won enough to beat out the Rams—the defending Super Bowl champions—in the NFC West title race.

Their performance set up a dramatic first-round playoff matchup: the Saints against the Rams at the Superdome in New Orleans. The smart money was on the Rams. The Saints had never won in the play-offs. Ricky Williams was out with an injury, adding to the pressure on Brooks. It was hard to envision him matching touchdown passes with Kurt Warner, the Rams' quarterback, a Super Bowl MVP.

A shrieking crowd filled the dome, hopeful of seeing the Saints overcome their playoff troubles. But the early minutes of the game only made the fans more nervous. Warner threw a touchdown pass. Joe Horn went out with an injury. It all seemed so familiar.

Undaunted, Brooks led two scoring drives and the Saints led at halftime, 10–7. Then Brooks threw three touchdown passes to the same receiver, Willie Jackson, in a fifteen-minute span. The Saints led 31–7, and the fans began to celebrate.

It almost proved premature. Warner rallied the Rams with a flurry of completions. Suddenly, the score was 31–28, and when the Rams' defense forced a punt, the Saints' collapse was nearly complete. But the Rams' Az-Zahir Hakim fumbled the punt, returning possession to the Saints, who ran out the clock. "One of the greatest victories I've ever been a part of," Brooks said.[15]

A week later, before the Saints and Vikings played in Minneapolis, Brooks and Culpepper crossed paths during warm-ups. They shook hands and embraced. Before that postseason, two Black starting quarterbacks had never faced each other in a playoff game.

Their teams were in different places. The Saints' season was already made; they were thrilled just to be in the final eight of the NFL playoff field. The Vikings sought grander rewards. They had won a lot of games under Denny Green but always experienced disappointment in the playoffs. They hoped that having a dynamic young quarterback would change their fortunes.

Culpepper immediately proved he was ready for the moment. On the Vikings' third offensive snap, he spotted Moss open far downfield and launched a pass that hit him in stride for a 53-yard touchdown.

Seeking a strong response, Brooks led his offense downfield, either throwing or running the ball himself on all but two snaps of a ten-play drive. It produced a field goal. The Saints hoped a close, back-and-forth game would evolve, but Culpepper was too much for them. He completed a pass to his running back, Robert Smith, for twenty yards, and another to Cris Carter for thirty-four yards. The drive stalled near the goal line, forcing the Vikings to kick a field goal, but Culpepper directed another drive near the end of the first half. He scrambled for a thirty-yard gain and hit Carter on a seventeen-yard touchdown pass.

On the third play of the second half, Culpepper hit Moss for a sixty-eight-yard touchdown that put the Vikings up 24–3. Brooks did what he could to rally the Saints, scrambling and throwing through the rest of the second half, but the Vikings had the game in hand.

Culpepper and Brooks congratulated each other on the field after the Vikings' 34–16 victory. Although Brooks had thrown two interceptions and not moved the ball as steadily, he had posted impressive numbers. La'Roi Glover, a defensive tackle for the Saints, suggested Culpepper "was the difference" in the game.[16] Culpepper's teammate, Robert Smith, agreed. "He looked fantastic making big plays and making smart plays," Smith said.[17]

Media accounts of the game did not mention that the quarterbacks who had combined for 597 passing yards and five touchdown passes were both young and Black.

The victory advanced the Vikings to the NFC championship game. They would play the Giants in New York, a tough assignment. The Giants had finished the regular season with five straight wins to earn the NFC's top playoff seed and then had beaten the Eagles to reach the championship game. Their quarterback, Kerry Collins, was not as exciting as Culpepper, but he was an effective veteran.

Confident going in, the Vikings were surprised when the Giants, a run-oriented team, came out passing. On their first possession, Collins tossed two completions for first downs and hit Ike Hilliard for a forty-six-yard touchdown. On the ensuing kickoff, the ball bounced between two Vikings, who scrambled to cover it. Culpepper raced onto the field, fully expecting to start heaving passes. But when the pile of players who had dived for the loose ball was untangled, a New York player was cradling it.

The turnover gave the Giants the ball at the Minnesota 18 yard line. On first down, Collins fired his second touchdown pass of a game that was barely two minutes old. The Vikings were down, 14–0, and they never recovered. Collins continued to shred their defense, and when Minnesota had the ball, New York's defense blanketed Culpepper's receivers and confounded him with new alignments. By early in the second quarter, the Giants led, 24–0. It was 34–0 at halftime and 41–0 when the final gun sounded.

In a truly nightmarish performance, Culpepper completed just thirteen of twenty-eight passes for seventy-eight yards, with three interceptions. "Definitely embarrassing," Culpepper said. "I can't even put it into words."[18]

He tried to find solace. "They say what doesn't kill you makes you stronger and I'm a firm believer in that," he said.[19]

But the monumental defeat generated strong aftershocks, impacting all involved. The Vikings collapsed the next season. Head coach Denny Green was fired. Culpepper would continue to play in the NFL for nearly another decade, but he only won one more playoff game and never made it to the Super Bowl.

The arc of Culpepper's career effectively illustrated the general experience for Black quarterbacks in the first decade of the 2000s. As encouraging as it was that opportunities for them finally had soared, they could not, as a group, sustain the promise they showed in 2000, when four started playoff games and it seemed they might take over the league. Before the decade ended, the rate of opportunity for them would stall and head down again. A full-on embrace by their sport would not come for years. In the meantime, while there would still be moments of magnificence that prior generations of Black quarterbacks never envisioned, a spate of searing lows lay just ahead. By the end of the decade, careers would be derailed, a life would be lost, and the specter of institutional racism would materialize as vividly and publicly as ever, calling into question whether the many gains were, in fact, illusory.

CHAPTER 21

Two years before he became the first Black quarterback selected with the first overall pick in the NFL draft, Michael Vick was not even sure he had a future at the position in pro football.

In hindsight, it would sound absurd that Vick, of all people, felt so uncertain about his potential. Throughout his pro career, which began when the Atlanta Falcons drafted him in 2001, he terrorized defenses and altered the norms of the position. He was the fastest quarterback ever, the best running quarterback ever, a playmaker like no one had ever seen at the position.

The Black quarterbacks who came after him did not emulate Doug Williams, Warren Moon, Steve McNair, or any of the others who helped open the door; they emulated Vick, the supernova who burst through the door in 2001 and made real NFL football seem like a video game.

But at age eighteen in the early spring of 1999, nearing the end of his first year on campus at Virginia Tech, in Blacksburg, Virginia, Michael Vick wondered whether he should just switch to defensive back. He wanted to play in the NFL, and he knew as well as anybody else how few Black quarterbacks had received legitimate opportunities in the league. "I went through so much mentally, thinking about changing my position; not wanting to waste my scholarship, waste my time," Vick said.[1]

Being a quarterback had worked for him to that point. He grew up in Newport News, Virginia, in a neighborhood dominated by gangs, drugs, and violence. "Anyone could get shot at any time," he later wrote in his memoir.[2] One summer, he heard gunfire every night. A youth football teammate was killed while walking to a store. "I wanted to escape," Vick wrote.[3] Playing quarterback at Warwick High School helped make it possible, luring scholarship offers from Virginia Tech, Syracuse, and East Carolina. "My escape came through football," he wrote.[4]

Even before he left for Virginia Tech, though, he doubted the long-range potential of his position choice.

One problem was he was not even the best quarterback in his district. "I don't know if you could project him being a pro quarterback at that time," Mike Smith, the head coach at Warwick's rival, Hampton High School, said a few years later.[5] Ronald Curry, Hampton's quarterback, was a bigger name. Tall, fast, and also dominant in basketball, Curry was deemed such a transcendent athlete that NFL Films sent a crew to cover him. "I've never seen a high school quarterback as good as Curry," Florida State's Bobby Bowden said.[6]

Vick never won a game against Curry, who went to North Carolina to play football and basketball. "I lived in his shadow," Vick wrote.[7] Vick was just as fast, with a strong throwing arm and smooth delivery, but at just over six feet tall, he was smaller. One day in high school, Antonio Banks, a linebacker who had attended Warwick and now played in the NFL, came to watch the current team practice. He studied Vick throwing passes. "You'll be a defensive back," Banks said.[8] Vick was shocked by Banks's casual dismissal of his prospects at quarterback. "It hurt me deeply inside but also motivated me; Antonio motivated me more than he would ever know. I got stereotyped by another Black man," Vick said.[9]

What most discouraged Vick, though, was the axiom about Blacks not being smart enough to play quarterback at the game's highest levels. He heard it so much that he started to believe it. "I was always a little scared, wanting to change my position. I heard about the stereotype," he said later. "I felt like I could throw the ball good, but [the stereotype] made me feel like I wasn't smart enough. I wasn't an honor student in school. I had a 2.4 GPA when I graduated. I wasn't a 3.0 student."[10]

His fears about his intelligence accelerated once he arrived at Virginia Tech in the fall of 1998. He had picked the Hokies in part because their head coach, Frank Beamer, wanted to redshirt him for a year, giving him time to pick up the program's complex offense, which featured multiple sets. Vick knew he had a lot to learn. But when that education began, he was overwhelmed. "They made it seem like [playing quarterback] was the ultimate thinking man's game; that was the only way you could play it," he said. "At first, it was a shock. I wanted to change my position. When I first got to college, as I put in time to handle running the offense, knowing where guys are going to be, being able to keep an eye on the play clock, knowing how to get in and out of the huddle, being able to read the signals from the sideline, do all of this in twenty-five seconds . . . I was like, 'Man, I can't do this.'"[11]

In the middle of a preseason practice, he told another quarterback he was going to ask the coaches to move him to defensive back. It depressed him to think there actually might be something to the stereotype about Blacks not being smart enough to play quarterback.

An assistant coach, Rickey Bustle, who oversaw the quarterbacks and was also the offensive coordinator, told Vick to calm down.

"You're a freshman. You're eighteen years old and you just got here. Why do you expect to do so much?" Bustle said.[12]

Vick said later, "My coach kept pushing me. My coach, he was white, kept pushing me, [saying], 'You can do it. You can do it. You're going to come to the meetings every day. You're going to travel with the team.' I didn't even know what was going on. Then one day, it just clicked. I learned defenses first. When I was a redshirt, I learned defenses. And then I had to learn the offense. I just pieced it together where I could do it. It took some time, but I found out I was smart enough."[13]

The following spring, he competed for the starting quarterback job with an upperclassman. It was not much of a competition. "I knocked him off in two weeks," Vick said. "Everything was mental. My decision-making was good. I wasn't just taking off and doing my thing. I was beating him in the passing game and the running game. [The coaches] saw that and respected that. That's when I put it all together."[14]

In a coincidence, just as his fears about his intelligence ebbed, so did his concerns about Black quarterbacks not receiving opportunities in the NFL. The 1999 draft taught him a lesson. "That draft did so much for me as a player, as an individual, as a Black man," Vick said later. "I felt like the game was trending, the position was trending, in a different direction. It was because of that draft."[15]

He had more than just a casual interest in the draft that year. Aaron Brooks, the University of Virginia quarterback selected by the Green Bay Packers in the fourth round, was his cousin; they were from the same neighborhood and had played pickup football together for years. Vick also knew Donovan McNabb, who went to the Philadelphia Eagles as the second overall pick. The two had met during Vick's recruiting visit to Syracuse and stayed in touch.

"I almost went to Syracuse because of him," Vick said. "When I saw him go number two, now I know, being a Black quarterback, I can actually make it. Now I've got a chance. At least I've seen someone I idolize get a shot. Once I saw Andy Reid take him and Akili Smith go high and Minnesota take Culpepper, and then Shaun King and Aaron also get picked, it was no longer about what [Antonio Banks] said; it was about how can I go out and produce and whether I'm worthy of being put in that [same] position."[16]

Soon enough, it was clear that, yes, he was worthy. In fact, he was more than just worthy. Vick would break through a barrier and solidify the ascent of Black quarterbacks by redefining the position, by playing quarterback like no one had seen it played before, in the process putting Black quarterbacks at the forefront of change. It was a long way from where they had always been before, trailing their white counterparts, just hoping to emulate and assimilate. Vick was having none of that.

═══

It is easy to pinpoint the moment when most football fans discovered Vick. On the night of January 4, 2000, Virginia Tech faced Florida State in college football's national championship game. Both teams were undefeated, but Florida State, a dominant program at the time, was favored by a touchdown.

Until that night, widespread understanding of Vick's phenomenal talent was mostly limited to the East Coast. Virginia Tech was on a magical run, and ESPN faithfully showed highlights of Vick making plays as the Hokies whipped Virginia (31–7), embarrassed Syracuse (62–0), and dominated Miami (43–10) during their perfect regular season. He ended up leading the nation in passing efficiency (yards per attempt), rushing for 682 yards, and finishing third in the Heisman Trophy voting; it was arguably the finest season ever by a freshman quarterback in major college football.

But the Hokies seldom played on national television. The championship game effectively served as his introduction to the football world at large. Vick gave a performance that "won't soon be forgotten," the *Baltimore Sun* wrote.[17] Florida State had more NFL-caliber players, far greater depth, and a longer track record of winning big games. More than a few experts predicted a rout, and when Florida State built a 28–7 lead in the first half, those predictions appeared on target.

Just before halftime, though, Vick ran around the right end, cut back across the field, and sped past several of Florida State's fastest defenders for a forty-three-yard gain. The drive ended with a touchdown that hinted that the game had not been decided.

The Hokies continued to rally in the second half. Vick "dazzled, ducked, and dashed his way all over the artificial turf," the *Washington Post* wrote, leading one scoring drive, then another.[18] He darted around some tacklers, sped past others, and tossed completions to sustain drives. "That year, Florida State had what I considered the best, and fastest, college defense I had ever seen," Tony Dungy would recall, but "it could not contain Michael as he threw, ran, and led his team back."[19]

Late in the third quarter, he scrambled twenty-two yards to set up a touchdown that put the Hokies ahead, 29–28. They were on the verge of a colossal upset, it seemed, with Vick having carried them to this point almost singlehandedly. Their fans' cheers filled the dome. Florida State defenders stood with their hands on their hips, breathing hard, in between plays; they were weary from chasing Vick around.

But the rally had exhausted the Hokies, and Florida State's superior depth proved decisive late. The Seminoles regained the lead and pulled away to a 46–29 victory. Their star wide receiver, Peter Warrick, was rightfully named the game's outstanding player; he made several key plays to decide the outcome. But only one true legend was hatched that night. In defeat, Vick had thrown for 225 yards and rushed for 145 yards; no one had ever really seen a quarterback so fast and unpredictable.

It was such a breathtaking performance that it all but guaranteed Vick would be leaving Virginia Tech for the NFL, and soon. As he began his sophomore season the next fall, he told *Sports Illustrated* he would "have to go" if it appeared he would get selected early in the draft.[20]

His second college season did not disappoint. He rushed for 210 yards in a road victory against Boston College. He sprinted fifty-five yards for the game-winning touchdown as the Hokies rallied from fourteen points down to win at Syracuse. Entering a crucial November contest against Miami, both teams were undefeated. The winner would likely end up in the national championship game.

But Vick was unable to start due to a sprained ankle. When Miami jumped out to a fourteen-point lead, Beamer put him in. He tried to start a rally, but his ankle was too sore and he ultimately had to return to the bench and watch Miami score a lopsided victory. Miami's players lined up to shake his hand after the game; his peers admired his talent.

The defeat dashed the Hokies' hopes of playing in another championship game and also dashed Vick's hopes of winning the Heisman Trophy—a goal that, he admitted later, had obsessed him to the point that he was tracking his statistics during games. After the Hokies finished the 2000 season with a 10–1 record and routed Clemson in the Gator Bowl, Vick considered returning for another season; he was having fun. But it was clear he would get selected near the top of the NFL draft. He announced he was turning pro.

Before the draft in April, he attended the combine, worked out privately for teams, and sat through interviews with personnel executives. His stock never wavered. He was universally regarded as the top prospect in the class at any position. "There was a lot of discussion that this guy was going to be the Michael Jordan of pro football. He was a special, special player, a special athlete," recalled Jimmy Raye III, the San Diego Chargers' director of college scouting at the time.[21]

Raye's father had been one of the first Black quarterbacks to achieve success at a major college program; an accurate passer and darting runner, he helped Michigan State win the Big Ten and a share of a national championship in the 1960s. But the pros had dismissed him as a quarterback prospect. Now, in a delicious coincidence, the elder Raye's son could help make up for the slight his father had experienced. The younger Raye's team, the Chargers, held the first pick in the 2001 draft. The football world assumed they would take Vick; they began contract negotiations with his agent weeks before the draft.

Quietly, though, the organization's top decision-makers had doubts. High picks commanded huge contracts—the NFL would not institute a cap on rookie salaries until 2011—and three years earlier, the Chargers had whiffed on Ryan Leaf, a quarterback from Washington State taken with the second overall pick. Peyton Manning, the top pick that year, was already a star for the Indianapolis Colts, but Leaf's career had disintegrated. In the wake of that colossal and costly mistake, the Chargers had signed thirty-eight-year-old Doug Flutie to stabilize their quarterback play in 2001.

Vick later wrote in his autobiography that he "heard" the Chargers also became skeptical about making him their quarterback after he brought a group of his friends to his private workout for the team in Blacksburg—friends the Chargers "did not trust to be positive influences," Vick wrote.[22] While acknowledging that "it was not professional" to bring his friends to a workout, he also said the Chargers were guilty of stereotyping people "they did not know."[23]

Whatever their rationale, the Chargers were interested in dealing the top pick, and they found a willing trade partner. Vick had impressed the Falcons' coaches and scouts during a private workout at the team's practice facility in suburban Atlanta. They liked his arm strength, his speed, and his throwing mechanics, but what sealed their opinion was his grasp of the game—his mind.

At one point during the daylong workout, Dan Reeves, the Falcons' head coach and a former NFL halfback, asked Vick to take a whiteboard in hand and explain how one of his favorite plays worked. Vick was ready. He drew up a play with four receivers split wide. "When we ran it, I always felt like it was something that an NFL quarterback would be running. This is an NFL play that we're running in college," Vick said, recalling the moment. "I understand it through and through—it's a lot of variables, a lot of things that could happen, and I could walk you through it front to back. I explained that play, and I remember walking out of there and everyone being very impressed."[24]

To obtain the top pick, the Falcons gave the Chargers their first-round pick—the fifth overall selection—and their third-round pick that year and second-round pick the next year. When the Chargers asked for Tim Dwight, a star kick returner, the Falcons added him to the haul to seal the deal.

On April 21, 2001, NFL commissioner Paul Tagliabue opened the draft, drawing cheers from a packed house of fans at Madison Square Garden in New York. The Falcons had ten minutes to make a selection, but Tagliabue quickly returned to the podium. "With the first selection in the 2001 NFL draft, the Atlanta Falcons select Michael Vick, quarterback, Virginia Tech," the commissioner said.[25]

The fans emitted a rumble of noise; it was not a surprise, but witnessing a dynamic player's future come together was still thrilling. And Vick's selection was historic. Donovan McNabb had gone second overall, and Steve McNair and Akili Smith had gone third, but never, until now, had a team taken a Black quarterback first overall.

It had only been a matter of time, given how many more Black quarterbacks were now receiving chances to play in college, but still, given the discrimination and obstacles prior generations had faced in the draft and throughout their careers, Vick's selection was momentous. It reinforced to the football world that a Black quarterback, from a personnel group long doubted, could be more than just worthy of a high pick—he could be the best of the best.

Two decades later, the significance of the Falcons' commitment still moved him. "Shout-out to them for having the faith in me, as a twenty-year-old Black man, to be the face of their franchise," Vick said.[26]

Initially, the racial implications were not his primary concern. "The only thing I was thinking about, it wasn't about being a Black quarterback going first; it was about not being a bust," he said. It was about "putting on display what I did at Virginia Tech and doing it at a higher level. At the time, I couldn't see the circumstances I was in, couldn't understand the value and power I had, the young kids who were watching me, that wasn't a focus. It was just, 'I've got to do my job.'"[27]

But as the reality of his circumstances became clear to him during his rookie season, the impact of being such a high-profile Black quarterback increasingly weighed on him.

His agent had negotiated the largest rookie contract in NFL history—a six-year, $62 million deal, with $15 million guaranteed. Even though the Falcons elected to stick with their incumbent starter, thirty-six-year-old Chris Chandler, ahead of Vick in 2001, there was no doubt Vick would soon have the job. It seemed he had it all—money, fame, an opportunity.

But as he settled into a routine with the Falcons, he was shocked by how much the pro game would demand of him.

Vick had impressed the Falcons' coaches before the draft with his explanation of a play, but the pro game was far more complex than what he had experienced in college. He could see he had a long way to go, which made him nervous. The stereotype about Black quarterbacks not being smart enough had concerned him in high school and at the outset of his college career, and now, it gnawed at him again. "It was a high-pressure situation, and I didn't want anyone looking at me like I was dumb, just because I'm a Black quarterback," he said.[28]

He was subdued around his teammates and coaches, his voice a whisper. He gazed down or into the distance to avoid looking anyone in the eye. His coaches and teammates dismissed it as typical rookie shyness; they would have been surprised to know Vick's self-confidence was ebbing because he feared not being able to grasp what his coaches wanted.

The Falcons were competitive with Chandler as their quarterback in 2001; he was three years removed from leading them to a Super Bowl appearance. Reeves utilized Vick as an occasional change-of-pace option, a not-so-secret weapon, but the coach mostly wanted his young quarterback to watch and learn rather than play.

When Chandler suffered an injury that left him unable to play one Sunday in November, Vick made his first start for the Falcons. Atlanta faced the Dallas Cowboys, who started Ryan Leaf—a white quarterback receiving a second chance, an opportunity seldom given to Black quarterbacks if their first chance went as poorly as Leaf's had in San Diego. It was immediately clear that day that Vick was not ready for full-time duty. The Cowboys thoroughly confused him with their changing defensive alignments and blitz packages. Although the Falcons won, Vick completed just four passes. Chandler reclaimed his starting job the next week.

"That Dallas game, I instantly learned, 'Man, this game is mental. I need to step away. I'm not ready to go in,'" Vick said. "I was honest. I told [Reeves], 'Man, this game is hard.' He's like, 'Man, you've got to mentally prepare yourself.' He started telling me things to look for in the defense. He said, 'The defense will tell you everything.'"[29]

Although Vick had learned to study film while at Virginia Tech, he had not relied on it because his natural athletic talent was so surpassing; he could make plays and win games relying strictly on that, without the knowledge that film study provided. His approach had changed little in his first months with the Falcons, partly because he was not on the field. After the Dallas game, though, he understood that he needed to start focusing more on the parts of pro football that he did not understand.

One day, before a meeting, Chandler and Vick were alone in a room. Vick asked, "What's the most important thing I can learn from you?"[30]

Chandler had been in the same position in Houston six years earlier; he was the starter when Steve McNair joined the Houston Oilers as a rookie. Chandler had not been especially helpful, he admitted later, not because he disliked McNair, but because he felt the Oilers had misled him by telling him they would not draft a quarterback.

This time, with Vick, he was more helpful. He pointed to his copy of that week's playbook, on which he had scrawled notes. "Learn to write down the plays exactly like this," he said.[31]

Vick looked at Chandler's playbook. The pages were annotated with notes about alignments, pre-snap motion, and other variables. Vick now began to understand what it really took to be a quarterback in the NFL. "By the time we got to practice Wednesday, all Coach Reeves had to do was tell Chris what he wanted run. Chris would match the formation with motion, the shift. I watched that and I was in amazement," Vick said. "I knew the task at hand was a mental task, a mental challenge. It was something I was going to have to really embrace. That leadership from Chris meant everything to me."[32]

The Falcons had a winning record when December began, but they lost five of their last six games, spiraling out of the playoff race. Vick received another chance to play in the final two games. He looked less awed. The Falcons had seen enough and cut Chandler that spring. Vick's time had arrived.

It became clear during the 2002 season that the trade between the Falcons and Chargers before the 2001 draft was a win-win, beneficial to both sides. The Chargers had come away with LaDainian Tomlinson, a running back from TCU, and Drew Brees, a quarterback from Purdue whose draft stock was discounted because he was just six feet tall. By 2002, Tomlinson and Brees had taken over the Chargers' offense, destined to become among the best players ever at their positions. Vick, meanwhile, made the Pro Bowl in his first year as a starter in 2002.

His performance in the Falcons' season opener was a preview of what lay ahead. At Lambeau Field, one of pro football's iconic venues, Vick took on the Green Bay Packers and Brett Favre, the game's preeminent quarterback, a three-time winner of the league MVP award. Though now thirty-three, Favre still had one of the game's most prolific arms, and he torched the Falcons' defense, passing for nearly three hundred yards and two touchdowns. But Vick matched him play for play, completing his first ten passes, throwing for 209 yards and a touchdown, and rushing for seventy-two yards and a touchdown. As seven-point underdogs, the Falcons led at halftime, fell behind in the third quarter, and rallied to take a late lead before finally losing in overtime, 37–34.

"Michael Vick has lived up to expectations. He gets my Pro Bowl vote," said the Packers' head coach, Mike Sherman.[33]

The Falcons lost again the next week and had a 1–3 record a month into the season, prompting grumbling from some fans about Vick. It would all dissipate, however, as the Falcons then went two months without a loss, winning seven games and tying one, with dynamic playmaking from Vick becoming a weekly occurrence. He either passed or ran for every yard of a late, game-winning drive in a 37–35 win against the Saints. Against the Steelers in Pittsburgh, he led a late rally from seventeen points down in a game that ended as a tie. "He's like a running back with a great passing arm," said Joey Porter, a veteran linebacker for the Steelers.[34]

He was not the NFL's first prolific running quarterback. Bobby Douglass had rushed for 968 yards with the Bears in 1972, and Randall Cunningham had gained 942 with the Eagles in 1990. Vick would end the 2002 season with 777, the third-highest total for a quarterback in league history. But never, safe to say, had any quarterback bedeviled NFL defenses so dramatically with his legs. The majority of his yardage came not on designed running plays, but rather after he had dropped back to pass and surveyed the field for open receivers. If he did not see an open target, he tucked the ball under his arm and took off.

The frustration he generated among opposing defenses was palpable. They could do everything right, force the Falcons into third-and-long situations, and blanket their receivers, and Vick would still gain the necessary yardage on impromptu playmaking.

The best example of the unique danger he posed came against the Vikings in Minnesota in early December. The Vikings harassed him into a poor passing performance; he completed just eleven of twenty-eight attempts. But he posted the highest single-game rushing total by a quarterback in NFL history—173 yards.

Three times, the Vikings, with Daunte Culpepper at quarterback, scored a touchdown to take the lead; three times, the Falcons responded with a touchdown that tied the score. The third time, Vick scrambled for gains of nineteen and thirteen yards to sustain the possession, then ran twenty-eight yards for a touchdown, dodging four defenders who thought they had him pinned.

When the game went to overtime, the Vikings had the first possession, but they punted after Culpepper was sacked. The Falcons started a drive at the Minnesota 48. After a run picked up two yards on first down, Vick dropped back to pass but quickly scrambled to his left and veered up the field. A cornerback and linebacker tried to cut off his running lane, but he sped through it untouched, cut back toward the middle of the field, and sped between three more defenders who lunged for him, only to hit each other. Two final defenders had no chance of catching him. Vick crossed the goal line, turned and backpedaled for a few strides, hurled the ball into the distance, and raised his arms in triumph. The game was over.

Barely slowing, Vick sprinted straight to the tunnel to the locker room and disappeared, leaving the Vikings' sellout crowd gasping, *What just happened here?*

When fans around the country and players and coaches on other teams saw the play later, they also gasped. "I had never seen a weapon like that at the quarterback position," said Tony Dungy, now the Indianapolis Colts' head coach after being fired by the Tampa Bay Bucs.[35]

The Falcons slumped after beating the Vikings, losing three of the last four games on their regular-season schedule, but they still secured a place in the NFC playoffs as a wild card entrant. They opened the postseason by returning to where their season had begun, at Lambeau Field in Green Bay. Few experts expected them to seriously challenge Favre and the Packers, who had won a division title and were viewed as Super Bowl contenders. The Falcons were young and excited just to be playing. But on the opening possession, Vick directed a seventy-six-yard touchdown drive, covering the final ten yards with a pass. A few minutes later, the Falcons scored another touchdown on a blocked punt, then added a third touchdown early in the second quarter after the Packers muffed a punt. The Falcons led, 21–0.

Vick took it from there, extending Atlanta drives by running and throwing for first downs. The Falcons would end up possessing the ball for some twelve minutes more than the Packers, leaving Favre few opportunities to start a rally. The Falcons won, 27–7. In Vick's postseason debut, he had helped deal the Packers their first-ever playoff defeat in Green Bay.

"Mike is amazing," Reeves said. "The tougher the situation, the better he plays."[36]

A week later, the Falcons were eliminated by McNabb and the Eagles in Philadelphia. Vick threw for 274 yards but was intercepted twice, and Jim Johnson, the Eagles' defensive coordinator, devised a shrewd scheme that limited his opportunities to run.

The loss was disappointing, but it was easy for Vick and the Falcons to find solace. He was just twenty-two. After just one year as a starter, he seemed bound for a long career filled with soaring highlights and elite achievements. Other Black quarterbacks had come into the NFL and helped change their position's look and norms, but Vick, it seemed, was his own category.

No one would have guessed, nor even imagined, that he had just experienced his highest high. Or that unspeakable off-field lows eventually would overtake his story.

CHAPTER 22

When Donovan McNabb and the Eagles eliminated Michael Vick and the Falcons from the 2002 NFC playoffs, McNabb was playing for the first time in weeks. He had missed six games with a fractured ankle. Although he played well, it was the Eagles' defense, one of the NFL's best, that carried the team against Atlanta.

The Eagles were the NFC's top seed, guaranteed of playing at home, in Veterans Stadium, until they reached the Super Bowl, if they made it that far. By beating the Falcons, they advanced to the conference championship game against the Tampa Bay Bucs. Their fans were giddy with excitement. The Eagles had not lost a game that mattered in more than two months (backups filled the field during a meaningless loss to the Giants in the season finale) and they had beaten the Bucs during the regular season. Their offense was led by Duce Staley, a thousand-yard rusher, and McNabb, by now a three-time Pro Bowl selection. Their defense featured All-Pro defensive backs Troy Vincent and Brian Dawkins.

The first plays of the championship game only made their trip to the Super Bowl seem likelier. After Brian Mitchell returned the opening kickoff seventy yards, Staley sliced through the Bucs' defense for a twenty-yard touchdown run. Two snaps into the game, the home crowd was close to delirious.

But the Bucs did not roll over. Their veteran quarterback, Brad Johnson, led touchdown drives of ninety-six and eighty yards, methodically spreading completions among an array of receivers. The fans grew quiet. The Eagles also moved the ball, but Tampa Bay's aggressive defense harassed McNabb into mistakes. Suddenly, he looked like a quarterback in just his second game back from a long layoff. Late in the second quarter, he lost a fumble while being sacked, denying the Eagles a shot at a field goal. He lost another fumble near midfield early in the third quarter. "I played poorly," he said.[1]

His final mistake came late. With the Eagles trailing by ten points in the fourth quarter, he drove the offense to Tampa Bay's 10 yard line. But the Bucs' Ronde Barber read his eyes, stepped in front of an intended receiver, picked off a pass, and ran ninety-two yards for a touchdown. The Bucs, not the Eagles, were going to the Super Bowl.

McNabb took responsibility. "Anytime a quarterback plays poorly, it makes it harder for everyone else," he said.[2]

At age twenty-six he was, by any measure, one of the NFL's best quarterbacks, already attaining the kind of success the Eagles had envisioned when they drafted him four years earlier. He had won twenty-nine of forty-two regular-season starts since becoming the full-time starter, and in those games had thrown more than twice as many touchdowns as interceptions. He also had a winning record in the playoffs, no easy feat; he had won four of seven starts for a team that was annually in the Super Bowl mix.

But while his nascent NFL career was impressive, it lacked a key piece. Each of the Eagles' three playoff runs with McNabb had ended short of a trip to the Super Bowl. He still had something to prove, not only as a Black quarterback intent on demonstrating that he was on par with the best white quarterbacks, but also, as of September 28, 2003, as an individual trying to overcome a very specific and public indignity that few other players had experienced.

The furor originated in the most innocuous of settings—ESPN's *Sunday NFL Countdown*, a pregame program featuring panels of analysts discussing issues and games being played that day. ESPN had brought in Rush Limbaugh, the fiery conservative radio host, as a regular panelist, hoping his edgy opinions would lure viewers, and on that Sunday in September, he took square aim at McNabb.

Expected to contend for the NFC title, the Eagles had started the 2003 season disastrously, losing two games in their new home stadium,

Lincoln Financial Field, by a combined score of 48–10, with McNabb registering the worst quarterback rating of any starter in the league. On the Sunday morning Limbaugh took on McNabb, the Eagles were in Buffalo to play the Bills, hoping to secure their first win of the season.

Limbaugh appeared on a roundtable panel with Chris Berman, the host of the show; Tom Jackson and Michael Irvin, former NFL players, who are Black; and Steve Young, the former quarterback, who is white. Discussing the Eagles' disappointing start, they turned to McNabb. "Sorry to say this, I don't think he's been that good from the get-go," Limbaugh said. "I think what we've had here is a little social concern in the NFL. The media has been very desirous that a Black quarterback do well. There is a little hope invested in McNabb, and he got a lot of credit for the performance of this team that he didn't deserve. The defense carried this team."[3]

Jackson fired back on the football aspect of the argument, saying McNabb had been "a very effective quarterback for this football team over the last two or three years."[4] But none of the panelists challenged Limbaugh's implication that McNabb was receiving undue credit because he was Black.

Limbaugh would later insist he was criticizing the media more than McNabb, and ESPN initially sought to defend him. But it soon became clear that many saw the hand of discrimination in his suggestion that a decorated Black quarterback was earning positive press strictly because of his race, as opposed to having earned the praise. ESPN received "thousands of negative email messages," the *New York Times* reported.[5] Politicians called for the network to fire Limbaugh. Sponsors threatened to withdraw ads. After ESPN eventually released a statement calling the comments "insensitive and inappropriate," Limbaugh resigned.[6]

The Eagles did not play the Bills until the late afternoon on that Sunday, so McNabb had several extra hours to digest Limbaugh's remarks before he played. He was stunned. Shaken. Disgusted. But despite having been sucked into an ugly controversy not of his making, he focused on his job. He completed a twenty-seven-yard pass on the Eagles' first offensive snap, then ran for twenty-five yards to set up a touchdown. The Eagles built a lead and held off a Buffalo rally to win, with McNabb looking more like his old self.

Asked about Limbaugh's comments after the game, he said, "It's sad that you've got to go to skin color. I thought we were through with that whole deal."[7]

It was not McNabb's first experience with "that whole deal." Far from it. His father, Sam, an electrical engineer, and his mother, Wilma, a nurse, had moved with Donovan and his brother from a tough neighborhood on Chicago's South Side to a mostly white suburb when Donovan was eight. "We were the first African-American family on the block, and the 'welcoming committee' was not very welcoming," Sam recalled. "They broke into my house, broke several windows, urinated on the carpeting, knocked holes in the walls inside the house and spray-painted the outside. It was their show of disapproval."[8]

The family eventually settled in, and the boys grew up in a supportive household in which their classwork and developing confidence were stressed. His parents' unyielding love "gets me through the tough times," McNabb would say.[9] He attended Mount Carmel High School, an all-male, Catholic institution, and blossomed into a star quarterback.

But most college recruiters wanted him as a running back or receiver. McNabb refused to switch from quarterback. "They'd get a little upset that you turned them down," he said. "They'd say, 'If you ever think about playing another position, put us on the list to be the first to call.'"[10]

He later referred to it as "kind of killing your dream," but his dream endured because Syracuse recruited him to play quarterback.[11] He became the starter, won games, and set records. Yet when he went second overall to the Eagles at the 1999 draft, Philadelphia fans on hand unleashed a vicious chorus of boos.

Some dream.

Hearing the boos that day, McNabb turned to check on his parents, who were with him in New York. Less accustomed to the venom fans could exhibit, Sam and Wilma reflexively wondered if their son was headed into a racially hostile environment. In fact, the fans had wanted the Eagles to draft Ricky Williams, a ballyhooed running back from Texas, who also was Black. They would have booed any pick other than Williams.

Nonetheless, the optics of mostly white fans viciously booing a Black quarterback were hard to shake. And now, four years later, McNabb was again being targeted negatively, this time strictly because he was Black.

——

On the weekend Limbaugh spoke out, seven of the NFL's thirty-two teams started Black quarterbacks and two other Black starters were out with injuries. There was no doubt the window of opportunity for Black quarterbacks had opened wide. But while that was encouraging, the Limbaugh incident made it clear that pro football's power structure was still as white as ever. It was chilling to see a white commentator take a racist potshot at a successful Black player without being rebuked on air or suffering consequences until the negative blowback became so fierce as to demand it.

McNabb received supportive phone calls from Warren Moon, Randall Cunningham, and James Harris, star Black quarterbacks who had preceded him, as well as the Reverend Jesse Jackson and comedian Bill Cosby. At his midweek news conference, he admitted he was shaken and could not just easily move on.

But as upsetting as it was, McNabb was equipped for the moment; he was mature, confident, a leader. In the years before social media hijacked the sports conversation, radio talk shows were a force, providing a forum for anyone wanting to voice opinions. Athletes had to learn to endure not only informed criticism but also uninformed criticism and baseless potshots. Playing in Philadelphia, where talk radio was popular and famously cranky, McNabb had learned that rising above criticism, in whatever form it came, was part of his job.

With his performance under scrutiny like never before, McNabb thrived. After beating the Bills, the Eagles won again, lost to the Cowboys, then won nine straight games, usually by a touchdown or more, to secure a third straight division title and the top seed in the NFC playoffs for the second straight year. McNabb's selection to the Pro Bowl was his fourth straight.

When the Eagles hosted Brett Favre and the Green Bay Packers in the divisional round of the playoffs, Favre threw two early touchdown passes and the Packers' defense doggedly protected the lead; McNabb would get sacked eight times and was booed when he lost a fumble in the first half. In a Packer-like windchill of thirteen degrees, it appeared another season of promise for the Eagles would end with a deflating elimination from the postseason.

But McNabb rallied the Eagles, throwing strikes to receivers and scrambling for gains when he eluded the Packers' relentless pressure. He would end the game with 248 passing yards and 107 rushing yards, the latter an NFL playoff record for a quarterback.

Still, with a minute and twelve seconds to play, the Packers led by a field goal, and the Eagles were about out of hope. On a last-ditch possession, McNabb and his offense faced fourth-and-26 at their 26.

McNabb dropped back as one of his receivers, Freddie Mitchell, ran down the middle of the field and into a seam in the Packers' zone defense. McNabb spotted him and hurled a pass that sailed between two defenders. Mitchell grabbed the ball and spun forward, just crossing the line needed for a first down. The fans unleashed a shattering roar.

The drive led to a field goal with ten seconds to play, forcing overtime. After the Eagles punted, Favre's first pass was intercepted by Brian Dawkins, who returned the ball to the Green Bay 34. McNabb threw for a first down, setting up a game-winning field goal.

As the Eagles celebrated in their locker room, they could not stop talking about McNabb's miraculous escape from fourth-and-26. It meant the Eagles would host the NFC championship game for the second straight season, this time against the Carolina Panthers. It was becoming hard not to see the force of destiny propelling McNabb and his team. A perfect narrative line was forming. In the year he had faced his most searing challenge, courtesy of Limbaugh, he could quell the doubts about his ability to lead a team to the Super Bowl. "If they win, it would be the proverbial icing on the cake," his father, Sam, told an interviewer.[12]

Sam was proud of his son's response to the controversy Limbaugh had created. "Donovan has shown people that he knows how to handle tough situations, and that he thinks before he speaks," Sam said.[13]

But Sam also understood that a victory in a football game would not alter the reality that his son faced an extra challenge simply because he was Black, a predicament to which most Black Americans could relate.

"I was in the service in Vietnam, and to go through so much over there and then come back and go through things in your homeland, it's a shame," Sam said. "It's not like things became bad just yesterday. We're talking about hundreds of years we've been going through this ordeal. We just don't have anything to show for it, and that's not good."[14]

As it turned out, McNabb did not enjoy a Hollywood-style ending in the 2003 playoffs. The Carolina Panthers brutalized the Eagles in the NFC championship game, scoring a 14–3 victory. McNabb suffered bruised ribs and threw three interceptions before being pulled in the second half, with the outcome in doubt, because the injury had left him unable to perform at his usual level.

Instead of McNabb, Carolina's Jake Delhomme started at quarterback for the NFC team in the Super Bowl. Two years older than McNabb, Delhomme had gone undrafted out of college and spent six years on the fringes of the pro game, most recently as the New Orleans Saints' backup quarterback, before signing with the Panthers in 2003, hoping he might finally get a chance to play. That chance had arrived, and he had made the most of it. (His backup was Rodney Peete, now thirty-seven but still in the league fourteen years after being slighted in the draft.) Delhomme could not come close to matching McNabb's career arc, but now he had a Super Bowl start and McNabb did not. (The New England Patriots defeated Carolina, 32–29.)

The Eagles' loss continued a disappointing trend for the generation of Black quarterbacks who had entered the NFL in the late 1990s and early 2000s and enjoyed significant success. None had led a team to the Super Bowl. In 1999, the Saints, with Shaun King at quarterback, had lost the NFC championship game to the Rams, who had Kurt Warner at quarterback. In 2000, the Vikings, with Daunte Culpepper at quarterback, had lost the NFC championship game to the Giants, who had Kerry Collins at quarterback. Now, the Eagles, with McNabb, had lost the NFC championship game for three straight years, falling to the Rams and Warner in 2001, the Bucs and Johnson in 2002, and the Panthers and Delhomme in 2003.

The media did not dwell on the fact that the NFC championship game had featured a white quarterback prevailing over a Black quarterback for five straight years. Or that Doug Williams was still the only Black quarterback to start the Super Bowl for an NFC team. Or that Steve McNair, with the Tennessee Titans in 1999, was the only Black quarterback to have started the Super Bowl for an AFC team.

The absence of championship laurels for Black quarterbacks provided ammunition for anyone still seeking to discount their abilities. Yes, they had proved in the past decade that they were just as capable as white quarterbacks of being starters in the NFL. But what had they won? The trend sparked echoes of the old Jim Crow doubts about their ability to lead.

McNabb's case was acute, but if anything, he was now accustomed to enduring disappointments and gearing up for another run. In the wake of the loss to the Panthers, the Eagles' front office helped him by acquiring Terrell Owens, one of the league's top receivers. In 2004, McNabb posted career highs in completion percentage, touchdown passes, and passing yardage as the Eagles won a fourth straight division title and McNabb was selected to a fifth straight Pro Bowl.

It was a terrific season for Black quarterbacks throughout the NFC. Culpepper and Michael Vick also made the Pro Bowl and helped their teams make the playoffs.

Culpepper and the Vikings came to Philadelphia for a divisional-round playoff game. At age twenty-eight, Culpepper was as dangerous as any quarterback in football. He had thrown thirty-nine touchdown passes and just eleven interceptions during the season and led the league in passing yardage. The Vikings were not a top team, but with Culpepper flinging touchdowns, they had made the playoffs as a wild card and defeated the Packers in an opening round game, with Culpepper tossing four touchdown passes.

But the Eagles, the top seed in the NFC, were a more well-rounded team. McNabb directed two early touchdown drives and the defense harassed Culpepper into two interceptions. The Vikings self-destructed with more than one hundred yards in penalties and the Eagles won easily. The win put them into the conference championship game for the fourth straight year—the third straight year at home. This time, they would play Vick and the Falcons.

Vick had spent the season demonstrating he was recovered from a serious knee injury that had sidelined him for most of the 2003 season. The comeback had gone well. Vick had only passed for about half as many yards as Culpepper in Minnesota, but he had rushed for nearly a thousand yards, bedeviling defenses with his impromptu scrambles. The Falcons won a division title with an 11–5 record, earning the No. 2 seed in the NFC playoffs.

McNabb and Vick had been friends since Vick's recruiting visit to Syracuse in 1998. Vick admitted later that he was so cocky as a young player that he rebuffed the counsel of Randall Cunningham and Steve Young, running quarterbacks willing to help him adjust to the pros. But he valued McNabb's thoughts. "He had a lot of influence on me," Vick said.[15]

Their matchup in the conference championship game was historic. Twenty-five years earlier, Black quarterbacks had started opposite each other for the first time in an NFL game when the Bucs, with Doug Williams, defeated the Bears, with Vince Evans, on September 30, 1979. There had since been several playoff games matching Black starters, but this was the first one with a trip to the Super Bowl on the line.

The matchup also represented a culmination of sorts for the generation of Black quarterbacks who had entered the league together in the late 1990s and early 2000s. Culpepper had quarterbacked two playoff teams and started a conference championship game. Shaun King also had quarterbacked two playoff teams and started a conference championship game. Aaron Brooks had quarterbacked one playoff team.

McNabb had quarterbacked five playoff teams and started four conference championship games. Vick, in 2004, was making his second appearance in the playoffs, and now he was in the conference championship game. It was an impressive record. But the fact remained: none had ever taken a team to the Super Bowl. For five straight years, one had been the losing starter in the NFC title game. With McNabb and Vick meeting, though, that streak would end. One way or another, a Black quarterback would start for the NFC team in the Super Bowl.

McNabb was under more pressure after the Eagles' recent playoff shortfalls, but at twenty-eight, at the end of his fifth full season as a starter, he was steeled for the challenge. It did not matter that Owens, his top receiver, was out with a broken ankle. It did not matter that key mistakes had characterized his recent performances in championship games. On January 23, 2005, he was nearly perfect against the Falcons.

He directed a long touchdown drive on the Eagles' second possession, setting up the score with a twenty-one-yard completion. Then he directed another long touchdown drive on the Eagles' next possession, setting up the score with a forty-five-yard completion.

Vick tried to keep up. He completed a long pass to set up a touchdown in the second quarter. The Falcons liked their chances at halftime, trailing by just four points. But Jim Johnson, the Eagles' defensive coordinator, had devised a game plan that shut down Vick's running lanes when he wanted to scramble. He would rush for just twenty-six yards in the game, well below his average. He also was sacked four times and threw an interception in the third quarter as the Falcons tried to rally.

Meanwhile, McNabb led the Philadelphia offense on a pair of drives that produced field goals in the third quarter, and then, with the Philadelphia fans cheering louder and louder, McNabb and the offense sealed the outcome with a methodical final drive lasting nearly seven minutes. Twice along the way, McNabb turned third downs into firsts with completions, and then he finished the drive with a short touchdown pass.

Finally, *finally*, it could be said: he was good enough to take a team to the Super Bowl.

CHAPTER 23

The NFL issued two thousand media credentials for Super Bowl 39, between the Philadelphia Eagles and New England Patriots, seemingly ensuring that no news angle would go uncovered. But the swarming media horde ignored one unusual aspect of the matchup before, during, and after the Patriots' 24–21 victory in Jacksonville, Florida, on February 6, 2005.

The Eagles had relied on Black quarterbacks more than any other franchise over the years. Randall Cunningham started 112 regular season and playoff games for them over eleven seasons starting in 1985, and when Donovan McNabb took the first snap in Super Bowl 39, he made his ninety-first start for the franchise in a regular-season or playoff game. These 203 starts by Black quarterbacks were far more than any other franchise's total, and also 203 more than the number the Eagles' opponents that day could claim. The Patriots had existed for forty-five years without once starting a Black quarterback.

The stark disparity went unreported, one could conclude, because the mainstream media believed race was no longer a factor in personnel decisions in the NFL. This was not the 1950s. Although every team owner was white and most head coaches and general managers also still were, the playing population was nearly two-thirds Black. Yes, that meant most of the Black players' careers depended on white approval, a depressing reality baked into the sport—and still true in many cases in 2023. But also true when the Eagles and Patriots met in the Super Bowl—and still true today—was the fact that a coach or GM was not likely to keep his job for long if he took *any* factor other than winning into account, such as a player's race, when building and operating his team.

The Patriots, clearly, were not *opposed* to Black quarterbacks. They had drafted Alabama A&M's Onree Jackson with a fifth-round pick in 1969, Howard University's Jay Walker with a seventh-round pick in 1994, Kansas State's Michael Bishop with a seventh-round pick in 1999, and LSU's Rohan Davey with a fourth-round pick in 2001, each time hoping a starting-caliber Black quarterback might blossom.

But none did, and meanwhile, a white quarterback drafted with a similarly modest pick in 2000 had blossomed into exactly what they were looking for—Tom Brady, a sixth-round pick from Michigan, won his third Super Bowl as a starting quarterback against McNabb and the Eagles.

The stark contrast between the Eagles and Patriots effectively summed up the prevailing conditions for Black quarterbacks in the NFL in the early 2000s. They had come a long way in terms of opportunity and respect since 1983, when the league's entire roster of Black quarterbacks consisted of one backup. But despite the gains, they still were not nearly on equal footing with white quarterbacks.

It was naïve to think race was no longer a factor at *their* position. Although the overall playing population was nearly two-thirds Black, only one-third of the quarterbacks were Black. Some old-school doubts about their mental acuity clearly still persisted; teams were far more likely to use white quarterbacks as backups. White quarterbacks also were likelier to receive more opportunities after their first chance ended.

Some Black quarterbacks received just one shot. After Ryan Leaf, the second overall pick in 1998, was deemed a bust and released by the Chargers, three other teams gave him a shot. But when Akili Smith, the third overall pick one year later, was deemed a bust and released by the Bengals, he never threw another pass in the NFL.

After Shaun King was replaced as the Bucs' starter in 2001, at age twenty-four, despite having taken them to the playoffs twice, he was never again an NFL starter. After throwing thirty-one more touchdowns than interceptions in six seasons with the Saints, Aaron Brooks saw his career abruptly end; he appeared in just eight more games after leaving New Orleans and threw his last pass at age thirty.

Although the Eagles, Atlanta Falcons, Tennessee Titans, and Minnesota Vikings were thriving with Black starting quarterbacks in the early 2000s, the Patriots and three other teams still had never given a Black quarterback a start. Through 2004, the Green Bay Packers, founded in 1919, the New York Giants, founded in 1925, and the San Francisco 49ers, founded in 1946, had played a combined 225 seasons with white starting quarterbacks only.

Aside from the doubts, Black quarterbacks also continued to endure racist hate mail, pejorative comments from fans, and the many challenges that came with being Black in America. When he started in the Super Bowl, McNabb was less than two years removed from being deemed overrated by Rush Limbaugh simply because he was Black—a withering moment of prejudice that could have brought a less sure athlete to his knees.

Going into the Super Bowl, McNabb's presence generated optimistic visions of a new normal. He was the third Black starting quarterback in Super Bowl history, after Doug Williams and Steve McNair, and only five years had passed since McNair became the second Black Super Bowl starter when he led the Tennessee Titans against the St. Louis Rams. "There were twelve years between Doug and me, and five years between myself and Donovan," McNair said. "The time gap is getting smaller, and it will continue to get smaller and become a regular occurrence. The league can see what guys like Donovan, Daunte Culpepper, Michael Vick, and others have brought to their teams and their ability to win, regardless of color."[1]

McNair was right that McNabb's generation had helped prove that Black quarterbacks were just as capable as their white counterparts; a lot had changed in the decade since McNair was drafted. But after the Super Bowl, with the Patriots and Brady celebrating their third title in four years, a disquieting aspect of the Black quarterback narrative simmered. If any owner, GM, or coach quietly believed they needed a white starting quarterback to win the Super Bowl, they did not lack for evidence supporting the thought.

In 1999, the Rams had turned to Kurt Warner, a white quarterback, after giving Tony Banks, a Black quarterback, three years to prove himself. They won a Super Bowl in Warner's first season as a starter. Traded to the Baltimore Ravens, Banks earned the starting job and held it for the first eight games of the 2000 season. But with the team's offense faltering, Banks was benched in favor of Trent Dilfer, a white quarterback, who ended the season by helping the Ravens to eleven straight wins, the last a rout of the New York Giants in Super Bowl 35.

The Bucs went to the playoffs in 1999 and 2000 with King, but after being eliminated shy of the Super Bowl twice, they turned to Brad Johnson, a veteran quarterback who was white, in 2001. A year later, they won the Super Bowl.

McNabb, with his start, was in a position to help change the narrative, and he played well enough against the Patriots, throwing for 357 yards and three touchdowns—one of the best statistical lines by a quarterback in Super Bowl history. Slight underdogs, the Eagles were tied with the Patriots late in the third quarter.

But McNabb faltered late, throwing two interceptions in the fourth quarter as the game slipped away. Afterward, it was rumored he had vomited on the field in the final minutes, prompting speculation that an ill-timed case of the nerves had struck. McNabb denied it.

Regardless, Brady delivered when the outcome was in doubt. Tall and seemingly nerveless, his statistical line showed twenty-three completions in thirty-three attempts with two touchdowns and no interceptions. A white quarterback had won the Super Bowl for the seventeenth straight year—another fact that went unreported.

———

Selected as the Super Bowl's Most Valuable Player for the second time, Brady, twenty-seven, was emerging as the most successful member of a generation of premier NFL quarterbacks that was almost entirely white—a generation that would continue to dominate the Super Bowl in the coming years. It was almost as if the league had, indeed, gone back to the 1950s, when Bobby Layne, Johnny Unitas, and Otto Graham ruled and the quarterback position was entirely white.

A year after Brady and the Patriots defeated McNabb and the Eagles, the Pittsburgh Steelers won the Super Bowl with a white starting quarterback in just his second year in the NFL. Ben Roethlisberger, burly and big armed, did not play well in the Super Bowl, totaling just 123 passing yards, but he was beginning a career worthy of the Pro Football Hall of Fame.

In 2006, Peyton Manning, in the middle of his own Hall of Fame–worthy career, finally added a Super Bowl victory to his superb resume. Manning, thirty, had been highly effective almost from the day he was drafted first overall in 1998, carrying the Colts to the playoffs multiple times only to fall short as others such as Brady and Roethlisberger made more plays when it mattered most. This time, though, the Colts outscored the Patriots in the AFC championship game and dominated the Chicago Bears in Super Bowl 41, with Manning leading the way.

When the Colts and Bears played on February 4, 2007, race in the NFL was a hot talking point. A Black head coach had never won the Super Bowl, and this matchup featured two Black head coaches, the Colts' Tony Dungy and the Bears' Lovie Smith. One was going to make history. It wound up being Dungy. After the Colts' 29–17 victory, Dungy was celebrated as a racial barrier-buster along the lines of Doug Williams. But Dungy's quarterback was the nineteenth straight white starter to win the Super Bowl.

A year later, Manning's younger brother, Eli, made it twenty in a row. Eli and the Giants were heavy underdogs in Super Bowl 42 against the Patriots, who were attempting to become pro football's first undefeated champions since the Miami Dolphins in 1972. But the Giants' defense pressured Brady, sacked him five times, and kept him from dominating. Eli delivered a game-winning touchdown pass in the final minute.

In 2008, the Steelers won another Super Bowl with Roethlisberger, and a year later, the Saints won with Drew Brees, who had become one of the sport's top quarterbacks after leaving the San Diego Chargers for New Orleans in 2006. After the Packers won with twenty-seven-year-old Aaron Rodgers at quarterback in 2010 and Eli and the Giants upset Brady and the Patriots again in 2011, white quarterbacks had won twenty-four straight Super Bowls and forty-five of forty-six since the game was first played in January 1967.

Doug Williams, the only Black starting quarterback to win the game, was now fifty-six years old.

The lack of triumphs for Black quarterbacks disappointed anyone invested in seeing them succeed. And other disappointments, ranging from unfortunate to tragic, dominated the Black quarterback narrative in the early 2000s.

Culpepper suffered a catastrophic knee injury in 2005, curtailing his career. He was twenty-eight when he went down, a three-time Pro Bowl selection coming off his finest season. In seven years with the Vikings, he had thrown for more than twenty thousand yards, with forty-nine more touchdowns than interceptions—stellar numbers. But the play on which he was injured was his last for the Vikings, who traded him before the 2006 season. Never the same after the injury, he won just three of seventeen starts for three teams over the next four seasons before retiring.

McNair's longtime employer also traded him before the 2006 season; the Titans sent him to the Ravens, ending an eleven-year run with Tennessee/Houston in which he fashioned a .595 winning percentage as a starter, nearly won a Super Bowl, and became the first Black quarterback to win the league's Most Valuable Player award—he shared the honor with Peyton Manning in 2003. It was a historic run, and McNair was still effective enough to make the Pro Bowl in 2005, but the Titans went 4–12, and it seemed their core had gone stale; they were ready for new blood.

The Ravens acquired him because they believed a solid veteran quarterback was all they needed to become a Super Bowl contender. McNair gave them exactly what they wanted in 2006, leading them to a 13–3 record, a division title, and the second seed in the AFC playoffs. But they lost to the Colts in the divisional round, and it turned out the one good season was all McNair had left. He retired after missing most of the 2007 season with an injury.

As he adjusted to life after football, he was shot to death in 2009, reportedly by a mistress, leaving behind his wife and their five children.

McNair's swan song performance with the Ravens in 2006 coincided with Vick's last season with the Falcons. But no one saw the end of his time in Atlanta coming. He was twenty-six, still an ascending player, one of the game's brightest stars. The Falcons' offensive coordinator, Greg Knapp, installed a set of designed runs giving him the option of keeping the ball or handing it off to a back. Utilizing the "zone read" scheme in 2006, Vick became the first NFL quarterback to surpass a thousand rushing yards in a season. Although the Falcons went 7–9, Vick was one of America's most unique and electrifying athletes, as evidenced by his endorsement deals with corporate powerhouses Nike and Coca-Cola.

Off the field and away from the spotlight, however, Vick was making a slew of bad decisions that were about to bring his burgeoning empire down. He had become "a master illusionist," he later wrote in his memoir, "and the illusion I had constructed would soon be revealed to the world."[2]

Vick had taken to hanging out with what he later called an "entourage of pretty questionable characters, some with their own criminal records."[3] He had sought to bring his family and friends from Newport News with him into the fabulous new life his money funded, and while his loyalty was admirable, he lost control of his surroundings. The Chargers had passed on drafting him in 2001 partly out of concern about his friends' influence on him, and those concerns were not off base, it turned out. "I spent late nights out with the guys at nightclubs, making a myriad of bad choices," he wrote. "Rather than lifting weights and running, I was out drinking and partying."[4]

Vick could have turned away from it all, but instead, he embraced it, later acknowledging he was fully responsible for his fall. "I had become a 'me' guy," he wrote. "Truth is, I just cared about my own time and not much else."[5]

In early 2007, he made headlines when he argued with an airport security guard over a water bottle and then skipped a scheduled appearance before Congress at which he was going to lobby for after-school programs. Far worse would follow.

In late April, a police dog alerted his tenders to the presence of marijuana in a car outside a nightclub in Hampton, Virginia. Police arrested one of Vick's cousins on charges of possession and distribution, and the home address the cousin provided was a property Vick owned. When police obtained a warrant and searched the property, they discovered a large-scale dogfighting operation. Behind a house where some of Vick's friends lived, there were barns, kennels, a blood-stained fighting pit, and more than four dozen dogs, some exhibiting injuries from fighting and restricted by chains.

Vick, it turned out, had been introduced to dogfighting as a child, and then had picked it back up once he was in the NFL. For the past five years, his Bad Newz Kennels had staged fighting events all over Virginia, Maryland, and North Carolina, drawing rowdy crowds of fans lusting for blood. Even though he lived in Atlanta, Vick was heavily involved, entranced by the violence and masculine environment. He developed an eye for dogs that could dominate and kill rivals in the ring. "I may have become more dedicated to the deep study of dogs than I was to my Falcons playbook. I became better at reading dogs than reading defenses," Vick wrote.[6]

Investigators turned up discoveries that outraged the public. According to a report by the US Department of Agriculture's inspector general, Vick and his associates "thought it was funny to watch the pit bull dogs belonging to Bad Newz Kennels kill or injure the other dogs" in fights.[7] Shortly before the ring was exposed, Vick and his associates killed "six to eight dogs" that had been deemed not adept at fighting, according to the inspector general's report.

Vick pleaded guilty to a federal charge related to running a dog-fighting ring and, in December 2007, was sentenced to twenty-three months in prison. Few superstar athletes had fallen faster or harder. Three years removed from signing a $130 million contract, Vick was as despised as any public figure in America.

He served most of his sentence at Leavenworth federal prison in Kansas, mopping floors, avoiding trouble, and ruminating on what he had done wrong. "I'm deeply sorry for everything . . . it was my fault," he wrote.[8]

He realized his litany of mistakes included an athletic crime: failing to fully realize his potential on the field. His athleticism was superior enough to have carried him to the NFL's upper reaches, so he slacked on the aspects of his craft that still needed developing. It was one reason the Falcons, so dependent on him, had fallen short of the pinnacle. "I should have been watching tape," Vick suddenly blurted to an Atlanta teammate who visited him in prison.

"What do you mean?" asked the teammate, a guard named Kynan Forney.

"I was doing just enough, going off instincts. We could have been much more dangerous," Vick said.[9]

Forney was shocked to hear that Vick had only recently figured this out; his Atlanta teammates had long recognized he could do more, but they had not interfered because he was so dazzling.

Vick pledged to be more professional if he received another chance in the NFL, but it was hard to imagine that materializing. The Falcons released him before he walked out of Leavenworth, free again, on May 20, 2009. Any team could sign him, but it was bound to provoke a public relations nightmare. How could you ask your fans to embrace a player who had abused animals?

But influential people were invested in seeing him get a chance to prove he was rehabilitated. Tony Dungy, recently retired from coaching, spent three hours with Vick on a high-profile visit to Leavenworth and let the football world know he thought Vick could make a positive impact on and off the field. The public agitation eventually would pass, Dungy said.

McNabb and Vick had been friends since Vick, as a high school senior, took a recruiting visit to Syracuse. When they spoke after Vick's release, Vick convinced McNabb that he was serious about receiving a second chance. McNabb spoke to Andy Reid, the Eagles' head coach. "Andy's reaction was, 'Are you sure?' and I said, 'Yeah,'" McNabb said. "He said, 'You know we're probably going to take a hit for it.' I said, 'I'm ready for it if you are.'"[10]

The timing was right for Reid to get on board. One of his sons had recently spent time in jail on a drug charge. Reid understood the importance of second chances.

The Eagles signed Vick with the idea that he would back up McNabb. Within a year, Vick had the starting job and McNabb was playing elsewhere.

The first decade of the 2000s saw a previous generation of quarterbacks receive their recognition as a new generation sought to blossom. In 2006, five years after he took his last snap, Warren Moon was voted into the Pro Football Hall of Fame, becoming the first Black quarterback to receive that honor.

In hindsight, Moon was an easy choice for the media panel that voted on Hall candidates. Even though he did not take a snap in the NFL until he was twenty-seven, he passed for nearly fifty thousand yards and earned nine Pro Bowl selections. He never won a Super Bowl, but he coolly and efficiently operated high-scoring offenses for well over a decade, using both his arm and legs to move the ball.

Speaking in Canton, Ohio, on the day he was inducted, Moon said, "All African American quarterbacks who played before me share in this. I don't want to make this a racial thing, but it's significant. It shows that we have arrived at the pinnacle of our sport."[11] He resisted using his speech to detail the prejudice he had faced, especially early in his career. Every NFL team had passed on him in the 1978 draft largely because the belief at the time was Black quarterbacks could not run complex offenses, provide leadership, or deliver in the clutch.

Although he did not win a Super Bowl, as Doug Williams did, or truly electrify fans, as Randall Cunningham did, Moon did more damage to that groupthink than anyone. "I accept the role of trailblazer now," he said in 2022. "I understand the part I might have played in what's going on in today's football with so many [Black quarterbacks] getting the opportunity to play, be drafted high, be highly endorsed. I feel like I played a small part in that, me and Doug and Randall, in really opening the minds up of a lot of those owners and general managers to say, 'Hey, these guys can play the game.'"[12]

The same year that Moon went into the Hall of Fame, the reigning group of Black quarterbacks was beginning to age and face injury and other woes. McNair and McNabb were in their thirties by then. Culpepper had torn up his knee. Vick's career would soon be halted by the dogfighting scandal.

The job market was favorable for younger Black quarterbacks, but the newest generation mostly failed to launch. Marshall's Byron Leftwich was drafted seventh overall by the Jaguars in 2003. Texas's Vince Young went third overall to the Titans in 2006. LSU's JaMarcus Russell went first overall to the Raiders in 2007. Each became their team's starter and experienced some success (not much in Russell's case), but they produced zero playoff wins between them and were gone from their original teams by age twenty-eight, never to be starting quarterbacks again.

Of the group, the most hope was invested in Young after he almost single-handedly produced a victory for Texas against a loaded Southern Cal team in the 2005 national championship game. He amassed 467 yards of offense, the last ten on a decisive and dramatic touchdown run in the final seconds.

But doubts about Young quietly arose. As a passer, he had plenty of arm strength but utilized a unique, sidearm motion and lacked accuracy at times. Then a rumor circulated about him posting a low score on the Wonderlic, an assessment test that teams used to gauge a player's ability to learn.

Years later, Young confirmed that he blew off the test. "I didn't take it serious, just wrote down anything," he said.[13] At the time, he did not see how an SAT-like standardized test had anything to do with his playing quarterback in the NFL. Other players agreed. "It has nothing that pertains to football. If you can read a defense, understand an offense, be able to comprehend your options within that offense, you can be successful," McNabb said about the Wonderlic.[14]

Though teams would continue using the Wonderlic as one of many tools for gauging players, they developed a far more nuanced view of it in the coming years, recognizing that it could penalize individuals who were not adept readers, which did not always correlate to the individual's ability to learn.

Before that became clear, Black players were more likely to see their draft stock suffer because of a poor Wonderlic score. "I didn't take it seriously and I guess [scouts] did," Young said.[15]

After the Texans passed on taking him first, Young went third overall to the Titans, who traded McNair to the Ravens two months later. Young became the starter and put on a show in 2006, winning eight of thirteen starts and capturing the Associated Press award for offensive rookie of the year. Although he was not as effective in 2007, throwing seventeen interceptions and just nine touchdowns, the Titans made the playoffs for the first time in four years.

After Young suffered a knee injury in the 2008 season opener, the Titans went on a roll with his replacement, veteran Kerry Collins, remaining unbeaten until November. That consigned Young to the backup role once he was healthy again. He did not like it, and his relationship with the Titans' head coach, Jeff Fisher, began to fray.

When Collins struggled early in the 2009 season and the Titans started 0–6, Young became the starter again. He played well enough to make the Pro Bowl for the second time and the Titans won eight of their last ten games, missing the playoffs due to their poor start without Young.

In 2010, Young dealt with a succession of injuries and then tore a tendon in his right thumb in November, ending his season and, it turned out, his tenure with the Titans as well. Even though he had compiled a 30–17 record for them as a starter over five seasons and made the Pro Bowl twice, they cut him during the off-season. Just twenty-seven, he was never again a starting quarterback. He spent one year as a backup with the Eagles and then was cut in successive years by the Bills, Packers, and Browns after training camp tryouts.

"I just got tired of the BS, taking the fun out of the game," he said, explaining why he retired at age thirty-one, having thrown his last pass three years earlier.[16]

===

On October 3, 2010, the best-known and highest-rated Black quarterbacks of their generation started opposite each other at Lincoln Financial Field in Philadelphia. McNabb was one, but weirdly, he was on the visiting team now, not the Eagles. They had traded him before the season to the Redskins, their NFC East rivals, clearing the way for Vick to take over as the Eagles' starter.

In an act of supreme selflessness, McNabb had helped his troubled friend get back into the NFL. As a result, his friend had ended up taking McNabb's job.

Their Week 4 matchup, with its soap-operatic story line, was eagerly anticipated in Philadelphia, but it did not live up to expectations. Vick went out early with an injury. McNabb completed just eight passes. The Redskins won, 17–12.

There were more fireworks when the teams played again in Washington six weeks later. Before a national audience on Monday Night Football, Vick threw four touchdown passes as the Eagles won easily, 59–28.

It was interesting to watch them compete, but to anyone invested in the success of Black quarterbacks, the enduring prominence of Vick and McNabb was discouraging in a way. Successors were not rising through the ranks. At the outset of the second decade of the new century, the NFL's quarterback population was, more than ever, primarily a study in white.

On January 24, 2010, Drew Brees and forty-year-old Brett Favre, now with the Vikings, squared off in a thrilling NFC championship game. The Saints won in overtime and then also won the Super Bowl over the Colts and Peyton Manning, who had won his fourth league MVP award that season.

The AFC was, in essence, the private domain of Brady, Roethlisberger, and Peyton Manning. Brees, Eli Manning, and Aaron Rodgers ruled the NFC.

During the 2010 regular season, the twelve quarterbacks who passed for the most yardage all were white. Among the top twenty, only McNabb, Vick, and the Tampa Bay Bucs' Josh Freeman, their 2009 first-round draft pick, were Black.

Where was the next generation?

The answer would come soon enough.

CHAPTER 24

I t all seemed simple enough, just a father trying to help his son, a high school quarterback with potential. Happens all the time.

But when Cecil Newton introduced his son, Cam, to Tee Martin, a private quarterback coach in Atlanta, Georgia, in 2006, the handshake between them was anything but simple. It was no less than a handshake between the past and future for Black quarterbacks in the NFL.

Martin had grown up in Mobile, Alabama, the son of a Black college quarterback, aware of the stereotypes and limitations they faced. "My dad had crazy ability, but he had to switch positions," Martin said in 2022.[1] Able to make plays throwing and running, Tee attended the University of Tennessee mostly because of its history of giving Black quarterbacks chances, and he had soared, succeeding Peyton Manning as the starter and achieving what Manning never could, leading the Volunteers to a national championship. But in an all-too-familiar tale, pro scouts found plenty about him not to like, the pro game itself was not as tailored to his talents, and his NFL career never took off. Now, at twenty-seven, he was beginning his second act in the sport.

Coaching came naturally to him. As a player, he had loved watching film and studying the philosophies underlying various decisions. Why did some offensive blueprints work better than others? What made a play tick? What made a *player* tick? "I'm kind of a football junkie when it comes to X's and O's and those things," Martin said in 2022.[2]

He was insightful enough to understand before his NFL career began that he probably was not destined for success. "The NFL games I watched in the 1990s were just boring," Martin said. "The quarterback just handed off or took a three-step or five-step drop [straight back] and threw. You had players like Donovan McNabb and Vick and myself lined up under center when we were so much more efficient in the shotgun, running systems that fit our skill set. I wondered, 'Am I even a fit for the NFL?'"[3]

It made him angry.

"I wanted to make it, but I felt like the NFL was behind what was happening in the college game with more open offenses," he said. "And then they were stubborn and blamed us [Black quarterbacks] instead of adjusting to these talented guys and doing things to help them. It was 'Let's just blame them because they can't do what we want.' I was, like, 'Screw you.' From the start of my time in the NFL, my mindset was 'I'm going to get what I can out of this [pro career] that'll help me when I become a coach.' I knew that's where I was headed."[4]

Heading into the 2000 draft, he earned a high grade from the Dallas Cowboys as a prospect and heard the Baltimore Ravens might take him in the second round. But he did not go until the Pittsburgh Steelers took him in the fifth round. "Surprised, hurt, disappointed, crushed," Martin said, recalling his reaction. "I thought there had to be a narrative about me that I didn't know about because guys being taken before me had not done nearly as much in college."[5]

He was excited about going to the Steelers. Years earlier, they had given Joe Gilliam, a Black quarterback, a chance to play; Martin's father had loved Gilliam's flashy style, and Martin wore uniform number 17 in Gilliam's honor. Also, the Steelers' current offense, with Kordell Stewart at quarterback, more closely resembled the varied college offenses Martin preferred. "Letting Kordell use his creativity was, at the time, regarded as an experiment around the league," Martin said. "But it was the only way Kordell had ever played. It was the only way I had ever played. High school quarterbacks were lining up in the shotgun, throwing on the move. Football was changing everywhere except in the NFL. You had to figure the day was coming. I know I was thinking that way. Looking back, my timing was not good in that respect."[6]

His timing was unfortunate in another respect: the Steelers had just signed Stewart to a lucrative contract the year before Martin was drafted. Although Stewart would leave after the 2002 season, he still had the organization's support during the two years Martin was in Pittsburgh. Martin only played in one game and never attempted a pass. "I just felt like my opportunity to win a job and play didn't exist," he said. "And once you're a low round pick, teams have no problem moving on from you."[7]

He spent a year on the Philadelphia Eagles' practice squad, a year with the Oakland Raiders, and two years with the Canadian Football League's Winnipeg Blue Bombers before deciding he was done playing. Settling in Atlanta, he became an assistant coach at a high school and worked at Nike quarterback camps as a "dual-threat" expert, as opposed to a "pro-style" expert, which was code for straight drop-back quarterback play. He eventually broke away from Nike and took on clients as a dual-threat quarterback coach in Atlanta, a college football hotbed, where he was recalled for his glory days at Tennessee rather than for his forgettable pro career.

His idea was to develop drills that introduced young quarterbacks to the skills and moves they would need and the situations they would face if they played like Martin had at Tennessee or Stewart did with the Steelers.

"Spinning away from the rush. Running around in the pocket, deciding whether to take off [running] or throw the ball," Martin said. "Just going through the different drop-backs and setups for throwing, making sure you kept your balance. When I did it in a game or saw others do it, the reaction [of coaches] was always, 'Wow, that was offbeat, great play, way to adjust.' In my mind, I'm going, 'Why don't we actually practice it?' No one did. But if you did, it would go in the player's toolbox and come out at some point, like when he was being rushed from the blind side, he could spin out and extend the play. He had practiced it."[8]

The style was an extension of the imaginary backyard football Martin had played as a youngster. In those days, he would spin around, jump over tires that he pretended were defenders. "My mom thought I was crazy," he said, "but they were the moves I used later. My idea was to create a curriculum for young quarterbacks made up of the moves they'd need later."[9]

He was thinking about molding quarterbacks for college football more than the pros when he began. The NFL seemed like a dead-end proposition to him, but the college game had a sizable population of dual-threat quarterbacks, many of them Black.

Getting Cam Newton into that population was what Cam's father, Cecil, wanted. As a junior in 2005, Cam was the starting quarterback for the Lions of Westlake High School, one of the top teams in Georgia. Their quarterback almost always played in college, and indeed, recruiters were interested in Cam. But Cecil was troubled by what they were saying. "I don't know how Cecil heard about me," Martin recalled, "but the first time we spoke, he kept saying, 'They're trying to switch his position. My boy, they're talking about switching him.'"[10]

It galled Martin. He knew that history. He knew how to translate what was being said. He knew the recruiters meant that they didn't believe Cam could handle the mental aspect of being a college quarterback.

A decade earlier, when Martin was being recruited out of Mobile's Williamson High School, he had established simple guidelines. If a school recruited him, only not as a quarterback, it was off his list. He would either play quarterback in college or play baseball, his favorite sport growing up. He was talented enough on the diamond to perhaps make the major leagues. If his football career petered out because no college would let him play quarterback, he was fine with playing baseball. It was certainly preferable to being forced to switch positions in football because some recruiter or coach doubted his intelligence. "One school recruited me by saying they had never had a Black quarterback before. I didn't think that was the right place for me," Martin recalled, chuckling.[11]

He picked Tennessee partly because it started out recruiting him as a quarterback and never wavered, and also because, among his many on-campus visits, it was the only one during which football X's and O's were brought up. He sat in on a meeting with Peyton Manning, the school's starting quarterback, destined to become famous for his obsessive film study, and David Cutcliffe, the offensive coordinator and quarterbacks coach, renowned as an expert teacher and mentor at the position. "I learned more in that one meeting than I had learned in my entire life in football up to that point," Martin said.[12]

After backing up Manning for two years, he was ready when his opportunity arrived. "I ran the same system Peyton did before he became the first [overall draft] pick [in 1998]," Martin said. "Called the same protections, ran the same two-minute drill. In fact, I had more on my plate than he did because they added some stuff [to the playbook] because of my skill set."[13]

It was laughable to think *this* Black quarterback was not smart enough to play in the NFL. But when he was not drafted until the fifth round, he believed the decades-old stereotype was one factor that had contributed to his stock dropping.

Nothing has changed, Martin thought.

A year later, after his rookie season in Pittsburgh, he had lunch with an event planner in Atlanta. Making conversation, he explained to her that he did not know the trailblazing Black quarterbacks who had come before him. The event planner's ears perked up. She contacted Warren Moon, James Harris, Marlin Briscoe, and others, and put together a weekend of events in Nashville. The Black quarterbacks played golf and planted a tree on the Tennessee State campus in honor of Joe Gilliam, who had died the year before. The weekend culminated with a lunch. "We ate, shut the doors, and Warren and the others started telling stories about what they went through," Martin said. "There was laughter. There were tears. Donovan and Culpepper and myself, young guys, we're sitting there, it's 2001, and we're going, 'This stuff is still happening. Nothing has changed, in a way.' Some guys were playing now, but there was so much in the NFL going against you. You're motivated to try to change it, but at the same time, if it hasn't changed after all these years, you feel a little helpless."[14]

That was what irked Martin five years later when Cecil Newton told him recruiters were talking about switching Cam from quarterback to tight end. Yes, that "stuff" was still happening. Martin told Cecil he would try to help, and Cecil brought Cam to a meeting.

"Wow, you're a big one," Martin said, looking Cam over as they shook hands.

"Yes, sir," Cam replied, flashing the megawatt smile the football world would soon know.[15]

A few years earlier, in middle school, Cam had been a scrawny kid wearing glasses. Then he started to grow. By his junior year, he was six feet three and 205 pounds. It was not a surprise: his older brother, Cecil Jr., was an offensive center, now playing at Tennessee State at more than three hundred pounds. But Cam had skills as well as size—foot speed, quickness, a deft passing touch.

"Cecil was upset about the possibility of him having to change positions. I said, 'No, just let me spend some time with him,'" Martin recalled. "We started out basic, just working on different drop-backs and footwork, the things you need as a quarterback playing out of the shotgun and throwing from different spots. He was the first guy I really got to work with. And I'm going, 'Wow, this guy, he's talented. Wow, this guy, he's really, really athletic.'"[16]

Martin had seen the future, it turned out, with his idea that pro football might soon follow the examples of college and high school football, where Black quarterbacks now used their skills more.

It would shock Martin and other keen observers of football's evolution when the pro game changed a few years later. "I never thought I would see the day when the college game influenced the NFL. It would always be the other way around, I figured, the NFL setting the example that the colleges and high schools would follow. But I was wrong about that," said Ozzie Newsome, who became the first Black general manager in NFL history, with the Ravens, in 2002, after a playing career that put him in the Pro Football Hall of Fame.[17]

A new style of quarterback play was coming to the NFL, tailored for a new generation of Black quarterbacks. And Cecil Newton's son would lead the way.

The Carolina Panthers did not wait long to make the first pick in the 2011 draft. They had ten minutes to consider their selection after Commissioner Roger Goodell opened the event at Radio City Music Hall in New York on a Thursday night in late April. Goodell practically sprinted back to the podium a minute later to announce the Panthers were taking Cam Newton.

The quick turnaround reflected the ease of the Panthers' decision. They had won just two games the year before, quite a fall for a team two years removed from a twelve-win season, and their quarterbacks had thrown more than twice as many interceptions as touchdown passes during the poor season. That fall, meanwhile, Newton delivered one of the finest performances in college football history, becoming the first Southeastern Conference quarterback to surpass two thousand passing yards and one thousand rushing yards in a season while leading Auburn to a national championship. At six feet six and 250 pounds, the winner of the Heisman Trophy balloting in a landslide, he looked like a grown-up toying with teenagers, more than ready to become a starter in the pros.

The Panthers did have some concerns and red flags to weigh before they selected Newton and made him the centerpiece of their rebuilding effort. When he signed with the University of Florida out of high school, the Gators already had a very good quarterback, adept at both running and passing—Tim Tebow won the Heisman in 2007 with Newton, then a freshman, backing him up. Unable to get on the field over two seasons in Gainesville, Newton had issues off the field. Police arrested him for stealing a laptop (charges were dropped when he completed a court-ordered pretrial diversion program) and then, according to the *New York Times*, he left the school after the fall semester in 2008 "rather than face suspension or expulsion in part because of three instances of academic cheating."[18] When the news of his academic problems surfaced two years later, Newton did not confirm or deny them in a statement released by Auburn, where he was then enrolled.[19]

After leaving Florida, Newton landed at Blinn College in Brenham, Texas, and helped the football team win a national junior college championship, igniting another recruiting battle, which Auburn won. But this round of recruitment spawned more controversy, which loomed over Newton as he played for Auburn in 2010. In a radio interview, a former Mississippi State football player alleged that Cecil Newton had told him it would cost a school "anywhere from $100,000 to $180,000" to sign Cam after his time at Blinn.[20] The NCAA investigated and alleged that Cecil had marketed Cam for pay.[21] Cecil denied any wrongdoing.[22] Auburn officials denied any involvement and maintained Newton also was not involved, and thus, eligible to play. The NCAA briefly declared Newton ineligible in December before reversing the decision, citing a lack of evidence, and letting him finish the 2010 season—gloriously, it turned out.[23]

Newton never played like someone under a cloud of controversy; he exuded joy as he dominated. When he scored a touchdown, he pantomimed ripping open his jersey to reveal another layer of clothing underneath—an imitation of Clark Kent's transformation to Superman. It was an audacious celebration, but Newton did it all with a smile, and most importantly, he backed it up. In their biggest game of the regular season, against Alabama, the Tigers fell behind, 24–0, threatening their perfect record. Newton led an epic winning comeback.

The Panthers were not concerned about the scandals of his college years as they weighed taking him with the first overall pick. They just wanted to make sure "Superman" was mature enough to handle being a starting NFL quarterback and serving as the face of a franchise. The two Black quarterbacks previously drafted first overall had not set the best example. Vick had been exciting and dynamic but eventually self-destructed. JaMarcus Russell had flunked out of the NFL in three years.

After spending time with Newton in the pre-draft process, the Panthers concluded he could handle the opportunity. The team's founder and owner, Jerry Richardson, signed off on drafting him first overall. But Richardson had stipulations, which he detailed several months after the draft during an appearance on *Charlie Rose*, an interview program on PBS.

Richardson was seventy-five years old, silver-haired, and spoke in a syrupy Southern drawl; he had made a fortune in the fast food industry and was popular in his native North Carolina for having brought NFL football to the region. Asked by Rose about Newton, Richardson recounted a snippet from their conversation before the draft. "He was dressed perfectly," Richardson said. "I asked him, 'Do you have any tattoos?' He said, 'No, sir, I don't have any.' I asked him, 'Do you have any piercings?' He said, 'No, sir, I don't have any.' I said, 'We want to keep it that way.'"[24]

Tattoos and skin piercings were common among young people. Richardson told Rose he thought he was being "reasonable," but to some ears, it sounded like a white master dictating to a Black enslaved person on a Southern plantation before the Civil War.[25]

The interview aired in August while the Panthers were in training camp, and it briefly generated headlines. But Richardson was close to bulletproof; a thirteen-foot statue of him would be erected outside the Panthers' stadium in 2016, and no lasting outcry ensued. Newton, who had signed a $22 million contract before joining the team, said the comments were being "blown out of proportion" and characterized his relationship with the owner as "A-1."[26]

But even though the story quickly disappeared, it revealed several enduring truths about the NFL. Two-thirds of the players were Black, but their careers still depended on the approval of white superiors; the league's ruling class, as white and lordly as ever, was comfortable wielding its immense, controlling power. And among that Black playing population, quarterbacks were held to a singular standard.

The Panthers, like all teams, had plenty of Black players with tattoos and piercings. Richardson had not scolded them about it. He just wanted Newton looking a certain way.

Most NFL owners did not mind having a Black starting quarterback now, provided the quarterback was not *too* Black.

———

Before the Panthers drafted Newton, the biggest question scouts had about him was whether he was polished enough as a passer. It did not take him long to provide an answer. Anointed as the starter heading into his rookie season, he tossed a seventy-seven-yard touchdown pass in the first quarter of his first game. He ended up throwing for 422 yards in a loss to the Cardinals. A week later, in his first home start, he threw for 432 in a loss to the Packers. In the history of the NFL, no quarterback had thrown for as many yards in his first two games.

Newton was still unhappy because he threw three interceptions against Green Bay, which proved costly, and he was unaccustomed to losing. But it was clear he was ready for the NFL.

More importantly, the NFL was ready for him.

The Panthers had hired a new head coach, Ron Rivera, to oversee their rebuilding. A thirty-nine-year-old former NFL linebacker, he had risen through the ranks as a defensive assistant to become one of the few Latino head coaches in league history. Familiar with the racial stereotyping that could hinder careers, he wanted no part of such labeling now, demanding that the Panthers make the most of Newton's varied talents, as opposed to boxing him into the accepted norms for NFL quarterbacks.

Rivera's offensive coordinator, Rob Chudzinski, stationed Newton in the shotgun, at the helm of a "read option" scheme. Sometimes he took the snap and ran with the ball, or handed it off to a back. Sometimes he ran laterally and threw. Sometimes he stayed in the pocket and threw. Although he struggled at times to command the offense as Chudzinski increased the size of the playbook during the season, the results were breathtaking. Newton surpassed four thousand yards passing for the season, and his season rushing total of 706 yards was the sixth highest by a quarterback in league history. The Panthers only won six games, but that was triple their win total from the year before, and their offense was chiefly responsible.

Selected to the Pro Bowl, Newton was on his way. He would end up fulfilling the promise the Panthers had envisioned, leading them to three division titles and a Super Bowl appearance while becoming the first Black quarterback to win the league's Most Valuable Player award outright. And he was not alone as a Black quarterback who entered the NFL in the early 2010s and forever altered fundamental notions about the position. Colin Kaepernick, drafted thirty-six slots after Newton in 2011, would make an even faster climb to the pinnacle of the NFL. Robert Griffin III and Russell Wilson, drafted in 2012, would stun the sport with how well they performed.

Never again would a snapshot of the NFL's quarterback population amount to a study in white.

CHAPTER 25

In late November 2012, the San Francisco 49ers faced a decision that gripped their locker room, their fans, and the entire NFL. Should they put their season in the hands of Alex Smith, their twenty-eight-year-old starting quarterback who had been playing the best football of his career before being sidelined for several games due to a concussion? Or should they start Colin Kaepernick, a second-year player who had displayed great upside while Smith was out?

A lot was at stake. The 49ers had almost made the Super Bowl the year before with Smith at quarterback, losing the NFC championship game in overtime, and they were serious contenders again in 2012, having forged one of the NFC's best records. The success of their season could hinge on whether they picked the right quarterback to lead them down the stretch and into the playoffs.

Jim Harbaugh, the 49ers' head coach, would make the call, assisted by input from his offensive coordinator, Greg Roman. The precepts of pro sports dictated that Smith was the choice. It was unfair, the thinking went, to take away a player's job just because he had suffered an injury. All Smith had done "wrong" was take a brutal hit to the head early in a Week 10 game against the St. Louis Rams, sending him to the sidelines. That he could lose his starting job as a result seemed wholly inappropriate, especially since he was ranked among the league's most efficient passers.

But Harbaugh was not a conventional thinker. Before becoming a coach, he had supplemented his relatively average physical skills as an NFL quarterback with a creative approach to the position's problems, enabling him to last fourteen years in the league. His ease with taking risks had also helped him make a rapid ascent in coaching. He had started out as the head coach at the University of San Diego, a job he held for three years. Then he was the head coach for Stanford for four years. The 49ers had hired him at age forty-eight in 2011.

Roman, who had come to the 49ers with Harbaugh from Stanford, was also an unconventional thinker. At a time when passing games were becoming a greater influence on offenses at every level, Roman's specialty was the running game. A short, squatty Midwesterner, he had only reached the NCAA's Division III level as a player (he was a defensive lineman at John Carroll University in Ohio) and was hardly an overnight sensation in coaching (he had recently worked for a year at his high school alma mater). But working with the like-minded Harbaugh had boosted his career; he was now one of the NFL's hottest assistants.

An experience from early in his coaching career informed Roman's use of his quarterbacks. He started out as an unpaid strength and conditioning coach with the Carolina Panthers when they were an expansion team in the mid-90s, playing in the NFC West. That meant they faced the 49ers and quarterback Steve Young twice a year.

Sitting in defensive staff meetings, Roman noted the coaches' frustration with their unit's inability to corral Young. "We were trying to cover [49er receivers] Jerry Rice, J. J. Stokes, and Terrell Owens, and we'd get them covered, and then Steve just tucks the ball in and runs for fifteen yards. It just breaks your spirit," Roman said in 2022. "You do everything right except maybe one guy gets out of his rush lane a bit, and Steve runs for a first down. It would definitely piss you off. When I observed what a problem he was for defensive coaches, that made a huge impact on me."[1]

In his offense, the quarterback was always on the move out of the shotgun or pistol formation, either throwing on the run or running with the ball himself when he did not hand it off to a running back. Young, one of the greatest running quarterbacks in NFL history, was his inspiration.

It was an ideal system for mobile Black quarterbacks, but also for white quarterbacks with the right skills. That became apparent when

Roman coached at Stanford under Harbaugh for two years. His arrival in 2009 coincided with the ascendance of Andrew Luck, a strong and precise passer with nimble feet and a quick mind. A lot went on before the snap in Roman's offense; the quarterback had to scan the defense and make a play call from among as many as a half-dozen options. Roman quickly realized he could ramp up the sophistication level with Luck at quarterback. "I was installing stuff at Stanford that I couldn't even run in the NFL later because it was so complex, but those kids were so smart," Roman said. "I would sit up there installing stuff I had never used before, and Andrew would just sit in the front row and write a couple of words down and never make a mistake on any of it. He was a freak that way, just so much brain power."[2]

Stanford went 5–7 the year before Luck became the starter; when he was a sophomore starter in 2010, the Cardinals went 12–1 and earned a top five national ranking. Luck finished second in the Heisman Trophy voting.

When Harbaugh and Roman jumped to the 49ers after that season, they inherited a starting quarterback with a similarly sharp mind. Alex Smith easily made quick reads and snap judgments at the line. But he had underperformed since the 49ers selected him with the first overall pick in the 2005 draft, winning just nineteen of fifty starts while never topping a modest three thousand passing yards in a season. Fans wanted the team to move on from him.

Operating Roman's offense in 2011, he was far more efficient and successful. The 49ers went 13–3 and fell just short of making the Super Bowl. Smith surpassed three thousand passing yards, threw just five interceptions all season, and finished third in the balloting for the Associated Press Comeback Player of the Year award.

In the first half of the 2012 season, he played like a former first overall draft pick should, completing more than 70 percent of his passes while leading the 49ers to a 6–2 record. Roman's running game was the heart of the offense and some fans still wanted anyone other than Smith at quarterback, but there was no denying his high level of play. On the last Sunday in October, he completed eighteen of nineteen pass attempts, with three going for touchdowns, in a road victory against the Arizona Cardinals. His only incompletion was a drop by an open receiver. Smith was "nearly perfect," the Associated Press reported.[3] It was hard to imagine him losing his job.

A week later, at home against the Rams, he completed seven of his first eight attempts. The 49ers surprisingly fell two touchdowns behind early, but Smith directed a touchdown drive to cut the deficit in half and the home fans felt a rally materializing. Suddenly, though, Smith was out of the game. He had taken a hit to the head. A team physician feared he had suffered a concussion and sent him to the locker room for further evaluation. He never returned.

The job of rallying the 49ers fell to Smith's young backup, who had never started an NFL game. Kaepernick grabbed his helmet.

━━━

Fans of the 49ers had cheered when the team drafted a quarterback with a second-round pick in the spring of 2011. Harbaugh and Roman had just arrived from Stanford a few months earlier and had not coached an NFL game yet; Smith's improved play in Roman's offense had not occurred.

The fans did not mind that the new quarterback was somewhat of an unknown, having played at the University of Nevada, or that he had a long name that was difficult to pronounce. You had to say it slowly at first to get it right: *Kapp . . . ur . . . nick.*

Nevertheless, Kaepernick's athletic gifts were impossible to miss. At six feet five and 225 pounds, he was big, with long legs that went on and on. Though not as quick as Steve Young or Michael Vick, he was among the fastest men on any field when he started running. His arm strength could be discerned from his background. He had thrown 90 mph fastballs as a high school baseball pitcher near Sacramento, California. The Chicago White Sox drafted him.

Nevada was the only college that offered him a football scholarship, and he had embarrassed those who doubted him, becoming the first quarterback in NCAA history to surpass ten thousand passing yards and four thousand rushing yards in his career. If it had happened in the Southeastern Conference, he would have been a first-round pick. Doubts about the quality of his opposition caused him to last until the second round, as did his elongated throwing motion. "He could rip intermediate throws, but with his release, he couldn't really get his elbow up and pull down on a ball, which sets its launch angle. He really wasn't very good at that," Roman said. "He could really rip the ball but couldn't put a lot of arc and pace on it. You had to work around that."[4]

Heading into the 2011 draft, the 49ers were open to finding Smith's successor. They had not had a winning season since 2002. Their fans, accustomed to better, were not happy. When they sent coaches and scouts to Nevada to interview Kaepernick, Roman tagged along. The 49ers would be installing his offense, after all; what he wanted and needed in a quarterback mattered.

Roman was impressed with the sophistication of Nevada's offense, which Kaepernick had mastered. And Roman was really impressed with Kaepernick, who was graduating on time with a business degree. He had been a standout student throughout high school and college. "Just a very intelligent guy, immediately apparent," Roman recalled in 2022. "He destroyed the whole Black quarterback thing about not being able to think or whatever, which was ridiculous, anyway. But I mean, I had had Andrew [Luck] and Alex [Smith], both of whom were as good as anyone at thinking their way through situations. And Colin was right there with them."[5]

The average football fan was not aware that Kaepernick's quick mind was one of his best assets. But as the world would learn soon enough, there was a lot about Kaepernick that was not apparent when you watched him play football.

Born in Milwaukee, Wisconsin, in 1987 to a white mother and Black father of African ancestry, he had been put up for adoption as an infant and taken in by Rick and Teresa Kaepernick, a white couple in nearby Fond du Lac. They had two older children but wanted another after losing two infant sons to heart defects. When Colin was four, the family moved to a mostly white suburb of Fresno, California, where Rick became vice president of a cheese company.

Although Colin was not especially dark skinned, he stood out in his family with his biracial ethnicity. He learned to joke about it, but the fact that his skin color prompted questions stuck with him. Sports were a realm in which he knew he belonged, but away from the playing fields, he searched for an identity. At Nevada, he believed some of his Black classmates resented him because his white parents paid his rent and supported him. But some white classmates resented him, he believed, simply because he was a person of color. As a result, he felt accepted nowhere, understanding that his skin color had put challenges in front of him that whites did not face. He pledged a Black fraternity, thinking it might help crystallize his outlook, and spoke at university events promoting diversity.

The 49ers were not concerned about any of that as the second round of the 2011 draft unfolded. They only cared that another team might take Kaepernick first, so they engineered a trade, sending three picks to the Denver Broncos for a pick earlier in the round. Watching on ESPN with his family outside Fresno, Kaepernick was delighted to go to a team less than two hundred miles away.

With typical rookie bravado, he started out saying he planned to compete for a starting job. But there was no competition once Smith took so well to Roman's offense. Kaepernick spent his rookie season almost entirely on the sideline, watching Smith lead the 49ers to their best season in nearly a decade.

The next year at training camp, Smith was the clearcut starter and Kaepernick competed for the backup job. But not for long. The 49ers' victory over the Minnesota Vikings in their exhibition opener was forgettable except for one play. On his second play after taking over for Smith, Kaepernick lined up in the shotgun, took the snap, and ran to his right. A hole opened and he angled through it and sprinted down the sideline, stiff-arming a defender to enable him to complete a seventy-eight-yard touchdown run. When he reached the end zone, he flung his arms wildly in celebration.

The coaches had seen hints of his explosiveness in practice, but seeing it in a game, even in August, opened their eyes. "I was like,

'Whoa, we've got lightning in a bottle here,'" Roman said.[6] He put in a set of plays with Kaepernick as a wildcat quarterback, running and throwing out of the shotgun, and used them as a change-of-pace option early in the season. Kaepernick attempted nine passes and ran for two touchdowns in the first eight games.

But when Smith went out with a concussion while playing against the Rams, Kaepernick suddenly was the 49ers' number-one quarterback, at least for the rest of that game. Roman simplified the calls, knowing it was Kaepernick's first game in charge. "We ran a very complicated, layered offense with Alex, with checks, audibles, and packages. He might come to the line and call seven different plays. We didn't start Colin out at that level, but he was able to do it; he was really, really good before the snap," Roman said. "He easily understood why you would want to check to this or that play. And the more he did it, the more he picked up on it."[7]

He was effective against the Rams, throwing for 117 yards and rushing for sixty-six yards and a touchdown. The 49ers trailed by ten points entering the fourth quarter, but Kaepernick led a rally and the game ended in a tie.

Smith hoped his doctors would clear him to return for the 49ers' next game, a Monday Night Football matchup against the Chicago Bears. But he was not cleared, so Kaepernick started.

The fact that a Black quarterback was starting for the 49ers received no media attention before the game. But a tale lurked. The 49ers had opened for business in 1946 as part of the All-America Football Conference and joined the NFL in 1950 when the AAFC folded. In their first sixty-four seasons, through 2009, they had started only white quarterbacks. Troy Smith, a twenty-six-year-old former Heisman Trophy winner, had become their first Black starting quarterback on October 31, 2010, when he led them to a victory over the Broncos.

No one was going to call it progress with the NFL a decade away from celebrating its centennial; the absence of Black starting quarterbacks was an appalling and enduring thread running through the histories of many teams and the league.

Kaepernick became the 49ers' second Black starting quarterback when he faced the Bears on Monday Night Football. The Bears were a solid team, headed for double-digit wins that season after winning the NFC Central the year before. Kaepernick picked their defense apart. On the game's third snap, he arched a perfect strike to his tight end, Vernon Davis, for a twenty-two-yard gain, setting up a field goal. A few minutes later, he threw deep for a receiver, Kyle Williams, who reeled in the pass for a fifty-seven-yard gain, setting up a touchdown. The 49ers led by twenty points at halftime and won, 32–7, with Kaepernick throwing for 243 yards and two touchdowns. He certainly did not look like he was making his first NFL start.

"He just lit it up completely," Roman said. "Everything on the money, everything sharp, and we steamrolled them. He just brought a different dimension. He didn't even run much in that game, but when he did, he was like a bullet train with his stride length and speed. You just had to get him going."[8]

But even though Kaepernick had put on a show, it was widely assumed Alex Smith would reclaim the starting job as soon as he was cleared to play. He was ranked first in the league in passing efficiency. The 49ers were in first place in the NFC West largely because of how well they had played with him.

When Harbaugh and Roman discussed what they would do, though, they did not weigh statistics. They weighed what they had seen against the Bears. "Colin was just so dynamic," Roman said.[9]

As the 49ers began preparing for their next game, it remained unclear whether Smith would be available. Harbaugh did not wait to find out. He informed both quarterbacks that Kaepernick would practice with the first team that week, an indication that he likely would start against the Saints in New Orleans.

"We went by instinct," Roman said. "A lot of people on the team were not happy with the decision. And some coaches. They just didn't feel somebody should lose their job with an injury. And I get that. But you have to weigh everything, and we just felt like there was an X factor with Colin. He gave us such a shot in the arm. We didn't know how it was going to go against the Bears. We were in 'wait and see' mode. And there he was, six five and a half, hitting all the throws, and when he started running, it was so impressive."[10]

He proved it again that Sunday, leading a second-half surge that produced a win in one of the NFL's toughest road environments. That was followed by his first hiccup, an average performance in a road loss to the Rams, but he bounced back impressively at home against the Miami Dolphins, completing eighteen of twenty-three passes and rushing for fifty-three yards and a touchdown.

With a month left in the season, the 49ers were in first place but feeling some heat; the Seattle Seahawks, young and feisty, were on a roll, forcing the 49ers to keep winning or risk losing a prime spot in the NFC playoffs. A Week 15 road game against the New England Patriots and Tom Brady loomed as pivotal. Brady was especially hard to beat at home.

Working on his offensive blueprint for the game, Roman faced a dilemma. He had kept under wraps several sets in the "pistol" formation, which really suited Kaepernick's skills. "I was saving a lot of stuff for the playoffs, didn't want to expose it," he said. "But we needed to win in New England to secure a spot, so I said, 'The heck with it. I'm hedging my bets here. I'm putting all the chips in and we're going to do all this stuff that he's good at.'"[11]

By early in the third quarter, the 49ers led, 31–3, and Kaepernick had thrown three touchdown passes. After a furious rally by the Patriots tied the score, Kaepernick went off script and hit an open receiver for a thirty-eight-yard touchdown that gave the 49ers the victory.

With a playoff berth secured, Roman put the sets that had battered the Patriots back on the shelf for the last two games of the regular season. The 49ers held off the Seahawks to win the division and earn the second seed in the NFC playoffs, which gave them a first-round bye.

Nothing was assured when they faced the Packers in a divisional-round game in San Francisco; the Packers had Aaron Rodgers and a defense that had not allowed a point until late in a first-round playoff win over the Vikings. The Packers struck first when one of their cornerbacks intercepted Kaepernick and returned it for a touchdown. "This is the great unknown in this matchup," Fox's Joe Buck said on the television broadcast, referencing Kaepernick.[12]

But the Packers could not corral him. He wound up passing for 263 yards and two touchdowns, and his running caused even more trouble. Roman's love of mobile quarterbacks traced to his early years as a coach, watching the Carolina Panthers' defensive staff grow frustrated with their inability to stop Steve Young from scrambling for gains. Kaepernick's performance against the Packers was the ultimate distillation of the advantage of having a quarterback who could run.

Quickly making amends for the interception, Kaepernick scrambled away from the pass rush and hit his running back, Frank Gore, with a perfect pass down the sideline. The play went for forty-five yards. A minute later, Kaepernick dropped back, found no open receivers, tucked the ball in, and ran twenty yards for a touchdown. No Packer touched him.

Rodgers had little trouble moving the ball with his passing and putting up points, but Kaepernick had two ways of moving the ball, with his legs as well as his arm. Whenever the Packers sent blitzers at him, he took off running for gains that kept drives going. With the score tied in the middle of the third quarter, Kaepernick ran around the right end, found a hole, and sprinted fifty-six yards for a touchdown. "Ran right through the whole defense," Roman said.[13] Then he locked up the victory in the fourth quarter with a deep pass to Vernon Davis, which set up a clinching touchdown.

No longer was he a "great unknown." And no longer could anyone question the 49ers' decision to go with him over Alex Smith. "I don't know that any of us had ever seen anyone quite like him. I mean, every player is different. But he was truly one of a kind," Roman said.[14]

He aced another test in the NFC championship game a week later. The Falcons, the NFC's top seed, were determined not to let him run wild, and Kaepernick adjusted, handing the ball off to Gore instead of trying to make all the plays himself. The 49ers trailed early in Atlanta, 17–0, but methodically caught up, went ahead, and held on to win.

The victory put the 49ers into Super Bowl 47 against the Baltimore Ravens, who were coached by Harbaugh's brother, John, and quarterbacked by Joe Flacco, a classic drop-back passer with a huge arm.

Kaepernick was the first Black quarterback since Donovan McNabb to make a Super Bowl start. Twenty-five years had passed since Doug Williams became the first—and still only—Black quarterback to win a Super Bowl. Logic had dictated that a ballyhooed talent such as Michael Vick or Vince Young would be the second, but with the 49ers favored to beat the Ravens, largely due to Kaepernick's sudden and spectacular emergence, it appeared a former second-round pick from the University of Nevada would succeed Williams.

But the Ravens were a formidable opponent led by a pair of veteran defensive stars headed for the Pro Football Hall of Fame, linebacker Ray Lewis and safety Ed Reed. They also were on a roll; they had dominated the Patriots to win the AFC championship game. The roll continued through the first half of the Super Bowl, played at the Superdome in New Orleans. Flacco had thrown eight touchdown passes and no interceptions in the AFC playoffs, and he threw three more touchdowns in the first half as the Ravens built a 21–6 lead. With Lewis and Reed orchestrating an agile defense, Kaepernick was kept largely in check.

When the Ravens' Jacoby Jones returned the opening kickoff of the second half for a touchdown, the Ravens had a 28–6 lead and it appeared the game would be a blowout. But Baltimore's momentum was halted by the strangest of forces—a power outage that delayed the game for thirty-four minutes. When the lights came back on and the game resumed, Kaepernick suddenly was all but unstoppable, throwing and running for gains as he engineered a massive rally.

Down by twenty-two points after Jones' kickoff return, the 49ers had the deficit down to just two after Kaepernick ran fifteen yards for a touchdown with some ten minutes to play. The 49ers went for two, seeking to tie the score, but the try failed.

Down by five with four minutes to play, the 49ers began a possession at their 20. Kaepernick ran for eight yards and completed a pass for twenty-four before Gore broke free for a forty-three-yard gain. With a new set of downs and the ball at the 7 yard line, the 49ers were seemingly on the brink of an epic comeback that would speak volumes about how the NFL had changed. A hot drop-back passer, embodying the classic stereotype, had put the Ravens in position to win. But a mobile Black quarterback, just as hot and truly a nightmare for defenses, was about to snatch the victory away.

It was hard to fathom what happened next. Kaepernick had run wild, but Lewis and Reed steeled their defense for a final stand. The 49ers' LaMichael James ran up the middle for two yards on first down, and Kaepernick threw incompletions on second down and third down. The game came down to fourth-and-goal at the five, and the Ravens brought an all-out blitz. Kaepernick threw quickly, lobbing a pass for a receiver, Michael Crabtree, rather than trying to make the defense stop him as a runner. There was contact between Crabtree and the Ravens' cornerback, Jimmy Smith, but the officials did not throw a flag and the ball fell to the ground.

Incomplete pass. The Ravens had won. More accurately, they had survived. But much like Steve McNair in the Super Bowl a dozen years earlier, Kaepernick had proven himself in defeat. It seemed all but certain that he would win a Super Bowl in time.

CHAPTER 26

Early in an NFC playoff game between the Seattle Seahawks and Washington Redskins on January 9, 2013, at FedExField outside Washington, DC, the Seahawks' Russell Wilson paced the team's sideline, exhorting his teammates to stay positive. The Seahawks had fallen two touchdowns behind, and the din made by eighty-three thousand fans, most of them rooting against the Seahawks, made it hard to think straight.

A new generation of Black quarterbacks had upended the NFL during the just-concluded regular season, exhibiting dynamic skills and uncanny poise while helping guide their teams to the playoffs. Wilson and the Redskins' Robert Griffin III had done it as rookies. Colin Kaepernick, with the 49ers, was in his second pro season. The Carolina Panthers' Cam Newton, also in his second season, had not taken his rebuilding team to the playoffs yet, but watching him puncture defenses with his running and passing, there was little doubt his time was coming.

The playoff matchup between the Seahawks and Redskins offered the clearest sign yet that a special group of Black quarterbacks had arrived. While many of the NFL's white starting quarterbacks watched from their couches that night, their seasons over, Wilson and Griffin went at it.

High above the field, in a broadcast booth on the press level, Warren Moon took everything in. *What a test for Russell*, he thought.

Moon, the only Black quarterback enshrined in the Pro Football Hall of Fame, was now an analyst on the Seahawks' radio broadcasts.

A Seattle resident, he worked every game, traveled with the team, and attended practices. He had spent hours conversing with Wilson since the Seahawks selected him in the third round of the 2012 draft earlier that year. They had a natural connection. Both had led their college teams to the Rose Bowl as seniors. Both had experienced disappointment in the NFL draft: Moon because he was not selected at all, Wilson because seventy-four players, including five other quarterbacks, were picked before him when he believed he had first-round talent. "When he got to Seattle, I was there for him as a sounding board," Moon said in a 2022 interview.[1]

There was one important difference in their stories. Moon went undrafted in 1978 almost entirely because NFL teams still wanted only white quarterbacks; it was discrimination, pure and simple, that denied him. Thirty-four years later, race was not involved in the calculus that sent Wilson tumbling to the third round. "His height was the only thing that scared people," Moon said. "At that time, teams were still looking for that cookie-cutter-sized [big] guy. If you were under six feet, like Russell, you were going to drop. On all other factors and intangibles, he had as much if not more than any other quarterback in that draft. Teams knew it. If he had been six feet or a little over, he'd have gone in the first round."[2]

Wilson had grown up in Richmond, Virginia, with football in his DNA: his father had been a fast, elusive wide receiver at Dartmouth, good enough to sign with the San Diego Chargers as an undrafted free agent in 1980 and catch a touchdown pass in a preseason game. Years later, Wilson employed the same darting style, only as a quarterback. His father, who became a successful attorney after the Chargers cut him, died of complications from diabetes in 2010, before Wilson reached the NFL.

Wilson signed with North Carolina State out of high school and played for the Wolfpack for three years before transferring to the University of Wisconsin, where he threw thirty-three touchdown passes and led the Badgers to the Big Ten championship as a senior. His leadership, handling of the offense, and ability to make plays outside the pocket impressed pro scouts. Although Wisconsin lost in the Rose

Bowl, Wilson passed for nearly three hundred yards and had a hand in three touchdowns.

Months later, there was a run on quarterbacks early in the 2012 draft. The Indianapolis Colts selected Stanford's Andrew Luck with the first overall pick. The Redskins selected Griffin second overall. Ryan Tannehill, from Texas A&M, and Brandon Weeden, from Oklahoma State, went later in the first round, and Brock Osweiler, from Arizona State, went in the middle of the second round.

It did not seem the Seahawks were looking for a quarterback. Before the draft, they had signed Matt Flynn, who had backed up Brett Favre and Aaron Rodgers in Green Bay and, at twenty-seven, was widely viewed as a potential starter needing only an opportunity. The Seahawks liked Flynn so much they gave him a three-year, $26 million contract. Tarvaris Jackson, their starter the year before, also was under contract for 2012.

But John Schneider, the Seahawks' general manager, liked Wilson enough to gamble that his many positives might outweigh the fact that he measured five feet eleven at the combine. "The Seahawks were fortunate to get a guy that good in the third round," Moon said. "But Russell also was fortunate. He went to the right place."[3]

The Seahawks were in year three of a rebuild guided by Schneider and Pete Carroll, the head coach, who had built a dynasty at Southern Cal before joining the Seahawks. After posting losing records in each of his first two seasons in Seattle, Carroll was hungry for better results. "He preached competition at every position, that was his thing," Moon said. "He was in his first couple of years there and wanted competition everywhere. Going to a team where the coach says everyone was going to compete for every job, Russell landed in a good spot."[4]

It meant the organization was open-minded about who might play quarterback even though Flynn had signed a large contract. And from Wilson's first days with the team, which took place at a rookie minicamp after the draft, he demonstrated that he just might be the right choice. "He really impressed me with how he handled things, his maturity, how he handled the huddle," Moon said. "A lot of times at a rookie camp, they throw so much at you that all you really know is how to call the play they just told you. You don't really know where everyone is going, where they line up. As soon as Russell got in, he commanded the huddle. They were in and out of the huddle with great rhythm and pace. When someone wasn't lined up properly, he motioned them to the right spot. Little things like that showed me you have maturity and command of what you're doing."[5]

When training camp began that summer, the coaches "just watched his work ethic and how quickly he picked things up," Moon said. "When you're thinking about putting in a rookie quarterback, you want to see if he can process the information you're going to give him. They saw from day one that it wouldn't be a problem. Russell studied hard. He was in the building before the coaches in the morning, and he was still there at night, when the equipment guys were the only ones left. He did everything right."[6]

The quarterback competition did not last long. Neither Flynn nor Jackson stood out in practices or the early preseason games, while Wilson made plays. Carroll named him the starter before the preseason ended. "It was an easy choice," Moon said. "He got there and made his presence felt and changed their minds."[7]

The Seahawks had Marshawn Lynch, one of the NFL's toughest running backs, and a young, hard-hitting defense. Wilson added athleticism and unpredictability to the offense. He moved the ball on designed runs and scrambles, avoided making mistakes, and threw accurately on the run and from the pocket. He also had inherited an authoritarian manner from his father; his teammates believed in him.

The Seahawks lost their season opener, won four of five, then lost two straight to give them a .500 record at midseason. Wilson occasionally looked like a rookie, but as he gained experience and became more comfortable, the offense took off, more than doubling its per-game point output in the second half of the season. A season-ending five-game winning streak included a 42–13 walloping of the San Francisco 49ers and Kaepernick.

The 49ers still won the NFC West, but the Seahawks made the playoffs as a wild card, setting up the first-round matchup with the Redskins. Inevitably, the game was framed as a meeting between rookie quarterbacks who were helping engineer the most sweeping wave of change at their position since George Halas installed the T formation in 1940.

The Redskins had paid a steep price for Griffin, giving up three first-round picks and a second-round pick to move up in the draft and take him. But they had churned through three starting quarterbacks over the previous three seasons, all of which ended with them in last place in the NFC East. They were looking for a savior, a cornerstone quarterback to build around, and they believed Griffin was the guy.

Unlike Wilson, who had to play his way into the starting job in Seattle, Griffin was effectively anointed the starter on the night he was drafted. The Redskins' head coach, Mike Shanahan, was a renowned advocate of the power running game (he had won two Super Bowls with it as the coach of the Denver Broncos), but he chiseled a set of run-pass option plays, or RPOs, into his offense, giving Griffin the option to hand off to a back, run with the ball himself, or pass after receiving the snap in the shotgun. Like Wilson, Luck, Kaepernick, and Cam Newton, Griffin was a departure from the NFL's classic drop-back norm even though he had set passing records at Baylor. Three inches taller than Wilson, he had been an All-American hurdler in track, his speed and power breathtaking as he sprinted down the lane.

Griffin passed for 320 yards and two touchdowns in his NFL debut, the Redskins' season opener, which they won on the road against the Saints. The next week, he passed for 206 yards and rushed for 82. In Week 6, he sealed a victory with a seventy-six-yard touchdown run in which he outran the Minnesota Vikings' entire defense along the sideline.

The Redskins still struggled at times, especially on defense, and their 3–6 record in early November suggested they would miss the playoffs. But like Wilson and the Seahawks, they pulled together late, winning their final seven games to capture their first division title since 1999. Griffin was named the NFL's offensive rookie of the year by the Associated Press after passing for 3,200 yards and twenty touchdowns and producing the fifth-highest season rushing total by a quarterback in league history (815 yards).

That Griffin and Wilson were opposing starters in a playoff game certainly reflected the changing norms at their position in the NFL. They had combined for 6,318 passing yards and 1,304 rushing yards while their teams combined to win twenty-one of thirty-two games. But they were not playing much differently than they had in college, where classic pocket passers had become relatively rare years earlier and many teams favored quarterbacks who could move as well as throw. What was different now, the most drastically changed norm, was how the teams that drafted Griffin and Wilson embraced how they played.

"Quarterback in the NFL was becoming a much more athletic position," Moon said. "You still had to be able to throw the football, but you also had to have more of an arsenal. It all came from college football. Basically, the NFL finally got smart and said, 'OK we're not going to force our offenses on these guys coming out of college anymore. Let's incorporate what they've been doing.' A lot of them had been running the run-pass option since high school. The NFL said, 'Let's put that in, make the learning curve easier for them. They can have more success early.' The NFL finally figured it out. Instead of trying to retrain these guys how to play, they said, 'Let's let them do what they've been doing.'"[8]

Classic pocket passers were not suddenly out of fashion; Tom Brady and Peyton Manning had ruled the league for more than a decade and still did. Teams that preferred the more traditional style argued that quarterbacks who liked to run inevitably would get injured in the NFL; pro defenders were faster, more agile, and hit harder than college defenders.

Their rationale received support when Griffin was injured in early December. In the fourth quarter of a game in which he had repeatedly frustrated the Ravens with his playmaking, he was smothered by a 350-pound defensive tackle, Haloti Ngata, while running downfield. Griffin suffered a knee sprain that forced him to sit out a game.

He returned a week later wearing a bulky brace that limited his mobility, but he still led the Redskins to back-to-back wins that clinched the division title.

Energized by their team's rookie quarterback, Washington's fans carried high hopes into the playoff game against the Seahawks. Griffin gave them plenty to cheer about early. On the game's first possession, he smartly drove his offense eighty yards to a touchdown. The Redskins' defense then sacked Wilson to end Seattle's first possession, and Griffin was right back at it, mixing passes and runs on another touchdown drive.

The Redskins led, 14–0, and the first quarter was not even over yet. "The Redskins were good. Robert was playing well. The place was really loud," Moon said.[9]

But the Seahawks' defense adjusted; noting Griffin's immobility, it focused on stopping the rest of the offense and began to dominate. Wilson, meanwhile, looked nothing like a rookie in his playoff debut. Poised and opportunistic, he scrambled for first downs, found open receivers, and led three straight drives that produced points. By halftime, the Seahawks only trailed by a point, 14–13.

That was still the score when the Seahawks began a possession early in the fourth quarter. They had blown an opportunity to take the lead earlier when Lynch fumbled at the Redskins' 1 yard line, and the crowd was roaring, imploring Washington's defense to continue to protect the slim lead. But Lynch ran up the middle for eighteen yards to get a drive started. Then, facing third-and-10 near midfield, Wilson completed a pass for twenty-two yards.

On third-and-5 at the Washington 27, Wilson handed the ball to Lynch, who bulled through two tacklers at the line. Wilson sprinted out of the backfield, wound up in front of Lynch, and cleared Lynch's path to the end zone by blocking a Washington safety. The touchdown put Seattle ahead—for good, it turned out.

"That just shows the kind of player he is," said Richard Sherman, a Seattle cornerback at the time. "It's the playoffs, and everyone has to do their part. It's not the first time he's thrown a block. He's a great quarterback. He should be offensive rookie of the year. I like RG3, too. But our guy has stepped up and showed up for us when we needed him."[10]

After Seattle's 26–14 victory, Shanahan received criticism for having continued to play Griffin when the rookie clearly was compromised. Griffin stayed in until his knee buckled as he tried to fall on a fumbled snap shortly after the Seahawks had taken the lead. He had suffered a more serious knee injury, it turned out. Unfortunately, what happened in the game would alter the trajectory of his career.

A week later, the Seahawks flew across the country again to play the Atlanta Falcons, the NFC's top playoff seed, in a divisional-round matchup. The Falcons' quarterback, Matt Ryan, was a prototypical drop-back passer, and he threw to an array of dangerous receivers. When the Falcons jumped all over the Seahawks early and led at halftime, 20–0, it appeared Wilson had taken his team as far as he could as a rookie.

But Wilson would earn a reputation for engineering epic comebacks, and he staged a classic in Atlanta. The Seahawks were down and, seemingly, out, but he picked them up and carried them, orchestrating one touchdown drive, then another, then a third. He would end the game with sixty rushing yards and 385 passing yards, and by the final minute of the fourth quarter, the Seahawks had the lead, 28–27.

But Ryan saved the Falcons, completing two passes to set up a game-winning field goal. In defeat, Wilson, emerging as a locker room leader, found reason for optimism. "That was an unbelievable comeback," he said. "Walking off the field, I got so excited for the next opportunity. I'm looking forward to what we have in the future."[11]

Warren Moon's eyebrows went up when he heard what Wilson had said. "That was a big-time situation, playoffs, on the road, way down, and nothing intimidated him. Then he was so positive after the game. You could just see that the Seahawks knew they had the right quarterback to go forward with and do big things. This was no ordinary rookie," Moon said.[12] The future Wilson was so excited about would live up to his expectations.

Pro football had opened wide to the skills that the new generation of Black quarterbacks possessed and the full range of possibilities they generated. The next fall, *Sports Illustrated*'s pro football preview issue had four different, regional covers, each featuring a different young quarterback, with the headline, "The New Kings." Three of the young quarterbacks—Wilson, Kaepernick, and Griffin—were Black, with Luck the fourth. The sub-headline on Wilson's cover read, "When you're barely six feet, it doesn't mean your career is six feet under."[13] He proved it in his second season in Seattle.

During the 2013 regular season, it became clear the Seahawks and 49ers were the class of the NFC along with Cam Newton and the Panthers. Newton had not received a personal *Sports Illustrated* cover going into the season because he had slipped as a second-year starter, but in 2013, he surpassed the form that made him a Pro Bowl selection as a rookie. The Panthers went 12–4 and won the NFC South. The 49ers also went 12–4 and finished second in the NFC West behind Seattle, which went 13–3.

After splitting their home-and-home series during the season, the Seahawks and 49ers met for a third time in the NFC championship game, with a berth in the Super Bowl at stake. "The thing I was happy about, no matter who won, there was going to be an African American quarterback in the Super Bowl," Moon said. "The more of us who could compete at a very, very high level, it was going to bring more credibility and help the next group of guys come in and get more opportunities."[14]

Although Wilson and Kaepernick had made the cover of *Sports Illustrated*, the game matched two of the league's top defenses, and they dominated before a rollicking crowd in Seattle. The Seahawks led at halftime, 10–3. Kaepernick threw a touchdown pass to give the 49ers the lead in the third quarter. Wilson threw a touchdown pass to put the Seahawks up in the fourth quarter. In the final minute, trailing by six points, Kaepernick led his offense deep into Seattle territory. On a first down at the 18, with thirty seconds to play, he lobbed a pass for Michael Crabtree; a touchdown probably would win the game.

The Seahawks intercepted.

Had Kaepernick and Crabtree connected, Kaepernick likely would have become the first Black quarterback to make two Super Bowl starts, after the 49ers' wild loss to the Baltimore Ravens the year before. Instead, Wilson became the fifth Black quarterback to make a start two weeks later, following Doug Williams, Steve McNair, Donovan McNabb, and Kaepernick.

"He downplayed it when the question came up. His response was, 'I just want to be a quarterback,'" Moon said. "I felt the same way when I played. That's something I always wanted, to be judged as just a quarterback, not a Black quarterback. And it wasn't like Russell was the first in the Super Bowl or anything, so it didn't hold that much significance. Doug Williams had done it many, many years before. I agreed with Russell, downplaying it as a point of emphasis. His play was going to make more of a statement than any actual statement he made in the newspaper."[15]

Indeed, his performance would be pivotal. Williams, now fifty-nine years old, was still the only Black winning quarterback in Super Bowl history, and the chances of Wilson becoming the second seemed long. The Seahawks were playing the Denver Broncos, who had dominated the AFC thanks largely to Peyton Manning giving the greatest passing performance in NFL history. At age thirty-seven, he had thrown for fifty-five touchdowns and 5,477 passing yards, setting new league records in both categories. His selection as the league MVP was a formality. "Peyton really had it going that whole season, with record on top of record," Moon said.[16]

The matchup set up a classic clash of old and new styles. Manning was rightfully acclaimed as one of the greatest quarterbacks ever, but Wilson had already rushed for far more yardage in two years than Manning had gained on the ground in fifteen seasons.

By the end of the Super Bowl, played in New York on February 2, 2014, both had the same number of Super Bowl triumphs.

Manning had hoped to win his second, but the Seahawks' defense swarmed him, shutting down the passing attack that had terrorized the league. "That defense had so much confidence, swagger, and speed," Moon said. "When you caught a pass, they knew how to rally to the football. A great tackling team hit you really hard. Intimidating players in the secondary. And they could get after the quarterback and make him get the ball out of his hands quickly. So they had everything you need to slow down an offense like Denver's."[17]

As Seattle's defense shut down Manning, Wilson methodically moved Seattle's offense with his usual blend of passes and runs. The Seahawks led at halftime, 22–0. It was 36–0 before the Broncos finally scored.

It had taken twenty-six years, but finally, another Black quarterback other than Doug Williams was a Super Bowl winner.

As the media swarmed him, Wilson fielded dozens of questions. Not one was about Black quarterbacks making progress. The subject never came up.

But what happened did matter when you considered the dated dogma about intelligence, poise, and leadership that had denied opportunities to so many Black quarterbacks. Six inches taller than Wilson, Manning was a classic embodiment of the white pocket-passer prototype that had prevailed for decades. But it was Wilson, not Manning, who proved himself poised and nearly perfect with a title on the line, completing eighteen of twenty-five passes for 206 yards and two touchdowns and no interceptions. Manning was the one who seemed rattled and failed to deliver.

Moon pulled Wilson aside later and congratulated him for making a point about Black quarterbacks. "I mentioned to him how proud I was of him," Moon said. "He didn't want to make a big deal out of it. But I felt I needed to say how proud I was of him, and how he had just helped the next generation of guys get more opportunities."[18]

The subject did come up when the Seahawks traveled to Washington, DC, to receive congratulations from President Barack Obama in a White House ceremony. "Russell became only the second African American quarterback to win a Super Bowl, and the best part about it was no one commented on it, which tells you the progress we've made, although we've got more progress to make," Obama said.[19]

Wilson beamed as he listened to the president. "I know history and I know football history," he wrote months later in a *Sports Illustrated* essay, acknowledging the obstacles Black quarterbacks before him had faced. But the NFL was becoming "more of a place where it's about ability first, second, and third," he wrote.[20]

Months after the Super Bowl, when the Seahawks reconvened for spring practices, they had five quarterbacks on their roster, all Black. They jokingly called themselves "The Jackson 5," but it was no laughing matter to anyone who knew history.

The Seahawks "didn't purposefully do it," Wilson wrote. "They put the best guys they could find on the roster to help the Seahawks win. But considering the history of the league and the quarterback position, how crazy is it that one team has five quarterbacks in camp, and they're all African-American? I believe that says so much about the state of the NFL today."[21]

CHAPTER 27

In the final minute of Super Bowl 49, Russell Wilson was poised to make history again by becoming the first Black quarterback to win two Super Bowls. His Seattle Seahawks had dominated Peyton Manning and the Denver Broncos the year before, and now their offense only needed to gain one yard to score a touchdown and take the lead against the New England Patriots and Tom Brady with twenty-six seconds to play.

If Wilson's spectacular NFL career to that point was any indication, the Seahawks would win. Wilson had established a pattern of producing epic comebacks and magical moments. Two weeks earlier in the NFC championship game, the Seahawks had trailed the Green Bay Packers by sixteen points at halftime and by twelve midway through the fourth quarter with Wilson having thrown four interceptions—a nightmarish performance. But then he led a rally and tossed a game-winning touchdown pass in overtime.

Wilson began the Super Bowl in a similar fashion. Twice, the Seahawks trailed the Patriots by a touchdown in the first half before taking the lead in the third quarter, only to see Brady lead a surge that gave the Patriots a four-point lead with two minutes to play. But Wilson, in classic form with the game on the line, moved the ball down the field with long completions until the Seahawks needed just one more yard.

But what followed was a play that would become infamous. Instead of giving the ball to Lynch, who seldom was stopped for a loss, Wilson tried to gain the yard through the air. Taking the snap in the shotgun, he zipped a pass for Ricardo Lockette, a reserve receiver, who had cut behind another receiver and was angling for the end zone. Malcolm Butler, a cornerback for New England, saw the "pick" play developing, cut in front of Lockette, and intercepted the pass.

"Unreal!" announcer Al Michaels shouted on NBC.[1]

Cris Collinsworth, Michaels's broadcast partner, immediately second-guessed the call on the air, suggesting a run by Lynch almost surely would have succeeded. Seattle's offensive coordinator, Darrell Bevell, had called the pass play at the 1, and Carroll had approved the call. Wilson was just following orders and threw the pass to the right place, but the fateful interception went on his statistical line.

Ever optimistic, Wilson said the Seahawks would not suffer because of the missed opportunity. But they were still reeling, it seemed, when the next season began. They opened 2015 with back-to-back losses and carried a 2–3 record into a mid-October game against the Carolina Panthers in Seattle.

The Panthers were unbeaten, having opened the season by winning four straight games with Cam Newton throwing seven touchdown passes and just two interceptions. Now twenty-six, Newton was a different quarterback than the one who had been drafted first overall in 2011. He was the same powerful runner with a strong throwing arm, but he had become savvier, more patient. Instead of locking in on one receiver, he scanned three or four options and picked the most promising. Also, instead of just taking off when he sensed pass rushers closing in, he used his mobility to stay in the pocket and wait for his receivers to get open, putting more pressure on opposing defensive backs.

Newton had experienced his share of success in his first four NFL seasons, leading the Panthers to the playoffs twice and earning two Pro Bowl selections. But he was under pressure to do more in his fifth season. Wilson and Colin Kaepernick, drafted a year after him, had played in championship games and gone to Super Bowls. A quarterback drafted first overall was supposed to do that, too.

Newton had never lacked for self-confidence or attention. He compared himself to Superman, concocted lengthy touchdown celebrations, and referred to himself as "an entertainer and an icon." His play heading into the Seattle game in 2015 suggested that he was about to start receiving attention for his actual on-field performance rather than for what came with it.

The Seahawks' defense gave him fits early, cutting off his running lanes and pressuring him to throw before he wanted. The Panthers trailed by thirteen points in the third quarter and by nine early in the fourth quarter, with Newton having thrown two interceptions and completed just eight of twenty-one passes. Seattle's raucous home crowd roared, smelling blood.

But Newton was undaunted by the hard hits he had absorbed. On a long drive that began with eight minutes to play, he missed his first pass attempt but then completed five in a row to four different receivers, setting up a short touchdown run. Then the Panthers' defense sacked Wilson to force a punt, and Newton had the ball again, trailing by three points with a little more than two minutes to play. Starting at his 20, he completed three passes to move the ball across midfield, then hit two more. At the 26, the Panthers were in position to kick a field goal and force overtime, but Newton went for the jugular. He found tight end Greg Olsen open deep and hit him in stride for a game-winning touchdown.

The result signaled a change at the top of the NFC. The Seahawks had won the conference for two straight years, but Newton's time had arrived. Even though the Panthers lacked several ingredients of a typically dominant team, especially on offense—their wide receivers were not difference makers and their line struggled to protect Newton at times—it did not matter with Newton playing so well. As the season rolled on, he threw five touchdown passes in three different games and piled up more than six hundred rushing yards. It was rare for the Panthers not to score thirty or more points in a game. They did not lose until December and finished with a 15–1 record to earn the top seed in the NFC playoffs.

Their divisional-round playoff game against the Seahawks reaffirmed that a new team now ruled the NFC. The Panthers rolled to a 31–0 lead and held off a typical Wilson-led rally to reach the conference championship game. A week later, they demolished the Arizona

Cardinals to earn a place in Super Bowl 50 opposite the Denver Broncos and Peyton Manning.

Leading up to the game, Newton dismissed as dated the suggestion that his Super Bowl start represented a triumph for Black quarterbacks. "I think we shattered that a long time ago," he said.[2] His take on the subject's news value was hard to dispute. For four straight years now, a Black quarterback had started for the NFC team in the Super Bowl.

Like Wilson, his hope was to erase race from how he was perceived. "I think we limit ourselves when we label ourselves just 'Black this, that,'" he said. "I want to bring awareness, but I don't want to be labeled just a Black quarterback."[3]

Try as he might, though, he could not escape the weight of history. The night before the game, he was announced as the winner of his sport's highest individual honor, the league's Most Valuable Player award. His selection was a foregone conclusion after his brilliant season, in which he participated in forty-five touchdowns, thirty-five as a passer and ten as a rusher. But he was the first Black quarterback to win the award outright (Steve McNair had shared it with Manning in 2003), a fact that reflected the brutal road Blacks at his position had traveled.

Many analysts expected Newton to conclude his nearly perfect season with a Super Bowl victory the next day. Manning, now thirty-nine, had palpably declined. Although Denver's defense, ranked first in the league, had carried the Broncos to this point, they were not a forbidding opponent and Newton surely would find a way to win, as he had all year.

But Denver's defense took advantage of the Panthers' offensive shortcomings, which Newton had overcome all year. Their line was overwhelmed by a fierce pass rush. Their receivers could not gain separation from coverage. Suddenly, it seemed Newton was all alone out there. He engineered a long touchdown drive late in the first quarter, but the Broncos stiffened after that. Newton was sacked six times, lost two fumbles, threw an interception.

Final score: Denver 24, Carolina 10.

As usual, Newton's behavior generated as much news as his running and passing. When he cut short his postgame press conference after sullenly responding to a handful of questions, he was criticized for being a poor loser. But photos taken on the field after the final gun showed him smiling as he congratulated Manning with a handshake. "He was very nice to me and I really appreciated that," Manning said.[4]

———

At the start of the 2016 season, Newton, Kaepernick, Griffin, and Wilson had already made their mark as the NFL's greatest generation of Black quarterbacks. They had revolutionized their position since entering the league as draft picks in 2011 and 2012. Three had made Super Bowl starts. And they were not even thirty yet; their future was exciting to contemplate.

But they also faced mounting issues. By 2016, Griffin and Kaepernick had fallen off, failing to sustain the brilliance of their early careers. And while all appeared well with Newton, coming off an MVP season, and Wilson, entrenched as the quarterback of a playoff contender, their best days with their original teams had already occurred; neither would appear in another Super Bowl wearing those uniforms.

Griffin's star fell with shocking suddenness. He was never as dynamic after undergoing surgery to repair torn knee ligaments suffered in the Redskins' playoff loss to the Seahawks in January 2013. Although he opened the next season as the starter, he struggled, reinjured his knee, and lost his starting job during a long losing streak. A dislocated ankle cut short his 2014 season and he never played in 2015 after suffering a concussion during training camp. The Redskins released him in 2016. He received a second chance when the Cleveland Browns signed him with the hope that he could rediscover his rookie form. But an injury ended his season.

Kaepernick's decline was not as precipitous. It had appeared he was the NFL's next big thing when he carried the 49ers to a Super Bowl appearance in 2012, and he helped them back to the NFC championship game the next year. But during his third season as a starter, in 2014, the 49ers went 8–8 as Jim Harbaugh feuded with the front office, leading to Harbaugh's departure after the season. Without Harbaugh and Greg Roman, the offensive coordinator who had helped turn him loose, Kaepernick was not nearly as effective in 2015 and eventually lost his starting job as the team won just five of sixteen games and finished last in the NFC West.

He was competing for the starting job at the 49ers' training camp in 2016, but football was not always foremost in his thoughts. He had followed the protests that roiled Ferguson, Missouri, after the death of an unarmed Black teenager at the hands of police in 2014, and also had watched the unrest in Baltimore a year later after the death of a twenty-five-year-old Black man in police custody. In December 2015, another twenty-five-year-old Black man, a suspect in a stabbing attack in San Francisco, was shot twenty times and killed after he allegedly ignored police orders to drop his knife. Kaepernick could no longer stand by idly. He wanted to protest police treatment of Blacks in America. Heading into training camp, he became more active on social media, tweeting and retweeting commentaries on race relations. Then, before the 49ers' first two preseason games, he sat on the bench, away from teammates, during the national anthem.

His protest initially received virtually no attention, but that changed after several reporters tweeted pictures of him sitting on the bench during the anthem before the 49ers' third preseason game. As news of his protest spread, it became a controversial issue across the country in the coming days.

In a locker room interview after practice, Kaepernick addressed the controversy directly. "I am not going to stand up and show pride in a flag for a country that oppresses Black people and people of color," he said. "To me, this is bigger than football and it would be selfish on my part to look the other way. There are bodies in the street and people getting paid leave and getting away with murder."[5]

His protest and comments drew intense criticism from those who claimed his actions represented disrespect for the flag and the military. "I am not looking for approval. I have to stand up for people that are oppressed," Kaepernick insisted. "If they take football away, my endorsements from me, I know that I stood up for what is right."[6]

Reaction swirled, ranging from wholehearted support to furious indignation. Among the myriad "takes" in the public realm, one stood out to Kaepernick. Nate Boyer, a former Army Green Beret who had served in Iraq and Afghanistan, wrote an open letter to the quarterback in the *Army Times*. Boyer was not a typical observer. After his army tour ended, he had tried out for the football team at the University of Texas and become the Longhorns' long snapper. That led to tryouts with the 49ers and Seahawks, who signed him in 2015. At age thirty-four, as the NFL's oldest rookie, he played in one preseason game before being cut. A lifelong fan of the 49ers, he wrote in his open letter to Kaepernick that "anger" was his initial reaction to the protest but that he was "trying to listen to what you're saying and why you're doing it."[7]

Intrigued by the measured response from an individual with backgrounds in both the military and NFL, Kaepernick contacted Boyer, who lived in Los Angeles. Boyer took a cab to San Diego and met with Kaepernick for several hours at the 49ers' hotel before the team's final preseason game against the Chargers. "We realized we had a lot more in common than we had differences, and a good amount of respect for each other," Boyer said.[8]

The conversation became a learning experience for Boyer.

"I had seen this image of him sitting on the bench, maybe heard a sound bite of him saying, 'I'm not going to stand for the anthem of a country that oppresses Black people, people of color.' I've been in some pretty oppressive places in the world, from the Middle East to Africa, where I saw genocide. I had a totally different impression of what oppression is like. I almost felt offended that word was used," Boyer said. "I also had this narrow-minded outlook that I was the one who had authority on what the definition of oppression is, what the definition of equality is. [I was] seeing that through a white person's lens. . . . It was a big moment for myself, a learning moment, through Colin and so many others, understanding that my perspective was purely based on my experiences and for me to pretend to know what it's like [to be a Black person in America] was very unfair."[9]

Kaepernick asked if Boyer had a suggestion for how he could continue to protest without offending so many people. "I said, 'No matter what you do, someone is going to be offended. But if you're asking my opinion, I think being by your teammates is the most important thing; not sitting back kind of isolated. If you're committed to not standing, I think kneeling is the only thing that makes logistical sense,'" Boyer said. "Also, it's a respectful gesture. I've never seen kneeling as anything but respectful. We kneel to pray, and to propose to our future spouse. When a player gets hurt on the football field, the other players kneel out of respect [while he is treated]."[10]

That night, a chorus of boos greeted Kaepernick during pregame warm-ups in San Diego. During the national anthem, he kneeled on the sideline, among his teammates, with Boyer standing beside him and a teammate, Eric Reid, kneeling beside him. Fans booed, then continued to boo during the game.

As attention increased and the protest became a national issue, Roger Goodell weighed in. It was not hard to discern that the NFL commissioner believed Kaepernick was disrespecting the flag and the military. "I support our players when they want to see change in our society, and we don't live in a perfect society," Goodell said. "On the other hand, we believe very strongly in patriotism in the NFL. I think it's very important to have respect for our country, for our flag, for the people who make our country better; for law enforcement and for our military who are out fighting for our freedoms."[11]

Undaunted, Kaepernick kneeled during the national anthem before the 49ers' season opener, and several players on other teams in other stadiums followed his lead. Their protest received modest attention amid the excitement of a new season beginning. The 49ers won their opener with Blaine Gabbert starting at quarterback.

Kaepernick was a backup, but he was the most scrutinized backup in the league as he continued to kneel during the anthem in the coming weeks. President Barack Obama weighed in, disappointing Kaepernick's side with a take that was not entirely supportive. "I want Mr. Kaepernick and others who are on a knee, I want them to listen to the pain that may cause somebody who, for example, had a spouse or a child who was killed in combat and why it hurts them to see somebody not standing. But I also want people to think about the pain he may be expressing about somebody who's lost a loved one that they think was unfairly shot," Obama said.[12]

Kaepernick reclaimed his starting job in October after the 49ers' season quickly went south with Gabbert. He would start the team's final eleven games and produce a solid statistical line, throwing sixteen touchdown passes to just four interceptions while generating an above-average quarterback rating. But the 49ers were awful. They lost twelve games in a row and finished with a 2–14 record.

On the 49ers' last offensive play of the season, Kaepernick threw a nine-yard touchdown toss to Garrett Celek, a tight end. The score brought the 49ers within two points of the Seahawks late in the fourth quarter of a game in Seattle, but the Seahawks took possession and ran out the clock to secure the win.

It would turn out to be the last pass of Kaepernick's career. He opted out of his contract after the season, but while other, lesser quarterbacks on the market signed with new teams, Kaepernick went unsigned. One possible explanation was teams did not want to put up with the headache of offending a chunk of their fan base by signing a player who did not stand for the national anthem. Another possible explanation was the owners of the NFL's thirty-two teams simply blackballed Kaepernick.

With Kaepernick out of the league, his protest simmered quietly at the start of the 2017 season. But Donald Trump, who had been elected president, brought it back into the limelight with a scathing commentary of kneeling players at a political rally in Alabama. "Wouldn't you love to see one of these NFL owners, when somebody disrespects our flag, to say, 'Get that son of a bitch off the field right now. Out! He's fired. He's fired!'" Trump shouted.[13]

The millions of fans offended by Kaepernick's protest loved it. But the players, furious, protested that Sunday. Hundreds either remained seated or kneeled during the anthem or stayed in the locker room while the song played. Several owners, a famously conservative group, protested alongside their players, either kneeling or linking arms.

When accused of disrespecting the flag and the military, the players clarified that they were trying to raise awareness of police brutality against Blacks and of social injustice. But nuance was all but impossible as Trump doubled down on his scathing criticism. Meanwhile, Kaepernick filed a grievance against the NFL, maintaining that the thirty-two teams had colluded to keep him out of the league. The two sides eventually reached a settlement in 2019 and signed a confidentiality agreement to keep the terms private.

Kaepernick was twenty-nine when he threw his final touchdown pass to Celek in Seattle. There is little doubt he had at least several years of good football still in him, certainly as a backup if not as a starter. Few quarterbacks in pro football history had exhibited the kind of dynamic playmaking he produced as a young pro.

As a Black quarterback denied the chance to play in the NFL, he had many predecessors. And like those before him, his denial was fundamentally rooted in the league's reaction to the fact that he was not white. But unlike the others, Kaepernick, with his activism, had the power to change the world. With his decision to kneel, he made activism, not touchdowns, the currency he traded. And in 2020, after the murder of George Floyd at the hands of police in Minneapolis initiated a new racial reckoning across America, his protest received far greater understanding from those who had opposed him.

Roger Goodell said he wished "we had listened earlier" to what Kaepernick was protesting, acknowledging that the protest had been "mischaracterized" and was "not about the flag."[14] Years too late, Goodell explained that Kaepernick and other protesting players were "exercising their right to bring attention to something that needs to get fixed." This altered response did not produce another chance for Kaepernick to play in the NFL, but according to Dr. Charles K. Ross, "what Kaepernick accomplished by taking a knee transcended the gridiron."[15]

CHAPTER 28

In one respect, the 2017 draft seemed to underscore how far Black quarterbacks had come from the days when they could not get on the field because teams believed white players were more equipped to handle their position. As the first round played out, two of the first twelve picks were Black quarterbacks, seemingly a clear indication that the white-only groupthink no longer existed. And no attention was paid to the racial implications of the drafting of Patrick Mahomes and Deshaun Watson, unlike in 1999, when the selection of three Black quarterbacks in the first eleven picks was viewed as historic. In 2017, Mahomes and Watson were viewed as just quarterbacks, not Black quarterbacks—the definition that trailblazers such as Doug Williams and Warren Moon had sought decades earlier.

In another respect, though, the 2017 draft served as a reminder that a reflexive preference for white quarterbacks could still be found in the NFL's nooks and crannies. It was hard not to conclude otherwise after the Chicago Bears, in search of a quarterback, traded up to claim the draft's second overall pick, then used it to draft not Mahomes or Watson, but rather, Mitchell Trubisky, a white quarterback who was not as accomplished.

Doug Williams, now a front office executive with the Redskins, just laughed in the team's draft room as he watched it all unfold. The Trubisky pick "told you all you needed to know," he would say later about the enduring presence of prejudicial thinking, however unconscious, at the quarterback position.[1] Three decades after Williams's landmark victory in the Super Bowl, NFL talent evaluators could still conjure far-fetched rationales for favoring white quarterbacks over talented Black prospects.

That had been apparent a year earlier, in 2016, when the Denver Broncos drafted Memphis's Paxton Lynch in the first round, the New York Jets took Penn State's Christian Hackenberg in the second round, the Cleveland Browns took Southern Cal's Cody Kessler in the third round, and the Oakland Raiders took Michigan State's Connor Cook early in the fourth round, all before the Dallas Cowboys took Mississippi State's Dak Prescott, a Black quarterback, near the end of the fourth round. All Prescott did as a rookie in 2016 was start immediately and lead the Cowboys to a 13–3 record and the NFC's top playoff seed, establishing himself as a winning pro quarterback worth building around. Lynch, Hackenberg, Kessler, and Cook would be long gone from the NFL when Prescott signed a contract making him one of the league's highest-paid players in 2021.

But Trubisky going before Mahomes and Watson in 2017 would look even more foolish in hindsight. Although Trubisky had thrown thirty touchdown passes to just six interceptions as a junior at North Carolina, that was his only season as a college starter. He had been a backup for two years before that. The Tar Heels won eight regular-season games with him in 2016 before losing to Stanford in the Sun Bowl. A quarterback without a bowl victory would not ordinarily wow pro scouts, but Trubisky impressed at the combine and other workouts. Standing six feet two, weighing 220 pounds, able to make all the throws, he fit the NFL's long-standing prototype. To scouts, what he might do going forward overruled his relatively modest record—the kind of optimistic projection white quarterbacks were likelier to receive.

Watson, meanwhile, had guided Clemson to college football's national championship game in each of his two seasons as a starter. Poised, smart, and strong, Watson could run and pass effectively and deliver in tense situations. He rushed and passed for 478 yards in his first national championship game appearance, a 45–40 loss to Alabama. A year later, again against the Crimson Tide, he totaled 463 yards of offense and hurled a game-winning touchdown pass in the final seconds.

Few Black quarterbacks had entered the NFL with a record that so disproved the tired dogma about them not being able to think, lead, or win. Watson was so beyond it that he scoffed at being called a "dual-threat" quarterback, labeling it racist code.

Mahomes had passed for more than eleven thousand yards in three seasons at Texas Tech, which favored a wide-open offense known as the "Air Raid," in which the quarterback lined up in the shotgun, at the center of a "spread" formation, and chose from between as many as five receivers. The Red Raiders were not into playing defense; they allowed an average of 43.6 points per game during Mahomes's sophomore and junior seasons. They just counted on outscoring the other team. Throwing on almost every play, Mahomes had averaged 421 passing yards and 3.4 touchdown passes per game as a junior.

At six feet two and 225 pounds, Mahomes had the size NFL teams wanted. Though not a flashy runner, he had nimble feet and a knack for escaping pressure and throwing accurately on the run. Any fan could see his arm was spectacularly strong; some scouts believed it was as strong as Brett Favre's legendary arm.

Why was he not regarded as the top quarterback in the class, or for that matter, the top prospect in the whole draft? It would become a fair question within several years, as Mahomes shot to the pinnacle of the NFL before he turned twenty-five. At the time, though, the comparison to Favre was, strangely, almost a negative. Favre was one of the most prolific quarterbacks in history, but some surmised that he only won one Super Bowl because he was too bold for his own good at times—a little too comfortable with casually taking low-percentage risks, some of which backfired, because he trusted his arm to make good things happen. "The operative word was gunslinger," said Leigh Steinberg, whom Mahomes had picked as his agent several months before the draft. "An NFL quarterback usually takes a three-step, five-step, or seven-step drop [before passing]. That was not Patrick in a spread offense at Texas Tech. The doubts about him were could he be a disciplined passer, a three-step, five-step, and seven-step guy, and not be a Brett Favre wild guy who was undisciplined."[2]

Mahomes did not mind the gunslinger label. In fact, he embraced it before the draft. "I threw the ball a lot at Texas Tech. That's definitely a gunslinger mentality," he said.[3]

But what he *was* in college did not matter; all that mattered now was what he *could be* as a quarterback in the NFL, and the scouts who were skeptical certainly did not give him the benefit of the same optimistic projection Trubisky received. "They missed on him initially. They couldn't project him," Steinberg said. "Drafts are supposed to be a projection, and they didn't get how smart he was, and they didn't get how the way he played at Tech was a response to the competitive nature of having a defense give up fifty points a game, so he had to try everything and took it on his shoulders."[4]

Having represented players for four decades, Steinberg was as experienced as any agent at shepherding prospects through the winding pre-draft process, with its many workouts and interviews, while helping them navigate the uncertainty. After soaring while representing star quarterbacks such as Warren Moon, Steve Young, Troy Aikman, Kordell Stewart, and Drew Bledsoe, Steinberg had crashed in the early 2000s amid legal battles with business partners, a divorce, bankruptcy, and a bout with alcoholism. Now sixty-six, he was sober, driven, and back in the game with Mahomes.

At the outset of the pre-draft season, no one was suggesting his newest client would become the NFL's next dominant quarterback. "There were scouting reports that said he'd never make it, that he lacked discipline and technique, that he wasn't applicable to taking the ball under center. So we started in the situation where a lot of predictions had him as a third-round pick," Steinberg said.[5]

Though sourced differently, the doubts were not unlike what Moon, Steinberg's first major client, had faced when he was eligible for the draft in 1978 after leading the Washington Huskies to a Rose Bowl victory as a senior. At the time, there were almost no Black quarterbacks in the NFL. "No one articulated the prejudice. It simply existed," Steinberg said. "A number of teams asked if Warren was willing to play wide receiver or running back. People were telling me he might get picked in the fourth round or sixth round or later as a quarterback."[6]

Moon, famously, went undrafted and played in Canada before returning to the United States and embarking on a career in the NFL that culminated with his induction into the Pro Football Hall of Fame. His stellar career, along with those of many other Black quarterbacks, had gradually opened minds and a window of opportunity, to the point that the landscape Mahomes encountered in 2017 was drastically different from what Moon faced. Few understood that better than Steinberg, who had represented many Black quarterbacks. "In the mid-90s, I had Kordell Stewart, who faced the same doubts as Warren with teams asking if he would change positions. Then he had to play the 'Slash' role for a few years, so he was a backup, before he got a chance and played at a very high level," Steinberg said. "That was a breakthrough and there were others with Warren, Doug Williams, Randall Cunningham, and the 1999 draft. I had Akili Smith that year. No one asked me a question about his skin color. It was not a factor and he went third overall."[7]

All issues for Black quarterbacks had not been resolved. "They had to be really talented and productive or there wasn't a place on the team for them; very few were backups," Steinberg said. "But as far as being completely denied the chance to play, that was over. It had been like the Berlin Wall. But the wall had crumbled."[8]

Unlike Moon, Mahomes had the benefit of a chance to improve his draft stock in the weeks before the draft. He made the most of that chance. At the combine, he threw accurately, handled the footwork on various drops, and impressed in interviews. At Texas Tech's Pro Day event, with scouts on campus in Lubbock, Texas, scrutinizing the Red Raiders' prospects, he threw a pass from his 25 yard line through the far end zone, a prodigious show of strength.

Mahomes even burnished his prospects when Steinberg put him through a media "carwash," a series of appearances designed to raise his profile. On ESPN's campus in Bristol, Connecticut, he stood in a courtyard in street clothes, with cameras rolling, and threw a ball completely over a second-floor walkway and into the lap of a dummy seated in a chair in the distance. On *The Dan Patrick Show*, he tossed a pass at a moving, life-size cardboard cutout of the host from eighteen yards away and literally hit the cutout on the nose.

"He was doing incredible things," Steinberg said.

With what effect on his draft stock?

"There was a meteoric rise," Steinberg said.[9]

=====

A career in pro football was not what Mahomes envisioned as a youngster in Whitehouse, a small town outside Tyler, Texas, east of Dallas. His father, known to sports fans as Pat Mahomes, was a major league pitcher who threw more than seven hundred innings over eleven seasons with the Minnesota Twins and five other teams. Being a major league pitcher's son formed the younger Mahomes's dreams. "When I was a little kid, I watched my dad play professional baseball and thought for sure that was going to be me," he said.[10]

His dream seemed realistic when radar guns clocked him throwing 90 mph fastballs for Whitehouse High School. When he was not pitching, he covered a wide swath of ground in center field and batted .500 as a senior. "He was one of the better athletes I've covered in my 15 years in East Texas," said a scout for the Detroit Tigers, who selected Mahomes in the thirty-seventh round of baseball's amateur draft in 2014, the year Mahomes graduated from high school.[11]

But that was a late selection for a player with major league bloodlines and obvious talent. Baseball's scouting world had decided by then that Mahomes preferred football—a correct assumption. "I had started playing football in seventh and eighth grade, and then really started in high school and fell in love with it," he said.[12]

He was a reserve quarterback as a high school freshman and sophomore before becoming the starter as a junior. Set loose in a wide-open offense, he was a scrambler who casually threw off his back foot and across his body, at odds with classic mechanics, yet he still piled up wins, statistics, and honors thanks to his arm. As a senior, he threw for fifty touchdowns, ran for fifteen more, and was named the Texas Associated Press Sports Editors high school player of the year—quite an honor given the competition in the state.

He was no less dominant on the basketball court and the baseball diamond, but football was his best sport and it seemed certain that top college programs would want him. But he was not ready to give up on baseball, and his desire to play both sports in college cooled the interest of programs where being a starting quarterback was a year-round commitment. Neither Alabama nor Clemson, the era's ruling national powers, seriously pursued him. Neither did Texas or Texas A&M, the most prestigious programs in his home state. In the end, only Texas Tech, Rice, and the University of Houston offered scholarships. Not a single school from outside Texas wanted Mahomes. He went with Tech, where the football coach, Kliff Kingsbury, agreed to let him play baseball.

Kingsbury did not expect the flirtation with baseball to last long. "I think he's just scratching the surface [as a quarterback], having played different sports throughout the year," he said after Mahomes signed. "When he really focuses on football the majority of the time, I think you could really see him take off at that position."[13]

Sure enough, Mahomes appeared in just two baseball games for the Red Raiders as a pinch hitter and made one infamous appearance as a pitcher. "I walked the first guy, hit the second guy, gave up a double, they scored a run, and I got taken out. I think I had an infinity earned run average," he said.[14] Meanwhile, he launched as a quarterback after becoming the starter late in his freshman season. In his fourth career start, he passed for 598 yards and six touchdowns against Baylor, ranked fifth in the country.

Those would have been outrageous statistics for a quarterback at any other school, but no team played like the Red Raiders. The Air Raid had been devised in the 1980s by Hal Mumme, a little-known but creative coach with Texas roots. His idea was to forgo running the ball, fill the field with receivers, try to create mismatches in the secondary, fill the air with passes, and see how defenses adjusted. Mumme polished his concept at high schools and small colleges before eventually becoming the head coach at Kentucky, and his protégé, Mike Leach, brought the offense to Texas Tech as the head coach starting in 2000. Kingsbury had played quarterback for Leach before becoming a coach.

The Air Raid presented Mahomes with an opportunity few Black quarterbacks had received. "For a long period, they were playing at the collegiate level in offenses that didn't translate to the NFL; run-based offenses like the Wishbone and Veer, where you could be physically smaller but play as long as you could move and run," Steinberg said. "They were good football players but not the kind of quarterback the pros were looking for. You didn't have many six feet four, strong-armed Black quarterbacks coming out of college. But by the time Patrick came along, the college game was becoming more of a passing game. At Tech, he was almost strictly a passer. That helped get the NFL's attention."[15]

Mahomes opened his sophomore season by throwing four touchdown passes in each of his first two games, and he never slowed, ending the season as the national leader in total offense. His junior season was even more outlandish—in one game, he attempted eighty-eight passes and completed fifty-two for 734 yards. He ended the season as the NCAA leader in every major passing statistic.

Some pro scouts were skeptical at first because, for all he had done, he still resembled the quarterback of Whitehouse High School, at times throwing across his body and off his back feet, habits that could get you in trouble in the NFL. Plus, Texas Tech had fielded powerhouse passing offenses for more than a decade, yet none of its record-setting quarterbacks had made it big in the NFL.

As the 2017 draft approached, though, scouts increasingly viewed Mahomes as an appealing package of pure athleticism and staggering arm strength. "His stock is rising faster than anyone's in the class," a draft analyst for SB Nation wrote.[16] Five teams told Steinberg they might take him in the first round.

Shortly after Roger Goodell opened the draft before a large crowd in Philadelphia, the Cleveland Browns took Myles Garrett, a defensive end from Texas A&M, with the first overall pick. Then came the shocker, the Bears taking Trubisky ahead of Mahomes and Watson. It felt like a throwback to the era when NFL teams really just wanted white quarterbacks.

Mahomes was not in Philadelphia; he was watching at home in Texas, seated on a couch between his mother and Steinberg, who just smiled when Trubisky was picked. The agent's phone was buzzing with communication from teams interested in Mahomes. Something would happen soon, Steinberg predicted. "I didn't care that Trubisky went first or any of that; I just wanted Patrick to go to the right place," Steinberg said.[17]

The fact that the New Orleans Saints held the eleventh pick in the first round brought the situation to a head. They were set at quarterback with Drew Brees, a no-doubt future Hall of Famer still performing at a high level. But he was thirty-eight, which meant it was about time for them to start finding another quarterback. They liked Mahomes. Meanwhile, the Buffalo Bills, picking one slot ahead of the Saints, did not want a quarterback.

The Kansas City Chiefs pounced. They had scouted Mahomes extensively, hosted him for a visit, discussed him internally for weeks. They loved his potential but knew he would be gone by the time they were scheduled to pick later in the first round. They had to make a major move up the draft board if they wanted Mahomes. They offered to swap first-round picks with the Bills and give Buffalo two other picks, including a first-round selection the next year. A deal was struck.

Having jumped ahead of the Saints, the Chiefs now had the tenth pick and did not wait long to finalize their selection. When Goodell announced they were taking Mahomes, the crowd in Philadelphia roared. Seated next to his client, Steinberg raised his hands in triumph and shook his fists in the air, practically vibrating with palpable excitement. "We could not have been happier," he said later. "People went absolutely crazy."[18]

The Chiefs' record on race was stellar in many respects. They had been in business for sixty-six years, dating to their days as original members of the American Football League, which, from its outset, had been more welcoming to Black players than the NFL. The Chiefs' first star was Abner Haynes, a Black running back. They were among the first teams to hire a full-time Black scout, who directed them to Willie Lanier, one of the first Black players given a chance to excel at middle linebacker, a position that, like quarterback, had long been deemed for whites only. Lanier and other Black stars such as Bobby Bell, Curley Culp, and Emmitt Thomas had played for the Chiefs on their way to being inducted into the Pro Football Hall of Fame.

But Black quarterbacks were still almost entirely missing from the Chiefs' history. Only once in their sixty-six years had a Black quarterback started a game for them. On November 26, 2000, Warren Moon, on his last legs at forty-four years old, filled in for the injured starter, Elvis Grbac, in a game at San Diego. Moon completed just twelve of thirty-one passes in a loss to the Chargers and retired after the season.

The fact that a barrier fell that day received little attention. Denial of Black quarterbacks had been a firmament on the NFL's landscape for so long that it was accepted with a shrug. A new generation, including Donovan McNabb and Kordell Stewart, were getting to play, but obstacles remained in place. On the day Moon started for the Chiefs, nine other teams still had never started a Black quarterback in a game.

But the careers of McNabb, Stewart, Culpepper, Michael Vick, Russell Wilson, Cam Newton, and others had forged profound changes by the time Mahomes was drafted seventeen years later. The Chiefs did not care one whit that he was Black; it was never part of their pre-draft calculus. Those days were over. Their history was irrelevant. They drafted Mahomes because they had a good team already, but wanted to be great, and saw Mahomes as the difference maker. A Black quarterback. No one cared. And no one was happier than Mahomes. "It was an ideal landing spot," Steinberg said.[19]

The Chiefs had won just one playoff game since 1993, churning through six head coaches in those years. In 2013, after enduring their fifth losing season in six years, they had hired Andy Reid, who had recently been fired by the Philadelphia Eagles after a long run of success that included nine playoff appearances but zero Super Bowl titles. Reid liked to move the ball through the air and favored quarterbacks who could throw on the run and scramble out of trouble. He immediately traded for Alex Smith, the former first overall pick who had lost his starting job to Colin Kaepernick in San Francisco. In Reid's first year in Kansas City, with Smith at quarterback, the Chiefs won eleven games—nine more than the year before—and made the playoffs, only to lose their opening game. They had since made the playoffs twice more in three seasons but had not advanced far.

By drafting Mahomes, the Chiefs acted on their hope that a dynamic young quarterback could provide the element they were missing. But Reid understood that patience was required, that Mahomes needed to marinate in the pro game and learn some of its nuances before he took over. As a rookie in 2017, he backed up Smith, attended meetings and practices, and watched games from the sideline, serving what amounted to an apprenticeship.

Rather than take offense at the idea of mentoring a player who would replace him, Smith embraced the situation and helped Mahomes learn the mechanics of being an NFL starter—how his workweek was structured, how to learn from studying film, what to look for in a defense. "Alex, by nature, was the greatest thing that ever happened to Patrick," Reid said later. "Alex let Patrick into his world without being forced."[20]

The Chiefs, with Smith starting and Mahomes backing him up, opened the 2017 season with five straight wins and captured the AFC West title with a 10–6 record. But when they failed to go deep in the playoffs for the fourth time in five years, fans clamored for change. The organization did not disagree that it was needed. Smith was traded to the Washington Redskins, clearing the way for Mahomes to become the starter in 2018.

Deshaun Watson had gone two picks after Mahomes in the 2017 draft. Needing a quarterback and beaten to Mahomes by the Chiefs, the

Houston Texans traded up and took Watson with the twelfth overall pick.

Watson had a far different rookie season than Mahomes. Unlike the Chiefs, the Texans did not have a veteran incumbent at the position. Watson started their season opener and immediately demonstrated that they had not erred by drafting him. By late October, he had thrown nineteen touchdown passes and the Texans were in the playoff picture. Although he missed the second half of the season with a torn knee ligament, he was clearly a quarterback to build around.

Anyone invested in the success of Black quarterbacks had to feel encouraged as the 2018 season began. A new generation was taking over. Prescott was established in Dallas. Mahomes's time had arrived in Kansas City. Watson's rehab went so well that he started the Texans' season opener. Each would lead their team to a division title that season, it turned out.

But the season did not pass without a reminder that Black quarterbacks might never entirely outrun the racism that had denied them for so long. After opening with a gritty loss to the Patriots, the Texans faced the Titans in Tennessee. Trailing late by a field goal, Watson drove the offense into scoring position, then held onto the ball so long while trying to make a play that the Titans did not have time to attempt a field goal and possibly force overtime. That evening, the superintendent of a school district outside Houston posted on Facebook that "when you need precision decision-making, you can't count on a black quarterback."[21]

The superintendent removed the post, but not before a reporter for the *Houston Chronicle* spotted it and wrote about it. Contacted by the paper, the superintendent said he "totally" regretted what he had written but was referencing the statistical success of Black quarterbacks. "Over the history of the NFL, they have had limited success," he told the paper.

It was a teachable moment for Watson, Mahomes, and Prescott. They had come along in a football world where Black quarterbacks played, making the denials that prior generations experienced seem like ancient history. But the notions that produced that denial had not vanished in America, not by any means.

=====

The Chiefs were optimistic heading into the 2018 season, but no one could have envisioned how well Mahomes's debut season as a starter would go. He was twenty-three, just five years removed from throwing fifty touchdown passes as a senior at Whitehouse High School. But he shredded NFL defenses in the same way.

In the opener, on the road against the Chargers, he threw four touchdown passes. He surpassed that a week later, throwing six against the Steelers in Pittsburgh, one of the NFL's toughest road environments. The Chiefs won their first five games, setting up a showdown with Tom Brady and the Patriots at New England. Nervous, Mahomes was intercepted twice in the first half. Then he threw four touchdown passes. Though the Chiefs lost, 43–40, Mahomes had the league's attention.

A week later, he threw four touchdown passes in a rout of the Cincinnati Bengals. Then he threw four touchdown passes again in a win over the Denver Broncos. Why Kansas City had been an "ideal landing spot" became clear. Mahomes's targets included Travis Kelce, a rugged tight end who had a knack for getting open and then battered the defenders trying to tackle him; Tyreek Hill, a wide receiver so quick he was almost impossible to cover; and Kareem Hunt, a running back as fast as Hill. Mahomes's connection with Kelce kept the first downs coming, and with Hill and Hunt, he was a threat to throw for a touchdown from any spot on the field.

Playing for Reid was the final piece of the puzzle. "He was a quarterback whisperer," Steinberg said, alluding to Reid's penchant for getting the most out of the players who ran his offense, which had been McNabb and Vick for the most part in Philadelphia before Alex Smith in Kansas City.[22] It was not just a function of Reid drawing up effective X's and O's. The key ingredient was the level of respect he offered, which Black quarterbacks had seldom experienced. "He was amazing at how he treated us and handled us and spoke to us and taught us," said Tee Martin, who spent a year with Reid while on the Eagles' practice squad in the early 2000s.[23]

McNabb was still relatively early in his tenure as Reid's starter in Philadelphia when Martin was around for a year, but Reid gave McNabb a measure of authority that stunned Martin.

"Before this, guys who played the position who looked like me, I don't think they felt free. In my experience, the quarterback coach always dictated to the quarterback. It was his way or the highway. But then in Philly we would sit at a table going over the plays for the week, and Andy would ask, 'You like this?' If Donovan said, 'Nah,' Andy just crossed it out. There was no, like, trying to convince him to see things his way," Martin said. "Donovan could say, 'Nah,' or 'I want to try this on third down,' and Andy would say, 'OK, I'll call that on the first third down on Sunday.' I appreciated that so much. I was thinking, 'Wow, Donovan has some control. He can speak his mind. His thoughts actually matter. He and the coach are actually building a relationship here.'"[24]

Mahomes now benefited from that. "Patrick had the exact same experience with Andy that Donovan did," Steinberg said.[25] The Chiefs rolled through the 2018 regular season, winning twelve games and earning the top seed in the AFC playoffs, with Mahomes throwing fifty touchdown passes—a figure that put him in elite company. Brady and Peyton Manning were the only quarterbacks who had previously thrown as many as fifty in a season.

The pressure on Mahomes was fierce in the Chiefs' playoff opener, but they sailed past the Indianapolis Colts, 31–13, to advance to the AFC championship game for the first time in a quarter-century. When they hosted Tom Brady and the Patriots a week later, an epic shootout unfolded, with Brady and Mahomes matching big plays in what amounted to a personal game of "top this."

The Patriots jumped ahead by two touchdowns. The Chiefs caught up. The lead went back and forth until both teams kicked a field goal in the final minute of the fourth quarter to force overtime. The Patriots won the toss, took the ball, and drove to a touchdown that decided the game. Thanks to the overtime rules in effect at the time, the Chiefs' chances ended without Mahomes touching the ball.

Despite that bitter disappointment, Mahomes, in his first season as a starter, had established himself as a dynamic force, one of the NFL's brightest stars. He was selected as the league's Most Valuable Player, becoming just the second Black quarterback, after Cam Newton, to win the award outright.

A year later, his explosiveness made the difference as the Chiefs won the Super Bowl for the first time in fifty years. In their playoff opener, they gave up the first twenty-four points to Watson and the Texans, then scored forty-one points in a row. A week later, they fell ten points behind Tennessee in the conference championship game before rallying to win by eleven. In the Super Bowl, they trailed the 49ers by ten points in the fourth quarter, then scored the game's final twenty-one points. Mahomes was voted the game's MVP.

Capitalizing on his success, he signed on as a pitchman for Head & Shoulders and State Farm Insurance, ubiquitous advertisers on NFL broadcasts. Appearing in humorous ads that showcased his personality, he became a familiar face to millions. "To have a predominately white country buy insurance and shampoo when a Black person is the endorser, that's progress," Steinberg said.[26]

But the biggest example of progress for Black quarterbacks was the gargantuan contract Mahomes signed with the Chiefs on July 6, 2020—a ten-year deal worth half a billion dollars, making Mahomes the highest-paid athlete in the history of American team sports. Steinberg, who negotiated the deal, could not help reflecting on the changes that had occurred since he took on Moon as a client in the 1970s. "When Warren came into the league, there were almost no Black quarterbacks. Now, you can't imagine the NFL without Black quarterbacks," Steinberg said. "The only reason Patrick faced questions coming into the league was because he ran a spread offense in college. The kinds of questions Warren faced, about his intelligence, it's hard to believe it happened. But it did."[27]

Steinberg had spent nearly a half-century trying to convince teams that they were wrong to believe Black quarterbacks could not think, lead, or win. "My role has been behind the scenes," he said, "but I'm happy I was able to talk to owners, talk to head coaches, and push back on this theory and get them to understand that they were the ultimate losers because they were missing generations of hyper-talented athletes who would have given them a better chance of winning."[28]

The progress was palpable and momentous, but sadly, even then, it was still premature to conclude that Black quarterbacks had been fully embraced and that Steinberg no longer needed to campaign against institutional doubt. A year after the Chiefs drafted Mahomes, another Black quarterback entering the league faced skepticism seemingly rooted in the 1950s. It was satisfying to see him soon become the ultimate distillation of what can happen when a team fully supports a Black quarterback instead of clinging to dated notions about race that extend beyond football. But that he did so amid the NFL's centennial celebration reflected the dogged persistence of intolerance, begging the question of whether a celebratory finish line for Black quarterbacks even exists.

CHAPTER 29

In the fall of 1969, thirteen-year-old Ozzie Newsome was late for his eighth-grade football tryouts in Muscle Shoals, Alabama. As his mother drove up to the field, he leapt from the car and sprinted toward where the players had separated into position groups.

Should he join the quarterbacks or receivers? It was a decision Newsome had thought about. Now he had to make the choice.

He had played quarterback in sandlot games around his neighborhood, and also on organized teams. His teammates and coaches wanted him at a premier position. He was big and fast and had a strong arm.

"I went to the all-Black school through fifth grade and then we had integration and my parents let me go to the predominantly white school," Newsome said in 2022. "Sports was the thing that gave me acceptance. I was a lineman [at the new school] for the first few days until people saw what I could do. After that, I was the quarterback."[1]

Continuing to play quarterback would have accelerated his acceptance, but when forced to choose a position at tryouts that day, Newsome lined up with the receivers. He made the decision in part because there was a talented quarterback one grade ahead of him, destined to play at Auburn. Also, another quarterback, just joining Newsome's team, had made it through several rounds of the NFL's "Punt, Pass & Kick" national skills contest.

But what most convinced Newsome to join the receivers was his understanding of what happened to Black quarterbacks at football's higher levels.

At thirteen, he was already a prodigious information gatherer, a trait that would later help him become a shrewd builder of rosters as the NFL's first Black general manager. "I was reading *Sport* magazine, the *Sporting News,* anything I could read," Newsome said. "I knew about Marlin Briscoe getting to play [quarterback] in Denver and then having to switch to receiver. I was aware that you always had to switch positions if you were a Black quarterback."[2]

Like many youngsters, especially those with his size and talent, he envisioned playing football in college and, possibly, the pros. It made sense to him that he should follow Briscoe's example and catch passes if he was not going to throw them. "I went to the receivers that day and never looked back," Newsome said. "It worked out pretty well."[3]

"Pretty well" is one way to put it: Newsome was such a standout pass catcher and blocker at Colbert County High School that Paul "Bear" Bryant recruited him to play at the University of Alabama, and he was such a standout during his four years with the Crimson Tide that the Cleveland Browns drafted him with a first-round pick in 1980. Over thirteen seasons as a tight end with the Browns, he caught 662 passes, forty-seven for touchdowns, and amassed nearly eight thousand receiving yards. He went into the Pro Football Hall of Fame in 1999. Yes, his decision worked out "pretty well."

Art Modell, owner of the Browns, thought Newsome's quiet intellect made him a candidate for front office work. Modell let him sample several jobs after he retired, and he took to scouting. He loved studying film and interviewing and analyzing prospects. The long hours, weeks on the road, and paperwork demands did not bother him. It turned out he had a feel for differentiating the players likely to make it from those likely to fall short.

When Modell moved the Browns to Baltimore and they became the Ravens starting in 1996, he put Newsome in charge of the roster and the draft. Newsome's capacity for the job was immediately apparent. The first player he drafted, a mountainous tackle named Jonathan Ogden, became an All-Pro and later made the Pro Football Hall of Fame. His second pick, a ferocious linebacker named Ray Lewis, became one of the NFL's all-time best defensive players.

There had never been a Black general manager in the NFL, largely due to the same stereotypes that had denied opportunities to Black quarterbacks and coaches for so long. Newsome's initial title in Baltimore was vice president of player personnel. He would not become the general manager until 2002, nearly two years after the Ravens had won a Super Bowl with a roster Newsome constructed.

Regardless of his title, though, he was in charge, with the power to use his opinions to shape the roster. And his opinions about Black quarterbacks differed from the stereotypes that had long prevailed in the NFL. While at Alabama, he had marveled at a rival quarterback, Tennessee's Condredge Holloway. Then he roomed with Doug Williams at the Senior Bowl and saw that Williams had "everything you wanted in a quarterback," Newsome said later.[4] To him, it was not a reflection on their talent that Holloway had to play in Canada or that Williams struggled to find a job in the NFL after his tenure with the Tampa Bay Bucs ended. Holloway, Williams, and other Black quarterbacks could play as well as many of the white quarterbacks in pro football, Newsome believed. All they lacked were opportunities to prove it.

During his years as a player, Newsome felt helpless to challenge the status quo. The lack of Black quarterbacks "was just something that was accepted," he said. "And that was what I saw at all levels—peewee, high school, college. Seeing it once I got to the NFL felt no different from seeing it at the other levels."[5]

But by the time he was in charge of the Ravens' roster in the 1990s and 2000s, college offenses were becoming more professional in style, with passing emphasized, and more college teams put Black players at quarterback, increasing the pool of candidates for NFL teams. The pro game was opening up, however slightly, to mobile quarterbacks. "You couldn't just have a statue back there [in the pocket] anymore," Newsome said. "It came from the college game. I used to think there was no way college football would ever influence NFL football, but the situation [for Black quarterbacks] began to change when the colleges started recruiting them without making them change positions. That eventually filtered up to the NFL."[6]

When Newsome took command of the Ravens' roster in 1996, twelve of the NFL's twenty-seven teams still had never started a Black quarterback in a game. Newsome's decision-making illustrated what could happen when a roster-builder with different opinions was in charge. In 1997, he drafted a Black quarterback, Penn State's Wally Richardson. In 1999, he traded for a Black starting quarterback, Tony Banks. In 2001, he signed thirty-eight-year-old Randall Cunningham as a backup. In 2002, he signed thirty-two-year-old Jeff Blake as a starter. In 2006, he traded for Steve McNair and drafted Ohio State's Troy Smith, a Heisman Trophy–winning Black quarterback. "Our head coaches always wanted athletic quarterbacks," Newsome said. "But it was all about winning, [not race]. Every guy we got was, in our mind, the best guy for the job."[7]

When McNair's career ebbed, Newsome drafted a classic pocket passer, Joe Flacco, with a first-round pick in 2008. Flacco, who was white, had played at the University of Delaware, far from college football's biggest stages, but he was six feet six and a pure thrower with a powerful arm. It was a brilliant pick. Flacco helped the Ravens reach the AFC championship game three times in his first five seasons; the bigger the stage, the better he played. In 2012, he threw eleven touchdowns and no interceptions during an epic playoff run as the Ravens swept to a Super Bowl victory.

That triumph was followed by five years of lesser results, though, as the Ravens made the playoffs just once. When Flacco turned thirty-one in 2017, Newsome quietly began entertaining thoughts of finding new blood at the position.

The 2018 draft offered a handful of touted candidates, all white and expected to become starters in the NFL, but they would be taken long before the Ravens selected later in the first round. Newsome was just as interested in a prospect who likely would still be available then: Lamar Jackson, a Black quarterback from the University of Louisville who had won the Heisman Trophy as a sophomore.

Jackson was a breathtaking playmaker, a startlingly fast and elusive runner who had thrown sixty-nine touchdown passes in three seasons at Louisville. But a classic drop-back passer he was not, and even though he could match career accomplishments with the other top prospects that year, he was not considered a sure thing.

Newsome believed he understood why. "If you studied him in college, he wasn't a very accurate passer. And you just wondered, because the coverage is going to be tighter [in the NFL] and with the kind of pressure he would see, is his accuracy going to get better or is it going to get worse? The thinking [of many talent evaluators] was it's going to get worse," Newsome said.[8]

Jackson faced more doubts as a draft prospect than other top Black quarterbacks of recent vintage. It was almost as if he had traveled back to the 1950s. Some pundits and talent evaluators thought he should play running back or wide receiver in the pros. In February, a scout for the San Diego Chargers asked him if he would run pass routes at the combine, a suggestion that inferred he might become a receiver in the pros. Jackson could hardly believe it. "I was like, 'What?' He caught me off guard with it. I thought he was trying to be funny," Jackson said.[9] He declined to run the forty-yard dash at the combine, fearing a fast time would increase the likelihood that he would be asked to switch positions.

Also contributing to the decline in his draft stock, almost surely, was his public persona. "He has a very kind of urban, African American persona. He has not cut his hair. He will wear braids. The way he communicates with the media is very similar to a young, urban African American. He could be a rapper. He could be a movie star. He could be a number of other things that fit into this kind of persona that he has," Dr. Charles K. Ross said.[10] Jackson was engaging, but "what was unspoken for years in the NFL was the quarterback should be someone the owner was comfortable taking to his country club and introducing around as the face of the franchise," Leigh Steinberg said, and Jackson was not that.[11]

The Ravens had no issues with Jackson's persona as they weighed him as a prospect. They just wanted to know if he really could supplant Flacco and become their starting quarterback. Newsome liked what he saw on the field during Jackson's final year at Louisville in

2017. Eric DeCosta, the Ravens' longtime assistant general manager, and the team's scouts received positive reviews from coaches who had worked with him; Jackson was a quick learner, they said. Heading into the draft, Newsome and DeCosta agreed to consider selecting Jackson if the right circumstances arose.

John Harbaugh, the Ravens' head coach, signed off on the idea, which was important. His offense would need to be overhauled if Jackson became the quarterback, and the team's record could suffer during the transition, possibly endangering Harbaugh's job. But Harbaugh embraced the potential risk, noting that few classic drop-back passers other than Tom Brady and Peyton Manning had won Super Bowls recently, yet a lot of high draft picks had been wasted trying to find another. His point: let's try something new if the opportunity presents itself.

The mood in the Ravens' draft room was charged on the night of the first round of the 2018 draft. On the job since 1996, Newsome had built two Super Bowl–winning teams and numerous playoff contenders, but now, at age sixty-two, he was set to retire in weeks, enabling DeCosta to become the general manager. This was Newsome's last time in command of the Ravens' draft. And for as much thought as he had given to Jackson, he did not think that finding a quarterback was an absolute necessity; the Ravens still had Flacco, and after missing the playoffs four times in the past five seasons, they had needs at other positions. Newsome took a tight end with the twenty-fifth overall pick. But as the first round wound down, Jackson was still available, and Newsome contacted the Philadelphia Eagles, who held the last pick in the first round. Newsome offered two picks for the Eagles' pick, and a deal was struck.

At the draft, before a giant crowd at the Cowboys' stadium in Dallas, Roger Goodell stepped to the podium and said, "With the thirty-second pick in the first round, the Baltimore Ravens select Lamar Jackson, quarterback, Louisville."[12]

The crowd roared. Jackson was a popular player, especially with younger fans; some of his weaving touchdown runs seemed to have come from a video game.

A loud cheer also erupted in the Ravens' draft room at the team's headquarters in Owings Mills, Maryland. "It felt like the building shook," Newsome said.[13] After giving Black quarterbacks opportunities for years, he finally had drafted one with a first-round pick in one of his final acts as a GM. "Everyone knew we'd done something special," he said.[14] Yes, that soon became clear.

As a youngster in Pompano Beach, Florida, Jackson played quarterback on powerhouse youth football squads. He was a natural, so fast that he could outrace entire defenses to the end zone. He could throw, too, and dreamed of becoming the next Michael Vick, the spectacular Black quarterback he watched on television. That he might follow Vick's path was hard to imagine, but his mother, Felicia Jones, tried to help. Her husband had died when Jackson was eight, leaving her to raise Jackson and a younger brother. Stepping into the stereotypical dad's role, Felicia ran backyard practices in which the boys tackled each other and flipped tires to gain strength.

Jackson's dream nearly ended before it began. He was not on the same page with the coaches at Santaluces Community High School and did not even play football as a sophomore, prompting him to transfer to Boynton Beach Community High School. "He changed high schools because he wanted to play quarterback," Newsome said.[15]

At his first practice, he sprinted around the end and ran sixty yards for a touchdown without being touched. "I looked at my offensive coordinator and said, 'We've got to change our offense . . . immediately,'" said Rick Swain, Boynton Beach's head coach. "He was so fast it was ridiculous."[16]

In two seasons at Boynton Beach, Jackson made dozens of long, weaving runs. At times it appeared he was almost impossible to corral. But recruiters from top college programs still envisioned him as a receiver or running back. Although he had success as a passer, his throwing motion was far from traditional; he would just fling the ball at times and deliver from different angles.

Bobby Petrino, Louisville's head coach, was willing to let him try to play quarterback, figuring Jackson could always help the Cardinals at another position if the quarterback experiment did not work out. Jackson liked the idea of learning from Petrino, who had been a head coach and offensive coordinator in the NFL and worked with Jackson's idol, Michael Vick.

Jackson's first months at Louisville were brutal; he did not understand the playbook or know how to learn from watching film. But he was a quick study. He became the starter early in his freshman season, and a year later so dazzled college football with his explosive playmaking that he won the Heisman Trophy at age nineteen, beating out Deshaun Watson and Oklahoma's Baker Mayfield. Vick, three years removed from his last NFL game, tweeted that Jackson was "5X better" than Vick was in college.[17]

Jackson was twenty-one when he was drafted, and when he arrived in Baltimore for spring practices soon after, it was immediately clear that he would not beat out Flacco anytime soon. When they lined up beside each other in passing drills, Flacco threw beautiful spirals while Jackson's tosses wobbled.

But Jackson was fast and elusive in scrimmages, and the Ravens' coaches quietly marveled at him. The offensive coordinator, Marty Mornhinweg, had held the same job with the Eagles when Vick was their quarterback. Also on the staff was Greg Roman, the run-game expert whose offense had helped launch Colin Kaepernick in San Francisco. Roman was coaching tight ends in Baltimore. "He wasn't very sophisticated when he first got here," Roman said of Jackson. "He came from a college system where they used, like, one-word [calls] and very static formations. So his learning curve was steep. Even with that, though, we saw right away that he was a gamer. When you put him in, he made things happen."[18]

Watching practice, Newsome was encouraged. "Lamar is like a point guard [in basketball]. You could see that right away when he got here. He just saw the field and where he was in relation to others, and what he needed to do," Newsome said.[19]

At the outset of his rookie season, he backed up Flacco. But Flacco suffered a back injury and Jackson made his first start against the Cincinnati Bengals in November. Before the game, he received a call from Doug Williams, who sought to encourage him. "The call was basically to tell him, 'Don't look back. Just keep going forward.' As a young African-American quarterback, sometimes the road might be a little more slippery for him than for other people," Williams recalled.[20]

Against the Bengals, Jackson just took off and ran rather than let plays develop; it was almost as if he were still at Boynton Beach Community High School. But he rushed for 125 yards and the Ravens won. Then they kept winning, surging into contention for a place in the AFC playoffs. "It wasn't always the prettiest. There'd be times when we'd work on something in practice and go, 'Jeez, I don't know how this is going to look in the game.' It didn't look good in practice. But then he'd just will something to happen," Roman said.[21]

When Flacco was ready to return, Jackson remained the starter and the Ravens wound up winning the AFC North title for the first time in six years. Shortly after the season, they went all in for Jackson, traded Flacco, fired Mornhinweg, and tasked Roman, the new offensive coordinator, with building an offense that suited Jackson's unusual talents.

It was a level of buy-in, wholehearted support, that few Black quarterbacks had ever experienced in the NFL. A half-century earlier, Marlin Briscoe had also come out of nowhere late in his rookie season to dazzle fans and teammates with a skill set totally out of place with the pro game's norms. But Briscoe's reward for playing well was being denied the chance to ever play quarterback again as a pro. Then, in the ensuing decades, although coaches typically tweaked their offenses to take advantage of a Black quarterback's mobility, they did not engineer a complete overhaul. The Ravens were doing that for Jackson. "It just made sense," Roman said, "to throw out the old stuff and put in stuff that would work for him. I had had some success with guys with his skill set, which, I think, helped give everyone some confidence that it might work."[22]

The Ravens' buy-in was based not only on Jackson's unique talent but also on his personality and approach. He was a football "gym rat" driven to succeed by the doubts of others. He was not self-satisfied, preferring to focus on his mistakes rather than what he did well. He never criticized a teammate. He was not a partier. "He is very transparent, owns up to his mistakes, just says, 'I've got to get better.' That says a lot to me about what kind of DNA he has, what kind of person he is," Dr. Charles K. Ross said.[23]

The new offense the Ravens debuted in 2019 was built around run-pass option plays out of the "pistol" formation. Jackson lined up in the shotgun, next to a running back. After receiving the snap, he read the defense and quickly decided between handing the ball off or running himself. There also were designed runs for him and passing plays with him both on the run and in the pocket.

Fundamentally, it was a run-based offense built around Jackson's legs. The rest of the league was skeptical of its chances of working. Vince Lombardi's Green Bay Packers had built a dynasty around a power running game in the 1960s, but in the decades since then, pro football had become a passing-oriented game. You had to throw to win, it seemed. Could the Ravens succeed with a run-based offense? Was Jackson effective enough as a passer?

Roman was confident. Jackson had a strong supporting cast. The Ravens' offensive line was dominant. They had three tight ends who could block and catch, and they had Mark Ingram, a running back who would gain more than a thousand yards that season. Jackson, in his second season, looked much more comfortable. "I told John Harbaugh, 'There are going to be times when we just light it up,'" Roman said. "I wasn't sure how consistent we'd be, or how mature, because we were young, but I told Harbaugh, 'There's gonna be some days when we just race over people.'"[24]

In their season opener, the Ravens routed the Dolphins in Miami, 59–10, with Jackson throwing five touchdown passes. After the game, Jackson listened as a reporter recounted his passing statistics as part of a question. Unable to resist taking a dig at his doubters, he deadpanned a classic response. "Not bad for a running back," he said.[25]

In early November, the Ravens hosted the New England Patriots on *Sunday Night Football*. Jackson had continued to play well after his hot start in Miami, helping the Ravens to a 5–2 record. But the Patriots were the ultimate test. They were the reigning Super Bowl champions and had not lost so far in 2019.

Fans around the country tuned in to see Jackson's electrifying skills tested, and he aced the test. The Ravens rolled to two touchdowns and a field goal in the first quarter as Jackson darted around defenders and zipped completions into narrow openings. The Patriots appeared helpless to stop him. The Ravens won by seventeen points. A week later, during a lopsided win in Cincinnati, Jackson produced the play of the year in the NFL. After racing into the secondary with the ball, he juked around a defender with a 360-degree spin straight out of basketball legend Michael Jordan's arsenal. "Lamarkable!!" CBS's Ian Eagle shouted.[26]

As the fourth quarter wound down, Baltimore fans who had made the trek to Cincinnati gathered behind the Ravens' bench and chanted, "M-V-P! M-V-P!" When the season opened, Jackson had been a long shot to win the league's highest individual award. But he emerged as the favorite as the Ravens pummeled opponents.

A game of media gotcha erupted as draft experts and pundits who had doubted Jackson admitted their mistake. Two years earlier, ESPN's Bill Polian, now a retired general manager in the Pro Football Hall of Fame, had said Jackson would fare better as a wide receiver in the NFL. "I was using the old notions of what a quarterback was," Polian said.[27]

New notions were now in vogue. "Lamar is not a Peyton Manning where he's just going to decipher and decode what the defense is doing and, bam, start to audible," Roman said. "We'll do a little bit of that, but it's after the snap where Lamar is special with his spatial awareness as a play unfolds, his vision, his ability to adjust."[28]

The Ravens won their final twelve games to finish with a 14–2 record. Jackson led the league in touchdown passes and rushed for 1,206 yards—the most ever by a quarterback in a season. Although the Ravens were upset in the playoffs, Jackson was named the league

MVP in a unanimous vote by a media panel, following Cam Newton in 2015 and Patrick Mahomes in 2018 as Black quarterbacks who had won the award outright.

"There were times during the season when he was so good it wasn't even fair, and that's hard to do in the NFL," Roman said. "It was just a great example of what can happen if you're really willing to throw out all the old stuff [that NFL offenses used] and start over with his skill set and say, 'What makes sense for this guy? How can he be successful?' It can work and it does work."[29]

———

Jackson accepted the MVP award at a league event held the night before Super Bowl 54 between the Kansas City Chiefs and San Francisco 49ers. His hair was braided. He looked sharp in a salmon-hued suit with a purple shirt, but it was not an outfit Brooks Brothers would feature. A large gold chain hung from his neck. "There's been a lot of doubt going on, me being a running back, a receiver, stuff like that," he said. "That came with me into the league. But I had a great organization with me."[30]

He thanked the Ravens' decision-makers, including Newsome, DeCosta, Harbaugh, and the owner, Steve Bisciotti, whom he referred to as "Mister Steve"—a touch of subjugation some Black fans perhaps did not appreciate.[31] But while he was not country-club polished, he thanked his mother and his teammates and came across as polite, humble, and genuine.

"I give the Ravens a lot of credit," Dr. Charles K. Ross said. "Your quarterback is your identity. You've got to be comfortable with it. And the Ravens clearly have not said to him, 'Lamar, we want you to change the way you kind of represent yourself,' just because he is representing the Baltimore Ravens. That is very important. Lamar brings a certain uniqueness that makes him a role model for young African American males across this country who struggle with certain kinds of expectations that have been forced on them in white society. They see Lamar and have visions and thoughts like, 'I can come from the inner city and I don't have to kind of change the way

I look, what I wear, how I communicate, and I can be as successful as him.'"[32]

The day after Jackson accepted the MVP award, the Chiefs rallied late to win the Super Bowl and Mahomes was voted the game's MVP. It was a fitting conclusion to the greatest season ever for Black quarterbacks in the NFL. Jackson was the league MVP. Mahomes was the Super Bowl MVP. Russell Wilson and Deshaun Watson had taken their teams to the playoffs. Jameis Winston and Dak Prescott had finished one-two in passing yardage. The Cardinals' Kyler Murray, the first pick in the 2019 draft, was voted Rookie of the Year.

Months after the 2019 season ended, the Eagles used a second-round pick in the 2020 draft on Jalen Hurts, a Black quarterback from Oklahoma, envisioning him strictly as a backup to Carson Wentz, a former second-overall pick who had recently signed a $128 million contract. But Wentz played so poorly that he was benched, giving Hurts an opportunity to play. Wentz never threw another pass for the Eagles as Hurts emerged as a far better pro than scouts envisioned. In 2022, he helped the Eagles to a 14–3 record, an NFC championship, and a Super Bowl matchup with the Chiefs and Mahomes—the first Super Bowl featuring two Black starting quarterbacks. Warren Moon, staunch keeper of the flame, tweeted before the game that he was "so proud" of Hurts and Mahomes and that Black quarterbacks "have come a long way."[33] Robert Griffin III, now working as a broadcaster after injuries derailed his playing career, tweeted, "Historically, Black QBs have been told they can get it done athletically but not mentally. That stereotype has always been wrong. Now, for the 1st time we have 2 BLACK QBs IN THE SUPER BOWL. They beat you athletically, with their arm and their brain. The NEW PROTOTYPICAL NFL QB."[34] When Mahomes and Hurts both performed brilliantly in the Chiefs' 38–35 victory, the tired question of whether Black quarterbacks could handle big-game pressure had definitively been answered.

A year after the Eagles drafted Hurts, the 49ers selected North Dakota State's Trey Lance third overall and the Bears took Ohio State's Justin Fields eight picks later—two more Black quarterbacks expected to lead their franchises into the future. Both were starters by the outset of the 2022 season. Lance suffered an ankle injury that ended his season in September, but Fields emerged as a dynamic playmaker, rushing for 1,143 yards—just short of the single-season rushing record for quarterbacks that Lamar Jackson had set in 2019.

With Fields and Hurts already excelling, Lance set to return in 2023, and top-tier Black college quarterbacks such as Alabama's Bryce Young, Ohio State's C. J. Stroud, and USC's Caleb Williams on the cusp of their pro careers, an impressive generation was forming. Black quarterbacks dominated the 2023 draft with Young, Stroud, and Florida's Anthony Richardson among the first four overall picks.

"College football has forced the NFL's hand," Dr. Charles K. Ross said. "If the NFL had its choice, it probably would stick with the model of Dan Marino, John Elway, and those kinds of players as the representatives of their respective teams. But because college football has overwhelmingly moved in the direction of Black quarterbacks, and with the success they've shown on the field, the NFL—reluctantly, in my opinion—has decided, 'OK, OK, we've got to make this transition.'"[35]

The most vivid illustration of how the situation has changed can be found not in the NFL, but rather, on the youth and high school fields across the country where young Black quarterbacks now dream—rightfully—of following their heroes into the pros. "Lamar coming on the heels of Mahomes had an electric effect," Leigh Steinberg said. "Players at the peewee and high school levels see things very differently now. They don't always know what went on before. They see Black quarterbacks at the top of the game and expect to be able to play quarterback as they make their way through the different levels of the game. And they *can* play quarterback at those different levels, all the way to the NFL. Everything has changed."[36]

EPILOGUE

After many decades when the status of Black quarterbacks shifted with the seasons, in 2022 it took nothing more complex than a list of NFL salaries to demonstrate they were here to stay. Aaron Rodgers was the league's highest-paid player, with an average annual salary of $50 million. The next four highest-paid after him were Russell Wilson, Kyler Murray, Deshaun Watson, and Patrick Mahomes—all Black quarterbacks with contracts worth more than $1 billion combined.[1] Lamar Jackson and Jalen Hurts joined the ranks of the highest-paid players in 2023, signing deals worth more than a half-billion dollars combined.

Receding into the mists of history were the many years when you only needed one hand, or no hands, to count the Black quarterbacks in the NFL. Ten Black quarterbacks started their team's opening game in 2022, and eight others had jobs as backups. Teams were building offenses and futures around them, drafting them with the intent of developing them, and in a few cases, paying them staggeringly well. "It's gratifying to see a different situation from what I encountered in the 1970s," Warren Moon said.[2]

In the years when most men who shaped NFL rosters still believed quarterbacks should be white, it did not take much to ruin a Black quarterback's pro aspirations. If there was a shred of doubt about his arm strength, his size, the caliber of opponents he faced in college, or his perceived ability to run an offense, he was denied a future. In many cases, the very color of his skin did the trick.

In 2022, though, teams readily overlooked such questions about Black quarterbacks and went to great lengths to obtain them. Even though Wilson was thirty-three, the Denver Broncos gave up three players and five high draft picks to obtain him from the Seattle Seahawks in a trade. Even though Trey Lance was from North Dakota State, a lesser program, the San Francisco 49ers traded four high picks, including three in the first round, to move up and draft him in 2021.

Teams were even willing to overlook legitimately troubling facts. Even though Watson was a defendant in two dozen civil lawsuits alleging sexual assault and sexual misconduct during massage sessions, the Cleveland Browns gave up five picks, including three in the first round, to acquire him from the Houston Texans. The Browns knew they would be heavily criticized for tacitly condoning Watson's alleged behavior by acquiring him when he was under such an ominous legal cloud, but that did not deter their pursuit. Watson eventually settled all but one of the civil cases in 2022 as the Browns doubled down on their support, signing him to the largest fully guaranteed contract in NFL history, worth $230 million.

When Watson's legal troubles led to him being suspended by the league for the first eleven games of the 2022 season, Jacoby Brissett, who also is Black, stepped into the starting role. Brissett was thirty, playing for his fourth team in his seventh NFL season. In a less obvious way, his career also illustrated improving conditions for Black quarterbacks.

While those with clear talent had received more opportunities since the 1990s, the market for Black backup quarterbacks had developed more slowly. Teams continued to prefer white quarterbacks in a role requiring discipline and patience. Dr. Charles K. Ross said, "When you've got Mahomes and Russell Wilson and Lamar, people say, 'We can accept this, the needle has been moved.' But what if you don't come in and set the world on fire like Michael Vick? Are you going to get the same treatment? Are you going to get the same opportunity to hang around for ten years, have a nice career, play a couple of games here and there as the backup? That doesn't happen as much."[3]

But it was happening more in 2022. Brissett had started just thirty-seven games in his first six NFL seasons; teams mostly viewed him as a backup or stopgap starter. But he threw more than twice as many touchdowns as interceptions, enabling him to continue signing contracts. He chose the Browns from among several teams that pursued him in 2022. The Washington Commanders signed him in 2023.

Wilson's departure from Seattle in 2022 also created an opportunity for a Black quarterback who had spent many years in the league primarily as a backup. Geno Smith was thirty-two, playing for his fourth team in his ninth pro season. He had started sixteen games for the New York Jets as a rookie in 2013, but after he was benched the next year, he became widely viewed as a backup. Entering 2022, he had started just five games since 2015. But he won Seattle's starting job and wound up helping the team make the NFC playoffs.

Tyrod Taylor, a Black quarterback who was the New York Giants' backup in 2022, had lasted even longer in the league than Brissett or Geno Smith despite seldom being viewed as a starter. He was thirty-three, on his sixth team in his twelfth pro season. He had been bitterly disappointed when ten quarterbacks were selected before him in the 2011 draft even though he had set a school record for total offense at Virginia Tech. (The Ravens drafted him in the sixth round.) In 2022, none of those ten quarterbacks, including neither Cam Newton nor Colin Kaepernick, were still playing, but Taylor, a nimble runner and accurate passer, had continually attracted interest.

This increase in the number of Black backup quarterbacks might also work to improve another area of the NFL where racial inequality has long dominated—the coaching ranks. "Getting to hang around for ten or twelve years in some capacity is how you become an expert in the pro game. The fact that Black quarterbacks have been denied that definitely has kept guys out of coaching," Doug Williams said. "You're seeing a few more now. I would expect that to pay dividends eventually."[4]

As the 2022 season began, racial inequality in NFL coaching received more attention than the shortfall of Black quarterbacks. There were just three Black head coaches, an embarrassing figure for a league with a playing population nearly 70 percent Black. "We're not doing a good enough job here," NFL commissioner Roger Goodell said.[5] Not only did Black coaches receive fewer opportunities, they were fired more quickly than their white counterparts. After the 2021 season, the

Miami Dolphins fired a Black head coach, Brian Flores, even though the team had a winning record with him in each of the prior two seasons.

Flores did not go quietly. He filed a racial discrimination lawsuit against the league and its teams, guaranteeing that the issue would continue to receive a deeper exploration.

But even though the quarterback position was no longer the primary focus of racial inequality in the NFL, Black quarterbacks still faced challenges. A 2010 study by two academics had revealed that Black and white quarterback prospects often were depicted in racially stereotypical language by major sports publications before the draft, with Blacks primarily described with words and phrases that emphasized their physical gifts and lack of mental prowess, and whites described as less physically gifted, but more mentally prepared and less likely to make mental errors.[6] These stereotypes, grievously unfair, still simmered in the football conversation in 2022, leaving Black quarterbacks with much to prove. James Harris, a witness to the situation since the 1960s, said reflexive doubts in the league about Black quarterbacks "continue to be an issue."[7]

Indeed, while progress was evident in the presence of eighteen Black quarterbacks on NFL rosters at the start of the 2022 season, that was still just 28 percent of the starting and backup jobs. There were more than twice as many white quarterbacks in the league—a near exact reversal of the racial breakdown at all other positions combined. Even though racist stereotypes about Black quarterbacks had been thoroughly disproved, they were not entirely out of play.

Old-school doubts had come back into the open as recently as 2018. That was the year Bill Polian said Lamar Jackson would be better in the pros as a wide receiver, and also the year a school superintendent near Houston questioned the mental acuity of all Black quarterbacks in a Facebook post that went viral.[8]

Another incident arose in the summer of 2022 after what seemingly was a triumph—Murray signing a contract extension with the Arizona Cardinals worth $230.5 million. It turned out the Cardinals had inserted in his deal a "homework clause" requiring him to spend at least four hours a week studying film during the season. Murray would not receive credit for studying "if he was simultaneously playing video games, watching TV or surfing the Internet" on his iPad, according to the clause.[9]

Murray, the first overall pick in the 2019 draft, was furious about what he perceived as a demeaning challenge to his professionalism. "To think I can accomplish everything that I've accomplished in my career and not be a student of the game and not have that passion and not take this serious, is disrespectful. It's almost a joke," he said.[10]

As the Cardinals were criticized for the patronizing language, race inevitably seeped into the conversation. Would a team ever ask a white quarterback to accept such a contract clause? If anything, it was a fair question.

Asked in 2022 if he believed he was evaluated differently because he was a Black quarterback, Mahomes gave a winding answer. "I don't want to go that far and say that," he said at first. But as he spoke, it became clear he believed Black quarterbacks were, in fact, singled out at times. "Obviously, the Black quarterback has had to battle to be in this position that we are, to have this many guys in the league playing. And I think every day we're proving that we should've been playing the whole time. We've got guys that think just as well as they can use their athleticism. So it always is weird when you see guys like me, Lamar, Kyler kind of get that [criticism] on them and other guys don't," Mahomes said.[11]

The reaction to Mahomes's comment was mixed, with some online responders supporting his view and others pointing out that all NFL quarterbacks received intense criticism in the age of social media. But Moon had spent decades witnessing, and experiencing, racist handling of Black quarterbacks, and refused to buy such equivalency. The homework clause was "a slap in the face to all African-American quarterbacks," Moon said. "It's something we were always accused of back in the day when they didn't let us play—that we were lazy, that we didn't study, that we couldn't be leaders, that we weren't smart. So all those different things just kind of came to the surface [again] after we had put all that stuff to bed over the years, and just because of this deal that's gone on between Arizona and Kyler."[12]

The Cardinals removed the homework clause from Murray's contract and the national media moved on to another subject. But "the damage has been done," Moon said. "He'll have this riding on him every time he does something wrong in a football game. They're going to say, 'See, that's the reason why that happened, because he didn't study enough film last week.'"[13]

To Moon and others familiar with the history of how Black quarterbacks were treated, the incident indicated that old-school thinking, whether conscious or unconscious, is still in play. "You look at the [mostly white] owners and GMs in the league and you can see the old-boy network still exists," Doug Williams said. "Mitch Trubisky getting drafted before Mahomes and Watson in 2017 tells you all you need to know. There's no way that ever should have happened."[14]

But while racism remains relevant, it also is clear that fundamental changes have impacted the quarterback position, and there are signs those changes will continue. "There is still racist thinking in pro football, but it's not at the level it was," Williams said. "The situation is getting better. Ten years from now, we might look up and see that half the quarterbacks in the league are Black."[15]

━━━

Jack Silverstein was frustrated. A Chicago sports historian and lifelong Bears fan, he feared his team simply did not want a Black starting quarterback—and had not for years.

To support his notion, he could recite several of the Bears' personnel moves that, in his view, certainly raised the possibility, especially when considered collectively. In 1999, they had wanted a quarterback and could have drafted Daunte Culpepper, a Black quarterback who became a star, with the seventh pick in the first round. Instead, they traded back and took a white quarterback, Cade McNown, later in the first round. McNown was a bust, traded within two years. Then, in 2003, they again wanted a quarterback and held the fourth overall pick, giving them a shot at Byron Leftwich, a sought-after Black quarterback. But again, they traded the pick and later drafted a white quarterback, Rex Grossman.

In 2017, they again wanted a quarterback and traded for the second overall pick, but instead of drafting Mahomes or Watson, who had set records and won championships in college and became immediate winners in the NFL, they drafted Trubisky, a white quarterback who had not won a college bowl game and was gone from Chicago after four seasons.

After reading a damning 2019 *Chicago Tribune* review of the process that led to the Bears taking Trubisky, Silverstein felt compelled to answer the question that had nagged him for years.[16] Were the Bears really opposed to Black quarterbacks? How did their racial history at the position compare to the racial history of other NFL teams at quarterback? "If you're a Bears fan, don't you want to know if your team is making bad quarterback decisions based on racism?" Silverstein asked. "I knew what I thought anecdotally, but what did the numbers actually say?"[17]

He saw the question as, potentially, part of a larger situation involving the Bears and race. In August 2019, he published an article suggesting that George Halas, the Bears' legendary founder, was at least partly responsible for the NFL's twelve-year ban on Black players that began in 1934. When the Bears announced they would wear 1936 "throwback" jerseys for a game in 2019, Silverstein wrote that the Black players on the current Bears team would be the first Black players to wear the 1936 uniform—an irrefutable point. George McCaskey, Halas's grandson, was the team's chairman in 2019, and although he declined to be interviewed for the article, he sent Silverstein copies of passages from the Bears' official one-hundred-year history, where it was noted that, at the very least, the Bears went along with the ban, which historians have attributed to the influence of the Redskins' George Preston Marshall, a notorious racist. Silverstein took that as a tacit acknowledgment from McCaskey that he was not wrong to question Halas.

"I think it is naïve, wishful thinking on the part of white people, Bears fans, to think that George Halas, who was so powerful in the league, able to do almost anything, could not overrule [Marshall] and was not involved himself," Silverstein said. "My question about the Bears' quarterback history was whether there were institutional forces that were still in play from his influence and his era."[18]

It was the deepest of research rabbit holes; Silverstein spent a year identifying every Black quarterback who had taken a snap in the NFL since 1953, using that starting point because it was the year George Taliaferro started two games for the Baltimore Colts, thus becoming the first Black starting quarterback in the modern NFL. As the 2020 season began, Silverstein published a comprehensive statistical report that brought unprecedented clarity to many aspects of the opportunities given to Black quarterbacks over the years in the NFL. The report included team-by-team breakdowns, draft histories, and a league-wide review measuring the ebb and flow of overall opportunity.[19]

Reaction was swift as fans of various teams discovered the information on Silverstein's website. "It started a lot of conversations, especially on Twitter," he said.[20]

The Bears, it turned out, had, indeed, offered fewer opportunities to Black quarterbacks than most teams. Black quarterbacks had started less than 5 percent of their games since 1953. Only nine teams had lower percentages, putting the Bears in the bottom third of the league. "The data supported what I'd thought was going on," Silverstein said.[21]

The New York Giants had the lowest percentage, having started a Black quarterback in just one game since their launch in 1925—a stunning fact. "You don't need to say anything more about it than that," Silverstein said.[22] The Green Bay Packers, who began play in 1919, before the NFL launched, had a similar record, giving just eleven starts to Black quarterbacks in more than a century of games. The New York Jets, Cleveland Browns, Miami Dolphins, Denver Broncos, Indianapolis Colts, New England Patriots, and Los Angeles Chargers also had started Black quarterbacks in less than 5 percent of their games.

At the other end of the spectrum, the Philadelphia Eagles had given more opportunities to Black quarterbacks than any team—starts in roughly a third of their games since 1953, with Randall Cunningham, Donovan McNabb, and Michael Vick logging most of the starts. The franchise that originated as the Houston Oilers, now known as the Tennessee Titans, also had started Black quarterbacks in roughly a third of their games, with Moon, Steve McNair, and Vince Young combining for twenty-six seasons as their starter.

Other teams at the top of the list included the Carolina Panthers, who began play in 1995 and had the highest percentage of games started by Black quarterbacks; the Tampa Bay Bucs and Seattle Seahawks, who had given more than 30 percent of their starts to Black quarterbacks; and the Baltimore Ravens, who were close to 30 percent.

Why had some franchises embraced Black quarterbacks more than others? "After compiling and studying this data, I feel confident in pointing to two reasons," Silverstein said. "One reason can be confirmed. The other is harder to confirm but I believe it's true."[23]

What could be confirmed, Silverstein said, was that the organizations at the top all had a key person at a certain point with the power to give a Black quarterback a chance to play, and a willingness to go against the grain of general thought in the league. Chuck Knox, as head coach of the Los Angeles Rams, made James Harris his starter for two seasons in the 1970s until, in effect, he was overruled by the team's owner. Andy Reid relied on Black starting quarterbacks for most of his long tenure as the Eagles' head coach. Ozzie Newsome just ignored the standard criticisms of Black quarterbacks as the Ravens' general manager starting in 1996.

Joe Gibbs was the key person for two franchises. As the Bucs' offensive coordinator in 1978, he advised the team's front office that Doug Williams was the best quarterback prospect in the draft that year—an opinion that led to Williams being drafted in the first round and starting for the Bucs for five seasons at a time when Black starters were extremely rare. Then, as the Redskins' head coach in 1986, Gibbs needed a backup and signed Williams—a move that led to Williams becoming the first Black quarterback to win the Super Bowl.

"The presence of a key person, a gatekeeper, is easy to objectify and confirm as helping Black quarterbacks receive opportunities," Silverstein said. "And then, though no one has confirmed this, what the numbers show is that once a franchise has success with a Black quarterback, the trend is it goes for other Black quarterbacks more readily. It's like the top comes off."[24]

Washington's history offers a vivid illustration. Founded by Marshall, an openly racist son of Confederate officers, the franchise, now known as the Commanders, were the slowest team to reintegrate after the league's all-white epoch ended in 1946; they did not employ a Black player at any position until 1961 and did not start a Black quarterback in a game until Williams in 1987. But after Williams led them to a Super Bowl victory, they became as open to Black quarterbacks as any team. Six others have started for them since Williams. Three times since 2005, they have drafted a Black quarterback in the first round. "Their record surprised me as much as anything I discovered in all of this data," Silverstein said.[25]

A comfort level with Black quarterbacks seemingly also helped in Philadelphia after Cunningham's superb career, which began in 1985; and with the Oilers/Titans after Moon's long run of success, which began in 1984. After Moon moved on and became the first Black quarterback to start for the Vikings in 1994—thirty-three years after the franchise's launch—eight other Black quarterbacks started in Minnesota over the next twenty years. For some of that time, the team had a Black head coach, Denny Green.

But even though his data clearly showed that some franchises had embraced Black quarterbacks and others had not, Silverstein warned against concluding that race was THE cause. "It's a nuanced situation," he said. "A number of teams that have low percentages [of Black starters] have enjoyed sustained excellence at quarterback for many years with [white] players who were Hall of Famers or longtime Pro Bowl types."[26] The Packers' quarterback history, for instance, includes Bart Starr, Brett Favre, and Aaron Rodgers—three iconic figures who have worn the uniform for forty years between them, leaving less room than usual for anyone else at the position. The San Francisco

49ers were among the last teams to give a Black quarterback a start (in 2010, sixty-four years after their launch), but they won five Super Bowls with Joe Montana and Steve Young, white quarterbacks now in the Hall of Fame, making it harder to fault their decision-making.

Although the Giants did not start a Black quarterback until Geno Smith in 2017, they were not always opposed to Black quarterbacks. In 1967, they signed Hank Washington, a talented quarterback from West Texas State who was Black and, not surprisingly, had gone undrafted even though he was six feet three, weighed 210 pounds, and had performed well against major college talent in an integrated all-star game. The Giants viewed him as a potential backup to Fran Tarkenton, and though they did not give him a roster spot as a rookie, they thought enough of him to retain his rights and loan him to a minor-league team, the Westchester Bulls of the Atlantic Coast Football League, for seasoning. He could have become the Giants' first Black starter decades before Smith, but he died of cancer at age twenty-four. Meanwhile, the Giants have reached five Super Bowls, winning four, with four different white starting quarterbacks—Phil Simms, Jeff Hostetler, Kerry Collins, and Eli Manning—a record that does not necessarily excuse the absence of Black quarterbacks from their history but does help explain it.

By contrast, the Bears, through the years, have won one Super Bowl and otherwise generally experienced more heartache than success with their long run of white quarterbacks. "The lack of Black starters over the years makes more sense for a number of other teams compared to the Bears," Silverstein said.[27]

But his premise about his favorite team still not wanting a Black quarterback suddenly was debunked in 2021 when the Bears drafted Justin Fields, a Black quarterback from Ohio State, with the eleventh overall pick, clearly expecting him to become a franchise cornerstone. Fields made several starts as a rookie and had the starting job in hand by his second season in 2022. If negative opinions about Black quarterbacks had previously prevailed in the Bears' front offices at any point, those opinions clearly no longer held sway.

Silverstein saw Fields's arrival as part of a reckoning on race that the Bears had recently experienced, orchestrated by George McCaskey. Since 2018, they also had become heavily involved in social justice initiatives, hired a senior vice president of diversity, equity, and inclusion, and put their roster decision-making in the hands of a Black general manager. McCaskey acknowledged his grandfather's mistaken thinking on race in a team-produced video.

"In my opinion, George McCaskey has led an effort to change the hiring policies and practices of his franchise," Silverstein said. "He is now doing some of the work to push his franchise away from the legacy of his grandfather. Drafting Justin Fields was part of that. I'm excited to see where it continues to go."[28]

Aside from unpacking each team's history with Black quarterbacks, Silverstein's data also told the story of overall opportunity through the years in the NFL.

"Such a sad story," he said.[29]

After the NFL opened for business in 1920, discrimination and exclusion ruled for decades at the game's pivotal position. There were no more than two Black starting quarterbacks in the league in any season through 1985. Moon was the only one in 1984. A decade later, he was still just one of four.

"Countless individuals along the way could have, and should have, had the opportunity that Moon and a few others received," Silverstein said. "These individuals had earned the opportunity by virtue of their talent, their intelligence, their work ethic, their commitment to the sport, their intangibles, leadership, all the things that quarterbacks are lauded for. To have NFL owners and teams not give them the opportunities they had earned was sad, most of all, for them, and also for their families and their fans. It makes me sad as a football fan because I always want the best people at things to do the thing. I want the best filmmakers to make movies. I want the best teachers to teach my children. I want the best athletes to play, the best coaches to coach.

Whatever the endeavor, art, entertainment, sports, I want the best people doing it. The idea that the best people are not playing the most important position in sports is sad to me, as a lover of sports. Imagine if we didn't get to see Warren Moon. Imagine if we didn't get to see Randall Cunningham. And we almost didn't."[30]

According to Silverstein's data, the largest spike in collective opportunity came in the late 1990s—fourteen Black quarterbacks started NFL games in the 2000 season. But that figure has never been surpassed. The total was still fourteen in 2007, but just half that in 2014. So much for the notion that Colin Kaepernick, Russell Wilson, Robert Griffin III, and Cam Newton ushered in a golden age.

In a historical sense, the presence of eighteen Black quarterbacks on NFL rosters at the outset of the 2022 season certainly represents improvement, especially when paired with the prodigious salaries the best Black quarterbacks now earn. Yet Silverstein, for one, is not celebrating. And no one should, really. The Black experience at quarterback during the NFL's first century was, for the most part, a long chronicle of misery mirroring the Black experience in many other realms of American life. The situation might be improved, producing hope for an even better future, but the past reveals dark forces simmering at the heart of America's favorite sport, a reality not easily reconciled.

"It's very easy for people to say Mahomes has the richest contract in the history of sports and Lamar is an MVP and it's going well in that Black quarterbacks are being given opportunities," Silverstein said. "But these are opportunities Black quarterbacks always deserved, opportunities that many earned and were denied. It should have happened all along, and the data really drives home how few were treated fairly. A lot of lives were changed because of the denial of opportunity. That's the story."[31]

ACKNOWLEDGMENTS

My thanks to Susan Canavan, my agent, for helping me frame the project and finding a home for it; Emma Berry, at Basic Books, for understanding that I had a lot going on; Brandon Proia and Lillian Duggan, for careful and insightful edits that made the book so much better; Patrick Gleason, for helping arrange interviews; Nestor Aparicio, for helping me contact Leigh Steinberg; Luke Rollfinke, for transcribing hours of interviews; and as always, Mary Wynne, for listening and understanding and a thousand other things.

NOTE ON SOURCES

None of my previous books covered this much narrative terrain—more than a century from Fritz Pollard to Lamar Jackson and beyond. To depict the lives and times of generations of Black quarterbacks, I relied on interviews and research. Ozzie Newsome, James Harris, Warren Moon, Doug Williams, Tee Martin, Greg Roman, Leigh Steinberg, Upton Bell, Jack Silverstein, Ron Wolf, and Dr. Charles K. Ross were especially generous with their time. As always when writing about the NFL, I could not have survived without pro-football-reference.com, which provided the final word on scores, statistics, play-by-play accounts of games, draft history, biographical facts, and more. A subscription to newspapers.com also helped me investigate and corroborate.

I owe a debt to the many writers who previously covered various aspects of the story. Greg Howard's "Big Book of Black Quarterbacks," published by Deadspin in 2014, is an online bible. A series of profiles on Black quarterbacks written for ESPN's Andscape site (formerly The Undefeated) helped me dig deeper, as did the work of Samuel G. Freedman, who has written eloquently about James Harris, and William Rhoden's 2005 oral history of the Black quarterback saga, *Third and a Mile*. I was fortunate to come across Jack Silverstein's excellent research shortly before I finished the manuscript.

I have sought to accurately source any words that appear between quotation marks in these pages and, also, any facts that might raise questions. I'm responsible for any errors.

BIBLIOGRAPHY

Allsopp, Ralph Cuffeea. *In Pro Football Black Quarterbacks and the N-Word Matters*. Denver: Outskirts Press, 2018.

Anderson, Sheldon, ed. *Twin Cities Sports: Games for All Seasons*. Fayetteville, AR: University of Arkansas Press, 2020.

Bowden, Mark. *Bringing the Heat: A Pro Football Team's Quest for Glory, Fame, Immortality, and a Bigger Piece of the Action*. New York, Knopf, 1994.

Carroll, John M. *Fritz Pollard: Pioneer in Racial Advancement*. Chicago and Urbana, IL: University of Chicago Press, 1992.

Eisenberg, John. *The League: How Five Rivals Created the NFL and Launched a Sports Empire*. New York: Basic Books, 2018.

Freedman, Samuel G. *Breaking the Line: The Season in Black College Football That Transformed the Sport and Changed the Course of Civil Rights*. New York: Simon and Schuster, 2013.

Gottehrer, Barry. *The Giants of New York: The History of Professional Football's Most Fabulous Dynasty*. New York: G. P. Putnam's Sons, 1963.

Gwynne, S. C. *The Perfect Pass: American Genius and the Reinvention of Football*. New York: Scribner, 2016.

Hurd, Michael. *Black College Football, 1892–1992: One Hundred Years of History, Education, and Pride*. Virginia Beach, VA: The Donning Company Publishers, 1993.

MacCambridge, Michael. *America's Game: The Epic Story of How Pro Football Captured a Nation*. New York: Anchor Books, 2005.

———. *Chuck Noll: His Life's Work*. Pittsburgh: University of Pittsburgh Press, 2016.

Moon, Warren, with Don Yaeger. *Never Give Up on Your Dream: My Journey*. Boston: Da Capo Press, 2009.

Rhoden, William C. *Third and a Mile: The Trials and Triumphs of the Black Quarterback*. New York: ESPN Books, 2007.

Rooney Jr., Art, with Roy McHugh. *Ruanaidh: The Story of Art Rooney and His Clan*. Pittsburgh: Arthur Rooney Jr., 2008.

Ross, Charles K. *Outside the Lines: African Americans and the Integration of the National Football League*. New York: New York University Press, 1999.

——. *Mavericks, Money, and Men: The AFL, Black Players, and the Evolution of Modern Football*. Philadelphia: Temple University Press, 2016.

Vick, Michael. *Finally Free: An Autobiography*. Brentwood, TN: Worthy Publishing, 2012.

Williams, Doug, with Bruce Hunter. *Quarterblack: Shattering the NFL Myth*. Chicago: Bonus Books, 1990.

NOTES

INTRODUCTION

1. Author interview with James Harris.
2. Samuel G. Freedman, *Breaking the Line: The Season in Black College Football That Transformed the Sport and Changed the Course of Civil Rights* (New York: Simon and Schuster, 2013), 258.
3. Author interview with James Harris.
4. Author interview with James Harris.
5. Samuel G. Freedman, "Football's Jackie Robinson," True Stories, OZY, January 18, 2014, www.ozy.com/true-and-stories/footballs-jackie-robinson/1476/.
6. Freedman, "Football's Jackie Robinson."
7. "Namath Says O.J. Is Going to Be Great," *Bridgewater (N.J.) Courier-News,* September 15, 1969.
8. *Sports Illustrated* cover headline, September 11, 1989.
9. Black QB starts by team (by Jack Silverstein/ReadJack), https://docs.google.com/spreadsheets/d/1V2TWQ6cnz0NwnUOW-tyzggS8SpgbkhJfmYuBXAC7sU8/edit#gid=634827050.
10. Myles Simmons, "Patrick Mahomes: It's Weird When Lamar Jackson, Kyler Murray, and I Get Criticism Others Don't," PFT Live, July 29, 2022, https://profootballtalk.nbcsports.com/2022/07/29/patrick-mahomes-its-weird-when-lamar-jackson-kyler-murray-and-i-get-criticism-others-dont/.
11. Author interview with James Harris.

CHAPTER 1

1. "Hammond Pros Win From Dayton," *Lake County Times,* October 8, 1923.
2. "Hammond Pros Win From Dayton."
3. "Hammond Pros Win From Dayton."
4. Edward McClelland, "Rogers Park/West Ridge Looks to Honor the Pollards, Its First Black Family," *Chicago,* November 11, 2021, www.chicagomag.com/city-life/rogers-park-west-ridge-looks-to-honor-the-pollards-its-first-black-family.
5. "Brown's Fritz Pollard Broke Yale Bowl's Racial Barrier 100 Years Ago," *New Haven Register,* November 6, 2015, www.nhregister.com/colleges/article/Brown-s-Fritz-Pollard-broke-Yale-Bowl-s-11348033.php.

6. John M. Carroll, *Fritz Pollard: Pioneer in Racial Advancement* (Chicago and Urbana, IL: University of Chicago Press, 1992), 137.

7. "Indians and Canton Play 0–0 Tie Game," *Akron Beacon Journal*, October 11, 1926.

8. "Sports Talks by William G. Nunn," *Pittsburgh Courier*, November 9, 1926.

9. Carroll, *Fritz Pollard*, 178.

10. Carroll, *Fritz Pollard*, 179.

CHAPTER 2

1. "Myers, N.Y.U. Guard, Used in Back Field," *New York Times*, October 17, 1929.

2. Arthur J. Daley, "Penn State Bows to N.Y.U. Eleven, 7–0, Before 30,000 Crowd at Yankee Stadium," *New York Times*, October 20, 1929.

3. "Meehan Will Not Use Myers Against Georgia," *New York Times*, October 24, 1929.

4. "Meehan Will Not Use Myers Against Georgia."

5. Ed Hughes, *Brooklyn Daily Eagle*, November 8, 1929.

6. John Eisenberg, *The League: How Five Rivals Created the NFL and Launched a Sports Empire* (New York: Basic Books, 2018), 101.

7. Eisenberg, *The League*, 102.

8. Eisenberg, *The League*, 102.

9. Bob Barnett, "Ray Kemp Blazed Important Trail," *Coffin Corner* 5, no. 12 (1983).

10. Barnett, "Ray Kemp Blazed Important Trail."

11. Barnett, "Ray Kemp Blazed Important Trail."

12. Eisenberg, *The League*, 102.

13. David Schwartz, "Let's Remember Ozzie Simmons," HawkeyeNation.com, October 26, 2017.

14. Kate Kelly, "Kenny Washington: Broke Color Line in NFL," America Comes Alive!, https://americacomesalive.com/kenny-washington-broke-color-line-in-nfl/.

15. Author interview with Jack Silverstein.

CHAPTER 3

1. Ben Donahue, "The Life and Career of Sammy Baugh (Complete Story)," Pro Football History, www.profootballhistory.com/sammy-baugh/.

2. Jack M. Silverstein, "Throwback: The Truth About George Halas and the NFL's Ban on Black Players," Windy City Gridiron, www.windycitygridiron.com/2019/8/28/20836166/chicago-bears-100-throwback-1936-jersey-truth-about-george-halas-nfl-12-year-ban-on-black-players.

3. Arthur Arkush, "Bears Don't Hide from History, Discuss 1936 Segregation-Era Jerseys," *Pro Football Weekly*, September 26, 2019.

4. John Eisenberg, *The League: How Five Rivals Created the NFL and Launched a Sports Empire* (New York: Basic Books, 2018), 252.

5. Barry Gottehrer, *The Giants of New York: The History of Professional Football's Most Fabulous Dynasty* (New York: G. P. Putnam's Sons, 1963), 211.

CHAPTER 4

1. Steve Milton, "Meet Bernie Custis: Football's First African-American Quarterback," *Toronto Star*, August 12, 2011.

2. Milton, "Meet Bernie Custis."

3. Milton, "Meet Bernie Custis."

4. Milton, "Meet Bernie Custis."

5. Milton, "Meet Bernie Custis."

6. Milton, "Meet Bernie Custis."

7. Milton, "Meet Bernie Custis."

8. Milton, "Meet Bernie Custis."

9. Milton, "Meet Bernie Custis."

10. "Behind the Marker," Willie Thrower Historical Marker, ExplorePAhistory .com, https://explorepahistory.com/hmarker.php?markerId=1-A-311.

11. Michael Carlson, "Willie Thrower," *The Guardian*, April 16, 2002.

12. George Taliaferro, "I Didn't Do It!," *Coffin Corner* 27, no. 5 (2005).

13. Taliaferro, "I Didn't Do It!"

14. Taliaferro, "I Didn't Do It!"

15. Taliaferro, "I Didn't Do It!"

16. Jerry Bembry, "George Taliaferro Played Quarterback and a Whole Lot More," Andscape, September 28, 2017.

17. Mike Klingaman, "Colts Star George Taliaferro, the First Black Player Drafted by the NFL, Dies," *Baltimore Sun*, October 10, 2018.

18. The 1955 Green Bay Packers, https://packershistory.homestead.com/1955 PACKERS.html.

19. John Maxymuk, "Before His Time: Charlie Brackins," https://packerspast perfect.wordpress.com/2015/11/01/before-his-time-charlie-brackins/.

20. Maxymuk, "Before His Time."

21. Maxymuk, "Before His Time."

22. Cliff Christl, "Final Cut in 1958: Dick Deschaine or Jim Taylor," Packers.com, January 11, 2018.

CHAPTER 5

1. Rustin Dodd, "The Legacy Bowl: How a Bold Scout, HBCU Talent Elevated Chiefs—and Football," *The Athletic*, February 4, 2021.

2. Fayette County Sports Hall of Fame, 1950–1959: Sandy Stephens (2009), http://fayettecountysportshalloffame.com/stephens.html.

3. African American Registry, "Sandy Stephens, Collegiate, and CFL Football Player born," https://aaregistry.org/story/university-of-minnesotas-first -black-quarterback-sandy-stephens/.

4. Fayette County Sports Hall of Fame.

5. Patrick Reusse, "U's Sandy Stephens Was Ahead of His Time," *Star Tribune* (Minneapolis), December 6, 2011.

6. Scott Dochterman, "Wilburn Hollis, Sandy Stephens and Perhaps the Most Significant Game in Big Ten History," *The Athletic*, November 14, 2019.

7. Associated Press, "Brown's TV Set Flashes Rosy Picture," *Akron Beacon Journal*, January 2, 1962.

8. Sheldon Anderson, ed., *Twin Cities Sports: Games for All Seasons* (Fayetteville, AR: University of Arkansas Press, 2020), 74–75.

9. Fayette County Sports Hall of Fame.

10. Heather Lloyd, "Sandy Stephens Paved Path for Quarterbacks of Today, Inspired Tony Dungy and Others Along the Way," Colts.com, February 22, 2018.

11. Lloyd, "Sandy Stephens Paved Path."

12. Lloyd, "Sandy Stephens Paved Path."

13. Lloyd, "Sandy Stephens Paved Path."

14. African American Registry, "Sandy Stephens."

15. African American Registry, "Sandy Stephens."

16. Lloyd, "Sandy Stephens Paved Path."

CHAPTER 6

1. Gregg Doyel, "Grandson Has the Potential to Create NFL Legacy That Dickey Was Denied," cbssports.com, September 18, 2013.

2. Clay Risen, "Karen Hastie Williams, 76, Who Broke Racial Barriers and Glass Ceilings, Dies," *New York Times*, August 5, 2021.

3. Risen, "Karen Hastie Williams."

4. Author interview with Upton Bell.

5. Author interview with Upton Bell.

6. Author interview with Upton Bell.

7. Author interview with Upton Bell.

8. Author interview with Upton Bell.

9. Author interview with Upton Bell.

10. Author interview with James Harris.

11. Author interview with Ron Wolf.

12. Michael Lee, "'We All Thought That He Would Be the One,'" *Washington Post*, November 12, 2021.

13. Author interview with Ron Wolf.

14. Author interview with James Harris.

15. Paul Gutierrez, "Why Mark Davis Chose Civil Rights Icon Tommie Smith to Light Raiders' Torch," ESPN.com, November 17, 2016, www.espn.com/blog/afc west/post/_/id/76558/why-mark-davis-chose-civil-rights-icon-tommie-smith -to-light-raiders-torch.

16. Jonas Shaffer, "'He Would've Been a Star': 50 Years Before Ravens QB Lamar Jackson, There Was Eldridge Dickey," *Baltimore Sun*, September 17, 2020.

17. F. M. Williams, "A&I, with Dickey Throwing, Planning on Passing Game Friday," *Nashville Tennessean*, September 10, 1967.

18. William C. Rhoden, *Third and a Mile: The Trials and Triumphs of the Black Quarterback* (New York: ESPN Books, 2007), 84.

19. Rhoden, *Third and a Mile*, 83–84.

20. Rhoden, *Third and a Mile*, 84–85.

21. "How Raiders View 'Exhibition' Games," *Santa Rosa Press Democrat*, August 21, 1968.

22. John Crittenden, "Eldridge Dickey: Quarterback-to-Be," *Miami News*, September 25, 1968.

23. Crittenden, "Eldridge Dickey: Quarterback-to-Be."

24. Crittenden, "Eldridge Dickey: Quarterback-to-Be."

25. Rhoden, *Third and a Mile*, 98.

26. Rhoden, *Third and a Mile*, 98.

27. Associated Press, "Quarterbacks a Miniature Scope of Black America's Aspirations," *Palm Beach Post-Times*, September 28, 1969.

28. Lee, "'We All Thought That He Would Be the One.'"

29. Doyel, "Grandson Has the Potential."

30. Ed Levitt, "Blanda's Last Shot," *Oakland Tribune*, August 4, 1969.

31. Lee, "'We All Thought.'"

32. Lee, "'We All Thought.'"

33. Lee, "'We All Thought.'"

34. Lee, "'We All Thought.'"

35. Blaine Newnham, "The Contribution Gap," *Oakland Tribune*, August 27, 1970.

36. Newnham, "Contribution Gap."

37. Rhoden, *Third and a Mile*, 84.

38. Newnham, "Contribution Gap."

39. Newnham, "Contribution Gap."

40. Newnham, "Contribution Gap."

41. Rhoden, *Third and a Mile*, 84–85.

42. Williams, "A&I."

43. Author interview with Upton Bell.

44. Author interview with Ron Wolf.

45. The Eldridge Dickey Story, www.eldridgedickey.com.

46. Ed Willes, "Inspiration: Brayden's Writing Next Chapter," *The Province* (Vancouver, BC), December 27, 2013.

CHAPTER 7

1. David Kiefer, "The Catalyst: Gene Washington and the Rise of Stanford Football," February 18, 2021, GoStanford, https://gostanford.com/news/2021/2/18/football-the-catalyst.aspx.

2. Kiefer, "The Catalyst."

3. Kiefer, "The Catalyst."

4. Kiefer, "The Catalyst."

5. Ben Swanson, "Marlin Briscoe's Path from Packinghouses to the Pros," DenverBroncos.com, February 23, 2021, www.denverbroncos.com/news/the-making-of-the-magician-marlin-briscoe-omaha-path-high-school-college.

6. Cliff Brunt, "First Black Starting QB Reflects on Change in Game, Society," Associated Press, September 25, 2018.

7. Vince Bzdek, "Lessons from Marlin Briscoe, the Bronco Who Broke Barriers," *The Gazette* (Colorado Springs), September 19, 2020, https://gazette.com/newslessons-from-marlin-briscoe-the-bronco-who-broke-barriers-vince-bzdek/article_2fc0ee20-f911-11ea-b903-07576b41e6f6.html.

8. Jack Dickey, "Where Are They Now?: Marlin Briscoe," *Sports Illustrated*, July 6, 2015.

9. William C. Rhoden, *Third and a Mile: The Trials and Triumphs of the Black Quarterback* (New York: ESPN Books, 2007), 88.

10. Charles Maher, "One of a Kind," *Los Angeles Times*, October 30, 1968.

11. Dickey, "Where Are They Now?"

12. John Sundvor, "Denver Squeaks Past Buffalo Bills," *Gazette-Telegraph* (Colorado Springs), November 25, 1968.

13. Rhoden, *Third and a Mile*, 92.

14. Alice George, "The 1968 Kerner Commission Got It Right, But Nobody Listened," *Smithsonian Magazine*, March 1, 2018.

15. Author interview with James Harris.

16. Bzdek, "Lessons from Marlin Briscoe."

17. James Harris on *5 Games* podcast, Talk of Fame Network, June 26, 2018, https://vokalnow.com/audio/1867.

18. Dickey, "Where Are They Now?"

19. Author interview with Doug Williams.

20. Billy Witz, "A Pioneering Black Quarterback's Lasting Legacy," *New York Times*, January 29, 2014.

21. "Marlin Briscoe Inducted into College Football Hall of Fame," University of Nebraska Omaha, www.unomaha.edu/news/2016/09/marlin-briscoe -the-magician-the-maverick.php#retrospective.

22. Author interview with Dr. Charles K. Ross.

CHAPTER 8

1. William C. Rhoden, "A Coach Who Symbolized a Golden Age of Football," *New York Times*, April 5, 2007.

2. Rhoden, "Coach Who Symbolized."

3. Rhoden, "Coach Who Symbolized."

4. Rhoden, "Coach Who Symbolized."

5. Michael Hurd, *Black College Football 1892–1992: One Hundred Years of History, Education, and Pride* (Virginia Beach, VA: The Donning Company Publishers, 1993), 113.

6. Author interview with James Harris.

7. Hurd, *Black College Football*, 113.

8. Author interview with James Harris.

9. Author interview with James Harris.

10. Author interview with James Harris.

11. Author interview with James Harris.

12. Author interview with James Harris.

13. Author interview with James Harris.

14. Samuel G. Freedman, "How One Man's Debut in a Crucial Game Made It OK for Black Athletes to Play Quarterback," *Washington Post*, September 22, 2014.

15. Freedman, "How One Man's Debut."

16. Freedman, "How One Man's Debut."

17. Author interview with James Harris.

18. James Harris on *5 Games* podcast, Talk of Fame Network, June 26, 2018, https://vokalnow.com/audio/1867.

19. Dan DeLong, "Rams Flatten Buffalo," (Pomona, CA) *Progress-Bulletin*, September 7, 1969.

20. Author interview with James Harris.

21. Harris on *5 Games* podcast.

22. Harris on *5 Games* podcast.

23. Craig Stolze, "Pro Football Has Talkers," (Rochester, NY) *Democrat and Chronicle*, November 11, 1969.

24. Craig Stolze, "Once No. 1, Harris on Taxi Squad," (Rochester, NY) *Democrat and Chronicle*, September 12, 1970.

25. William C. Rhoden, *Third and a Mile: The Trials and Triumphs of the Black Quarterback* (New York: ESPN Books, 2007), 115.

CHAPTER 9

1. Sunni Khalid, "Pioneering QB Chuck Ealey Doesn't Look Back," Andscape, September 20, 2016.

2. Khalid, "Pioneering QB."

3. Khalid, "Pioneering QB."

4. Author interview with Dr. Charles K. Ross.

5. Khalid, "Pioneering QB."

6. David Jones, "Jimmy Jones, 50 Years After He Left for USC: On McKay, Bama-1970 and Helping to Break the QB Color Barrier," Pennlive.com, August 27, 2018.

7. Author interview with Upton Bell.

8. Author interview with Upton Bell.

9. Author interview with Upton Bell.

10. Ian MacDonald, "Als vs. Lions Tonight: The Walking Wounded Meet Each Other," *Montreal Gazette*, September 11, 1973.

11. Mark McCarter, "Holloway Appreciated Bryant's Honesty That Alabama 'Wasn't Ready' for Black Quarterback," al.com, February 20, 2011.

12. McCarter, "Holloway Appreciated Bryant's Honesty."

13. McCarter, "Holloway Appreciated Bryant's Honesty."

14. McCarter, "Holloway Appreciated Bryant's Honesty."

15. Author interview with Ozzie Newsome.

16. Seth Schwartz, "The Johnnie Walton Story," National Football Post, October 30, 2014.

17. Schwartz, "Johnnie Walton Story."

18. Schwartz, "Johnnie Walton Story."

19. Author interview with James Harris.

CHAPTER 10

1. Bill Christine, "Colts Learn Why No. 273 is No. 1," *Pittsburgh Post-Gazette*, September 16, 1974.

2. Art Rooney Jr. with Roy McHugh, *Ruanaidh: The Story of Art Rooney and His Clan* (Pittsburgh: Arthur Rooney Jr., 2008), 350.

3. Christine, "Colts Learn Why."

4. Joe Gilliam, interview by James Brown, *Real Sports with Bryant Gumbel*, HBO, Season 6, episode 1, posted January 24, 2000, www.youtube.com/watch?v =Ee8bmp124UY.

5. Terry Bradshaw, interview by James Brown, *Real Sports with Bryant Gumbel*.

6. Samuel G. Freedman, "Remembering Legendary Tennessee State Assistant Joe Gilliam," *Sports Illustrated*, January 11, 2013.

7. Phil Musick, "Gilliam Clinches Starting Job, 41–15," *Pittsburgh Press*, September 6, 1974.

8. Maury Z. Levy, "Terry Bradshaw: The Playboy Interview," *Playboy*, March 1980.

9. Author interview with Upton Bell.

10. Author interview with Upton Bell.

11. Author interview with Dr. Charles K. Ross.

12. Roy Blount Jr., "Gillie Was a Steeler Driving Man," *Sports Illustrated*, September 23, 1974.

13. Blount Jr., "Gillie Was a Steeler Driving Man."

14. Vito Stellino, "Steelers, Broncos Struggle to 35–35 Tie," *Pittsburgh Post-Gazette*, September 23, 1974.

15. Phil Musick, "Madden Makes Best of Situation," *Pittsburgh Press*, September 30, 1974.

16. Musick, "Madden Makes Best of Situation."

17. Phil Musick, "Oakland Raid Wipes Out Steelers," *Pittsburgh Press*, September 30, 1974.

18. Musick, "Madden Makes Best of Situation."

19. Joe Gilliam, interview by James Brown, *Real Sports with Bryant Gumbel*.

20. Gilliam, interview by Brown.

21. Gilliam, interview by Brown.

22. Gilliam, interview by Brown.

23. Al Abrams, "Is Winning the Only Thing?" *Pittsburgh Post-Gazette*, October 21, 1974.

24. Vito Stellino, "Bradshaw and Steeler Fans Rekindle an Old Romance," *Pittsburgh Post-Gazette*, October 29, 1974.

25. Michael MacCambridge, *Chuck Noll: His Life's Work* (Pittsburgh: University of Pittsburgh Press, 2016), 202.

26. MacCambridge, *Chuck Noll*, 202.

27. Gilliam, interview by Brown.

28. Bradshaw, interview by Brown.

29. Jerry Bembry, "Joe Gilliam Represented Much More Than 'Pittsburgh's Black Quarterback,'" Andscape, November 2, 2017.

CHAPTER 11

1. Author interview with James Harris.

2. Steve Wulf, "All Hell Broke Loose," *ESPN The Magazine*, February 3, 2014.

3. Samuel G. Freedman, "Chuck Knox Should Be Remembered for Making James the NFL's First Black Starting QB," Andscape, May 22, 2018.

4. James Harris on *5 Games* podcast, Talk of Fame Network, June 26, 2018, https://vokalnow.com/audio/1867.

5. Harris on *5 Games* podcast.

6. Harris on *5 Games* podcast.

7. Wulf, "All Hell Broke Loose."

8. Freedman, "Chuck Knox Should Be Remembered."

9. Headline, *Los Angeles Times*, November 25, 1974.

10. William N. Wallace, "Los Angeles Forces 3 Fumbles and 3 Interceptions for First Playoff Victory Since 1951," *New York Times*, December 23, 1974.

11. Wulf, "All Hell Broke Loose."

12. Wulf, "All Hell Broke Loose."

13. Freedman, "Chuck Knox Should Be Remembered."

14. Freedman, "Chuck Knox Should Be Remembered."

15. Associated Press, "New Look Coming Up for Rams," (Spokane, WA) *Spokesman-Review*, January 7, 1976.

16. Associated Press, "New Look Coming Up for Rams."

17. Wulf, "All Hell Broke Loose."

18. Skip Bayless, "The Ram Family: A House Somewhat Divided," *Los Angeles Times*, January 28, 1977.

19. Erwin Baker, "Harris Furor Spreads to the L.A. City Council," *Los Angeles Times*, February 15, 1977.

20. Skip Bayless, "The Sacking of James Harris . . . as Viewed by James Harris," *Los Angeles Times*, July 21, 1977.

21. Wulf, "All Hell Broke Loose."

22. Harris on *5 Games* podcast.

23. Wulf, "All Hell Broke Loose."

24. Wulf, "All Hell Broke Loose."

CHAPTER 12

1. Author interview with Doug Williams.

2. Doug Williams with Bruce Hunter, *Quarterblack: Shattering the NFL Myth* (Chicago: Bonus Books, 1990), 10.

3. Author interview with Ron Wolf.

4. John McKay Quotes, Sports Feel Good Stories, www.sportsfeelgoodstories.com/john-mckay-quotes/.

5. Author interview with Doug Williams.

6. Rick Gosselin, "Joe Gibbs Opened the Door for African-American Quarterbacks," Talk of Fame Network, SI.com, September 27, 2020.

7. Eddie Robinson from *A Football Life: Doug Williams*, NFL Network, Season 8, episode 10, December 7, 2018.

8. Lisa Zimmerman, "Doug Williams Reflects on the Importance of HBCUs and the Foundation of Success He Was Given," http://nfl-pe.azurewebsites.net/next/articles/doug-williams/.

9. Author interview with Doug Williams.

10. Author interview with Doug Williams.

11. Williams, *Quarterblack*, 92.

12. Author interview with Doug Williams.

13. Williams, *Quarterblack*, 95.

14. Williams, *Quarterblack*, 93.

15. Williams, *Quarterblack*, 93.

16. Williams, *Quarterblack*, 94.

17. Jerry Bembry, "Vince Evans Was Steadfast on Playing Quarterback in the Pros," Andscape, October 19, 2017.

18. Mike Tierney, "An Unheralded but Historic Happening in Chicago," *St. Petersburg Times*, September 26, 1979.

19. Ron Rapoport, "Black QB Duel No Big Deal Now," *Chicago Sun-Times*, reprinted in *Shreveport Journal*, September 28, 1979.

20. Author interview with Doug Williams.

21. Rapoport, "Black QB Duel."

22. Williams, *Quarterblack*, 96.

23. Author interview with Doug Williams.

24. Williams, *Quarterblack*, 98.

25. Author interview with Doug Williams.

26. John Feinstein, "Fishbowl Life Is Magnified for Black NFL Quarterback," *Washington Post*, reprinted in *Fort Worth Star-Telegram*, October 8, 1980.

27. Feinstein, "Fishbowl Life."

28. Feinstein, "Fishbowl Life."

29. Feinstein, "Fishbowl Life."

30. Williams, *Quarterblack*, 105.

31. Williams, *Quarterblack*, 106–107.

32. Author interview with Dr. Charles K. Ross.

33. Author interview with Doug Williams.

34. Williams, *Quarterblack*, 107–108.

35. Author interview with Doug Williams.

CHAPTER 13

1. Warren Moon, interview by Clifton Brown, "Not Bad for a 'Running Back,'" February 8, 2021, in *Black in the NFL* podcast, episode 9.

2. Author interview with Warren Moon.

3. Author interview with Warren Moon.

4. Author interview with Warren Moon.

5. Author interview with Warren Moon.

6. Author interview with Warren Moon.

7. Author interview with Warren Moon.

8. Author interview with Warren Moon.

9. Warren Moon with Don Yaeger, *Never Give Up on Your Dream: My Journey* (Boston: Da Capo Press, 2009), 53.

10. Moon, *Never Give Up*, 50.

11. Author interview with Leigh Steinberg.

12. Author interview with Leigh Steinberg.

13. Author interview with Warren Moon.

14. Author interview with Warren Moon.

15. Author interview with Warren Moon.

16. Ray Turchansky, "Racial Issue Helps Land Moon," *Edmonton Journal*, April 13, 1978.

17. Moon, *Never Give Up*, 79.

18. Moon, *Never Give Up*, 81.

19. Author interview with Warren Moon.

20. Author interview with Warren Moon.

21. Author interview with Warren Moon.

22. Author interview with Leigh Steinberg.

23. Author interview with Leigh Steinberg.

24. Author interview with Leigh Steinberg.

25. Rick Reilly, "On the Road to Riches with Moon," *Los Angeles Times*, February 9, 1984.

26. Author interview with Leigh Steinberg.

27. Author interview with Warren Moon.

28. Author interview with Leigh Steinberg.

29. Reilly, "On the Road to Riches."

30. Author interview with Dr. Charles K. Ross.

31. Reilly, "On the Road to Riches."

32. Reilly, "On the Road to Riches."

33. Author interview with Warren Moon.

34. Author interview with Leigh Steinberg.

CHAPTER 14

1. Warren Moon, interview by Clifton Brown, "Not Bad for a 'Running Back,'" February 8, 2021, in *Black in the NFL* podcast, episode 9.

2. Paul Domowitch, "To Pass, or Impasse?," *Philadelphia Daily News*, June 11, 1985.

3. Charean Williams, "'You're Not Called a Black Quarterback Anymore,'" *Orlando Sentinel*, August 1, 1999.

4. Victor Bryant, "Santa Barbara's Great Cunningham Brothers," *Santa Barbara Independent*, June 17, 2021.

5. Bryant, "Santa Barbara's Great Cunningham Brothers."

6. Hal Bock, "QB of the '90s: Randall Cunningham Looks Like Best of Present and Future," Associated Press (published in *Los Angeles Times*, September 3, 1989).

7. Bock, "QB of the '90s."

8. Mark Bowden, *Bringing the Heat* (New York: Knopf, 1994), 362–363.

9. Neil Paine, "How Randall Cunningham Taught NFL Quarterbacks to Fly," FiveThirtyEight.com, November 17, 2016.

CHAPTER 15

1. William Weinbaum, "The Legacy of Al Campanis," ESPN.com, March 29, 2012.

2. Author interview with Doug Williams.

3. Author interview with Doug Williams.

4. Author interview with Doug Williams.

5. William C. Rhoden, *Third and a Mile: The Trials and Triumphs of the Black Quarterback* (New York: ESPN Books, 2007), 154.

6. Author interview with Doug Williams.

7. Doug Williams with Bruce Hunter, *Quarterblack: Shattering the NFL Myth* (Chicago: Bonus Books, 1990), 145.

8. Williams, *Quarterblack*, 147.

9. Williams, *Quarterblack*, 148.

10. Williams, *Quarterblack*, 149.

11. Liz Clarke, "Doug Williams's Super Bowl Win 30 Years Ago Changed the Game for Black Quarterbacks," *Washington Post*, January 30, 2018.

12. Williams, *Quarterblack*, 149.

13. Mike Bianchi, "Dumbest Question Was Never Asked," *Orlando Sentinel*, January 30, 2007.

14. Author interview with Doug Williams.

15. Doug Williams, "The Legendary Doug Williams Talks Super Bowl XXII," episode 21, in Washington Commanders' *WOW: Women of Washington* podcast.

16. Rhoden, *Third and a Mile*, 154.

17. Rhoden, *Third and a Mile*, 155–156.

18. Author interview with Dr. Charles K. Ross.

19. Author interview with Doug Williams.

20. Skip Miller, "Doug Williams Writes to Explain Pain and Anger," (Long Beach, CA) *Daily Press*, September 16, 1990.

CHAPTER 16

1. Randall Cunningham Monday night football, YouTube, posted July 30, 2019, www.youtube.com/watch?v=QaZ2FixDfw4.

2. Michael Weinreb, "Randall Cunningham and the Journey of the Black Quarterback (October 10, 1988)," Throwbacks (Substack newsletter), June 9, 2020.

3. Will Weiss, "Classic MNF: Randall's World," ABC Sports Online, October 17, 2001.

4. Ray Didinger, "Randall Cunningham's Magical Escape Against the Giants," philadelphiaeagles.com, December 5, 2019.

5. Didinger, "Randall Cunningham's Magical Escape."

6. William C. Rhoden, *Third and a Mile: The Trials and Triumphs of the Black Quarterback* (New York: ESPN Books, 2007), 182.

7. Neil Paine, "How Randall Cunningham Taught NFL Quarterbacks to Fly," FiveThirtyEight.com, November 17, 2016.

8. Vito Stellino, "Warren Moon's Home Team," *Baltimore Sun*, October 30, 1988.

9. Doug Williams with Bruce Hunter, *Quarterblack: Shattering the NFL Myth* (Chicago: Bonus Books, 1990), 173–174.

10. Author interview with Doug Williams.

11. Author interview with Doug Williams.

12. Author interview with Doug Williams.

13. Author interview with Doug Williams.

14. Stellino, "Warren Moon's Home Team."

15. Stellino, "Warren Moon's Home Team."

16. Author interview with Warren Moon.

17. Tim Kawakami, "Another Barrier Falls," *Philadelphia Daily News*, January 25, 1989.

18. Kawakami, "Another Barrier Falls."

19. Kawakami, "Another Barrier Falls."

CHAPTER 17

1. Mark Whicker, "Lions' Pick of Peete Scores Points, Counterpoints," *Orange County Register*, published in *Detroit Free Press*, April 26, 1989.

2. Jerry Bembry, "Rodney Peete Stood the Test of Time," Andscape, November 9, 2017.

3. Brad Smith, "Why, Major?," mountaineersports.com, June 9, 2019.

4. Mike White, "Harris 12th Round Selection Not Major Upset," *Pittsburgh Post-Gazette*, April 24, 1990.

5. White, "Harris 12th Round Selection."

6. White, "Harris 12th Round Selection."

7. Jerry Bembry, "Andre Ware Isn't Just an Analyst, He's the First Black Quarterback to Win the Heisman," Andscape, November 23, 2017.

8. Geoff Hobson, "Bleak to Blake: Hope Emerges," *Cincinnati Enquirer*, October 31, 1994.

9. Mike Lupica, "The Road to Dreamville," *Newsday*, November 17, 1994.

10. Dave Caldwell, "Jeff Blake (6 Feet) Has Been Standing Tall," *Philadelphia Inquirer*, December 11, 1994.

11. Dadio Makdook, CJ Exclusive: interview with former Bengals QB Jeff Blake, cincyjungle.com, August 11, 2015.

CHAPTER 18

1. S. L. Price, "Air McNair: Steve McNair Is the Best Quarterback—Black or White, Big School or Small—in College Football," *Sports Illustrated*, September 26, 1994.

2. John Shearer, "McNair Dazzled Chamberlain Field Fans on Sept. 10, 1994," thechattanoogan.com, July 11, 2009.

3. Steve McNair Biography, https://biography.jrank.org/pages/2358/McNair-Steve.html.

4. Thomas George, "Deep in the Heart of Mississippi, a Halo Glows over Alcorn State," *New York Times*, August 28, 1994.

5. Associated Press, "McNair Brought Spotlight to Small School," ESPN.com, July 5, 2009.

6. Talk of Fame Network, "Jameis Winston: Charlie Ward Could've Been Russell Wilson," si.com, April 24, 2017.

7. Bruce Lowitt, "Two Arms. One Trophy.//McNair," *Tampa Bay Times*, September 28, 1994.

8. Ken Rosenthal, "McNair's the One," *Baltimore Sun*, October 27, 1994.

9. George, "Deep in the Heart."

10. Ira Berkow, "McNair and Alcorn Wind It Up Throwing," *New York Times*, November 26, 1994.

11. Justin Tinsley, "Steve McNair Went Third in the NFL Draft 25 Years Ago. We May Never See Another HBCU Player Go As High," Andscape, April 22, 2020.

12. Bill Polian, "Building an NFL Franchise Part 2 and the 1995 Draft Decision between Kerry Collins and Steve McNair," episode 11, August 5, 2020, in *Inside Football Podcast with Hall of Fame GM Bill Polian*.

13. Tennessee Titans, "Jeff Fisher Shares His Memories of Steve McNair," September 12, 2019, www.tennesseetitans.com/video/jeff-fisher-shares-memories-of-steve-mcnair.

14. Polian, "Building an NFL Franchise Part 2."

15. Steven J. Gaither, "Too Good to Pass Up: Steve McNair Defied the Odds in 1995 NFL Draft," HBCU Gameday, April 13, 2020, https://hbcugameday.com/2020/04/13/steve-mcnair-1995-nfl-draft-houston-oilers/2/.

16. Gaither, "Too Good to Pass Up."

17. Gaither, "Too Good to Pass Up."

18. David Boclair, "Reese Made the Most of Picks That Mattered Most," All Titans, si.com, August 21, 2021, www.si.com/nfl/titans/news/tennessee-titans-floyd-reese-first-round-nfl-draft-success.

19. Transcript, "Hearing Footsteps," *Outside the Lines*, ESPN.com, August 26, 2001, www.espn.com/page2/tvlistings/show74transcript.html.

20. Transcript, "Hearing Footsteps."

21. Tennessee Titans, "Jeff Fisher Shares His Memories."

22. Paul Kuharsky, "McNair-Style Apprenticeships Likely History," ESPN.com, July 7, 2009.

23. Steve McNair Biography.

24. Tennessee Titans, "Jeff Fisher Shares His Memories."

25. Tennessee Titans, "Jeff Fisher Shares His Memories."

26. Phil Sheridan, "For Titans' McNair, Patience Pays Off Big," *Philadelphia Inquirer*, January 27, 2000.

27. Brian Schmitz, "Skinny on McNair," *Orlando Sentinel*, January 26, 2000.

28. "The Tackle (Rams vs Titans 1999 Super Bowl XXXIV)," posted by Daniel Leu, June 1, 2016, www.youtube.com/watch?v=R3eukxNnm0M.

29. Jim Wyatt, "Steve McNair Left Lasting Impression in Super Bowl XXXIV," tennesseetitans.com, February 3, 2017.

30. Wyatt, "Steve McNair Left Lasting Impression."

CHAPTER 19

1. Author interview with Doug Williams.

2. Author interview with Leigh Steinberg.

3. Author interview with James Harris.

4. Author interview with Ron Wolf.

5. Author interview with Ron Wolf.

6. Charean Williams, "'You're Not Called a Black Quarterback Anymore,'" *Orlando Sentinel*, August 1, 1999.

7. "Steve Young's Famous 49-Yard Game-Winning Touchdown vs. Vikings, October 30, 1988," official49ers, posted June 24, 2013, www.youtube.com/watch ?v=LbPwwmEcws0.

8. Author interview with Leigh Steinberg.

9. Jerry Bembry, "Kordell Stewart and the Legend of Slash," Andscape, January 4, 2018.

10. Gerry Callahan, "All-Purpose Weapon Steeler Kordell (Slash) Stewart, A Passer/Runner/Receiver, Is Disarming Pittsburgh's Foes," *Sports Illustrated*, December 11, 1995.

11. Callahan, "All-Purpose Weapon."

12. Bembry, "Kordell Stewart."

13. Bembry, "Kordell Stewart."

14. Martenzie Johnson, "Tony Banks Had All the Potential in the World," Andscape, December 28, 2017.

15. Johnson, "Tony Banks."

16. Johnson, "Tony Banks."

CHAPTER 20

1. David Fleming, "Home Boy Near the Playing Fields of His Youth, Unflappable Rookie Quarterback Shaun King Led the Bucs to Another Crucial Win, Against the Lions," *Sports Illustrated*, December 20, 1999.

2. Staff reports, "Redskins-Bucs Notes: King Shows Poise Despite Struggling," DailyPress.com, January 16, 2000.

3. Staff reports, "Redskins-Bucs Notes."

4. Jenna Laine, "How the Bucs' Bert Emanuel Overcame the Non-Catch That Forged His Legacy," ESPN.com, January 23, 2020.

5. Laine, "How the Bucs' Bert Emanuel."

6. Laine, "How the Bucs' Bert Emanuel."

7. Laine, "How the Bucs' Bert Emanuel."

8. Charean Williams, "'You're Not Called a Black Quarterback Anymore,'" *Orlando Sentinel*, August 1, 1999.

9. Williams, "'You're Not Called.'"

10. Associated Press, "Culpepper's Adoptive Mother Passes Away," ESPN .com, May 6, 2007.

11. Associated Press, "Culpepper's Adoptive Mother."

12. Martenzie Johnson, "Long Before Drew Brees, There Was Aaron Brooks," Andscape, December 14, 2017.

13. Aaron Brooks, in "Aaron Brooks & Jeff Blake on the Black History of the Saints Quarterback Position," neworleanssaints.com, www.neworleans saints.com/video/aaron-brookes-jeff-blake-new-orleans-saints-quarterback -black-history.

14. Johnson, "Long Before Drew Brees."

15. Johnson, "Long Before Drew Brees."

16. H. A. Branham, "Culpepper's Plays Are 'Unbelievable,'" *Tampa Tribune*, January 7, 2001.

17. Branham, "Culpepper's Plays."

18. Kent Youngblood, "Words As Elusive As a Touchdown," (Minneapolis) *Star Tribune*, January 15, 2001.

19. Youngblood, "Words As Elusive."

CHAPTER 21

1. Michael Vick, interviewed on *Skip and Shannon: Undisputed*, Fox Sports 1, September 18, 2020.

2. Michael Vick, *Finally Free: An Autobiography* (Brentwood, TN: Worthy Publishing, 2012), 5.

3. Vick, *Finally Free*, 5.

4. Vick, *Finally Free*, 5.

5. Damon Hack, "Back in High School, Vick Was Far from Being the Running Man," *New York Times*, November 24, 2002.

6. Jim Wilkie, "QB Curry Can Escape 'Noles Only So Often," *Tampa Bay Times*, October 26, 1999.

7. John Ed Bradley, "A Cut Above the Rest," *Sports Illustrated*, August 14, 2000.

8. Vick, interviewed on *Skip and Shannon*.

9. Vick, interviewed on *Skip and Shannon*.

10. Michael Vick, interview by DeSean Jackson, *Fade the Booth* podcast, episode 2, September 21, 2021.

11. Vick, interview by DeSean Jackson.

12. Bradley, "Cut Above the Rest."

13. Vick, interview by DeSean Jackson.

14. Vick, interview by DeSean Jackson.

15. Vick, interviewed on *Skip and Shannon*.

16. Vick, interview by DeSean Jackson.

17. John Eisenberg, "Hokies Get Trapped in Morass of Florida State's Depth," *Baltimore Sun*, January 4, 2000.

18. Rachel Alexander, "Seminoles Make Their Claim for National Title," *Washington Post*, January 5, 2000.

19. Tony Dungy, foreword to Vick, *Finally Free*, xi.

20. Bradley, "Cut Above the Rest."

21. Lindsay Jones, "The 2001 NFL Draft Trade That Changed the Falcons, Chargers and QB Play Forever," *The Athletic*, April 27, 2021.

22. Vick, *Finally Free*, 56–57.

23. Vick, *Finally Free*, 56–57.

24. Jones, "2001 NFL Draft Trade."

25. "NFL Draft 2001," posted by Michael Charles, June 30, 2021, ww.youtube.com/watch?v=VPvr-W2TI7Y.

26. Vick, interview by DeSean Jackson.

27. Vick, interviewed on *Skip and Shannon*.

28. Vick, interview by DeSean Jackson.

29. Michael Vick, "Michael Vick: Walking in His Truth," on *Huddle and Flow* podcast, NFL Podcast Network, December 24, 2020.

30. Vick, "Michael Vick: Walking in His Truth."

31. Vick, "Michael Vick: Walking in His Truth."

32. Vick, "Michael Vick: Walking in His Truth."

33. Packers-Falcons Recap, Packers.com, September 9, 2002, www.packers.com/news/packers-falcons-recap-2477301.

34. Alan Robinson, "Wild Finish Results in Tie for Steelers, Falcons," *Latrobe Bulletin*, November 11, 2002.

35. Dungy, foreword to Vick, *Finally Free*, xii.

36. Associated Press, "Behind Vick, Falcons End Pack's Home Playoff Rule," ESPN.com, January 5, 2003.

CHAPTER 22

1. Associated Press, "Ineffective McNabb Leads Eagles to Ruin," (Middletown, NY) *Times Herald-Record*, January 20, 2003.

2. Associated Press, "Ineffective McNabb."

3. ESPN.com news services, "Limbaugh Comments Touch Off Controversy," ESPN.com, October 1, 2003.

4. "What Limbaugh Actually Said," transcribed by Brian S. Wise, American Partisan, www.american-partisan.com/cols/2003/wise/qtr4/1006a.htm.

5. Richard Sandomir, "Limbaugh Still Has a Fallback Position," *New York Times*, October 3, 2003.

6. ESPN.com news services, "Limbaugh Comments."

7. ESPN.com news services, "Limbaugh Comments."

8. ESPN.com news services, "Sam McNabb Recalls Past Racist Incidents," ESPN.com, January 17, 2004.

9. ESPN.com news services, "Sam McNabb."

10. Rob Maaddi, "Eagles Legend Donovan McNabb Says Black QBs Have Always Faced Doubt," June 24, 2021, NBC Philadelphia, www.nbcphiladelphia.com/news/sports/eagles/donovan-mcnabb-black-quarterbacks-jalen-hurts/2858889/.

11. Maaddi, "Eagles Legend Donovan McNabb."

12. ESPN.com news services, "Sam McNabb."

13. ESPN.com news services, "Sam McNabb."

14. ESPN.com news services, "Sam McNabb."

15. Michael Vick, interview by DeSean Jackson, *Fade the Booth* podcast, episode 2, September 21, 2021.

CHAPTER 23

1. Jim Wyatt, "McNabb Third Black QB to Start a Super Bowl," (Nashville) *Tennessean*, January 31, 2005.

2. Michael Vick, *Finally Free: An Autobiography* (Brentwood, TN: Worthy Publishing, 2012), 86.

3. Vick, *Finally Free*, 85.

4. Vick, *Finally Free*, 86.

5. Vick, *Finally Free*, 91.

6. Vick, *Finally Free*, 101–102.

7. Kelly Naqi, "In Virginia Facing State Dogfighting Charges, Vick's Involvement Revealed," ESPN.com, November 21, 2008.

8. Vick, *Finally Free*, 113.

9. Seth Wickersham, "The View from Within," ESPN.com, August 26, 2011.

10. Donovan McNabb, interviewed in *Vick (Part 2)*, 30 for 30 documentary film series, Season 3, episode 36, ESPN+ and ESPN Films.

11. CBC Sports, "Warren Moon Enters Hall of Fame," February 4, 2006, www.cbc.ca/sports/football/warren-moon-enters-hall-of-fame-1.604021.

12. Author interview with Warren Moon.

13. Vince Young, interviewed in *Fear of a Black Quarterback*, VICE Versa documentary film series, VICE TV, 2021.

14. Donovan McNabb, interviewed in *Fear of a Black Quarterback*.

15. Young, interviewed in *Fear of a Black Quarterback*.

16. Young, interviewed in *Fear of a Black Quarterback*.

CHAPTER 24

1. Author interview with Tee Martin.

2. Author interview with Tee Martin.

3. Author interview with Tee Martin.

4. Author interview with Tee Martin.

5. Author interview with Tee Martin.

6. Author interview with Tee Martin.

7. Author interview with Tee Martin.

8. Author interview with Tee Martin.

9. Author interview with Tee Martin.

10. Author interview with Tee Martin.

11. Author interview with Tee Martin.

12. Author interview with Tee Martin.

13. Author interview with Tee Martin.

14. Author interview with Tee Martin.

15. Author interview with Tee Martin.

16. Author interview with Tee Martin.

17. Author interview with Ozzie Newsome.

18. Pete Thamel and Ray Glier, "Newton Faced Suspension at Florida," *New York Times*, November 9, 2010.

19. Thamel and Glier, "Newton Faced Suspension."

20. FOX Sports, "More Scandalous Claims in Newton Case," November 11, 2010, www.foxsports.com/stories/college-football/more-scandalous-claims-in-newton-case.

21. Mark Memmott, "Auburn QB Cam Newton Cleared to Play by NCAA," The Two-Way, NPR, December 1, 2010, www.npr.org/sections/thetwo-way/2010/12/01/131729406/auburn-qb-cam-newton-cleared-to-play-by-ncaa/.

22. Chris Low and Mark Schlabach, "Cash Sought for Cam Newton," ESPN, November 4, 2010, www.espn.com/college-football/news/story?id=5765214.

23. Memmott, "Auburn QB."

24. Jerry Richardson, interview by Charlie Rose, "NFL Team Owners," *Charlie Rose*, August 23, 2011, https://charlierose.com/videos/15597.

25. Richardson, interview by Rose.

26. Joseph Person, "Newton: Relationship with Richardson 'A-1,'" *Charlotte Observer*, August 26, 2011.

CHAPTER 25

1. Author interview with Greg Roman.
2. Author interview with Greg Roman.
3. Bob Baum, "49ers' Smith Is Almost Perfect," Associated Press, published in (Tucson) *Arizona Daily Star*, October 30, 2012.
4. Author interview with Greg Roman.
5. Author interview with Greg Roman.
6. Author interview with Greg Roman.
7. Author interview with Greg Roman.
8. Author interview with Greg Roman.
9. Author interview with Greg Roman.
10. Author interview with Greg Roman.
11. Author interview with Greg Roman.
12. "Kap Puts On a Dual-Threat Clinic! (Packers vs. 49ers 2012, NFC Divisional Round)," NFL Throwback, posted January 18, 2022, www.youtube.com /watch?v=Mp8w_5LDQtY.
13. Author interview with Greg Roman.
14. Author interview with Greg Roman.

CHAPTER 26

1. Author interview with Warren Moon.
2. Author interview with Warren Moon.
3. Author interview with Warren Moon.
4. Author interview with Warren Moon.
5. Author interview with Warren Moon.
6. Author interview with Warren Moon.
7. Author interview with Warren Moon.
8. Author interview with Warren Moon.
9. Author interview with Warren Moon.
10. Jim Corbett, "Seahawks Knock Off Redskins in Slugfest Wild-Card Game," *USA Today*, January 7, 2013.
11. Danny O'Neil, "Seahawks Rookie Russell Wilson Dazzles Even in Defeat to Falcons," *Seattle Times*, January 14, 2013.
12. Author interview with Warren Moon.
13. Ben Eagle, "Colin Kaepernick, Andrew Luck, Robert Griffin III, Russell Wilson on Sept. 2 Covers of SI," August 28, 2013, si.com, www.si.com/nfl /2013/08/28/colin-kaepernick-andrew-luck-robert-griffin-iii-russell-wilson -sports-illustrated-cover.
14. Author interview with Warren Moon.
15. Author interview with Warren Moon.
16. Author interview with Warren Moon.
17. Author interview with Warren Moon.

18. Author interview with Warren Moon.

19. Russell Wilson, "From the Akron Pros to the Seattle Seahawks: Race and the NFL," *Sports Illustrated*, July 9, 2014.

20. Wilson, "From the Akron Pros."

21. Wilson, "From the Akron Pros."

CHAPTER 27

1. "Worst Play Call in Super Bowl History?," NFL Network, posted February 3, 2015, www.youtube.com/watch?v=CZSqjfYaX4M.

2. Scott Polacek, "Cam Newton Comments on Race, Being a Role Model for Kids," Bleacher Report, February 2, 2016.

3. Polacek, "Cam Newton."

4. Daniel Kramer, "Peyton Manning Comments on Cam Newton After Super Bowl 50 Win vs. Panthers," Bleacher Report, February 8, 2016.

5. Victor Mather, "A Timeline of Colin Kaepernick vs. the N.F.L.," *New York Times*, February 15, 2019.

6. Marissa Payne, "Colin Kaepernick Refuses to Stand for National Anthem to Protest Police Killings," *Washington Post*, August 27, 2016.

7. Nate Boyer, "An Open Letter to Colin Kaepernick, from a Green Beret-Turned-Long Snapper," *Army Times*, August 30, 2016.

8. Nate Boyer, interview by Clifton Brown, "Shut Up and Play," *Black in the NFL* podcast, episode 1, October 6, 2020.

9. Boyer, interview by Brown.

10. Boyer, interview by Brown.

11. USA Today Sports, "Roger Goodell on Colin Kaepernick: 'We Believe Very Strongly in Patriotism in the NFL,'" September 7, 2016, www.usatoday .com/story/sports/nfl/2016/09/07/goodell-doesnt-agree-with-kaepernicks -actions/89958636/.

12. *TIME*, "The Difference Between President Trump and President Obama's Reactions to the NFL Kneeling Movement," September 24, 2017, time.com/4955050 /trump-obama-nfl-nba-kaepernick-kneeling/.

13. Bryan Armen Graham, "Donald Trump Blasts NFL Anthem Protesters: 'Get That Son of a Bitch Off the Field,'" *The Guardian*, September 23, 2017, www .theguardian.com/sport/2017/sep/22/donald-trump-nfl-national-anthem -protests.

14. ESPN, "Roger Goodell: 'Wish We Had Listened Earlier' to What Colin Kaepernick Was Protesting," August 23, 2020.

15. Author interview with Dr. Charles K. Ross.

CHAPTER 28

1. Author interview with Doug Williams.

2. Author interview with Leigh Steinberg.

3. Joe Rutter, "Gunslinger Label Saddles Texas Tech's Big-Armed QB Mahomes," tribLIVE.com, April 16, 2017.

4. Author interview with Leigh Steinberg.

5. Author interview with Leigh Steinberg.

6. Author interview with Leigh Steinberg.

7. Author interview with Leigh Steinberg.

8. Author interview with Leigh Steinberg.

9. Author interview with Leigh Steinberg.

10. Patrick Mahomes, interviewed on *The Dan Patrick Show*, February 23, 2017.

11. Jason Beck, "Former Tigers Pick Mahomes Talk of NFL Draft," mlb.com, April 27, 2017.

12. Mahomes, interviewed on *Dan Patrick Show*.

13. Don Williams, "Kingsbury Keeping Fingers Crossed Regarding Mahomes' Uncertain Plans," *Lubbock Avalanche-Journal*, February 6, 2014.

14. Michael Shapiro, "Patrick Mahomes Details 'Infinity ERA' in Texas Tech Baseball Appearance," si.com, February 3, 2021.

15. Author interview with Leigh Steinberg.

16. Christian D'Andrea, "Patrick Mahomes' Stock Is Rising Faster Than Anyone's in the 2017 NFL Draft," sbnation.com, April 17, 2017.

17. Author interview with Leigh Steinberg.

18. Author interview with Leigh Steinberg.

19. Author interview with Leigh Steinberg.

20. Pete Sweeney, "The Tale of Alex Smith's Mentorship of Patrick Mahomes Resurfaced This Week," arrowheadpride.com, May 11, 2022.

21. Joshua Rhett Miller, "School Superintendent on Texans Star: 'You Can't Count on a Black QB,'" *New York Post*, September 18, 2018.

22. Author interview with Leigh Steinberg.

23. Author interview with Tee Martin.

24. Author interview with Tee Martin.

25. Author interview with Leigh Steinberg.

26. Author interview with Leigh Steinberg.

27. Author interview with Leigh Steinberg.

28. Author interview with Leigh Steinberg.

CHAPTER 29

1. Author interview with Ozzie Newsome.

2. Author interview with Ozzie Newsome.

3. Author interview with Ozzie Newsome.

4. Author interview with Ozzie Newsome.

5. Author interview with Ozzie Newsome.

6. Author interview with Ozzie Newsome.

7. Author interview with Ozzie Newsome.

8. Author interview with Ozzie Newsome.

9. Alec Nathan, "Lamar Jackson Says Chargers Scout Told Him About Interest in Him as WR," Bleacher Report, June 23, 2018.

10. Author interview with Dr. Charles K. Ross.

11. Author interview with Leigh Steinberg.

12. "Picks 21–32: Lamar Jackson Gets Drafted, & WR's Go off the Board! (Round 1)—2018 NFL Draft," NFL Network, posted April 26, 2018, www.youtube.com/watch?v=UthBRYlIX3o.

13. Author interview with Ozzie Newsome.

14. Author interview with Ozzie Newsome.

15. Author interview with Ozzie Newsome.

16. Ryan DiPentima, "Before NFL Dominance, Lamar Jackson's Star Shined Bright in Palm Beach County," *Palm Beach Post*, January 8, 2020.

17. Alysha Tsuji, "Michael Vick Says Louisville QB Lamar Jackson Is '5 Times Better' Than He Was at Virginia Tech," ForTheWin, USA Today Sports, September 17, 2016, https://ftw.usatoday.com/2016/09/michael-vick-louisville-qb-lamar-jackson-praise.

18. Author interview with Greg Roman.

19. Author interview with Ozzie Newsome.

20. Daniel Oyefusi, "'It's a Big Deal': With Young Black Quarterbacks on the Rise, Ravens' Lamar Jackson Having a Season for the Ages," *Baltimore Sun*, January 8, 2020.

21. Author interview with Greg Roman.

22. Author interview with Greg Roman.

23. Author interview with Dr. Charles K. Ross.

24. Author interview with Greg Roman.

25. "Lamar Jackson: Not Bad for a 'Running Back,'" BaltimoreRavens.com, www.baltimoreravens.com/video/lamar-jackson-not-bad-for-a-running-back.

26. Good Morning Football (@gmfb), "Ian Eagle used the term 'Lamarkable' on the @Ravens CBS broadcast. How'd our crew feel about it? What do you think?," Twitter.com, November 18, 2019, 6:00 a.m., https://twitter.com/gmfb/status/1196412906998382592?lang=en.

27. Sean Wagner-McGough, "Bill Polian Finally Admits He Was Wrong to Say Lamar Jackson Should Switch from Quarterback to Receiver," cbssports.com, November 6, 2019.

28. Author interview with Greg Roman.

29. Author interview with Greg Roman.

30. "Watch Lamar Jackson's MVP Speech After Unanimous Win," NFL.com, www.nfl.com/videos/watch-lamar-jackson-s-mvp-speech-after-unanimous-win.

31. "Watch Lamar Jackson's MVP Speech."

32. Author interview with Dr. Charles K. Ross.

33. Warren Moon (@WMoon1), "I'm so proud to see Jalen and Patrick as the first 2 African American QBs to face each other in the Super Bowl! We have come a long way," Twitter, January 29, 2023, 10:58 p.m., https://twitter.com/WMoon1/status/1619938194799366144.

34. Robert Griffin III (@RGIII), "Historically, Black QBs have been told they can get it done athletically but not mentally. That stereotype has always been wrong. Now, for the 1st time we have 2 BLACK QBs IN THE SUPER BOWL. They beat you athletically, with their arm and their brain. The NEW PROTOTYPICAL NFL QB," Twitter, January 30, 2023, 10:34 a.m., https://twitter.com/RGIII/status/1620113360040910850.

35. Author interview with Dr. Charles K. Ross.

36. Author interview with Leigh Steinberg.

EPILOGUE

1. Vincent Frank, "12 Highest-Paid Quarterbacks in the NFL: Struggles Define the Top of the List," SportsNaut.com, December 28, 2022, https://sportsnaut.com/highest-paid-quarterbacks-in-the-nfl/.

2. Author interview with Warren Moon.

3. Author interview with Dr. Charles K. Ross.

4. Author interview with Doug Williams.

5. "Roger Goodell: 'We're Not Doing a Good Enough Job Here,'" yahoo!sports, February 9, 2022, https://sports.yahoo.com/roger-goodell-not-doing-good-223156865.html.

6. Eugenio Mercurio and Vincent F. Filak, "Roughing the Passer: The Framing of Black and White Quarterbacks Prior to the NFL Draft," *Howard Journal of Communications* 21 (2010): 1, 56–71, www.tandfonline.com/doi/abs/10.1080/10646170903501328.

7. Author interview with James Harris.

8. Joshua Rhett Miller, "School Superintendent on Texans Star: 'You Can't Count on a Black QB,'" *New York Post*, September 18, 2018.

9. Cale Clinton, "Warren Moon Calls Kyler Murray's Film Study Clause a 'Slap in the Face' to Black Quarterbacks," *USA Today*, July 31, 2022.

10. Clinton, "Warren Moon."

11. Myles Simmons, "Patrick Mahomes: It's Weird when Lamar Jackson, Kyler Murray, and I Get Criticism Others Don't," PFT Live, July 29, 2022, https://profootballtalk.nbcsports.com/2022/07/29/patrick-mahomes-its-weird-when-lamar-jackson-kyler-murray-and-i-get-criticism-others-dont/.

12. Clinton, "Warren Moon."

13. Clinton, "Warren Moon."

14. Author interview with Doug Williams.

15. Author interview with Doug Williams.

16. Dan Wiederer and Rich Campbell, "Why Did the Bears Draft Mitch Trubisky over Patrick Mahomes and Deshaun Watson?" *Chicago Tribune*, November 12, 2019.

17. Author interview with Jack Silverstein.

18. Author interview with Jack Silverstein.

19. Jack Silverstein, "The Complete History of Black NFL Starting Quarterbacks—Ranks by Franchise," readjack.com, September 17, 2020.

20. Author interview with Jack Silverstein.

21. Author interview with Jack Silverstein.

22. Author interview with Jack Silverstein.

23. Author interview with Jack Silverstein.

24. Author interview with Jack Silverstein.

25. Author interview with Jack Silverstein.

26. Author interview with Jack Silverstein.

27. Author interview with Jack Silverstein.

28. Author interview with Jack Silverstein.

29. Author interview with Jack Silverstein.

30. Author interview with Jack Silverstein.

31. Author interview with Jack Silverstein.

INDEX

ABC, 46, 167

Abrams, Al, 120

Adams, Bud, 154, 156, 185, 208–209

Adams, Joe, 158

Adventures of Huckleberry Finn, The (book), 144

Aikman, Troy, 191–192, 196–197, 208, 325

Akron Beacon Journal (newspaper), 17

Akron Indians, 13–15, 21

Akron Pros, 10–17, 21

Alabama A&M University, 264

Alcorn State University, 200–205, 207

All-America Football Conference (AAFC), 35–40, 43, 65–66, 131, 137, 294

Allen, Eric, 181

Allen, Kevin, 161–162

Alstott, Mike, 230

American Association, 28

American Football Conference (AFC)
    championship games, 125, 128, 172, 211, 222, 231, 260, 267–275, 298, 309, 332–335, 341, 346
    origin of, 124–125

American Football League (AFL)
    beginnings of, 53–54
    drafts, 54, 58, 90
    early years of, 53–54, 69–73, 79, 83–87, 90–97, 114, 124, 331
    first Black quarterback drafted in, 58
    first Black quarterback in, 82–90
    integration of, 54, 63
    merger of, 54, 65–68, 74, 124–125
    MVP award, 69–70

American Professional Football League, 14. *See also* National Football League

Arizona Cardinals, 106, 199, 286, 290–291, 314–315, 350, 355–357

Arizona State University, 148–149, 168, 223, 302

Army Times (newspaper), 318

Associated Press (AP), 3, 57, 74, 98, 180, 274, 290–291, 304, 327

Astrodome, 182, 209

Atlanta Falcons, 68, 139, 239, 245–253, 261–262, 265, 269–271, 297, 307

Atlantic Coast Conference, 194

Auburn University, 106, 194, 283–284, 338

Baltimore Colts, 38, 43–44, 46–48, 65–66, 72, 75–77, 83, 96, 105, 115–116, 124, 129–130, 135, 359

Baltimore Ravens, 89, 199, 222, 266, 268, 274, 278, 298–299, 305, 309, 339–349, 354, 360

Baltimore Sun (newspaper), 204, 243

Banks, Antonio, 240

Banks, Carl, 178–179

Banks, Tony, 223–224, 266, 341

Barber, Ronde, 254

Bartkowski, Steve, 139

baseball
    color line in, 46
    Hall of Fame, 46
    integration of, 4, 28–29, 36, 42–43, 167–169

baseball (*continued*)
major league baseball, 10, 14–18,
22–30, 33–36, 42–43, 46, 55, 81,
167–169, 202, 291, 327–328
minor league baseball, 20
racism and, 28–29, 33–36, 46, 167–169
segregation and, 10, 33–36
semipro baseball, 16, 25
basketball
all-Black team, 19
college basketball, 55, 202–203, 240,
328
pro basketball, 81, 153, 204, 348
Batch, Charlie, 224
Battle, Bill, 107
Baugh, Sammy, 32–34, 38
Bayless, Skip, 132
Baylor University, 304, 328
Beamer, Frank, 241, 244
Bell, Bert, 28, 65–66, 114
Bell, Bobby, 331
Bell, Ricky, 140, 142–143
Bell, Upton, 65–67, 77, 105, 114–115
Benhart, Gene, 193
Benjamin, Guy, 136–137, 151
Berman, Chris, 255
Bettis, Jerome, 222
Beuerlein, Steve, 207
Bevell, Darrell, 312–313
Big Ten, 28, 44, 56–61, 92, 245, 301
Biletnikoff, Fred, 72
Birmingham Stallions, 158
Bisciotti, Steve, 349
Bishop, Michael, 224–225, 264
Black History Month, 46
Black Panthers, 69
Black quarterbacks
first Black quarterback, 9–12
first Black quarterback drafted in
AFL, 54, 90
first Black quarterback selected in
first round of NFL draft, 68–77
first Black quarterback in AFL, 54,
82–90
first Black quarterback in CFL, 42–43
first Black quarterback in Hall of
Fame, 272–273

first Black quarterbacks in NFL, 1–6,
9–19, 36, 43–46, 63–83, 88–102,
124–129
first Black quarterback in Pro Bowl, 129
first Black quarterback winning Grey
Cup, 101–103
first Black quarterback winning
Heisman Trophy, 194
first Black quarterback winning
MVP award, 268, 286, 315
first Black quarterback winning
Super Bowl, 4–5, 46, 88, 183–186,
228, 360
first Black starting quarterback in
NFL playoffs, 127
first Black starting quarterbacks in
NFL, 3–6, 88–102, 124, 127–129,
178–183, 186–188, 232, 257, 263
first Black starting quarterbacks in
Pro Bowl, 186–188
first Black starting quarterback in
Super Bowl, 171–175, 260, 268,
298, 309–310, 322
history of, 1–6, 9–19
number of, 1–6, 354–364
see also specific quarterbacks
Blackbourn, Lisle, 51
Blake, Jeff, 195–200, 221, 234, 341
Blanda, George, 43, 45, 54, 70, 72–75
Bledsoe, Drew, 325
Blinn College, 283–284
Blount, Mel, 110
Blount, Roy Jr., 117
Boise State University, 163
Bono, Steve, 160–161
Booker T. Washington High School, 63
Boozer, Bob, 81
Boselli, Tony, 207
Boston Celtics, 153
Boston College, 160, 244
Boston Globe (newspaper), 27
Boston Patriots, 82–83, 85, 88, 98–99.
See also New England Patriots
Bowden, Bobby, 240
Boyer, Nate, 318–319
Boynton Beach Community High
School, 344, 346

Boys & Girls Clubs of America, 88
Brackins, Charlie, 49–52, 67
Bradley, Hal, 22
Bradshaw, Terry, 111–122, 128
Brady, Tom, 265–268, 275, 296, 305, 312, 334–335, 343
Braman, Norman, 161, 165
Bratkowski, Zeke, 44
Brees, Drew, 249, 267–268, 275, 330
Brigham Young University, 136, 219
Briscoe, Marlin, 2, 4, 46, 51, 73–74, 78–89, 95–99, 102, 139, 166, 281, 339, 346
Brissett, Jacoby, 353–354
British Columbia Lions, 87, 105, 194
Brooklyn Daily Eagle (newspaper), 23
Brooklyn Dodgers, 22–23, 36
Brooks, Aaron, 224, 234–235, 242, 261, 264–265
Brown, Jim, 59
Brown, Paul, 40–42, 58–59, 66, 114
Brown, Roosevelt, 49
Brown, Willie, 75
Brown Bombers, 34
Brown University, 13
Browner, Joey, 219
Bruce, Isaac, 212–213
Bryant, Paul "Bear," 106–107, 339
Buchanan, Buck, 54, 75, 90
Buck, Joe, 297
Buffalo Bills, 1–3, 54, 72–74, 85–88, 94–99, 105, 108, 114, 123, 127, 135, 211, 255–257, 274, 330
Bustle, Rickey, 241
Butler, Malcolm, 313
Butler, Sol, 16–19, 36, 42

Calgary Stampeders, 86–87, 105
California Eagle (newspaper), 35
Camp, Walter, 13
Campanis, Al, 167–168, 171
Campbell, Hugh, 150, 153, 155
Campbell, Marion, 164–165
Canadian Football League (CFL)
  beginnings of, 41–43
  first Black quarterbacks in, 42–43, 103–104

Grey Cup and, 43, 101–107, 151–155
integration of, 41–43
MVP awards, 101, 151–152
segregation and, 103–104
teams of, 42–45, 59, 86–87, 101–107, 150–155, 160, 184, 194–196, 225, 279
Caniglia, Al, 82, 87
Canton Bulldogs, 16–21, 42
Carlos, John, 86
Carlson, Cody, 177
Carlson, Jeff, 192
Carolina Panthers, 192, 205–207, 258–260, 283–286, 289, 297, 300, 308, 313–315, 360
Carr, Joe, 20–21, 27, 30
Carroll, Pete, 302, 313
Carroll High School, 92
Carson, Harry, 178
Carter, Cris, 232, 236
Carter, Ki-Jana, 205, 207
Cavanaugh, Matt, 136–137, 151
CBS, 116, 142, 348
CBS Evening News (TV show), 116
Celek, Garrett, 320–321
Chandler, Chris, 208–209, 247–249
Charlie Rose (TV show), 284
Chicago Bears, 14, 22, 26, 28, 31–34, 37–38, 43–45, 51, 140–142, 146, 159, 165, 170–171, 182, 185–187, 250, 261, 267, 294–296, 322, 329, 350, 357–359, 362
Chicago Cardinals, 21–22, 24–27, 38
Chicago Cubs, 14
Chicago Fire, 108
Chicago Sun-Times (newspaper), 141
Chicago Tribune (newspaper), 358
Chicago White Sox, 291
Chuck Noll: His Life's Work (book), 121
Chudzinski, Rob, 286
Cincinnati Bengals, 82–83, 177, 182, 196–199, 207–210, 216, 221, 225, 234, 264, 334, 346, 348
Cincinnati Enquirer (newspaper), 197
Cincinnati Reds, 25
Civil Rights Act, 68
civil rights activists, 86, 93, 157, 168, 171
civil rights movement, 68–69, 86, 93

Clarion-Ledger (newspaper), 172
Clark, Gary, 174
Clemson University, 244, 323, 328
Cleveland Browns, 35–38, 40–41, 51, 58–59, 65–66, 107, 112–113, 120, 144, 196, 274, 316, 323, 329, 339, 353–354, 359
Cleveland Rams, 34–35
Coca-Cola, 269
Colbert County High School, 339
college basketball, 55, 202–203, 240, 328
college football
    Big Ten teams, 28, 44, 56–61, 92, 245, 301
    Black coaches in, 90–91
    first Black starting quarterback for major program in, 40–41
    Hall of Fame, 12
    integration of, 28, 55, 60–61, 90–96
    racism and, 13, 55–58
    rule changes for, 30–32
    scoring points in, 30–33
    segregation and, 57, 60–61
    white coaches in, 90–91
Collier, Reggie, 158
Collins, Kerry, 206–207, 237, 260, 274, 362
Collinsworth, Cris, 313
color line
    in baseball, 46
    breaking, 27–35, 43–46, 67–94, 100–166
    in football, 10, 27–28, 34–35, 43–46, 67–94, 100–166
    see also racial barriers
Columbia University, 32
Columbus Panhandles, 20
Comeback Player of the Year award, 290
Conerly, Charlie, 37
Continental Football League, 108
Cook, Connor, 323
Corso, Lee, 205
Cosby, Bill, 257
Cosell, Howard, 91–92
Coslet, Bruce, 196–198
Cotton Bowl, 48
Cowher, Bill, 221–222
Crabtree, Eric, 85

Crabtree, Michael, 299, 308
Crowder, Eddie, 44
Culp, Curley, 331
Culpepper, Daunte, 216–217, 224, 226, 231–237, 242, 251, 260–261, 265, 268, 281, 331, 357
Culpepper, Emma, 232–233
Culverhouse, Hugh, 134–137, 143–146, 154, 156, 176
Cumbee, Glenn, 206
Cunningham, Anthony, 163
Cunningham, Bruce, 163–164
Cunningham, Randall, 4, 160–166, 168, 176–183, 186–188, 193–194, 220, 224, 232, 250, 257, 261–263, 272–273, 326, 341, 360–361, 364
Cunningham, Sam "Bam," 163
Curry, Ronald, 240
Custis, Bernie, 40–43, 51, 55, 58, 103
Cutcliffe, David, 281

Dallas Cowboys, 65, 74, 114, 125, 129–130, 144–145, 158–159, 183, 191–192, 196–197, 200, 208, 233, 248, 257, 278, 323, 333, 343
Dallas Texans, 43, 48, 54
Dan Patrick Show, The (radio program), 326
Darragh, Dan, 98
Dartmouth College, 12
Davey, Rohan, 264
Davidson, Cotton, 70, 73
Davis, Al, 67, 69–72, 74–76
Davis, Ernie, 55, 58
Davis, Mark, 69
Davis, Mouse, 195
Davis, Vernon, 295, 297
Dawkins, Brian, 253, 258
Dawson, Len, 54, 59
Dayton Triangles, 9–10, 17
Decatur Staleys, 14
DeCosta, Eric, 343, 349
Delhomme, Jake, 259–260
Denver Broncos, 2, 73, 79, 82–88, 95–97, 105, 117–118, 166, 172–174, 218–220, 293–294, 304, 309–312, 315, 323, 334, 339, 353, 359

Deschaine, Dick, 51
Detroit Lions, 37–38, 88, 95–96, 125, 159, 170, 180, 192, 194–195, 208, 224, 228, 234
Detroit Tigers, 327
Dickey, Eldridge, 63–81, 94, 99–102, 110–112, 218
Dickinson, Parnell, 135–136
Dickson, Judge, 56
Didier, Clint, 171, 174
Dierdorf, Dan, 178–179
Dilfer, Trent, 227–228, 266
Dilweg, Anthony, 192
Dorow, Al, 44
Douds, Forrest "Jap," 24–26
Douglas, Karl, 104–105
Douglass, Bobby, 159, 250
Draft Advisory Board, 203
Duke University, 192
Dungy, Tony, 60–62, 138, 218, 226–231, 243, 251, 267, 271
Dwight, Tim, 246
Dyson, Kevin, 211, 214

Eagle, Ian, 348
Ealey, Chuck, 101–104, 107–109, 152
East Carolina University, 195, 197, 240
East Texas State University, 110
Ebony Film Corporation, 12
Edmonton Eskimos, 150–155
Edmonton Journal (newspaper), 151
Edmonton Oilers, 152
Edwards, Harry, 168
Elizabeth City State University, 108
Elkins, Mike, 192
Elway, John, 158, 160, 172–174, 218, 220, 351
Emanuel, Bert, 230–231
Enke, Fred, 47
Epstein, Jack, 148
Esiason, Boomer, 198
ESPN, 162, 178, 181, 193, 205–207, 226, 243, 254–255, 293, 326, 348
Evans, Vince, 135, 140–141, 261

Facebook, 333, 355
Faulk, Marshall, 212

Favre, Brett, 205, 249–252, 258, 275, 302, 324, 361
Fayette County (Pennsylvania) Sports Hall of Fame, 60
FedEx Field, 300
Feinstein, John, 144
Ferragamo, Vince, 132
Fields, Justin, 350–351, 362–363
Fisher, Jeff, 205, 207–212, 214, 274
Fisk University, 79
Flacco, Joe, 298, 341–346
Flaherty, Ray, 32
Flores, Brian, 355
Flores, Tom, 2, 54, 95, 98
Florida A&M University, 63, 91
Florida State University, 82, 197, 203, 240, 242–244
Floyd, George, 321
Flutie, Doug, 160, 245
Flynn, Matt, 302–303
Fontes, Wayne, 195
Forbes Field, 24–25
Ford, Len, 38
Forney, Kynan, 271
Fouts, Dan, 133
Fox Sports, 231, 297
Frankford (Pennsylvania) Yellow Jackets, 21
Freeman, Josh, 276

Gabbert, Blaine, 319–320
Gabler, Wally, 103
Gabriel, Roman, 108, 123–124
Gaither, Jake, 91
Garrett, Myles, 329
Gator Bowl, 244
George, Eddie, 209, 212–213
Georgia Dome, 213
Gibbs, Joe, 137, 139, 168–170, 173–175, 182–183, 360
Gibson, Bob, 81
Gilberton Catamounts, 15, 17
Giles, Jimmie, 137, 178–179
Gilkerson's Colored Giants, 19
Gill, Turner, 160
Gilliam, Joe, 110–122, 128, 135, 278. 281
Gilliam, Joe Sr., 64, 112

Gilliam, Ruth, 112
Gilliam, Sonia, 112
Gillman, Sid, 164
Gillom, Horace, 36, 38
Glover, La'Roi, 236
Goodell, Roger, 283, 319–321, 329–330, 343, 354
Gordon, Clemente, 194
Gore, Frank, 297, 299
Graham, Jeff, 192
Graham, Otto, 38, 41, 114, 267
Grambling State University, 1, 3, 54, 63, 66–68, 75, 90–93, 108–110, 124, 136–139, 175, 194, 201–202
Grange, Red, 28
Grayson, Dave, 76
Grbac, Elvis, 331
Great Depression, 23
Green, Darrell, 171, 229
Green, Denny, 232–237, 361
Green Bay Packers, 17, 31, 49–52, 69, 112, 125, 142, 153, 158–159, 180–182, 212, 224, 234, 242, 249–252, 258, 261, 265, 268, 274, 286, 296–297, 302, 312, 347, 359, 361
Green Bay Press-Gazette (newspaper), 50
Greene, Joe, 110
Grey Cup, 43, 101–107, 151–155
Griffin, Robert III, 62, 287, 300–308, 316, 350, 364
Groomes, Melvin, 37
Grossman, Rex, 358
Gruden, Jon, 106

Hackenberg, Christian, 323
Hackett, Paul, 141
Haden, Pat, 131
Hadl, John, 124–126, 131
Hakim, Az-Zahir, 235
Halas, George, 14, 22, 28–30, 32–34, 38, 43–45, 49, 304, 358–359
Hall, Nickie, 158
Hamilton High School, 147–148, 150
Hamilton Spectator (newspaper), 42
Hamilton Tiger-Cats, 42–43, 101–104, 152
Hammel, Todd, 193
Hammond Pros, 9–11, 15–17, 21

Hampton High School, 240
Hanratty, Terry, 111, 113–114, 120
Harbaugh, Jim, 288–291, 295, 298, 316–317
Harbaugh, John, 298, 343, 347, 349
Harding, Halley, 35–36
Harris, Franco, 111, 118–119
Harris, James, 1–6, 46, 51, 67–68, 74, 79, 86–88, 92–102, 108–109, 114, 123–135, 139–141, 154, 162, 186, 217, 257, 281, 355, 360
Harris, Major, 193–194
Harvard University, 64
Hastie, Karen, 64–65
Haynes, Abner, 331
HBO, 119
Head & Shoulders, 336
Heisman Trophy winners, 55, 58, 89, 102, 135–136, 160, 191, 194, 200, 203–205, 283, 290, 294, 341, 345
Henderson, Barbara, 232–233
Henderson, Thomas, 233
Herber, Arnie, 31
Herzeg, Ladd, 155
Hess, Wally, 16–17
Hill, Herman, 35
Hill, Tyreek, 334
Hilliard, Ike, 237
Hollas, Don, 196
Hollis, Wilburn, 57
Holloway, Condredge, 100, 104–107, 109, 340
Hollywood Bears, 29
Holm, Tony, 25
Holt, Torry, 212
Horn, Joe, 234–235
Hostetler, Jeff, 362
Houston Chronicle (newspaper), 333
Houston Oilers, 54, 66, 85, 97, 137, 154–157, 177, 181–185, 195–198, 206–209, 221, 249, 360–361. See also Tennessee Titans
Houston Texans, 332–333, 336, 353, 355
Howard University, 264
Humphrey, Claude, 66–68
Hunt, H. L., 53
Hunt, Kareem, 334
Hunt, Lamar, 53–54

Hurts, Jalen, 5, 350–351, 352
Hutson, Don, 31–32
Hyde, Harvey, 164

"I Have a Dream" speech, 93
Indiana University, 16, 37, 112, 161
Indianapolis Capitols, 108
Indianapolis Colts, 61, 177, 211, 245,
   251, 267–268, 275, 302, 335, 359
Ingram, Mark, 347
integration
   baseball and, 4, 28–29, 36, 42–43,
      167–169
   college football and, 28, 55, 60–61,
      90–96
   football and, 27–43, 51–55, 60–78,
      90–96, 156–160, 234–235, 338–364
   military and, 36
   NFL and, 27–43, 51–55, 60–78, 95–96,
      156–160, 234–235, 338–364
   schools and, 64, 338
Irsay, Robert, 124
Irvin, Michael, 255
Ivor Wynne Stadium, 101

Jack Murphy Stadium, 172
Jackson, Harold, 128
Jackson, Jesse, 61, 257
Jackson, Lamar, 5, 66, 76–77, 89, 148,
   341–350, 352–356, 364
Jackson, Onree, 264
Jackson, Tarvaris, 302–303
Jackson, Tom, 255
Jackson State University, 63–64, 68, 91,
   112, 201
Jacksonville Jaguars, 195, 207, 211, 231,
   273
James, Don, 149
James, LaMichael, 299
Jaworski, Ron, 125–126, 130–131, 161, 165
Jim Crow era, 94, 104, 260
John, Butch, 172
John Carroll University, 289
Johnson, Brad, 253, 260, 266
Johnson, Henry, 79
Johnson, Jim, 252, 262
Johnson, Lyndon, 86

Jones, Cardell, 202
Jones, Felicia, 344
Jones, J. J., 135
Jones, Jacoby, 298
Jones, Jimmy, 100, 104–105, 135
Jones, June, 139
Jones, Mike, 214
Jones, Terrence, 194
Jordan, Michael, 179, 207, 245, 348

Kaepernick, Colin, 5, 287–288, 291–300,
   303–304, 308–309, 313, 316–321,
   332, 345, 354, 364
Kaepernick, Rick, 292
Kaepernick, Teresa, 292
Kansas City Chiefs, 5, 54, 59, 66, 74–77,
   82, 86, 120, 139, 142, 186, 220,
   330–337, 349–350
Kansas State University, 224, 264
Karlis, Rich, 174
Kelce, Travis, 334
Kelly, Brian, 152
Kelly, Jim, 158
Kemp, Jack, 2, 54, 87, 95, 97–98
Kemp, Ray, 24–26, 34
Kennedy, Robert, 86
Kerner Commission, 86
Kessler, Cody, 323
King, Martin Luther Jr., 86, 93, 157, 171
King, Shaun, 224, 226–233, 242,
   260–261, 264, 266
Kingsbury, Kliff, 328–329
Kiper, Mel Jr., 206
Klingler, David, 196, 198
Knapp, Greg, 269
Knox, Chuck, 124–126, 129–131, 154, 360
Knox, Shirley, 131
Koppel, Ted, 167
Kramer, Erik, 195
Ku Klux Klan, 16
Kupp, Craig, 193

Ladd, Ernie, 75
Lake County Times (newspaper), 11
Lambeau Field, 249, 251
Lamonica, Daryle, 69–74, 76–77
Lance, Trey, 350–351, 353

Landry, Greg, 159, 180
Landry, Tom, 208
Lanier, Willie, 66, 331
Layne, Bobby, 38, 267
Leach, Mike, 328
Leaf, Ryan, 245, 248, 264
LeClair, Jim, 82
Lee, Carl, 219
Lee, Robert E., 106
Lee, Spike, 197
Leftwich, Byron, 273, 358
Leland College, 90
Lewis, David, 144
Lewis, Frank, 110
Lewis, Ray, 298–299, 339
Liberty Bowl, 209
Lillard, Joe, 24–28, 34, 36
Limbaugh, Rush, 254–259, 265
Lincoln Financial Field, 255, 275
Lincoln High School, 50
Lincoln University, 13
Liske, Pete, 86–87
Little, Floyd, 85–86
Lombardi, Vince, 49, 69, 347
Long Beach State University, 192
Los Angeles Chargers, 359
Los Angeles City College, 141
Los Angeles Coliseum, 35–36, 127, 130
Los Angeles Dodgers, 167
Los Angeles Dons, 36–37
Los Angeles Express, 154, 219
Los Angeles Police Department, 29
Los Angeles Raiders, 154, 187, 193–194, 209, 273. *See also* Oakland Raiders
Los Angeles Rams, 3, 29, 33–36, 47–49, 54, 65, 79, 93, 108–109, 123–133, 135, 142–143, 154, 180, 183, 223, 360. *See also* St. Louis Rams
Los Angeles Times (newspaper), 127, 132
Los Angeles Tribune (newspaper), 35
Lott, Thomas, 159–160
Louisiana Negro Normal and Industrial Institute, 90
Louisiana State University (LSU), 138, 202, 264, 273
Louisiana Tech University, 111
Louisville Colonels, 21

Luck, Andrew, 290, 292, 302, 304
Luckman, Sid, 32–34, 38
Lynch, Marshawn, 303, 306, 312–313
Lynch, Paxton, 323

MacCambridge, Michael, 121
Mack, Tom, 128–129, 132
Macon, Eddie, 38
Madden, John, 74–76, 118, 231
Madison Square Garden, 216, 246
Mahomes, Pat, 327
Mahomes, Patrick, 5, 155, 205, 322–336, 349–353, 356–358, 364
major league baseball
    games played, 14–18, 22–30, 55, 202, 291, 327–328
    integration of, 28–29, 36, 42–43, 167–169
    racial barriers and, 28–29, 33–36, 46, 167–169
    segregation and, 10, 33–36
    sharing names, 22–23
Manhattan-Bronx championship, 22
Mann, Bob, 37
Manning, Archie, 105
Manning, Eli, 267–268, 275, 362
Manning, Peyton, 245, 267, 275, 277, 280–281, 305, 309–312, 315–316, 335, 343, 348
Mara, Tim, 28
Mara, Wellington, 37
Marchetti, Gino, 48–49
Marchibroda, Ted, 44, 108, 161
Marino, Dan, 158, 161, 205, 233, 351
Marshall, Bobby, 10
Marshall, George Preston, 26–28, 30, 32, 45, 358–361
Marshall University, 273
Martin, Tee, 277–282, 335
Masterson, Bernie, 32
Matson, Ollie, 38, 45
Mayfield, Baker, 345
Mayfield, Curtis, 115
McCaskey, George, 34, 358, 363
McClain, Lester, 107
McCormick, John, 82
McCutcheon, Lawrence, 124, 133
McKay, John, 134–144

McKay, Rich, 229
McNabb, Donovan, 216–217, 224, 226, 234, 242, 246, 252–265, 271–278, 281, 298, 309, 331, 334–335, 360
McNabb, Sam, 256–259
McNabb, Wilma, 256–257
McNair, Fred, 202
McNair, Lucille, 201–203
McNair, Steve, 46, 199–215, 221, 224, 231–233, 239, 246, 249, 260, 265, 268–269, 273, 299, 309, 315, 341, 360
McNown, Cade, 357–358
McPherson, Don, 194
Mecom, John, 154
Meehan, Chick, 22–23
Memorial Stadium, 47–48
Merritt, John "Big John," 63–64, 67, 70, 73–76, 91, 110, 112
Miami Dolphins, 84–85, 88–89, 99, 113, 131, 135–136, 161, 210–211, 267, 296, 348, 355, 359
Miami News (newspaper), 72
Michaels, Al, 214, 313
Michigan State University, 43–44, 57, 79, 92, 108, 223, 245, 323
Mid-American Conference, 102
Milwaukee Badgers, 15
Minnesota Gophers, 56–60
Minnesota Twins, 327
Minnesota Vikings, 59, 120–121, 126–128, 139, 159, 170–171, 185, 216–219, 224, 227–228, 231–237, 242, 250–251, 260–261, 265, 268, 275, 296, 304, 361
minor league baseball, 20
minor league football, 15, 28–29, 34, 48, 72, 101, 108, 194, 362
Mississippi State University, 284, 323
Mississippi Valley State, 68, 135
Mitchell, Brian, 253
Mitchell, Freddie, 258
Modell, Art, 339
Molesworth, Keith, 47–48
Monday Night Football, 104, 178–179, 228, 275, 294–295
Montalbán, Ricardo, 131
Montana, Joe, 218–220, 362

Montreal Alouettes, 42, 59, 105–106
Montreal Concordes, 160
Montreal Expos, 106
Montreal Gazette (newspaper), 105
Moon, Warren, 4, 46, 51, 103, 130, 147–159, 168, 176–177, 181–188, 193–194, 207, 221, 224, 232, 239, 257, 272–273, 281, 300–310, 322, 325–326, 331, 336, 350–352, 356–357, 360–364
Moore, Shawn, 194
Morgan State University, 49, 66, 68
Mornhinweg, Marty, 345–346
Morrall, Earl, 105
Mortensen, Chris, 207
Moses, Haven, 97–98
Moss, Randy, 232, 236
Most Valuable Player (MVP) awards
 in AFL, 69–70
 in CFL, 101, 151–152
 first black quarterback winning, 268, 286, 315
 in NFL, 5, 46, 89, 123–124, 129, 175, 180–183, 196, 214, 235, 249–250, 266–268, 275, 286, 309, 315–316, 336, 348–350, 364
Motley, Marion, 36, 38
Mount Carmel High School, 256
Mount Olive High School, 202
Mumme, Hal, 328
Munn, Clarence "Biggie," 44
Munsey, Bill, 56
Murray, Kyler, 5, 106, 350, 352, 355–357
Musburger, Brent, 142
Myers, Dave, 22–24, 34

Namath, Joe, 72, 74, 96–97, 110, 132
National Basketball Association (NBA), 81, 153, 204, 348
National Collegiate Athletic Association (NCAA), 136, 226, 233, 284, 289–291, 329
National Football Conference (NFC)
 championship games, 124–131, 139–145, 169–173, 178–187, 195, 228–237, 251–263, 288–297, 300–317, 325, 350, 354
 origin of, 124–125

National Football League (NFL)
  color line in, 10, 27–28, 34–35, 43–46, 67–94, 100–166
  commissioners of, 65–66, 95–96, 114, 137, 207, 246, 283, 319–321, 329–330, 343, 354
  drafts, 1, 4–5, 32, 36–38, 40–60, 65–111, 125–126, 131–145, 150–155, 158–164, 168, 172, 176, 181, 191–197, 202–212, 216–229, 232–234, 239–249, 254–259, 264–276, 278–287, 290–293, 301–305, 313–316, 322–332, 337–363
  early years of, 1–6, 9–78
  first Black coach winning Super Bowl, 61, 267
  first Black general manager in, 107, 282, 338–345, 360
  first Black head coaches, 12, 69, 187
  first Black players drafted in, 40–52, 65–81
  first Black quarterbacks in, 1–6, 9–19, 36, 43–46, 63–83, 88–102, 124–129
  first Black starting quarterbacks in, 3–6, 88–102, 124, 127–129, 178–183, 186–188, 232, 257, 263
  former name of, 14
  history of, 1–6, 9–19, 33–36
  integration of, 27–43, 51–55, 60–78, 95–96, 156–160, 234–235, 338–364
  merger of, 54, 65–68, 74, 124–125
  MVP awards, 5, 46, 89, 123–124, 129, 175, 180–183, 196, 214, 235, 249–250, 266–268, 275, 286, 309, 315–316, 336, 348–350, 364
  Player of the Year awards, 124, 180
  presidents of, 20–21, 27, 30
  racial barriers and, 10–19, 25–46, 67–94, 100–166, 170–188, 242–247, 267–272
  racism and, 2–19, 25–46, 50–58, 67–94, 100–166, 170–197, 216–247, 263–272, 277–286, 315–324, 330–333, 340, 350–364
  Rookie of the Year awards, 38, 98, 350
  rule changes for, 30–33
  segregation and, 27–40, 54, 103–104, 138, 223
  whitewashing of rosters, 10, 28, 33–40
National Hockey League (NHL), 152
NBC, 313
Neal, Lorenzo, 211
New England Patriots, 105–107, 163, 224, 259, 263–268, 296–298, 312–313, 333–335, 348, 359. *See also* Boston Patriots
New Jersey Generals, 154
New Orleans Saints, 126, 154, 182, 199, 234–236, 250, 259, 264–265, 268, 275, 295, 304, 330
New York Giants, 18, 26, 28, 37, 49, 142, 154, 159, 165, 169, 172, 177–180, 183, 236–237, 253, 260, 265–268, 354, 359, 362
New York Jets, 3, 72, 74, 84, 96–97, 130, 135, 158, 160, 195–196, 323, 354, 359
New York Times (newspaper), 18, 22–23, 127, 204, 255, 283
New York Titans, 58–59
New York University (NYU), 22–23
New York Yankees, 36, 43
Newsome, Ozzie, 107, 139, 144, 282, 338–345, 349, 360
Newton, Cam, 5, 46, 76, 277, 280–287, 300, 304, 308, 313–316, 331, 336, 349, 354, 364
Newton, Cecil, 277, 280–282, 284
Newton, Cecil Jr., 282
NFL Films, 240
Nied, Frank, 13–14, 16–18
Nielsen, Gifford, 136
Nightline (TV show), 167, 171
Nike, 269, 279
Noll, Chuck, 110–121
North Carolina A&T, 61
North Carolina Central University, 141
North Carolina State University, 301
North Dakota State University, 350, 353
North Texas State University, 110

Northwestern University, 12, 28
Notre Dame High School, 101
Notre Dame University, 111
Nunn, Bill, 66, 110–111

Oakland Raiders, 54, 67–81, 86, 94–99,
    112, 118–119, 162, 218, 234, 273,
    279, 323. *See also* Los Angeles
    Raiders
Oakland Tribune (newspaper), 74–75
Obama, Barack, 89, 310, 319–320
O'Brien, Davey, 191
O'Donnell, Neil, 198, 210, 221–222
Ogden, Jonathan, 339
Ohio State University, 57–58, 202, 341,
    350–351, 362
Oklahoma Outlaws, 146, 168
Oklahoma State University, 191, 302
Olsen, Greg, 314
Olympics, 17–18, 35, 86
O'Neal, Ron, 115
Oregon State University, 192
Osweiler, Brock, 302
Ottawa Rough Riders, 106, 152, 160
Owen, Steve, 37
Owens, Terrell, 260, 262, 289

Pacific Coast League, 29
Pacific Lutheran University, 193
Page, Alan, 128
Pardee, Jack, 185
Pastorini, Dan, 105
Paterson (New Jersey) Panthers, 28
Payton, Walter, 141, 200
PBS, 284
Peete, Rodney, 191–192, 195, 259
Penn State University, 13, 23, 86, 111,
    193, 205–206, 323, 341
Petrino, Bobby, 345
Philadelphia Daily News (newspaper),
    161
Philadelphia Eagles, 5, 28, 38, 65–66,
    79, 109, 140–142, 161–166, 169,
    177–183, 194, 216, 233–237, 242,
    250–267, 271–275, 279, 331–332,
    335, 343–345, 350, 360–361
Philadelphia Phillies, 55

Pittsburgh Courier (newspaper), 18, 35,
    66, 110
Pittsburgh Pirates (pro football team),
    24–26, 28, 30
Pittsburgh Pirates (major league
    baseball team), 55
Pittsburgh Post-Gazette (newspaper),
    120, 193–194
Pittsburgh Steelers, 38, 60–61, 110–122,
    128, 135, 180, 198, 221–223, 250,
    267–268, 278–281, 334
Plum, Milt, 58
Plummer, Jake, 223
Plunkett, Jim, 105
Polian, Bill, 205–206, 348, 355
Pollard, Amanda, 12
Pollard, Artemisia, 12
Pollard, Frederick Douglass "Fritz,"
    9–19, 28, 34–36
Pollard, Hughes, 12
Pollard, John, 12
Pollard, Leslie, 12
Pollard, Luther, 12
Pollard, Naomi, 12
Porter, Joey, 250
Portsmouth Spartans, 25
Powell, Colin, 186–187
Prairie View A&M, 49–50
Prescott, Dak, 5, 62, 323, 333, 350
Pro Bowl, 3, 69, 81, 88, 129, 169,
    178–180, 185–188, 198, 253,
    258–260, 268, 272–274, 308, 313,
    361
Pro Football Hall of Fame, 4, 37–38,
    46, 74, 133, 158, 164, 192, 215, 267,
    272–273, 282, 298, 300, 326, 331,
    339, 348, 361
Purdue University, 57, 249

Quarterblack (book), 134

racial barriers
    baseball and, 28–29, 33–36, 46,
        167–169
    breaking, 27–35, 43–46, 67–94,
        100–166, 183–188, 197, 242–247,
        267–272, 330–331

racial barriers (*continued*)
   college football and, 13, 55–58
   color lines, 10, 27–35, 43–46, 67–94,
     100–166
   NFL and, 10–19, 25–46, 67–94,
     100–166, 170–188, 242–247,
     267–272
racial inequality, 86, 91–92, 153,
   354–358
racial justice, 86, 318–321. *See also*
   social justice
racial profiling, 102, 167–168
racial reckoning, 168, 321–322, 363–364
racism
   activists and, 10, 61–65, 86, 93, 157,
     168, 171, 319–321
   baseball and, 28–29, 33–36, 46,
     167–169
   college football and, 13, 55–58
   color lines, 10, 27–28, 34–35, 43–46,
     67–94, 100–166
   NFL and, 2–19, 25–46, 50–58, 67–94,
     100–166, 170–197, 216–247,
     263–272, 277–286, 315–324,
     330–333, 340, 350–364
   stereotyping and, 4, 41, 52, 91,
     100–166, 179–187, 218, 232,
     240–247, 277–286, 299, 340, 350,
     355
Ralston, John, 80, 118
Rather, Dan, 116
Rauch, John, 70–71, 95–99
Raye, Jimmy, 79, 108, 245
Raye, Jimmy III, 245
Real Sports with Bryant Gumbel (TV
   show), 119
Reed, Ed, 298–299
Reese, Floyd, 207–209
Reeves, Dan, 35, 246, 248–249, 252
Reich, Frank, 160
Reid, Andy, 242, 271–272, 331–332,
   334–335, 360
Reid, Eric, 319
Rhome, Jerry, 207–208
Rice, Jerry, 289
Rice University, 50, 328
Richardson, Anthony, 351

Richardson, Jerry, 284–285
Richardson, Wally, 341
Rivera, Ron, 286
Riverfront Stadium, 197
Robeson, Paul, 10, 15
Robinson, Abie, 35
Robinson, Eddie, 1–3, 67, 90–95, 99,
   124, 138, 175, 201
Robinson, Jackie, 4, 28–29, 36, 42, 46,
   132, 167, 175
Robinson, John, 141
Rock Island (Illinois) Independents,
   21–22
Rodgers, Aaron, 215, 268, 275, 296, 302,
   352, 361
Roethlisberger, Ben, 267, 275
Roman, Greg, 288–298, 317, 345–348
Rookie of the Year awards, 38, 98, 350
Rooney, Art, 26, 28, 30, 110–111
Rose, Charlie, 284–285
Rose Bowl, 12–13, 31, 56–60, 141,
   149–150, 191, 206, 301–302, 325
Rosenbloom, Carroll, 124, 130–132
Ross, Bobby, 228
Ross, Dr. Charles K., 89, 103–104, 116,
   145, 155, 175, 321, 342, 347, 349,
   351, 353
rosters
   integrating, 28–43, 51–55, 156–160,
     338–341, 352–364
   shaping, 77, 339–341, 352–364
   whitewashing, 10, 28, 33–40
Rote, Tobin, 50–51, 54, 180
Rozelle, Pete, 95–96, 137
Russell, JaMarcus, 273, 284
Rutledge, Jeff, 183–184
Ryan, Buddy, 165
Ryan, Matt, 307
Rypien, Mark, 182–183

Saban, Lou, 73, 82–85, 87–88
St. Louis Cardinals, 81, 130, 159–160
St. Louis Rams, 210–214, 223–224,
   229–231, 235, 260, 265–266, 288,
   291, 294–296. *See also* Los Angeles
   Rams
St. Petersburg Times (newspaper), 141

Salaam, Rashaan, 205
Sam Houston State University, 204
San Antonio Wings, 109
San Diego Chargers, 54, 75, 84–85,
    88, 124, 132–133, 140, 194, 221,
    245–249, 264, 268–269, 301,
    318–319, 331, 334, 342
San Diego State University, 98
San Diego Union-Tribune (newspaper),
    172
San Francisco 49ers, 38, 43–45, 61,
    79, 131, 158, 183, 218–221, 265,
    288–299, 303, 309, 316–320, 332,
    336, 345, 349–353, 361–362
Sanders, Barry, 191
Sanders, Ricky, 171, 174
Santa Barbara High School, 163
Santa Rosa Press Democrat (newspaper),
    71
Santaluces Community High School,
    344
Sapp, Warren, 230
Saskatchewan Roughriders, 101
Sayers, Gale, 81–82
Sayers, Roger, 82
Scarbath, Jack, 44
Schneider, John, 302
Schroeder, Jay, 168–170, 173, 176
Scott, Darnay, 196–197
Scott, Tom, 152
Seattle Mariners, 202
Seattle Seahawks, 154–155, 185, 197,
    224, 296, 300–321, 353–354, 360
segregation
    baseball and, 10, 33–36
    college football and, 57, 60–61
    military and, 33, 36
    NFL and, 27–40, 54, 103–104, 138,
        223
    schools and, 48, 50, 68, 92
semipro baseball, 16, 25
semipro football, 45, 122
Shanahan, Mike, 304, 307
Shaughnessy, Clark, 32
Shaw, Dennis, 98–99
Shelburne, John, 16
Shell, Art, 70, 75, 187

Sherman, Mike, 250
Sherman, Richard, 306
Shula, David, 197
Shula, Don, 75
Shuler, Heath, 203
Silverstein, Jack, 29, 34, 357–364
Simmons, Lon, 220
Simmons, Oze, 28–29
Simms, Phil, 362
Simpson, O. J., 94–96, 144
Singletary, Mike, 187–188
Slack, Reggie, 194
Slater, Duke, 10, 15, 21–22
Smith, Akili, 216–217, 224–226, 242,
    246, 264, 326
Smith, Alex, 288, 290–295, 297, 332, 334
Smith, Geno, 354, 362
Smith, Jimmy, 299
Smith, Lovie, 267
Smith, Mike, 240
Smith, Robert, 236
Smith, Timmy, 174
Smith, Tommie, 86
Smith, Troy, 294, 341
Snow, Jack, 127
Snyder, Bob, 36
social justice, 86, 228–229, 318–321, 363
social media, 257, 317, 333, 345, 350,
    355–356, 359
social unrest, 68–69, 86, 317
Solomon, Jesse, 219
Southeastern Conference, 100, 106, 194,
    283, 291
Southern Cal, 80, 94, 100, 104–105,
    130–135, 140–141, 149, 163, 191,
    273, 302, 323, 351
Southern Methodist University, 53
Southern University, 110, 201
Southwest Conference, 51
Southwestern Athletic Conference
    (SWAC), 200–204
Spagnola, John, 164
Sport (magazine), 339
Sporting News (magazine), 339
Sports Illustrated (magazine), 4, 100,
    104–105, 117, 154, 180, 200, 204,
    224, 244, 307–308, 310

Spurrier, Steve, 135–136
Stabler, Ken, 69–72, 74, 76–77
Staley, Duce, 253
Stallworth, John, 121
Stanford University, 13, 79–80, 136, 138, 149, 151, 289–291, 302, 323
Star Wars (film), 157
Starr, Bart, 361
State Farm Insurance, 336
Staten Island Stapletons, 22–23
Staubach, Roger, 74, 130, 159
Steinberg, Leigh, 150, 152–155, 157, 216, 221, 324–327, 329–331, 334–337, 342, 351
Stephen F. Austin State University, 193
Stephens, Sandy, 55–62, 103, 109
Stewart, Kordell, 199, 221–224, 278–279, 325–326, 331
Stiles, Lynn, 161
Stokes, J. J., 289
Stram, Hank, 59, 75, 77
Strode, Woody, 36
Strong, Ken, 23
Stroud, C. J., 351
Stuyvesant High School, 22
Sun Bowl, 323
Sunday NFL Countdown (TV show), 254–255
Sunday Night Football, 181, 184, 348
Sunday Night Football (TV show), 181
Super Bowl
    first Black coach winning, 61, 267
    first Black quarterback winning, 4–5, 46, 88, 183–186, 228, 360
    first Black starting quarterback in, 171–175, 260, 268, 298, 309–310, 322
    first games of, 3, 67–69, 72–74
    upsets in, 72, 96, 173–175, 218, 268
    victories, 3–5, 46, 61, 67–69, 72–74, 88–89, 96–97, 120–122, 125, 128–130, 142–143, 156–159, 165–176, 179–185, 192, 196–198, 211–216, 218–229, 235, 248–254, 258–268, 272–275, 298–316, 322–324, 336, 340–343, 348–351, 360–362

Super Fly (film), 115–116
Superdome, 235, 298
Swann, Lynn, 117
Syracuse University, 40, 55, 194, 216, 240, 242–244, 256, 261, 271

Tagliabue, Paul, 207, 246
Taliaferro, George, 37, 43–49, 83, 135, 359
Tampa Bay Bandits, 162
Tampa Bay Buccaneers, 61, 134–146, 154–155, 158, 168, 177, 219, 224–233, 251–254, 260–261, 264–266, 276, 340, 360
Tangerine Bowl, 102
Tannehill, Ryan, 302
Tarkenton, Fran, 127, 129, 159, 362
Taylor, Tyrod, 354
Tebow, Tim, 283
Tennessee A&I University, 63–64, 66–67, 76, 110
Tennessee Oilers, 209. *See also* Tennessee Titans
Tennessee State University, 63–64, 66–67, 76, 110–112, 158, 281–282
Tennessee Titans, 209–213, 231, 260, 265, 268, 273–274, 333, 336, 360–361. *See also* Houston Oilers
Tennessee Volunteers, 100, 106–107
Tensi, Steve, 82, 84–85, 87
Texas A&I University, 104
Texas A&M University, 302, 328–329
Texas Christian University (TCU), 32, 249
Texas Tech University, 192, 324–326, 328–329
Theismann, Joe, 156, 208
Thomas, Emmitt, 331
Thorpe, Jim, 17–18, 20
Three Rivers Stadium, 110, 116, 118
Thrower, Willie, 43–46
Toledo Rockets, 102
Tolliver, Billy Joe, 192
Tomczak, Mike, 221
Tomlinson, LaDainian, 249
Toronto Argonauts, 152, 225
Tournament of Roses, 13

Troy University, 204
Trubisky, Mitchell, 322–325, 329–330, 357–358
Truman, Harry, 36
Trump, Donald, 154, 320–321
Tulane University, 158, 194, 224, 226–227, 230
Tunnell, Emlen, 37, 45
Twain, Mark, 144
Twitter, 359

UCLA, 28–29, 36, 58–59, 153, 160, 168, 191
Uniontown High School, 55
Unitas, Johnny, 38, 52, 105, 124, 191, 267
United States Football League (USFL)
    as new league, 145–146, 153
    playing in, 122, 146, 153–155, 158, 162, 168, 184, 219
    teams of, 122, 146, 153–155, 158, 162, 168, 219
University of Alabama, 25, 31, 69, 106–109, 284, 323, 339–340, 351
University of California, 149, 153
University of Central Florida, 216, 233
University of Chattanooga, 44, 201
University of Colorado, 205, 207, 221
University of Delaware, 341
University of Detroit Mercy, 44
University of Dubuque, 17
University of Florida, 135, 283
University of Georgia, 23, 44
University of Houston, 194, 196, 328
University of Illinois, 36, 61
University of Iowa, 28, 37, 57
University of Louisville, 89, 341–343, 345
University of Maryland, 44, 160
University of Memphis, 323
University of Miami, 197, 202, 243–244
University of Michigan, 37, 221, 264
University of Minnesota, 25, 55–60
University of Mississippi, 37, 103, 138
University of Nebraska, 57, 132, 160, 202
University of Nevada, 160, 163–165, 291, 298
University of North Carolina, 323

University of Notre Dame, 44, 111
University of Oklahoma, 44, 152, 158–160, 345, 350
University of Omaha, 73, 81–82, 87
University of Oregon, 25, 216
University of Pittsburgh, 136–138, 151
University of San Diego, 289
University of San Francisco, 38
University of Southern California (USC), 80, 94, 100, 104–105, 130–135, 140–141, 149, 163, 191, 273, 302, 323, 351
University of Southern Mississippi, 158
University of Tennessee, 100, 106–107, 203, 277, 279–280, 340
University of Texas, 273, 318
University of Toledo, 101–102
University of Virginia, 194, 224, 234, 242
University of Washington, 57, 149, 325
University of Wisconsin, 301–302
Upshaw, Gene, 71, 76

Vainisi, Jack, 49–52
Van Brocklin, Norm, 47–48
Vanguard High School, 233
Vermeil, Dick, 108–109
Veterans Stadium, 178, 253
Vick, Michael, 5, 46, 76, 180, 239–253, 260–262, 265, 269–278, 284, 291, 298, 331, 334, 344–345, 353, 360
Vincent, Troy, 253
Virginia Military Institute, 44
Virginia Tech University, 239–244, 246–248, 354

Wake Forest University, 192
Walker, Jay, 264
Walsh, Bill, 219
Walsh, Chile, 35–36
Walton, John, 107–109, 140, 161
War Memorial Stadium, 96
Ward, Charlie, 203–204
Ware, Andre, 194–195, 203, 206
Warmath, Murray, 56
Warner, Kurt, 212–215, 230, 235, 260, 266

Warrick, Peter, 244
Warwick High School, 240
Washington, Gene, 79–81
Washington, Hank, 362
Washington, Kenny, 28–29, 36, 45, 54
Washington Commanders, 354, 361.
   See also Washington Redskins
Washington Federals, 122
Washington Huskies, 149, 325
Washington Post (newspaper), 144
Washington Redskins, 27–28, 32–33,
   45, 54, 127, 156, 159, 168–177,
   181–185, 203, 229, 275, 300–306,
   316, 322, 332, 358, 360–361. *See also*
   Washington Commanders
Washington State University (WSU),
   13, 245
Waterfield, Bob, 33, 38
Watson, Deshaun, 66, 322–324,
   329–333, 336, 345, 350–353,
   357–358
Watts, J. C., 152, 158, 160
Weber State University, 192
Weeden, Brandon, 302
Wells, Lloyd, 66
Wells, Warren, 72
Wentz, Carson, 350
West Los Angeles College, 148–149
West Texas State University, 362
West Virginia State University, 112
West Virginia University, 193
Westbrook, Michael, 207
Western Illinois University, 193
Westlake High School, 280
Wharton, Dr. Clifton R., 186
White, Dwight, 110
Whitehouse High School, 327, 329, 334
whitewashing, 10, 28, 33–40
Whitt, Rick, 201
Wilder, Douglas, 187
Wilhelm, Erik, 192
Wilkinson, Tom, 151
William & Mary, 44, 98
Williams, Caleb, 351

Williams, Chuck, 80
Williams, Doug, 4–5, 46, 88, 134–146,
   151, 154–158, 162, 168–173,
   176–188, 193–194, 200, 204, 216,
   228, 239, 260–261, 265–268,
   272–273, 298, 309–310, 322, 326,
   340, 346, 354, 357, 360–361
Williams, Inky, 10–11, 16
Williams, Karen Hastie, 64–65
Williams, Kyle, 295
Williams, Ricky, 234, 257
Williams, Tom, 66
Williamson High School, 280
Willis, Bill, 36, 38
Wilson, Russell, 5, 62, 76, 102, 300–316,
   331, 350, 352–354, 364
Winnipeg Blue Bombers, 45, 279
Winston, Jameis, 203, 350
Winters, Jonathan, 131
Wolf, Ron, 67–68, 70, 77, 136, 218
Women of Washington (podcast), 173
Wonderlic test, 273–274
World Football League (WFL),
   108–109, 131
World War II, 19, 26, 28–29, 33, 35, 40,
   91
Wrigley Field, 26
Wycheck, Frank, 211
Wycoff, Doug, 23

Yale University, 13
Yankee Stadium, 23
Yewcic, Tom, 44
Young, Alva "Doc," 15–17
Young, Bryce, 351
Young, Buddy, 36–37, 95–96
Young, Steve, 218–221, 255, 261, 289,
   291, 297, 325, 362
Young, Vince, 273–275, 298, 360
Younger, Paul "Tank," 49, 93, 108, 124
Youngstown State University, 125, 205

Zeier, Eric, 228
Zuger, Joe, 103

John Eisenberg is an acclaimed sportswriter and the author of ten books. A newspaper columnist for almost three decades at the *Dallas Times Herald* and the *Baltimore Sun*, Eisenberg has covered major events like the Super Bowl, NCAA Final Four, World Series, Olympic Games, and more. He has also taught sports journalism at Towson University and written for publications such as *Sports Illustrated*, *Smithsonian*, and *Details*. Eisenberg's previous books include *The Streak* (a finalist for the Casey Award and short-listed for the PEN/ESPN Award for Literary Sports Writing) and *The League*. He lives in Baltimore, Maryland.